5⚾⚾ BALLPARKS

From Wooden Seats to Retro Classics

5⚾⚾⚾ BALLPARKS

From Wooden Seats to Retro Classics

Eric Pastore
Digitalballparks.com

THUNDER BAY
P·R·E·S·S

THUNDER BAY
P·R·E·S·S

Thunder Bay Press
An imprint of the Baker & Taylor Publishing Group
10350 Barnes Canyon Road, San Diego, CA 92121
www.thunderbaybooks.com

ISBN-13: 978-1-60710-293-9

ISBN-10: 1-60710-293-5

Library of Congress Cataloging-in-Publication Data available upon request.

Printed in China.

1 2 3 4 5 15 14 13 12 11

Design: Danny Gillespie Greene Media
Artwork Illustrations: Mark Franklin
                       Colin and David McCarthy

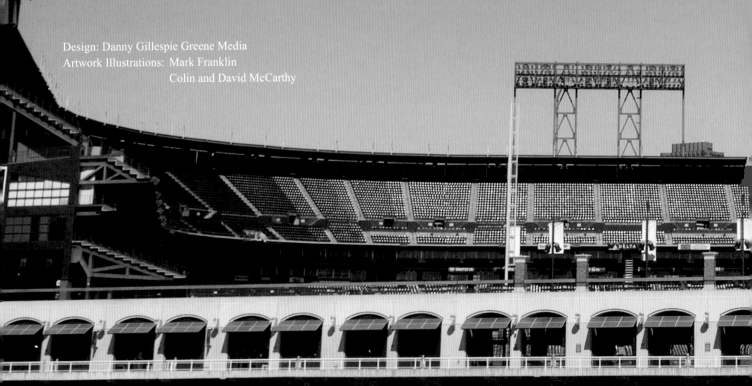

PAGE 1: PNC Park in Pittsburgh is among the most picturesque ballparks in the majors today.

PAGES 2–3: The Pima-Maricopa Nation's Salt River Field at Talking Stick was Digitalballparks.com's Ballpark of the Year for 2011.

THIS PAGE: The sculpture of Willie McCovey at McCovey Point looks back to AT&T Park across McCovey Cove. On game days, a flotilla awaits splash hits.

Contents

ABOVE: Fenway Park at dusk. One of the most beautiful ballparks in the world is also the oldest ballpark used by professional baseball in the United States.

Since the nineteenth century the United States has been at the forefront of architectural development, leading the world with modern approaches to design. From skyscrapers to Art Deco, Frank Lloyd Wright to Frank Gehry, the American contribution to world architecture has been remarkable.

However, there is one form of architecture in which the United States is not just great but unbeatable: the ballpark. Sure the stadium can be traced back to the days of the Roman Colosseum (we even built our own version in Los Angeles), but that monster doesn't reflect the serene, almost bucolic simplicity of the typical ballpark. The green grass and the four bases surrounded by the grandstand seem to create something greater than the sum of its parts: the perfect oasis, a mixture of architecture and garden, of grandstand and field, that draws us in and brings us back to a simpler time.

Our national pastime has since gone on to become an international phenomenon, and the visions that other cultures bring to ballpark design are often exciting. There seems to be an endless number of combinations of how grandstand and field can be put together—to suit rookie league ballparks that may seat only a thousand, all the way to the monstrous major league facilities that seat over 50,000.

What is it about the ballpark draws us in? It is something about the different combinations of grandstand and field, of wood, aluminum, concrete, and steel, and the different types of grass or even pseudo-grass (though the purists are convinced that AstroTurf was the evilest thing ever brought into a baseball stadium). Each stadium is intriguing and idiosyncratic, unique and original—sufficiently different to make some of us to want to visit and experience as many of these masterpieces as possible. This can become an obsession, and if you are reading this, then I'm assuming you are one of us: one of those who have on the top of their bucket list the goal to see every major league stadium, or to see every stadium ever used for professional baseball. For those who are obsessed, here is a primer to ballpark history past and present. It is a brief examination of most of the major league teams' ballparks throughout time, as well as their spring training facilities and their top minor league affiliates. A little history of some other important parks is here as well, such as some Negro League parks, the monstrous College World Series stadiums in Omaha, representative WPA buildings, and the nearly perfect Little League World Series ballpark, Lamade Stadium in Williamsport. Wherever possible—and within economic constraints—these have been photographed.

So much has changed since the original ballparks of the nineteenth century, but most of us will admit that those were in fact the most exciting. In the days of yesteryear, ballparks (even the major league ones) were made almost exclusively of wood. While their beauty could be attributed to the same quality one would find in a log cabin, their inherent problem was obvious. Wood burns. The number of beautiful wooden ballparks that have burned to the ground is astounding. Keep in mind that in those days, smoking a cigarette at a ballgame was commonplace and cost many a team their home. Soon enough it was realized that concrete and steel would stand the test of time—and not just cigarettes but the weather as well. Mother Nature hasn't been so kind to America's most beautiful architectural achievement either.

Concrete and steel brought the modern ballpark. Development was a slow and steady process until the mid-1930s. America was lost in the throes of the Great Depression. In an effort to create jobs, the Works Progress Administration (WPA) began to build things: big populist things, like ballparks. The WPA built them everywhere—all over the country, whether the city had a minor league team or not. Because of this, many towns were suddenly awarded professional baseball as these new WPA ballparks allowed teams to compete in modern new stadiums. The WPA meant that the U.S. government was suddenly the new chief architect of our grand game. Amazingly, these new WPA parks that suddenly sprang up all over the country were not only well made and able to withstand the elements, but they were warm and rustic and had a simple beauty that we've been trying to recapture ever since. Many of these WPA projects have survived and still exist today, and even a handful of the old wooden ballparks can be found if you look hard enough. The largest all-wooden ballpark still standing is Olympic Stadium in Hoquiam, Washington. Digitalballparks.com personally helped secure its historical marker.

In recent years the "retro movement" has attempted to bring back some of the warmth from the WPA era that we lost in the 1970s "doughnut stadium" movement, where cookie-cutter ballparks such as Veterans Stadium in Philadelphia, Three Rivers Stadium in Pittsburgh, Fulton County Stadium in Atlanta, Riverfront Stadium in Cincinnati, Busch Stadium in St. Louis, and Shea Stadium in New York took over from classic ballparks such as Redland-Crosley Field in Cincinnati, Forbes Field in Pittsburgh, and Sportsman's Park in St. Louis. This retro movement created new stadiums using red brick and dark green elements that certainly did help bring the ballpark back to life. The trouble is that the retro ballpark became the modern version of the doughnut stadium. They were copied and cloned everywhere, and too many looked too similar.

Happily, today there is a new movement that aims to bring something modern and unique to the table, yet retains the classic elements and is still respectful to the grand game. New blood has come into the ballpark architecture scene after being dominated by the same designers for so many years. Exciting new ballparks in Columbus, Ohio; Glendale, Arizona; and the new Talking Stick, built on the grounds of the Salt River/Pima Indian reservation are simply breathtaking. It is great to be saying that again: "breathtaking." I haven't said it since the first time I saw Fenway Park. Built at a time when ballparks were fitted into neighborhoods, Fenway Park had to be squeezed into a small area. An asymmetric vintage beauty rose up to become what many ballparks aspire to be. Luckily for us, I think we are coming closer than ever before.

Welcome to the ballpark!

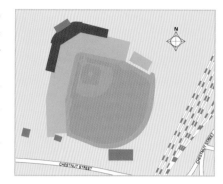

ABOVE: The drawings show the footprint of the stadium in question, its north–south orientation, and any roads or railroads nearby. The colors represent:

Light gray = buildings
Dark gray = covered seating
Pink = open seating
Brown = dirt
Green = grass/synthetic grass

BELOW: The new Salt River Fields at Talking Stick was designed by HKS Architects of Dallas, Texas, one of the largest firms in the country.

23rd Street Grounds

Location: Chicago, IL
Status: Defunct
Opened: 1872
Closed: 1877
Capacity: 2,000 (estimated)
Dimensions: N/a

23rd Street Grounds, sometimes known as State Street Grounds and 23rd Street Park and sometimes spelled out in full as Twenty-third Street Grounds, first hosted baseball in the 1872–1873 season. The stadium was rented by the Chicago White Stockings at a time when the club was trying to overcome its financial problems following the catastrophic 1871 Chicago Fire. For their part, the Chicago White Stockings played baseball for their first two years at the stadium in the National Association and the latter two in the National League.

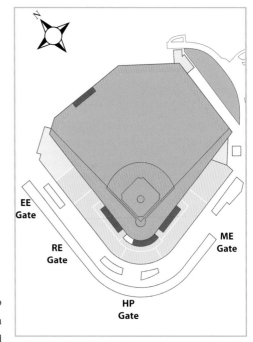

59th Street Bridge

Location: Between E 59th and 60th Streets; between First Avenue and the East River, New York, NY
Aka: "The Sandlot"
Status: Defunct
In use: Mid-1930s

The New York Cubans of the Negro National League were a reincarnation of Alex Pompez's Cuban Stars and played their home games on this diamond under the 59th Street Bridge in an area known as "The Sandlot" in 1939. The overarching bridge technically made the park the first major league covered stadium. The infield was covered with cinders. The Cubans were a Negro league baseball team that played in the Negro Leagues during the first half of the 1930s until suffering a losing season in 1936. The Cubans did not field a team for the next two seasons but returned to the Negro National League in 1939 and played every season until 1950, winning the World Series in 1947. However, the Negro National League folded following the 1948 season and the Cubans joined the Eastern Division of the Negro American League.

BELOW: The 59th Street Bridge in the late 1930s—the ballpark was on the Manhattan side.

Location: 250 Evans Avenue, Reno, NV

Status: Current home of the Triple-A Reno Aces

Architect: HNTB

Opened: April 17, 2009

Capacity: 9,100

Dimensions:

Left Field 345 ft

Center Field 400 ft

Right Field 339 ft

The relatively new Aces Ballpark—groundbreaking work commenced on February 25, 2008, and the official grand opening took place on the first day of the 2010 season—is home to the Aces who play in the PCL, and cost $50 million to build. Located by the Truckee River, it is at the heart of the downtown Reno redevelopment effort known as the Freight House District. The idea of a new stadium first surfaced in 2002 but construction work on what was tentatively called Sierra Nevada Stadium did not begin until early 2008. It was renamed Aces Ballpark once the Reno Aces were earmarked to take up residence, and they played their first home game on April 17, 2009, although construction work to complete phase two of the build resumed the following September.

ABOVE: View toward home plate. (Amanda Lippert Merzbach, BaseballStadiumReviews.com)

OPPOSITE, ABOVE LEFT: Footprint of Aces Ballpark.

BELOW: Aces Ballpark has great views of Reno from the right-field grass. (Amanda Lippert Merzbach, BaseballStadiumReviews.com)

Ainsworth Field

Location: 24th Street at Washington Place, Erie, PA
Status: Amateur
Opened: 1947; renovated 1980
Capacity: 3,500
Dimensions:
Left Field 320 ft
Center Field 390 ft
Right Field 320 ft

Built in 1938, Ainsworth Field was the home for professional Erie baseball for almost sixty years and it remains a great vintage ballpark with a tremendous history. Unlike major or minor league teams, Negro league teams sometimes had between three and six home stadiums throughout a regular season and so Ainsworth Field hosted many Negro league teams in the 1940s.

In 1938 the Erie Sailors entered the Middle-Atlantic League, as affiliates of the Boston Braves, switching their affiliation to the Cincinnati Reds in 1939. The Sailors returned to the Middle-Atlantic League in 1941, where they played for two seasons, before being interrupted in 1943 by the war. They resumed play in 1944, switching leagues to the New York Penn League, and then transferring to the Middle-Atlantic League in 1945, where they remained until its closure in 1951. In 1954 they rejoined the NY Penn League, where they would stay for the rest of Ainsworth Field's professional life.

The Sailors had a checkered career during the 1950s and 1960s, affiliating with a variety of teams ranging from the Senators and the Minnesota Twins to the Detroit Tigers. And worst of all, for fourteen years from 1967 the Sailors did not field a team, until they were reborn as the Erie Cardinals under the wing of the St. Louis Cardinals. From 1987 to 1989 they played as the Erie Orioles, and in 1992–1993 Erie was briefly awarded the Florida Marlins Single-A franchise for a single season. The Texas Rangers were the last affiliated team ever to use Ainsworth Field because in 1995 Erie was the beneficiary of a brand new ballpark, built in the downtown area, the Jerry Uht Park.

Ainsworth Field had one last hurrah. In 1994, Erie joined the Independent Frontier League and played a full season at Ainsworth before giving way to the new downtown ballpark. Fans came out in response to Ainsworth's final season and the team drew an impressive 64,000 throughout 1994. The Erie Sailors not only sold out the final game, but recorded their highest attendance in a seventy-one-year professional history: almost 5,000 fans.

BELOW: Footprint of Ainsworth Field.

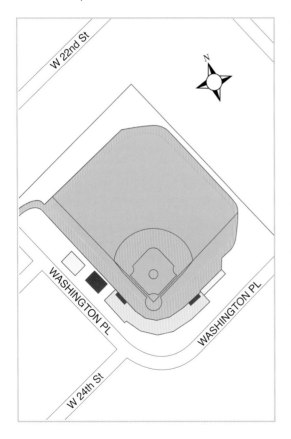

ABOVE RIGHT and RIGHT: View toward and from home plate. Ainsworth Field was built, and is still owned, by the Erie School District. Rumor has it that Babe Ruth once hit a home run during an exhibition game here that cleared that giant chimney and the school below it!

Location: N. Dale Mabry Highway, Tampa, FL
Status: Demolished 1989
Opened: 1955
Capacity: 4,000
Dimensions:
Left Field 340 ft
Center Field 400 ft
Right Field 340 ft

LEFT: Alfonso Ramon "Al" Lopez was a catcher and manager who was inducted into the Hall of Fame in 1977. There's a statue of him in nearby Al Lopez Park.

BELOW: Footprint of Al Lopez Field.

Built at a cost of $287,901 ($2.1 million in today's dollars), Al Lopez Field was named in honor of Tampa-born Hall of Famer Al Lopez in 1954, at a time when he was the manager of the White Sox. Owned by the Tampa Sports Authority and home to the Florida State League's Tampa Tarpons, the park's most noteworthy feature was a grandstand that had a high, curved roof with no obstructing columns to block a fan's view. However, the Sox moved elsewhere near the end of the decade and their replacements, the Cincinnati Reds, stayed longer but eventually left for more up-to-date facilities in Plant City after 1987's spring training program.

The Tarpons again reached an affiliation agreement with the Chicago White Sox for the 1988 season, but the Tampa Sports Authority's revenue from leasing the ballpark to them did not cover expenses and it would not agree to a lease longer than a year. The authority moved forward its redevelopment plans and demolition of the ballpark started in March 1989. Raymond James Stadium rose on the site and opened for business in 1998.

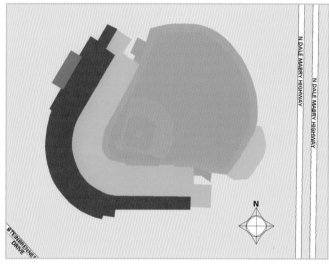

BELOW: The field (in the background of this photograph) was razed in 1989, and the Raymond James Stadium (foreground) expanded.

Al Lang Field (1947)

Location: 80 Second Avenue SE, St. Petersburg, FL

Status: Largely demolished in 1977

Opened: 1947

Capacity: 7,227

Dimensions:

Left Field 309 ft

Center Field 400 ft

Right Field 305 ft

St. Petersburg's Al Lang Field was the second of three incarnations of this ballpark which have occupied the spectacular waterside site. Torn down in 1947, the original wooden structure of the St. Petersburg Athletic Park was replaced by a new concrete ballpark, the Al Lang Field, named after the mayor of St. Petersburg who, in 1914, convinced the St. Louis Browns to move to the Sunshine State for spring training.

Al Lang, a former Pittsburgh laundry owner, moved to St. Petersburg in 1910. He became the business manager of a ballpark and tried to attract a major league team for spring training. His success is shown by the great heritage we can look back on today: St. Petersburg has been home to at least one team for spring training for some eighty years. Al Lang benefited, too. In 1916 and again in 1918, he was elected the mayor of St. Petersburg. He died in 1960 at age 89.

At the inaugural game of the new $300,000 ballpark in 1947, the St. Louis Cardinals beat the New York Yankees, and the stadium went on to host a succession of major league teams, including the New York Mets from 1962, the Baltimore Orioles, the Yankees, and the ever-loyal Cardinals. The New York Giants stayed for the 1951 season, before returning to their spring home in Phoenix, Arizona. Great baseball players continued to run the bases in St. Petersburg, among them Joe DiMaggio, Mickey Mantle, Stan Musial, and many others.

In 1977 the stadium underwent a major refit, and the building was demolished to make way for a new concrete-roofed structure, replacing the asymmetric grandstand and the press box, which had been positioned on the third base line, instead of behind home plate.

TOP LEFT: The St. Louis Cardinals are most known for making use of Al Lang, in all of its forms. They began using it in its wooden state when it was still called Waterfront Park in 1938. Waterfront Park was torn down in 1947, and this new concrete ballpark was created in its place. Perched on the edge of Tampa Bay, you can understand why Al Lang Field attracted the majors.

CENTER LEFT: Al Lang Stadium, in this configuration, lasted from 1947 until 1977. Note the asymmetric grandstand that was replaced in the rebuild.

LEFT: Al Lang was the "father of modern spring training" but the stadium named for him was looking long in the tooth after thirty years and needed a makeover.

The new stadium that opened in St. Petersburg in 1977 was the winter home to two major league teams, the St. Louis Cardinals and the New York Mets. Although newspaper publisher Jake Lake suggested introducing a local major league team to the city in the same year, it was not until 1995, almost twenty years later, that St. Pete was awarded a major league franchise, and the Tampa Bay Devil Rays were formed. Unlike most other teams, they didn't have far to go when moving from spring training to the full season home.

In the intervening years, the stadium hosted a number of minor league teams from the Florida State League, such as the St. Petersburg Cardinals, who played from 1966 to 1997, and the St. Petersburg Devil Rays, who were the last to use it in 2000.

In 1998 the Tampa Bay Devil Rays took over the stadium, using the city as their home all year round, for both spring training and the regular season. Their summer base is at Tropicana Park, just over a mile to the west. The Cardinals were happy to move out, relocating to their brand-new Jupiter home. The stadium's name was changed to Florida Power Park in the same year, as the local utility company purchased the naming rights to the site. The company's name was changed to Progress Energy in 2003, so the stadium became Progress Energy Stadium at Al Lang Field.

The Rays played the last spring training ballgame at the stadium on March 28, 2008, and moved their spring training home to Port Charlotte. Progress Energy Park was without a spring training contract for the first time in many years, and its future is currently uncertain.

Location: 180 Second Avenue SE, St. Petersburg, FL
Aka: Florida Power Park (1998–2003), Progress Energy Stadium at Al Lang Field (from 2003)
Opened: 1976
Status: Home to FC Tampa Bay of the North American Soccer League
Opened: March 13, 1947
Capacity: 7,227
Dimensions:
Left Field 320 ft
Center Field 412 ft
Right Field 315 ft

LEFT: Al Lang Field was the springtime home of the Mets for twenty-six years (eleven years at the second Al Lang), until their new stadium was built in Port St. Lucie in 1988. The Cardinals began playing at Al Lang in 1938. They took a break in 1942 due to travel restrictions during the war when they played in Cairo, Illinois, and then came back to play here from 1946 to 1997.

BELOW: With its palm-lined fences and yacht harbor views, Progress Energy Stadium at Al Lang Field 22is the perfect place to gear up for the upcoming season. It seats just over 7,000 but the berm means that crowds of over 11,000 have watched games.

Location: University Boulevard and Avenida Cesar Chavez, Albuquerque, NM

Status: Demolished 2000

Architect: Max Flatlow

Opened: March 1, 1969

Capacity: 10,500

Dimensions:

Left Field 360 ft

Center Field 425 ft

Right Field 350 ft

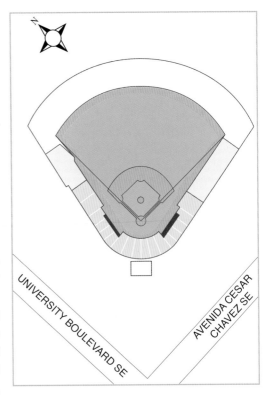

RIGHT: Footprint of Albuquerque Sports Stadium.

BELOW: Albuquerque Sports Stadium had a seating capacity of 10,510 but could accommodate more. It was replaced by Isotopes Park.

Albuquerque Sports Stadium was constructed at a cost of $1.4 million as a replacement for the aging Tingley Field, home of professional baseball in Albuquerque since the Great Depression, but was itself demolished after little more than thirty years' service. The ballpark's first tenants were the Albuquerque Dodgers of the Double-A Texas League but the city gained a Triple-A team franchise, the PCL's Albuquerque Dukes, in 1972 and they remained at the stadium for the next twenty-eight years.

The stadium was the second oldest in the league by the end of the 1990s and showing its age. The team's owner sold the franchise to Portland in 2000, the stadium was soon torn down, and Isotopes Park was built in its place. The latter was supposed to be a remodeling of the old stadium, but was built virtually from scratch and only the playing field of its predecessor remains.

Location: Baton Rouge, LA

Aka: Formerly LSU Varsity Baseball Field (1938–1943)

Status: Demolished 2010

Opened: March 12, 1938

Capacity: 7,760

Dimensions:

Left Field 330 ft

Center Field 405 ft

Right Field 330 ft

Constructed in 1938 and home of the Louisiana State University's Fighting Tigers for seventy years, Alex Box Stadium was also the spring training ground of the New York Giants (1938–1939), and home to two minor league teams—the Baton Rouge Red Sticks and Cougars. When the stadium opened in 1938 it was known as the LSU Varsity Baseball Field, but was renamed in honor of Simeon Alex Box, an alumni killed in World War II.

The Fighting Tigers have one of the most avid fan bases in the history of collegiate baseball. The team has led the nation every year in NCAA attendance since 1994. With a capacity of 7,700, the stadium set the all time NCAA record in 2003, with 291,000 through the gate in only thirty-nine games. From 1984 until 2007, the LSU Tigers drew over four million fans to the "Box." The LSU Tigers have always been very successful at their home ground, and have brought five championship titles home to the Baton Rouge campus. In fact, their winning percentages practically defy logic. From 1998 to 2005, LSU had a

655–162 record—an .801 winning percentage! Their best season ever at home was 1998, when they went 32–3 for an astounding .914 winning percentage.

Many former Fighting Tigers have gone on to the major leagues, including several who are currently playing today. Two former LSU alumni took center stage in the 2007 playoffs, when Paul Byrd pitched for the Cleveland Indians in the showdown against the Boston Red Sox. A new player came into the spotlight during the World Series, as Brad Hawpe showcased his talents for the Colorado Rockies.

The most infamous element of this venerable stadium must have been the "Intimidator," the large billboard showing a ferocious tiger and the Fighting Tigers' greatest victories in the College World Series.

In 2008 LSU decided that Alex Box had become obsolete, and commissioned a new stadium, also called Alex Box, which opened in 2009.

ABOVE, BELOW, and OPPOSITE, BELOW: The first Alex Box Stadium was built in 1937–38 under the Works Progress Administration, which was an important New Deal agency that helped build a number of ballparks such as "The Rockpile" in Buffalo, Roosevelt Stadium, in Jersey City, and Civic Stadium, in Eugene,

Alex Box Stadium (2009)

Location: Nicholson Drive at
N. Stadium Road, Baton Rouge, LA
Aka: The new "Box"
Status: Home of Louisiana State
University
Architect: Grace & Herbert; DLR and
Jeffrey L. Bruce & Company
Opened: 2009
Capacity: 10,150
Dimensions:
Left Field 330 ft
Center Field 405 ft
Right Field 330 ft

RIGHT, BOTTOM, and OPPOSITE, ABOVE: The new "Box" is a splendid stadium with all the amenities you'd expect from such a well-patronized team.

BELOW: Footprint of Alex Box Stadium.

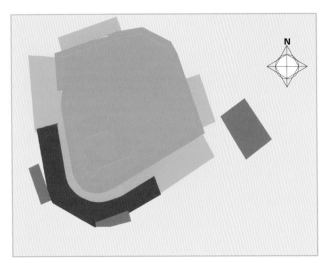

The new "Box," built just 200 yards south of the old one, is a vision of metal and concrete, with state-of-the-art facilities designed to maintain LSU's position as one of the premier college baseball teams. The new stadium gives fans a taste of major league facilities, with air-conditioned club lounges located under the grandstand seating. The ancillary facilities are all more elaborate than in their old home, with larger lockers room and new, improved batting cages.

LSU is rightly proud of its loyal fan base, who return year after year, giving the team one of the best college baseball attendance records in the country. Over the past twenty-six seasons the Tigers have lured nearly five million fans to their games, and from 1996 to 2009 Alex Box Stadium maintained its position with the best attendance statistics in the country. During the first year of operations the new Alex Box Stadium drew a record 403,056 fans.

The new stadium has a capacity of 10,150, with nearly 4,000 seats in the covered grandstand and 6,000 on bleachers. It incorporates a touch of the old, with the great "Intimidator" billboard in right field, depicting a roaring tiger over the dates of LSU's six national championships. The new stadium fuses the best of the Tigers' traditions with a modern facility that appeals to fans and players alike.

All Sports Stadium was located at the city's State Fairgrounds and was the home of the Oklahoma City 89ers until 1990, when the team was renamed the Oklahoma Red Hawks and began playing at the AT&T Bricktown Ballpark. All Sports Stadium was the follow-up to the beautiful ballpark known as Holland Park, which hosted Texas League baseball from 1924 to 1957. All Sports Stadium didn't have much of the classic charm of the old wooden facility, but it was up to the code of the American Association, which meant that for the first time ever Oklahoma City could host Triple-A baseball. All Sports Stadium had some odd design quirks, but Oklahoma City was thrilled to have baseball back after five long years without a team.

Over the following decades the 89ers would sign partnership deals with the likes of the Houston Astros, the Cleveland Indians, and the Philadelphia Phillies but the All Sports Stadium was looking increasingly tired and plans were made to find a site for a new ballpark. Finally, in 1997, it was announced that the plans were finally completed and all the hurdles had been jumped to bring a brand-new stadium to the Bricktown section of Oklahoma City. The new Bricktown Ballpark would be a welcome sight for fans.

Location: Oklahoma City, OK
Status: Demolished 2005
Opened: 1961
Capacity: 12,000
Dimensions:
Left Field 340 ft
Center Field 415 ft
Right Field 340 ft

All Sports Stadium

BELOW: The view over home plate.

BELOW: At the very top of the stadium sat a blue building which housed the press box and broadcasters, as well as all concessions, bathrooms, and services. It was basically the worst seat in the house because it was the farthest away from the action that you could get in the whole stadium. It was, however, air conditioned.

Location: 99-500 Salt Lake
Boulevard, Honolulu, HI
Status: Football field
Architect: The Luckman Partnership
Opened: September 12, 1975
Capacity: 50,000
Dimensions:
Left Field 325 ft
Center Field 420 ft
Right Field 325 ft

RIGHT: Miss Hawaii 1996 Melissa Ann Short sings the national anthem before a game between the St. Louis Cardinals and the San Diego Padres on April 19, 1997.

BELOW: Aerial view of Aloha Stadium. (Courtesy Gerald Ako)

Aloha Stadium was built in the mid-1970s at a cost of $37 million as a multi-purpose replacement for the increasingly outdated Honolulu Stadium and is currently home to the University of Hawaii Warriors football team. With regard to baseball, the stadium served as the home of the Triple-A Hawaii Islanders of the Pacific Coast League from 1975 to 1987, the year when the team moved to Colorado Springs. Major League Baseball's San Diego Padres played an exhibition series here against the Seibu Lions of Japan's Pacific League in 1995, and a three-game regular season series between the St. Louis Cardinals and San Diego Padres was held at the same venue two years later. The stadium was permanently configured for football in early 2007.

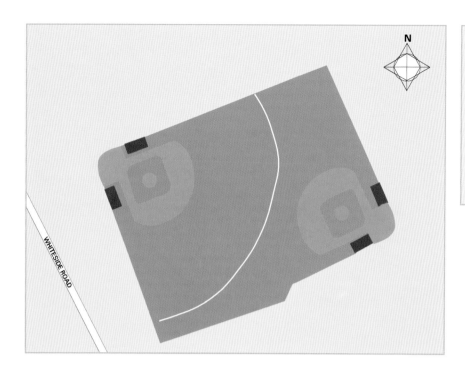

Location: 2217 Bedford Avenue, Pittsburgh, PA
Aka: Josh Gibson Field
Status: Amateur
Opened: 1928; renovated 2008–2009

LEFT: The footprint the new Josh Gibson Field, transformed at a cost of $300,000.

BELOW: A statue to Josh Gibson of the Homestead Grays stands in the center field plaza of Nationals Park in Washington, DC.

BOTTOM: The Pittsburgh Crawfords pose for a photo in Ammon Field c. 1928.

In 2008 Ammon Field was renamed Josh Gibson Field to honor Baseball Hall of Fame player Josh Gibson. Located in the city's Hill District, it is said to have served as the home of the Negro National League's Pittsburgh Keystones in 1922, the team's only season in the league, but the date makes this seem unlikely.

Gibson began his career at Ammon Field in 1929 while playing with the Pittsburgh Crawfords, who were visiting the Keystones, and continued playing there, as the both the Crawfords and the city's Homestead Grays, Gibson's other team, regularly played at Ammon.

The Josh Gibson Foundation, a non-profit organization based in the city that preserves the history of the Negro National League, began a major renovation of the field in 2008, costing $300,000. The grass fields were resurfaced, the four dugouts and bleachers renovated, and scoreboards, sprinklers, and a concession stand were installed.

Anaheim Stadium (1966)

Location: 2000 Gene Autry Way, Anaheim, CA

Aka: The Big A

Status: Still in use after major changes in 1980 and 1997–1999

Architect: N. Herzberg; constructed by Del Webb Company

Opened: April 19, 1966

Capacity: 43,250

Dimensions:

Left Field 333 ft

Left Center 375 ft

Center Field 406 ft

Right Center 375 ft

Right Field 333 ft

World Series: None

All-Star Game: 1967

RIGHT: Anaheim Stadium in 1966—note the scoreboard supported by the huge A-frame. Now in the parking lot, it is twenty-three stories tall and weighs a hefty 210 tons. The halo lights up when the Angels win a game.

BELOW: Anaheim Stadium was built on a parcel of about 160 acres of flat, agricultural land in a suburban area.

First constructed in 1964 (at a cost of $24 million) and currently in its third incarnation, the home of baseball in Anaheim has always been affectionately known as the "the Big A." When the ballpark first opened as Anaheim Stadium in 1966, it became home to the American League's California—now Los Angeles—Angels. The team started up in 1961 and spent its first year playing at Wrigley Field in Los Angeles before moving to then-new Dodger Stadium for four seasons.

The original ballpark seated just over 43,000 primarily on three tiers that stretched down the length of both foul lines. The defining feature of the park was found beyond the outfield wall—a giant A-frame scoreboard that led to the obvious nickname "the Big A."

As originally set up, Anaheim measured 333 feet down both foul lines and 406 feet to straightaway center. Over the years, the team tinkered with the playing field's dimensions as a result of studies conducted to find the fairest balance for both pitchers and hitters, ultimately ending up slightly smaller than the original dimensions.

The stadium had many memorable moments in its early years, including the 1967 All-Star Game—the first in which home runs accounted for all the scoring and the first to be shown on prime-time television. Other highlights included two of baseball legend Nolan Ryan's seven career no-hitters and Alex Johnson becoming the first Angel to win a batting title in 1970, on the season's final day against the Chicago White Sox.

Major changes came in the late 1970s when a deal was struck to bring the NFL's Los Angeles Rams to Anaheim. The $30 million changes to the stadium enclosed the stadium. This caused problems for baseball fans. In particular, they lamented the loss of great views—spectators could previously see the local mountains from their seats. A new scoreboard was installed on the facade of the outfield roof and the famous "Big A" scoreboard moved to the parking lot, to be used for electronic marquee advertising. The new scoreboard was not up to the job and was replaced by a Sony Jumbotron color video board in 1988; black and white matrix scoreboards were later installed above the right field upper deck and the infield upper deck. The changes were completed in time for the 1980 NFL season, with the capacity duly increased to around 65,000. The first NFL game was played on September 7, 1980, and the dual usage would last for fifteen years.

The Angels had many memorable moments at the stadium in the 1980s: In 1982 and 1986 the team won Western Division titles; in 1984 a crowd of nearly 29,000 watched home favorite Reggie Jackson hit his 500th career home run; and in 1986 more than 37,000 fans cheered Angels pitcher Don Sutton to his 300th career victory. The Big A hosted its second All-Star Game in 1989—a Bo Jackson show, the hitter helping to secure the second of back-to-back All-Star Games for the American League.

Damaged in the Northridge earthquake on January 17, 1994, the scoreboard collapsed onto several hundred seats, but there was no loss of life because the stadium was empty. At the end of the same year, the last NFL game took place on December 24, after which the Rams moved to St. Louis. Once again the Angels were the sole inhabitants: changes were needed to improve the stadium and take it into the new century.

Location: 2000 Gene Autry Way, Anaheim, CA
Aka: Renamed Edison International Field in 1998
Status: Rebuild of stadium to show football
Opened: April 11, 1980
Capacity: 64,593
Dimensions:
Left Field 333 ft
Left Center 374 ft
Center Field 404 ft
Right Center 374 ft
Left Center 333 ft
World Series: None
All-Star Game: 1989

BELOW and BOTTOM: The enclosed, dual-usage stadium in 1981. Note the rooftop scoreboard that mimicked the A-frame original, which can now be seen in the parking lot.
(Below left and right courtesy of All-Star pitcher and broacaster Jerry Reuss, Jerryreuss.com)

Angel Stadium of Anaheim

Location: 2000 Gene Autry Way, Anaheim, CA

Aka: Edison Field, "Big Ed" (1997–2003)

Status: Home of the Los Angeles Angels of Anaheim

Architect: Populous

Opened: April 19, 1997; renovated 1997–1999

Capacity: 33,851 (1997); 45,050 (1999)

Dimensions:

Left Field 330 ft

Left Center 370 ft

Center Field 400 ft

Right Center 387 ft

Right Field 330 ft

World Series: 2002

All-Star Game: 2010

THIS PAGE and OPPOSITE: Views of Angel Stadium.
ABOVE RIGHT AND BELOW: The "Outfield Extravaganza."
BELOW: Looking out over the field from above home plate towards the batter's eye.
OPPOSITE, TOP: The ballpark became Angel Stadium in 2003. Note the baseball bats holding up the entrance porch.
OPPOSITE, CENTER: Footprint of Angel Stadium.
OPPOSITE, BELOW: Fans at Angel Stadium watch the Angels' 5–4 victory over the Yankees in extra innings in game 3 of the 2009 ALCS.

The end of the dual-usage arrangement saw a deal struck with the city of Anaheim, ensuring the Angels could stay at their home until 2031, although they have an option to leave thirteen years early. Part of the deal included a new stadium, back in its original baseball-only format. The renovations cost $118 million, reduced capacity by 20,000 spectators, and took two years to complete. Indeed, the Angels played the 1997 season in the stadium when it wasn't even finished.

The new stadium briefly became Edison International Field, and was known to fans as "Big Ed." At the same time the Angels were renamed the Anaheim Angels, but neither of the monikers would last; Edison pulled out of the deal in 2003—a year after the Angels captured their first World Series (against San Francisco) and the stadium was renamed Angel Stadium. The team reverted to the Los Angeles Angels for the 2005 season.

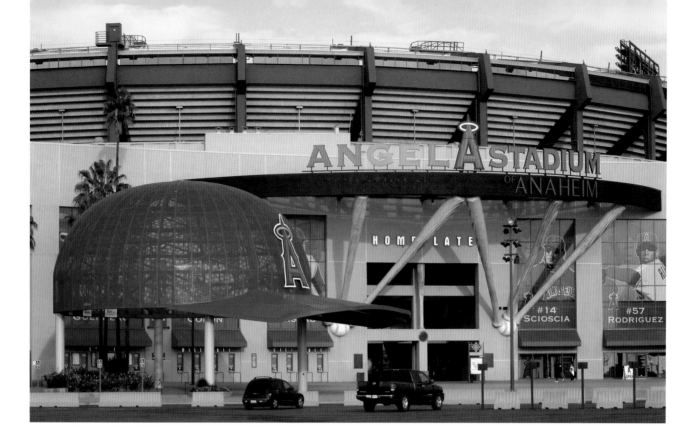

With the Walt Disney Company owning the Angels, and plowing almost $1 million into the park's rebuilding costs, there are a few telltale signs of their input—for example, the sign at the front facade of the stadium is held up by six giant baseball bats, and there is the "Outfield Extravaganza" behind the left center field fence. It consists of a mountainside covered in real trees and artificial boulders that house geysers that erupt to send streams of water cascading down the slope.

Fans should also look out for an attraction that lies just outside the home-plate gate—a full-size brick infield. The bricks at each player's position are engraved with the name of the player who played there on the opening day of each season since 1961, while the other bricks have messages from fans.

The new stadium has seen highs and lows—the worst collapse in their history in 1995 saw the Angels blow an eleven-game lead and lose a playoff with the Mariners for the division title; however, in 2002 the Angels tasted success with their first World Series.

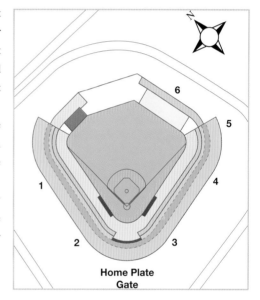

Home Plate
Gate

Angels Stadium

Location: 1901 E. Baristo Road, Palm Springs, CA
Aka: Polo Grounds (1949–1961), Palm Springs Stadium (since 1996)
Status: Home of Palm Springs Power
Opened: 1949; extended in the 1950s
Capacity: 5,185
Dimensions:
Left Field 347 ft
Center Field 377 ft
Right Field 345 ft

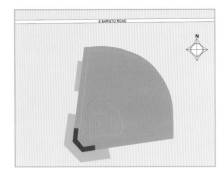

ABOVE: Footprint of Angels Stadium.

ABOVE RIGHT and BELOW: A beautiful setting makes Angels Stadium a great place to watch a ballgame. When the Palm Springs Suns of the independent Western League played here, the park was known as Suns Stadium. In July 1983 Gene Autry put up the money to get the stadium lights.

This amazing little ballpark was built in 1949 and named the Polo Grounds. Interestingly, it continued to serve as a polo ground after the grandstand was completed, but the first baseball team to utilize the ballpark for spring training was the Seattle Rainiers in 1950. This was an important moment, because the PCL was being considered as another major league. It never happened, partly because the westward migration of teams from Philadelphia, New York, and Brooklyn would satisfy the need for major league baseball on the West Coast.

Despite a brief period in 1952 when the major league Chicago White Sox used the Polo Grounds for spring training, it remained as spring training facility for the Seattle Rainiers until 1955. Several other PCL teams would begin training at this ball field until 1960, when the Rainiers returned.

In 1961 two new teams joined the American League, notably the Los Angeles ("California") Angels, owned by Gene Autry. Autry announced that he would be taking over the Polo Grounds in 1961 and making it the Angels' permanent spring training home. He renamed the ballpark Angels Stadium and began a relationship that would last for thirty-two years. The Angels would train here until 1992, making this one of the longest relationships of any spring training facility and host team.

In 1986, the California Angels announced that they would be moving their Single-A team, the Redwood Pioneers, to Palm Springs, and Angels Stadium hosted its first minor league baseball team. When the Angels left town for Anaheim, Palm Springs would now continue to host baseball all season long, for the California League.

The Palm Springs Suns used the stadium for two seasons, renaming the ballpark Palm Springs Stadium in 1996, before moving to Oxnard in 1997. The ballpark lay dormant for almost a decade before a collegiate summer league took over the facility. It is now home to the Palm Springs Power of the SCCBA, and the city has finally repainted the stadium and the field.

With the reputation of being the hottest place to play baseball (thanks to temperatures often reaching the 100s), Arlington Stadium—then named Turnpike Stadium—was practically still under construction right up to the first pitch! But while the baselines were still being chalked just hours before the first game began in 1965, the plan for a stadium to serve Dallas-Fort Worth had first been devised in 1959.

The location of the new park was a natural hollow in the centrally located suburb of Arlington, adjacent to the freeway and next door to an amusement park—ideal for visitors who wanted extra entertainment on their Texas visits.

Upon completion, the new ballpark—built some forty feet below ground level—was named Turnpike Stadium. The Dallas-Fort Worth Spurs were in the Double A league and eased Turnpike in with minor league baseball. While their seven-year tenure saw only mixed success, they had a tremendous fan following and it was soon clear the original capacity of 10,500 was too small. The City of Arlington (which owned the facility) doubled the capacity to 20,000 in 1970.

The park's increased size and close proximity to a tourist attraction were to prove useful selling points two years later when the Washington Senators decided to relocate and chose Arlington as their destination. They were to be renamed the Texas Rangers and the ballpark was also to get a new moniker—Arlington Stadium. A major renovation and expansion would take place in 1971.

Location: 1500 South Copeland Road, Arlington, TX
Aka: Turnpike Stadium
Status: Demolished in 1994
Opened: April 23, 1965, as minor league ground
Capacity: 10,050 (as built); 20,500 (1970)
Dimensions:
Left Field 330 ft
Left Center 380 ft
Center Field 400 ft
Right Center 380 ft
Right Field 330 ft
World Series: None
All-Star Game: None

Arlington Stadium (1965)

BELOW: 1965 panorama of one of the hottest places ever to watch baseball!

BOTTOM: Capacity would be increased in 1970 to accommodate the strong local support.

31

Location: 1500 South Copeland Road, Arlington, TX

Status: Demolished in 1994

Opened: April 21, 1972, first major league game

Closed: October 3, 1993

Capacity: 35,700 (1972); 41,000 (1979); 43,500 (1992)

Dimensions:

Left Field 330 ft

Left Center 380 ft

Center Field 400 ft

Right Center 380 ft

Right Field 330 ft

World Series: None

All-Star Game: None

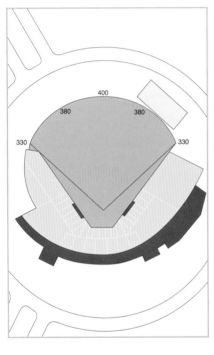

The fourth former minor league park converted for use by a major-league team—the others being Baltimore's Memorial Stadium, Kansas City's Municipal Stadium, and Minnesota's Metropolitan Stadium—the stadium's capacity was increased in the wake of MLB arriving in Arlington, pushing the seating to almost 36,000. A new scoreboard was also added, but the look of the stadium became somewhat distorted due to the continued additions of tiers—some fans started calling it a "mistake." The steel seats, combined with the severely hot Texan weather, also gained it the unenviable nickname of "the world's largest open-air roaster." Indeed, it was so hot in Arlington Stadium that most of the Rangers' games—even those on Sundays—were scheduled for night. It is strange but true that this oven of a stadium also boasted the largest bleachers in the major leagues, extending from foul pole to foul pole.

Further renovations took place in 1978: an upper tier was added, expanding the seating to over 41,000. This also stopped the ability to convert the facility to a football stadium by swinging the seating from the third-base grandstands.

The Rangers beat the California Angels in their first game in Arlington and went on to provide the crowds with many highlights. In 1981, Rick Honeycutt set a club record with his fourth consecutive shutout, a 7–0 five-hitter over the Royals, while in 1989 local boy and legend Nolan Ryan recorded his 5,000th strikeout against Rickey Henderson. The seemingly ageless strikeout king followed that feat with his seventh and final career no-hitter against the Blue Jays in 1991 at the grand old age of 44—the oldest man in MLB history to do so.

On the whole, the Rangers never delivered any real team success, but as one fan put it, "It's hard to be a Rangers fan, but it's not hard to love Arlington Stadium." However much it was liked, the combination of the heat playing a major part in games and the fact the stadium was starting to show its age meant that plans for a new stadium a few hundred yards away were passed. The last game at Arlington was played on October 3, 1993, against the Royals, ending in a 4–1 defeat for the Rangers, and the park was demolished the following year. The site is now a parking lot for the Rangers' new stadium.

LEFT: Footprint of the stadium.

ABOVE and BELOW: With three tiers in places, Arlington Stadium could house over 40,000 by 1992.

ABOVE: Arlington Stadium on Nolan Ryan Day during a Texas Rangers game in 1993. The "Ryan Express" had 5,714 strikeouts in a twenty-seven-year career and today is CEO of the Texas Rangers.

Armory Park—the brainchild of oil magnate Charles J. Strobel—was home to the minor league Toledo Mud Hens and their predecessors from 1897 until the mid-season of 1909. When it opened, Armory Park immediately replaced one of the two existing Toledo ballparks, Ewing Street Park, although weekend games continued to be played at the second, Bay View Park, until the end of the 1900 season. Thereafter and for the next eight and a half seasons, Armory Park was the Mud Hens' exclusive home but the final game was played there on July 2, 1909, and Swayne Field, its replacement, opened the very next day.

Armory Park stood on Spielbusch Avenue, the site of the United States District Courthouse today, and had the Ohio National Guard Armory on the left-field side. Eventually there were grandstands along the baselines and bleachers in right field and the ballpark became Toledo's first permanently established grounds. As elsewhere, the blue laws meant it could not show games on Sundays and the Mud Hens had to play at Casino/Bay View Park, but this changed in 1901.

Major league baseball came to Armory Park twice in 1903: the American League Detroit Tigers played New York and Philadelphia.

Armory Park became too small after some thirteen years and Swayne Field—with almost twice its capacity—took over.

Location: South corner of Spielbusch Avenue and Beech Street, Toledo, OH
Aka: Military Park
Status: Demolished in 1909
Opened: May 29, 1897
Capacity: 3,000; 4,000 (1902); 7,000 (1908)
Dimensions:
Left Field 350 ft
Center Field 450 ft
Right Field 230 ft

Armory Park

Location: 8400 Kirby Drive, Houston, TX

Aka: Harris County Domed Stadium

Status: In use, but not for baseball

Opened: April 12, 1965

Capacity: 42,217 (opening day); 54,816 (current)

Last MLB game: October 9, 1999

Architect: Hermon Lloyd & W.B. Morgan and Wilson, Morris, Crain & Anderson

Dimensions:

	Initial 1965	Final 1999
Left Field:	340 ft	325 ft
Left Center:	375 ft	375 ft
Center Field:	406 ft	400 ft
Right Center:	375 ft	375 ft
Right Field:	340 ft	325 ft

World Series: None

All-Star Game: 1968, 1986

OPPOSITE, ABOVE: Jim Beauchamp of the Houston Astros is congratulated at home plate by teammates after hitting the team's first home run in Houston's new domed stadium, April 10, 1965.

OPPOSITE, BELOW: Inside the Astrodome a full house of over 50,000 enjoys a game in 1995.

BELOW: View of the exterior as it looked in 1975.

Initially named the Harris County Domed Stadium, the name didn't roll off the tongue. When the Colt .45s moved from their temporary home at Colt Stadium to their new home in 1965, it was felt they needed a shiny new name to go with their shiny new stadium: accordingly they were renamed the Houston Astros.

In its time, the Houston Astrodome was an amazing architectural feat that overrode the troubles and constraints of the Texan climate, namely sweaty heat and biting mosquitoes of summer—but over the period it was used it came to represent everything that modern baseball parks try to avoid.

The Astrodome was the first indoor ballpark, cost $35 million to build, and used a completely artificial surface—Astroturf. The stadium could seat 42,000 people and Texans hailed it as the Eighth Wonder of the World. Never before had major league baseball been played indoors. To combat the Texas climate, the Astrodome was air-conditioned, so the heat was no longer a problem. The dome, however, was built as a facility for a number of sports; in 1965 the University of Houston football team started using the venue, as did the NFL's Houston Oilers.

The playing surface was intended to be grass, but it didn't thrive. The clear glass of the dome was supposed to help the grass grow but had to be painted a translucent white after players complained about the glare coming through roof panes blinding them as they tried to track fly balls. The grass started dying, so artificial Astroturf was laid instead.

The Astrodome hosted two All-Star Games; the first in 1968 was won by the NL and although traditionalist spectators hated having the midsummer classic indoors, the Astrodome again hosted the All-Stars in 1986 when 46,000 watched the AL win 3–2.

In 1989, the Astrodome enjoyed a $60 million expansion that enlarged seating capacity by extending the upper decks into the outfield. To assist the extra numbers, two external pedestrian ramps were added. There were other major changes: the Astroturf was replaced with a Magic Carpet system; the scoreboard and home run spectacular were replaced by two Diamond Vision screens, a large matrix board, two auxiliary matrix boards, and a game-in-progress board.

The Astros stayed at the Astrodome for thirty-four years without managing to bring the city a World Series. In 1996 the Houston Oilers left for Tennessee following a dispute over a new stadium; the Astros finally left the Astrodome in 1999 when they moved into Minute Maid Park. Unexpectedly, the Astrodome's finest hour was after sport left the Dome altogether: in 2005 it sheltered refugees from Hurricane Katrina that ravaged New Orleans; the Dome also aided victims of Hurricane Rita later in the year.

35

Location: 24 Willie Mays Plaza, San Francisco, CA

Aka: Pac Bell Park (2000–2003), SBC Park (2004–2005), AT&T Park (since 2006)

Status: Home of the San Francisco Giants

Architect: HOK Sports

Capacity: 41,503

Opened: April 11, 2000

Dimensions:

Left Field 339 ft

Left Center 384 ft

Center Field 399 ft

Right Center 366 ft

Right Field 309 ft

World Series: 2002

All-Star Game: 2007

ABOVE: Aerial view highlighting the proximity of McCovey Cove to the action. There's a public waterfront promenade alongside and fans can get a free view of a game through the archways.

BELOW: The scoreboard features a Mitsubishi HD screen and was billed as the highest-quality outdoor scoreboard in the country when unveiled in 2007.

The San Francisco Giants were about to be poached by Florida in 1992 when local businessmen, led by Peter Magowan, managed to put together an ambitious plan for a classic but state-of-the-art urban ballpark to keep the Giants in San Francisco. Originally opening as Pacific Bell Park, then becoming SBC Park, the Giants' stadium changed its name for the third time in six years when it was officially renamed AT&T Park on March 1, 2006.

When Pac Bell Park opened it was the first MLB ballpark since Dodger Stadium in 1962 to be built using private funding—a cost of $319 million. The approach to the ballpark along King Street is announced by two huge clock towers that rise up to 122 feet and then are topped by forty-five-foot flagpoles. Inside, the three-tiered grandstand provides seating for some 41,000 spectators and runs left and right from home plate to the foul poles; additionally, there are 868 luxury suites above the club level. The only bleachers are behind

the left-field fences, with a magnificent backdrop of San Francisco Bay over McCovey Cove.

Fans sitting in the first row of seats are forty-eight feet from home plate, and twelve feet closer to the batter than the pitcher! The twenty-four-foot right-field wall is named in honor of Willie Mays; the wall is topped with four pillars that erupt with fountains of water whenever the Giants hit a home run or win a game.

Perhaps the most distinctive feature is the Coca-Cola Fun Zone above the left-field bleachers that has an eighty-foot-long Coca-Cola bottle containing childrens' slides inside and blows bubbles and lights up whenever the Giants hit a home run—at the same time a foghorn blasts out. The other high-visibility novelty is a giant replica of a catcher's mitt made of steel and fiberglass. Meanwhile in right center field is a genuine San Francisco cable car resplendent with a banner proclaiming "No Dodger Fans Allowed."

For many fans the modern retro-style AT&T Park is one of the very best in baseball. It is located near downtown San Francisco and has spectacular views out over the urban landscape.

Purpose-built for baseball, the sight lines for spectators are unhindered, and from the upper deck across right field fans can enjoy stunning views of the East Bay hills and the Bay Bridge. Ideally, even better views of the bay would have been available but the architects resisted the temptation in order to keep wind levels down within the stadium. The smallish field is asymmetric with the right-field brick wall only 309 feet from home plate—giving AT&T Park the closest foul pole in the majors—with McCovey Cove on the other side (named after the Giants' Hall of Fame first baseman Willie McCovey). Few players have splash hits to their credit, although Barry Bonds managed the feat thirty-five times. Nautical fans like to wait there in boats and kayaks in the hope that a home run ball will come flying out over the right-field fence.

Thankfully not as cold and windy as Candlestick Park, it can still be a chilly ballpark. On the bay side of the ground a statue of Willie McCovey looks out over his cove, while at the main entrance a statue of Willie Mays greets arriving fans—he is one of four nine-foot-high statues around the park, the others being pitcher Juan Marichal, Orlando Cepeda, and a statue of a seal with a baseball on its nose to honor the memory of the San Francisco Seals. The statues of the four Hall of Famers were created by sculptor William Behrends of North Carolina.

ABOVE: The Coca-Cola Fun Zone features a huge bottle and an old-style fielder's mitt behind the left-field bleachers.

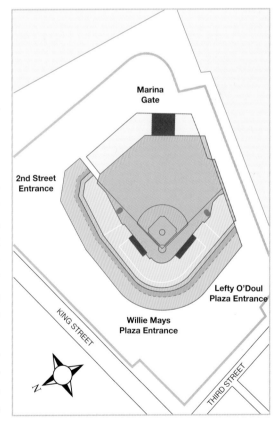

ABOVE: Footprint and entrances to AT&T Park.

Location: Seventh Street and Tennessee Avenue, Indianapolis, IN
Aka: Tinker Park; later Seventh Street Park
Status: Demolished

The home of the Indianapolis Hoosiers, Tinker Park was named for Tinker Street and when that name changed to Seventh Street, so did the ballpark. Used by the National League club from 1887 to 1889, it saw action weekdays. Because of the blue laws, Sunday games were played outside the city limits, at Bruce Grounds (1887) and Indianapolis Park (1888–1889).

RIGHT: The 1888 Indianapolis Hoosiers came seventh in the National League with a 50–85 record. In the background, Boston's South End Grounds.

Location: 1125 North Florida Avenue, Lakeland, FL
Aka: Later Henley Field Ball Park and Clare "Doc" Henley Ball Park (1942 to present)
Status: Home of the Florida Southern College Moccasins
Opened: March 17, 1922; renovated 2002
Capacity: 1,000
Dimensions:
Left Field 325 ft
Left Center 365 ft
Center Field 420 ft
Right Center 385 ft
Right Field 330 ft

Built in 1922, Lakeland's Henley Field is one of the great historic spring training ballparks of Florida. Originally known as Athletic Park, it was renamed in 1942 in honor of Clare Henley, the driving force behind the park's construction.

The first team to use it was the Cleveland Indians in 1923, who stayed until 1927, when they moved to New Orleans. The ballpark stayed dormant for six years until 1934, when the Detroit Tigers began an association with Lakeland that still exists today. The Tigers utilized the ballpark for spring training 1934–1942, 1946–1965, and again in 2003. Tiger fans are lucky that the ballpark is still standing today. Spring training ballparks generally don't have much staying power: historically they have often been rebuilt or completely demolished once the major league team has moved on. In fact, although the Detroit Tigers moved out to the larger Joker Marchant Stadium in 1966, they returned to their original home in 2003 while Joker Marchant underwent an $11 million renovation.

Henley Field continues to host collegiate or Independent games. Florida Southern College (FSC) saw gold here at Henley Field. They moved in as soon as the Tigers left, and have been there ever since playing in the SSC. Because of this, Henley Field remains in fantastic shape more than eighty years later. Henley Field recently received new clubhouses and restrooms. The original locker rooms are now used strictly for storage. The place where Al Kaline and Hank Greenberg used to hang their hats is still there, deep inside the grandstand.

The Single-A Florida State League has also utilized this facility on and off since it opened in 1922. In 1960, the Cleveland Indians became the first affiliated minor league ballclub to play at Henley Field.

The Tigers' 2003 return restored Henley Field to its 1922 opening day condition and meant that vital renovation could take place, including new aluminum bench seating and some nice new brickwork in the picnic area.

LEFT: Henley Field today, much improved by its 2003 facelift.

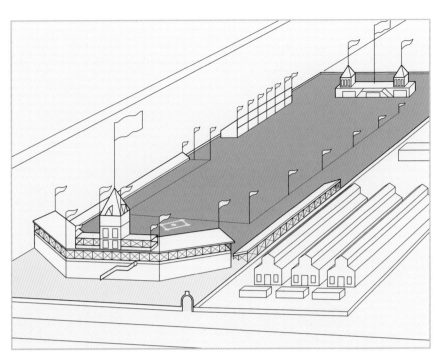

Location: 3000 N. Eighth Street, Milwaukee, WI
Aka: Brewers Park (in the 1920s); Borchert Field (1928–53)
Status: Demolished 1953
Opened: 1888
Capacity: 6,000 (opening); 13,000 (1952)
Dimensions:
Left Field 267 ft
Left Center 435 ft
Center Field 392 ft
Right Center 435 ft
Right Field 268 ft

Athletic Park, Milwaukee

LEFT: Artist's impression from a postcard showing Athletic Park.

Athletic Park opened on May 20, 1888, as the home for the Milwaukee Creams of the Western League, who remained in existence until 1894. The original ballpark resembled the Polo Grounds in New York, another urban facility which had been stretched thin in order to fit into a city block.

The Milwaukee Brewers were founded in 1891, but with the demise of the American Association, they had a rocky start. In 1901 the Brewers entered the new American League, but just a year later, they relocated to St. Louis and became the St. Louis Browns. Finally, in 1902, a new Triple-A Brewers franchise was launched that proved more permanent, and the team remained in the American Association for over fifty years.

Athletic Park was improved in 1902, with a separate clubhouse for the players and a new grandstand, which had wire netting fitted to the center part so that "women need have no fear of being hit by the ball." At their inaugural game, on May 11, 1902, the Brewers won 3–2 before a crowd estimated at 7,000, who braved a northeast wind which chilled "the spectators to the marrow, benumbing the fingers of the players," according to the *Evening Wisconsin* report. The stadium design was never ideal, and in his biography, the colorful Brewers' owner (1941–45) Bill Veeck called Borchert Field "an architectural monstrosity . . . so constructed that the fans on the first-base side of the grandstand couldn't see the right fielder, which seemed perfectly fair in that the fans on the third-base side couldn't see the left fielder. 'Listen,' I told them. 'this way you'll have to come back twice to see the whole team.' "

Athletic Park hosted the Milwaukee Bears during their single year of existence in the Negro National League in 1923, and the Green Bay Packers for their first year in 1933. In 1928 the park was renamed for the late owner and former brewer, Otto Borchert. With the Brewers' success, Borchert Field became too small to accommodate a major league team and in 1953 the Brewers relocated to Toledo, becoming the Toledo Mud Hens.

BELOW and BELOW LEFT: Borchert Field was similar in shape to New York's Polo Grounds. The lights were added in 1935.

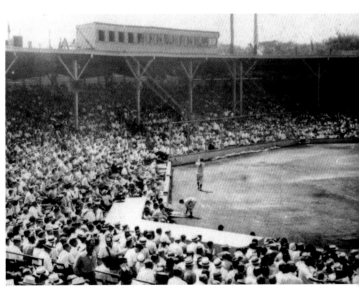

Location: South of Jackson Street, along Fifth Avenue, Nashville, TN

Aka: Sulphur Spring Bottom, later Sulphur Dell

Status: Demolished 1969

Opened: 1870; renovated 1927

Closed: 1963

Capacity: 8,500

Dimensions:

Left Field 334 ft

Center Field 421 ft

Right Field 262 ft

RIGHT: Athletic Park was in a low-lying area that flooded when the Cumberland River broke its banks. It was renamed for the sulphur water well on the ballpark's southern boundary.

ABOVE: Renovation of grandstand in 1927.

BELOW: A packed house in the main grandstand.

Baseball has belonged in Nashville since the late nineteenth century when the city had a team called the Americans, who were founding members of the Southern League in 1885. Then in 1901 Nashville helped found the new Southern Association (it lasted sixty-one years) in which the Volunteers (or Vols for short, from the "Volunteer State") played at Sulphur Dell Park.

The ground was substantially remodeled in 1927 and the Vols thrived. Starting in 1938 the Vols became affiliated with the Brooklyn Dodgers and by 1940 their championship team is recognized as one of the greatest in minor league history—four championships in 1948, 1949, 1950, and 1953. Despite such success, when the Southern Association folded after the 1961 season, Nashville lost its baseball for a season. In 1963 they had a one-year flirtation with the South Atlantic League but ended the season in last place. Years passed until 1978, when the Nashville Sounds joined the Southern League when it expanded from eight to ten clubs. The Nashville Sounds moved on to Herschel Greer Stadium.

Location: 521 Capitol Avenue, Atlanta, GA
Aka: Atlanta-Fulton County Stadium, the Launching Pad
Status: Demolished in 1997
Architect: Heery, Heery & Finch
Opened: April 12, 1966
Last MLB game: October 24, 1996
Capacity: 52,000
Dimensions:

	Original 1966	Final 1996
Left Field:	325 ft	330 ft
Left Center:	385 ft	385 ft
Center Field:	402 ft	402 ft
Right Center:	385 ft	385 ft
Right Field:	325 ft	330 ft

World Series: 1991, 1992, 1995, 1996
All-Star Game: 1972

ABOVE: View of Fulton County Stadium in 1996.

This multi-purpose stadium was one of the famous "cookie cutter" venues which became so popular in the 1960s and 1970s. Discussions about building a ballpark started as early as the 1930s but it was the mid-1950s before ideas started to solidify and even then fans had to wait another decade before the dream became a reality. Finally, after a spend of $18 million and fifty-one weeks of construction, in spring 1965 Atlanta Stadium finally opened in time for the new season. The first game on April 12, 1966, was in front of 51,500 Braves fans cheering on their team against the Pittsburgh Pirates. The first team in was the International League Atlanta Crackers, and after a year they made way for the relocating MLB Milwaukee Braves and the NFL's Atlanta Falcons.

The multi-use stadium was fully enclosed with three tall tiers of blue wooden seats. Situated at the foothills of the Appalachian Mountains, at 1,050 feet the stadium had the highest elevation above sea level of any team at the time: the thin air helped home-run hitters and led to its nickname of "the Launching Pad."

Attendance grew as the first season progressed but then tailed off until it was renowned for its "ghost town" atmosphere. A soccer team, the Atlanta Chiefs, also used the stadium and the playing surface inevitably suffered: until 1989 the Atlanta municipal street-maintenance crew was responsible for the surface. The lowest point came in 1976 when a crowd of under a thousand came through the gates to watch a doubleheader between the Braves and the Houston Astros. Then multimillionaire Atlanta businessman Ted Turner bought the Braves and introduced wrestling contests into the mix: there was no upturn in spectator numbers.

BELOW: The classic cookie-cutter from above.

In the early 1990s a professional groundsman was finally hired and the surface improved enormously: the Falcons left and the Braves improved. Suddenly they became successful, winning six consecutive divisional titles and becoming World Series contenders. The fans returned as the Braves won their first championship in thirty-eight years. In 1996 the Olympic Games were held in Atlanta and Atlanta-Fulton was refurbished to provide the venue for the Olympic baseball competition. The Braves moved out of Atlanta-Fulton and into their new home next door. Atlanta-Fulton Stadium was imploded in summer 1997 and leveled to make a parking lot for Turner Field.

Location: 200 Union Avenue, Memphis, TN
Status: Home of the Memphis Redbirds
Architect: Looney Ricks Kiss and HOK Sport
Opened: 2000
Capacity: 14,320
Dimensions:
Left Field 319 ft
Left Center 360 ft
Center Field 400 ft
Right Center 373 ft
Right Field 322 ft

RIGHT: The dramatic entrance to AutoZone Park.

BELOW: Footprint of AutoZone Park—note the Truegreen Bluff grass seating area in left field.

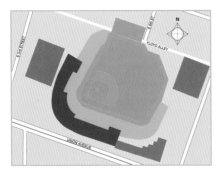

OPPOSITE, TOP: Looking along the skyboxes toward the city.

BELOW: This panorama looking toward home plate shows the great sight lines throughout the asymmetric grandstand.

AutoZone Park is a spacious modern ballpark that opened in 2000. It combines the traditional characteristics of some of America's great ballparks, such as Wrigley Field and Fenway Park, with state-of-the-art facilities for fans and players alike.

Designed by HOK Sports, the architectural firm responsible for many of the early ballparks of the twenty-first century, AutoZone cost $80 million, which is currently the highest sum spent on a minor league ballpark. A redbrick building in downtown Memphis, it is built to major league standards and has a capacity of 14,320. It has an open concourse, enabling fans to stroll around without losing sight of the game, in addition to two upper club levels with forty-eight luxury suites. The video board is one of the largest in minor league baseball, and at 127 feet, or thirteen stories high, it towers over the stadium.

Both the Redbirds and AutoZone Stadium are owned by the Memphis Redbirds Foundation, a charitable body which aims to provide sporting opportunities to children and young people, so the Redbirds are highly unlikely to relocate to another city. In an arrangement unique to Memphis, profits from the Redbirds' games go to support the charity, some $5 million from their first eight seasons.

In addition to hosting the Redbirds, AutoZone Park was home to the inaugural Civil Rights Games in 2007 and 2008, a major league exhibition that marks the unofficial end of spring training and honors the history of civil rights in the United States.

The Redbirds are the Triple-A affiliates to the St. Louis Cardinals, and since their founding in 1998 have made it to the playoffs of the Pacific Coast League three times, winning the title in 2000 and 2009.

Bader Field was located at the airport of the same name. High point was in 1944 when the New York Yankees held spring training there—something the Philadelphia Athletics had also considered. John Boyd Stadium, with a football field and track, was built at a cost of $350,000 just north of the ballpark's left-field wall. Home to the Atlantic City High School football from 1949 until 1994, it was demolished in February 1998. That year, The Sandcastle baseball stadium was built at Bader Field, and professional baseball returned to the airport site. In 2006 it was renamed Bernie Robbins Stadium after a jewelry chain bought the naming rights. The $15 million ballpark was home to the Atlantic City Surf, who played there through 2008—the last two years in the Can-Am League—before the team ceased operating, leaving the ballpark without a team. The field is unused today save for the occasional music concert.

Location: 545 North Albany Avenue, Atlantic City, NJ
Aka: John Boyd Stadium, later the Sandcastle, Bernie Robbins Stadium
Status: John Boyd demolished 1998; the Sandcastle extant but unused
Opened: Bader Field 1920; John Boyd October 22, 1949; the Sandcastle 1998; Bernie Robbins Stadium 2006
Capacity: Bader 4,000; John Boyd 6,000
Dimensions: (for John Boyd)
Left Field 309 ft
Center Field 400 ft
Right Field 309 ft

Bader Field

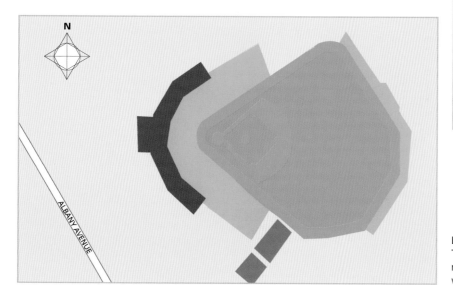

LEFT: Bader Field footprint. There was a runway to the northeast when the airfield was functioning.

Location: 1701 Myrtle Avenue, Jacksonville, FL

Aka: Myrtle Avenue Ball Park; later Joseph E. Durkee Field (1926–85); James P. Small Memorial Stadium (1985–)

Status: Extant

Opened: 1912; renovated 1936, 1985, 2006

Dimensions:

Left Field 337 ft

Center Field 375 ft

Right Field 285 ft

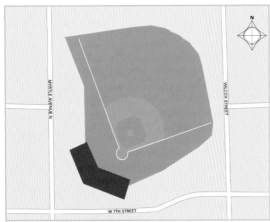

THIS PAGE: Today Barrs Stadium is known as J.P. Small Stadium and is Jacksonville's oldest ballpark. The photo below and footprint above show an unusual feature of this ballpark: the asymmetric layout of the field. The point at which home plate is located is to the right of the center of the grandstand. It's quite unusual, because all of the foul territory normally behind the plate is to the right of the plate, with the center of the ballpark lining up in right center. The press box, too, is off center.
(Top and Below Right photos courtesy Brian Merzbach Ballparkreviews.com.)

In 1919 the Brooklyn Dodgers and the New York Yankees arrived at Barrs Field, Jacksonville, Florida, for spring training, following in the footsteps of the Pittsburgh Pirates and the Philadelphia Athletics. The arrival of these great northern teams fueled the city of Jacksonville's desire for their own full-time professional ball club, but the problem was they didn't own a field.

In 1911, Dr. Jay Durkee gave control of his field to businessman and president of the Jacksonville Baseball Association, Amander Barrs, who created Jacksonville's original ballpark. In 1926, the city gained control of Barrs Field and renamed it Joseph E. Durkee Athletic Field, finally paying $348,000 for it in 1932. Durkee Field was not used again for spring training, but was instead given over to Jacksonville's minor league team, and was the city's main municipal park. The original stadium burned down in 1936 and the city immediately rebuilt a larger version.

In 1926, the Jacksonville Tars joined the Southeastern League and minor league baseball began in Jacksonville. In 1936, the Tars jumped ship and moved over to the Southern League (then known as the South Atlantic League). With the exception of a ten-year stint with Triple-A ball (International League), they remain an integral part of the Southern League to this day. In 1937 the Tars were the Class B affiliates of the Washington Senators, and in 1942, they joined the New York Giants' organization.

Durkee Field was also home to Jacksonville's only Negro League team, the Jacksonville Red Caps, who used the park as their home field from 1938.

The stadium suffered a decline in the 1970s, but fortunately the city of Jacksonville recognized its historical value and it was renovated in 1985, when it was also renamed J. P. Small Memorial Stadium after a local coach who taught at Stanton High School. Further work—including the addition of a museum—took place in 2006, and today the ballpark remembers the great Negro League Hall of Famers who played here.

Location: 300 Stadium Way, Davenport, FL
Status: Demolished 2005
Opened: February 7, 1988
Capacity: 8,000
Dimensions:
Left Field 330 ft
Center Field 410 ft
Right Field 330 ft

Formerly the spring home of the Kansas City Royals and home of the Baseball City Royals (Single-A Florida State League), Baseball City was more than just a ballpark. Baseball City was a baseball theme park, complete with over thirty rides and attractions, including its own roller coaster. This stadium was designed to bring together all the excitement of the amusement park atmosphere of neighboring Orlando and baseball (including major league spring training). Sadly, it was also a complete failure.

When the ballpark was built at a cost of $13,000,000 in 1988, Baseball City was able to lure the Kansas City Royals away from Fort Myers' vintage Terry Park, where the Royals had trained since 1969. Millions of dollars were spent to create the ultimate baseball paradise. And on the ballpark level, it was a decent success: Baseball City Stadium had more character than many of the ballparks that were built during this era. But as a theme park, it simply could not compete with Disney.

The two teams that used Baseball City as home between 1988 and 1993 provided inspiring games and featured several future impact major league players, such as Kevin Appier, Jeff Conine, Joe Vitiello, Joe Randa, Jon Leiber, and Shane Halter. However, in 1993, after five seasons, Baseball City Stadium's owners—Anheuser-Busch—dismantled the failing theme park and the Single-A Royals moved north to Wilmington, Delaware. The Kansas City Royals, meanwhile, continued to make Baseball City their spring home, since it was still a very good ballpark. The Royals would pull in strong and steady crowds over the next decade.

However, in 2002 the Royals were lured to new spring training facilities in Arizona, and Anheuser- Busch sold the stadium—just as Disney opened its baseball-themed Wide World of Sports. In 2004 Baseball City, a fine ballpark only fifteen years old, was demolished, having been sold to housing developers.

THIS PAGE: Three views of Baseball City Stadium—a good-looking ballpark which was sold by owner Anheuser-Busch to condo developers, who quickly went to work making it an Orlando suburb housing complex.

Location: 301A Philip Randolph Boulevard, Jacksonville, FL

Status: Home of the Jacksonville Suns

Architect: HOK Sport (now Populous)

Opened: 2003

Capacity: 11,000

Dimensions:

Left Field 321 ft

Center Field 420 ft

Right Field 317 ft

Winner of the 2004 Digitalballparks Ballpark of the Year Award

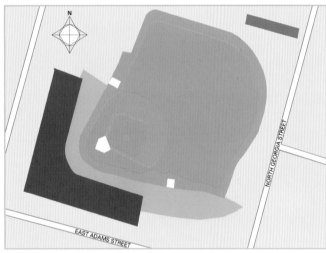

ABOVE: Footprint of the stadium.

TOP and BELOW: A lovely sunset, a good-looking ballpark, and a clean field, kept cleaner by its deliberate lack of advertising. (Photos courtesy, Paul Crumlish Littleballparks.com)

The Baseball Grounds of Jacksonville is a retro park and it replaced the historic Sam W. Wolfson Park, itself as historic a ballpark as could be found in baseball. The new stadium was the brainchild of the Bragan family, who have owned the Suns for many years. The family did its best to make sure that the new ballpark was as memorable as the former: features include a putting green, a terraced berm, and an interesting large hill in left field. The Baseball Grounds of Jacksonville is also the only ballpark in the world to be built onto the grounds of a historic church!

The new stadium looks and feels steeped in history but it also has state-of-the-art training areas, including an indoor batting area hidden beneath the stands. One thing noticeably absent from the ballpark is advertising. This has been kept to a minimum, especially on the outfield walls.

The Suns play in the Southern League and the team is—since 2009—the Double-A affiliate of the Florida Marlins, having enjoyed affiliation to the Cleveland Indians (1962–1963, 1971), St. Louis Cardinals (1964–1965), New York Mets (1966–1968), Kansas City Royals (1972–1984), Montreal Expos (1970, 1985–1990), Seattle Mariners (1991–1993), Detroit Tigers (1994–2000), and Los Angeles Dodgers (2001–2008).

Location: 20 America's Cup Avenue, Newport, RI
Aka: Now known as Cardines Field
Status: Home of the Newport Gulls
Opened: 1908; stadium built 1936
Capacity: 3,250
Dimensions:
Left Field 315 ft
Center Field 395 ft
Right Field 285 ft

LEFT: Exterior of this famous old ballpark that looks a lot sprightlier after its $1 million facelift.

BELOW: Footprint of Cardines Field.

Now known as Cardines Field and home of the Newport Gulls of the New England Collegiate Baseball League, baseball has been played at the site from at least 1908, when local railroad workers formed a league of six teams and began playing at Basin Field. The amateur Sunset League began using this ballpark in 1925 and its teams still use it today. The New England Collegiate Baseball League also plays at this vintage ballpark. Cardines Field, named after Bernardo Cardines, a Newport baseball player who died in World War I, was often visited by barnstorming Negro National League teams throughout the early 1940s. The ballpark faced demolition in 1980 when there were plans to turn it into a parking lot, but funds were raised for renovation work that brought it back into playing condition. Today it is almost a new ballpark, having had nearly a million dollars spent on it. The effect on attendance has been dramatic, with average figures topping 40,000 annually.

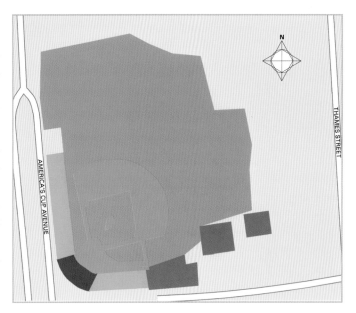

LEFT: Basin Field was renamed for Bernardo Cardines, a Newport baseball player who died during World War I. The city bought the field in 1937 and the Works Progress Administration built the bleachers after that; the grandstand was built around 1941.

Bay Street Ball Grounds

Location: Bay Street near Webster Avenue, Rochester, NY

Opened: 1908

Closed: 1928

Capacity: 13,000 (opening day, May 15, 1909)

BELOW, from LEFT to RIGHT:

LEFT: Opening day 1909 drew a substantial crowd—some 13,000.

CENTER: Rochester Bronchos playing Newark in 1910.

RIGHT: The Bronchos became the Hustlers in 1912

(All Albert R. Stone Collection, Rochester Museum and Science Center)

Two versions of Culver Field were the first homes to many Rochester teams—the International League Rochester Bronchos played there from 1899 to 1907—but the first burned down in 1892 and the second collapsed in 1906. The Rochester Bronchos sold the ground and moved to the new Bay Street Ball Grounds (or Ballpark) that opened in 1908. The Bronchos brought in good crowds but their first year performance didn't live up to expectations and they came last in their league.

The turnround in 1909 was complete. They went from last to first and won the championship from the Newark Indians, the first for the Bay Street Ball Grounds. Two more International League titles would follow in 1910 and 1911. Then, in 1912, the team committed what every superstitious sports fan knows to be a cardinal error: in the middle of this great run they changed their name—to the Rochester Hustlers. They came second that year and did so again the next year. They were not able to hit the heights again.

The Rochester Hustlers became the Colts in 1921 and by 1926, now called the Rochester Tribe, they began receiving complaints that Bay Street Ball Grounds was not able to keep up with fan demand. In fact, it seemed to be decaying rapidly. The team announced that they would move to a new stadium in 1928. Silver Stadium (aka Red Wings Stadium when the team changed its name yet again after they moved to the new ballpark) would be home to Rochester professional baseball for almost seventy years until it was replaced by Frontier Field in 1997.

BellSouth Park

Location: 201 Power Alley, Chattanooga, TN

Aka: Renamed AT&T Park in 2007

Opened: 2000

Status: Home of the Chattanooga Lookouts

Capacity: 6,362

Dimensions:

Left Field 330 ft

Center Field 400 ft

Right Field 325 ft

RIGHT: Most of the seating is on the right-field side of the ballpark as can be seen from this view of the asymmetric grandstand.

BellSouth Park was designed to take Chattanooga into the twenty-first century, taking over from historic Engel Stadium. Lookouts team president and general manager Frank Burke has created a unique modern ballpark designed to fit in with the beautifully revitalized Riverfront district. With an interstate highway running right through the site, except for the small bleacher-like section and a couple of rows of box seats behind the dugout, there isn't a left-field line grandstand and almost all of the seating capacity runs from home plate to right field. The name changed following Bell's acquisition by AT&T.

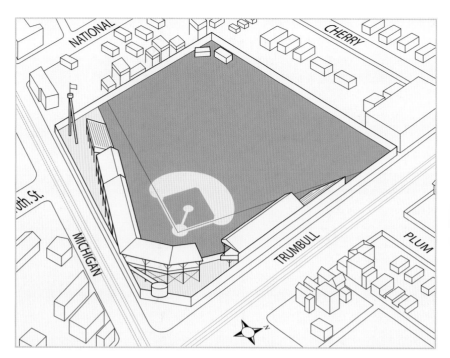

Location: Corner of Michigan and Trumball, Detroit, MI
Opened: 1896
Status: Demolished 1912
Capacity: 5,000 (1896); 14,000 (1911)
Dimensions:
Left Field 285 ft
Center Field 390 ft
Right Field 324 ft
World Series: 1907, 1908, and 1909

LEFT: Artist's impression of Bennett Park.

Bennett Park, in the Corktown district of Detroit, was named after major league catcher Charlie Bennett, the Detroit catcher of the late 1800s who lost both legs in a train accident in 1894. It was home to the Detroit Tigers, a team that started in the minor Western League and debuted there in April 1896. A few months after this, Bennett Park brought night baseball games to Detroit on September 24, 1896.

There was one main problem with Bennett Park. It faced west and the setting sun was always in the batter's eye. It also did not occupy a complete block and was restricted in left field. Between the 1911 and 1912 seasons, the Tigers acquired the rest of the block, demolished some unofficial bleachers and Bennett Park itself, and built Navin Field on the same site, though the new stadium was shifted by ninety degrees with home plate located where the left-field corner had formerly been—thus solving the problems with the setting sun.

LEFT: Bennett Park in 1896 shortly after opening.

BELOW: The seven-game 1909 World Series between the Detroit Tigers and Pittsburgh Pirates was played at Forbes Field (three games) and Bennett Park (four). Top attendance at Bennett was on October 11 (pictured here) when the crowd was 18,277 strong. The Tigers lost the last game and so became the first American League team to lose three straight World Series.

Bethel Park

Location: Eugene, OR
Opened: 1950
Status: Demolished 1969
Capacity: 6,000

Bethel Park was built in west Eugene just off the intersection of Seneca Road and Roosevelt Boulevard in 1950. The first professional baseball team to use Bethel Park was the Eugene Larks of the Far West League, who played there in 1950 and 1951. Then pro ball stopped for three years until the creation of the Eugene Emeralds in 1955.

The Eugene Emeralds, aka the Ems, started as charter members of the Northwest League in 1955 and played at Bethel Park. The ballpark was renowned for its huge outfield and subsequent lack of home runs. Then in 1969 the Ems were promoted to the Triple-A Pacific Coast League. Needing a bigger venue, they accordingly left Bethel Park for Civic Stadium, which could accommodate over a thousand more fans.

Bethel Park was demolished in 1969, as it was in the way of the westward extension of Roosevelt Boulevard.

Beyerle Park

Location: Newburgh, Cuyahoga County, OH
Aka: Forest City Park (1894–1920)
Opened: 1883
Status: Demolished 1912

Beyerle Park was built as an amusement park by George William Beyerle in forty-seven acres in a ravine in the Washington Park area. It opened in 1883. A baseball diamond was one of the many attractions, along with a beer hall and a shooting gallery. In 1888 it hosted the American Association Cleveland Blues. In 1894 the name was changed to Forest City Park.

Beyerle Park also was used by the Negro leagues—the Tate Stars in 1922, the Browns in 1924, the Elites in 1926, and the Hornets in 1927.

Binghamton Municipal Stadium

Location: 211 Henry Street, Binghamton, NY
Aka: Later NYSEG Stadium
Opened: 1992
Status: Home of the Binghamton Mets (aka the B-Mets)
Capacity: 6,000
Dimensions:
Left Field 330 ft
Center Field 400 ft
Right Field 330 ft

RIGHT: The impressive home of the New York Mets' Double-A team since it opened in 1992.

Originally known as Binghamton Municipal Stadium, NYSEG Stadium is one of the newer breed of ballparks that have taken over the game in the past decade. It has been the home of the New York Mets' Double-A team since it opened in 1992. Located just off Route 7 in downtown Binghamton, NYSEG Stadium has country mountain views from every vantage point of the stadium.

While Binghamton is a fairly large city, between 1968 and 1992 it was without baseball. The former Binghamton team, the Triplets, were located in Johnson City and the ballpark had been demolished to make room for Route 17. Before NYSEG Stadium was built, the Double-A Mets played out of Smith Wills Stadium in Jackson, Mississippi, for the Texas League. The Mets wanted their young future stars a little closer to home and Binghamton was a great untapped market in upstate New York. It seemed like the obvious choice in which to build their new stadium.

Located in the heart of downtown Binghamton, NYSEG Stadium is a "blue collar" ballpark. Binghamton's commercial rail yards are located just over the left-field fence.

Home run hitters aim for the locomotives and coal containers that pass by constantly throughout the game—with the ball carrying on to Pennsylvania.

All of the seating in NYSEG Stadium is located either behind the plate or down the lines. This makes the stadium look relatively big compared to other Double-A parks that may have outfield seating. NYSEG has a capacity of about 6,000, the minimum for Double-A ball.

If you look in the corner by the right-field foul pole, you'll see a little white box with an opening. This is where the relief pitchers hang out to watch the game. They have their own little secret booth tucked away inside the outfield wall.

Location: 1000 Park Avenue, Altoona, PA
Status: Home of the Altoona Curve
Architect: L.D. Astorino Companies, Pittsburgh
Opened: 1999
Capacity: 7,200
Dimensions:
Left Field 325 ft
Left Center 365 ft
Center Field 405 ft
Right Center 375 ft
Right Field 325 ft

Built in 1999, Blair County Ballpark is home to the Eastern League Altoona Curve, named after a dangerous horseshoe-shaped section of the Allegheny Mountain railroad track that leads into the town of Altoona.

The Altoona Curve are an affiliate of the nearby Pittsburgh Pirates. Blair County Ballpark is a big field, double-decked—the only such in the Eastern League—and its capacity of 7,200 is well short of its highest crowd figure. The largest regular-season crowd was 9,255 on August 10, 2003. But perhaps the most interesting feature of this ballpark is its view: just past the left-field fence is a huge white roller coaster, part of Lakemont Park.

Blair County Ballpark almost never came to be. It was not the first choice when the Eastern League was awarded an expansion. In fact, Springfield, Massachusetts, the original home of the Triple-A and Eastern League Springfield Rifles, was to be awarded this franchise. But their ballpark burned down in 1965 and Springfield has been without a team since as the city was unable to acquire the land or the capital needed to build a new ballpark. Altoona suddenly was thrust to the forefront. Developers and lawmakers quickly put together a plan and proposed it to the Eastern League. Their offer was accepted and Blair County Ballpark was built.

Altoona was one of the first cities in the country to be awarded a major league team. Altoona's Columbia Park was the home of the Altoona Mountain Citys (aka Altoona Pride) of 1884, before they moved to Kansas City. Professional baseball finally returned to Altoona in 1995 after a more than a century's absence when the Altoona Rail Kings played for the Heartland League at Vets Field.

TOP: The roller coaster in Lakemont Park.

ABOVE LEFT: Inside the spacious home of the Altoona Curve. At the time this photograph was taken, capacity was 6,200. That has since risen above 7,000.

BELOW: Footprint of Blair County Ballpark.

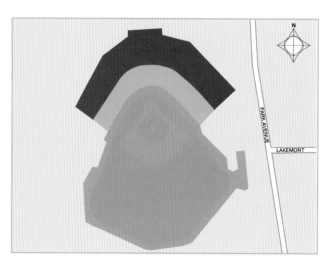

Location: 4700 Deukmejian Drive, Long Beach, CA

Status: Home of the Long Beach State 49ers

Opened: April 11, 1958; renovated 1992, 1999

Capacity: 3,200

Dimensions:

Left Field 348 ft

Center Field 400 ft

Right Field 348 ft

ABOVE: The Chicago Cubs left Blair Field after a year, but it is a fine facility: indeed, better than most of the spring training facilities in use during the mid-1960s. (Photo courtesy of Amanda Lippert, Merzbach BaseballStadiumReviews.com)

BELOW and BOTTOM:
Blair Field footprint and entrance.
(Photo courtesy of Amanda Lippert, Merzbach BaseballStadiumReviews.com)

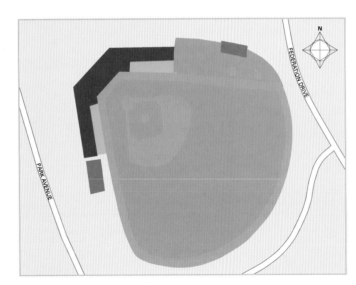

Originally opened in 1958 at a cost of $500,000, Blair Field is in Recreation Park, a sports and leisure area in the southeast of Long Beach. Recreation Park itself was already established as a baseball landmark and the new ballpark was named after a local sports editor, Frank Blair, who had battled all his life to have a ballpark in Long Beach.

With a capacity of 3,200, it has earned a reputation as the center for local amateur baseball, but also hosted spring training for the Chicago Cubs in 1966. Blair Field has seen brief periods of professional play, when the Dodgers played one game in 1967, and a handful of exhibition games between the Angels and the Indians in 1967.

Although many future professionals, such as Jeff Burroughs, Bobby Grich, and Tony Gwynn, began their careers at Blair Field, the facility was long neglected by the city authorities, until it was given a $1.5 million makeover 1992. With a new roof, improved drainage, new seating, and Triple-A standard lighting, the field is now regarded as one of the finest collegiate facilities in the country. The city of Long Beach continues to invest in Blair Field, recently adding a new $300,000 scoreboard with a large clock and an "old-time" look. Other renovations include 774 new box seats, located in the first five rows between first and third base. In 2008, Long Beach State and the city also funded a new scoreboard with a full LCD color video screen and LED score displays. *Baseball America* has recognized this ballpark as one of the top fifteen facilities in North America.

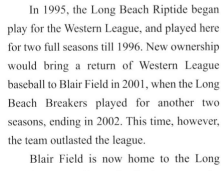

In 1995, the Long Beach Riptide began play for the Western League, and played here for two full seasons till 1996. New ownership would bring a return of Western League baseball to Blair Field in 2001, when the Long Beach Breakers played for another two seasons, ending in 2002. This time, however, the team outlasted the league.

Blair Field is now home to the Long Beach State's 49ers, fondly known as the "Dirtbags," who became the stadium's first full-time tenants in 1993.

After the end of the 1888 season a new all-wooden ballpark was rapidly built at Woodlawn Avenue over the winter months for the start of the next professional baseball season. The fences and wooden grandstand were removed from Olympic Park and moved by horse and wagon to the main entrance of the new site at the corner of Summer Street and Richmond Avenue. Open stands flanked both sides of the grandstand.

Initially called Buffalo Baseball Park, it was the home of the Buffalo Bisons of the International League. Over the years it was rebuilt twice, ruined by fire and built again, but by the 1920s it was showing its age. In 1920 Frank J. Offermann had become the principal owner of the Bisons and the main mover behind the development of a new stadium: he became the Bisons' president in 1928.

During the 1923 season the grandstand was slowly demolished around the crowd with different parts of the ground cordoned off as necessary. For the following season a new canopied, concrete-and-steel stadium appeared on the site, able to accommodate 15,000 fans. It cost $265,0000 and was designed by Louise Blanchard Bethune, who was the first female member of the American Institute of Architects. Now called Bison Stadium, the first game was played on April 3, 1924.

Unfortunately, the first season was a disaster with the rainy weather meaning fifteen games were washed out and the seasonal attendance was unsurprisingly low. In 1930 the first night game was played on July 3 in front of over 11,000 fans, unfortunately it was a loss to Montreal 5–4. Many of the minor league venues also installed lights that year, five years before the professionals did. The initial reason for lighting the game was to attract as many paying customers as possible as the Depression was starting to take serious effect.

In 1935 the stadium was renamed Offermann Stadium in memory of owner Frank J. Offermann following his untimely death at age 59 just before the start of the season.

By 1960 the city of Buffalo wanted the stadium site for a new school, and even though they didn't want to move, the Bisons were forced out of Offermann under threat of demolition. The facility was sold and the Bisons left for War Memorial Stadium after narrowly losing the Junior World Series. The last game at Offermann was on September 17, 1960.

Offermann Stadium was quickly demolished in 1960 and Woodlawn Junior High School built over its footprint.

Location: On the corner of Michigan and East Ferry, Buffalo, NY
Aka: Later (1935) Offermann Stadium (aka Bison Stadium)
Status: Demolished 1960
Architect: Louise Blanchard Bethune (Offermann Stadium stands)
Opened: 1889; rebuilt 1924
Capacity: 4,000; final 13,000
Left Field 321 ft
Left Center 345 ft
Center Field 400 ft
Right Center 365 ft
Right Field 297 ft

BELOW: Frank J. Offermann was the principal investor in the Buffalo Bisons. He bought the team in 1920, and died aged 59 just before the 1935 season. The board voted to rename the stadium after him.

Buffalo Baseball Park

Location: 11th and Y Streets (now Riverside and Broadway), Sacramento, CA
Aka: Moreing Field (1920–1935); Cardinal Field (1935–1944); Doubleday Park (1944); Edmonds Field (from 1945)
Status: Burned down July 11, 1948; rebuilt 1949; demolished 1964
Opened: March 9, 1910
Capacity: 5,000 (1910); 10,000 (1920)
Dimensions:
Left Field 310 ft
Center Field 405 ft
Right Field 280 ft

BELOW: A plaque commemorating Edmonds Field is in the parking lot where home plate used to sit.

BELOW RIGHT and BOTTOM: Interior and exterior views of the "new" home of the Solons, the latter during reconstruction in 1949.

The main ballpark in Sacramento was built in 1910 and was originally known as Buffalo Park. It was named in honor of the Buffalo Brewing Company, the owner of the city's team, the Sacramento Senators, who played in the Pacific Coast League. Originally all dirt, grass was planted the next year in the outfield and by 1912 the park was entirely grassed.

In 1920 the club was purchased by local builder Lew Moreing, and the park was renamed Moreing Field. Moreing expanded the accommodation and invested $100,000 in his new ballpark, building a concrete-and-wood grandstand in addition to the original wooden bleachers, and providing seating for 10,000 fans.

When the Senators became part of the St. Louis Cardinals' franchise in 1935, the park was renamed Cardinal Park, while the Senators became the Sacramento Solons. In 1944 a newspaper contest resulted in another name change, this time to Doubleday Park, but only a year later in 1945, it became Edmonds Field after former *Sacramento Union* sports editor Dick Edmonds.

When the original structure burned down in 1948, the stadium which replaced it retained the name and opened on the same site in 1949. The name may have been the same, but the structure was entirely different. The grandstand was constructed of concrete and, unlike the old wooden structure, lacked a roof. The advertising hoardings, left-field bleachers, and lights survived the fire, so the new stadium was not entirely unfamiliar to Sacramento's die-hard fans.

By the late 1950s, the owners of the Solons, in common with many other franchise owners, were in financial difficulties as the public deserted ballparks for their new television sets. With losses mounting, the Solons were sold in 1961 and became the Hawaii Islanders.

The last game played at Edmonds Field was a classic match in 1964, an exhibition game between the San Francisco Giants and the Cleveland Indians. After home runs by Willie Mays and Willie McCovey, the lights dimmed for the last time on Edmonds Field before the facility was demolished to make way for a discount store.

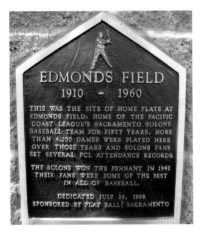

The minor league Buffalo Stadium was built on the East End of Houston, bounded by Leeland Street, St. Bernard Street (present-day Cullen Boulevard), Coyle Street, and Milby Street. It was named after the Buffalo Bayou, which divides Houston. The railroad tracks leading to Union Station, site of the Houston Astros' current ballpark, ran behind the center field wall. It was a well-appointed ballpark for its time with a Spanish-style tiled-roof entryway with large pictures of buffaloes on the adobe wall, and in the late 1950s, ladies' rooms became air-conditioned.

The stadium opened on April 11, 1928 with Houston's then-record baseball crowd of 15,000. Some 12,000 fans attended the first night game on July 22, 1930. The cost of the lighting structures was $250,000—a sizable amount when you consider the overall construction cost was $400,000.

It was used by the Texas League Houston Buffaloes 1928–1958, the Negro American League Houston Eagles 1949–1950, and the Houston Buffs of the American Association 1959–1961. The Houston Buffs were a farm team for the St. Louis Cardinals and the ballpark was later a practice field for the Houston Oilers from the early 1960s. Before Buff Stadium, the team had played at West End Park from 1907 until 1927 at the north corner of Bagby and Jefferson on the southwest edge of downtown.

Briefly renamed Busch Stadium in the 1950s, it was damaged by Hurricane Carla in 1961 and, because it was too small for the majors—Houston had been granted an expansion franchise that saw the Colts (now the Astros) arrive in 1962—it was subsequently sold to furniture mogul Sammy Finger. The stadium was demolished and turned into Finger's Furniture Showroom and Warehouse. The store included a museum dedicated to Houston sports history, with Buff Stadium's home plate position marked on the floor.

Location: Houston, TX
Aka: Buff Stadium; later Busch Stadium
Status: Demolished 1961
Opened: April 11, 1928
Capacity: 12,000; 14,000 (1938)
Dimensions:

	Original 1928	Final 1938
Left Field	344 ft	345 ft
Center Field	430 ft	440 ft
Right Field	344 ft	325 ft

ABOVE, ABOVE RIGHT, and TOP RIGHT: Late 1950s interior views of Buffs Stadium. The press box was added later and the lights in 1930.

BELOW: Opening day, April 11, 1928, a 7–5 victory over the Waco Cubs. Some 15,000 people turned out for that game, the largest single gathering for a baseball game in Houston at that time.

Location: 1501 NW Third Street, Miami, FL

Aka: Renamed Miami Orange Bowl (1959)

Status: Demolished May 14, 2008

Architect: City of Miami Public Works Department

Opened: December 10, 1937

Capacity: 74,476

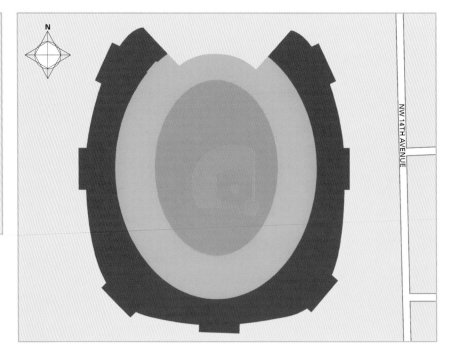

N

NW 14TH AVENUE

BELOW and BOTTOM: The Orange Bowl in its baseball (below) and football (bottom) configurations.

Burdine Stadium, an outdoor athletic stadium that cost $340,000 to construct, was primarily home to the Miami Hurricanes college football team. It also hosted the professional Miami Dolphins for their first twenty-one seasons and was the temporary home of Florida International University football while their stadium underwent expansion during the 2007 season.

It was surfaced in grass (1937–1969 and 1976–2008), experimenting with PolyTurf 1970–1975.

The minor league Miami Marlins baseball team occasionally played games here from 1956 to 1960, and in 1956, 57,000 turned out to watch

Satchel Paige, the largest ever minor-league crowd. The twentieth Caribbean Series of Baseball was played at the Orange Bowl in 1990—an experiment that was not repeated.

The Orange Bowl was best known, of course, for its football—five Super Bowls (II, III, V, X, XIII) were played here—and Burdine Stadium was renamed in 1959 as the Miami Orange Bowl. Despite some controversy and dismay among Hurricanes fans, the Dolphins are set to move into a new ballpark, Miami Stadium, being built on the site. The Orange Bowl was demolished to make way for a new 37,000-seat retractable-roof baseball stadium that is set to open in 2012.

BELOW: Burdine Field was renamed the Orange Bowl in 1959. It's seen here in football configuration.

Burns Park was opened in 1900, specifically to accommodate Sunday baseball games for the Detroit Tigers, who played for the rest of the week at Bennett Park. The ballpark was situated in Springwells, just outside Detroit, and so was not affected by the blue laws, which banned entertainment on Sundays within Detroit's city limits. It was named after the team's owner, the brick manufacturer James D. Burns, who used a plot of his land for the ballpark, and the Tigers played here for just two years.

The all-wooden ballpark was built in a hurry, and it showed. Shortly after it was opened, a strong wind blew the grandstand roof onto the field. The Detroit Tigers, then a popular minor league team, always attracted a good crowd, and the stadium's capacity of 3,000 was frequently exceeded. The grandstand was expanded within a year of opening, and the following year, in 1902, a long line of bleachers was installed to cope with the growing number of fans. The park's popularity may have had something to do with its location next to the saloons and stockyards outside the city's jurisdiction, but it did nothing for the team's reputation. The American League was keen to avoid association with brawling, gambling, hard-drinking fans, and strongly advised the Tigers to move away. Games at Burns Park accounted for approximately one-third of all Tigers' ticket sales between 1900 and 1902, but from 1907, Sunday games were played at Bennett Park and the stands at Burns Park were demolished. The Tigers' attendance figures for Sunday games were reflected in the move: they dropped from around 4,500 to 2,500.

Location: Dix Street, Detroit, MI
Aka: Formerly West End Park
Status: Demolished
Team: Detroit Tigers
Opened: April 28, 1901
Capacity: 3,000; (1901) 5,000
Dimensions:
Left Field 305–315 ft
Center Field 380–390 ft
Right Field 355–365 ft

Burns Park

Busch Stadium

Location: 700 Clark Street, St. Louis, MO

Aka: New Busch Stadium; Busch Stadium III

Status: Home of the St. Louis Cardinals

Architect: HOK Sport (now Populous)

Opened: April 4, 2006

Capacity: 46,861

Dimensions:

Left Field 336 ft

Left Center 375 ft

Center Field 400 ft

Right Center 377 ft

Right Field 335 ft

World Series: 2006

All-Star Game: 2009

RIGHT and OPPOSITE, ABOVE:
Panoramas of the stadium in 2011. The views of downtown St. Louis include the spectacular Gateway Arch—which is engraved in the turf through the skill of the ground staff.

BELOW: Footprint and entrances of Busch Stadium.

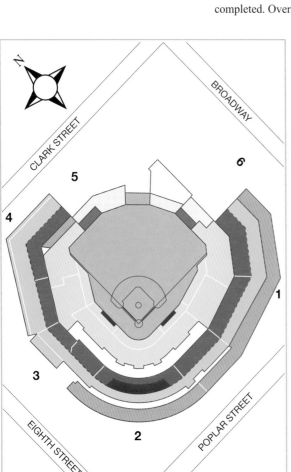

Considered to be one of the most attractive MLB ballparks and sitting almost on top of the old Busch Memorial Stadium, the "new" Busch Stadium is a circular, multipurpose ultramodern venue. It had been a battle to secure the funding but finally agreement was reached between the owners, the State of Missouri, and the city of St. Louis for the creation of a new ballpark in the city. Construction cost $370 million and was in three phases: first the south side of the stadium; then over winter 2005 the old Busch Memorial Stadium was demolished; finally, the north side of the stadium was built. By opening day, April 4, 2006, the bleachers were in place and the field and terrace level seating for about 37,000 people completed. Over the next month the rest of the seating area was finished.

Busch Stadium is constructed from a creative mixture of redbrick, glass, concrete, and shiny steel, and in homage to its previous incarnation, the stadium also has ninety-six open arches as its principal architectural feature. Also the bronze statues from the old stadium were relocated, including, of course, Cardinals legend Stan "the Man" Musial, who now stands outside the third base entrance; the other statues are positioned outside the team store at the corner of Clark and Eighth Streets. The old scoreboard from Busch Memorial Stadium is now positioned on the main concourse. The new stadium also retains the Cardinals' signature green fencing and the old red seat color. A fifty-two-foot-wide by thirty-two-foot-high integrated LED video and scoring system shows footage, scores, and messages. Home plate is in the southwest corner and a main-level concourse encircles the entire ballpark so the play can be viewed from 360 degrees. Parking is next door, over the old Busch Stadium footprint.

Busch Stadium is designed in retro-classic style with panoramic views of downtown St. Louis and, in particular, the Gateway Arch. It accommodates some 2,886 standing fans and 43,000 seated spectators in two red-seated decks; additionally it has 3,706 club seats and 61 luxury suites. On their new grass surface and in the first season at their new home the Cardinals saw a home World Series victory—for the first time since 1923.

The stadium has proved immensely popular with the fans and in the debut season every game was a sell-out and the trend has continued. Other than baseball, the stadium has proved itself as an arena for huge concerts.

64

LEFT: 2011 view of a packed stadium. The Cardinals have been the pride of St. Louis since 1900. They were originally called the Brown Stockings, and then the "Perfectos," before finally settling on the Cardinals at the turn of the century. Since then the Cardinals have been to the post-season more than twenty times. Annual attendance is always over three million, with a 2005 high of just over 3.5 million—that's an average of over 43,000 a game.

BELOW: Exterior of Busch Stadium.

Location: 10710 West Camelback Road, Phoenix, AZ

Status: Home of the Arizona League Dodgers

Opened: March 1, 2009

Capacity: 13,000

Dimensions:

Left Field 345 ft

Left Center 380 ft

Center Field 410 ft

Right Center 380 ft

Right Field 345 ft

BELOW: Footprint of Camelback Ranch, the largest ballpark in the Cactus League.

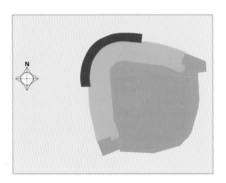

Camelback Ranch—all 141 acres of it, boasting more than 118,000 square feet of major and minor league clubhouse space, thirteen full baseball fields, and three half-fields—is owned and operated by Glendale, Arizona. Holding 13,000 people (10,000 seated and 3,000 on the grass berm), it has the largest capacity of any ballpark in the Cactus League. The ballpark replaced Holman Stadium in Vero Beach, Florida, as the Dodgers' spring training home and Tucson Electric Park in Tucson, Arizona, as the White Sox equivalent. To help them feel at home, two of the twelve practice fields (four major league, eight minor league) are replicas of Dodger Stadium and U.S. Cellular Field. A lake filled with fish separates the two major league teams' facilities. The park, which has a playing field sunk some twelve feet below ground level to give better sight lines, is also home to the rookie level minor league affiliate Arizona League Dodgers, who moved to Camelback Ranch with the major league team in 2009.

TOP: Spring training in 2011 saw thirty games played at Camelback Ranch. This view shows the press boxes and suites housed in a wooden structure reminiscent of Frank Lloyd Wright's desert home at Taliesin West in Scottsdale.

LEFT and BELOW: These photographs give a good idea of the size of the ballpark and attendance levels.

Location: 300 South Main Street, Akron, OH
Status: Home of the Akron Aeros
Architect: Populous
Opened: April 10, 1997
Capacity: 9,000
Dimensions:
Left Field 331 ft
Left Center 376 ft
Center Field 400 ft
Right Center 375 ft
Right Field 337 ft

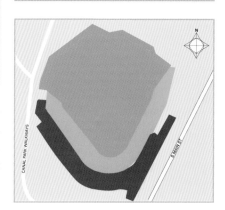

The home of the Akron Aeros is right in the heart of downtown Akron—a green oasis and a centerpiece for this Ohio city. Originally named the Canton-Akron Indians, they had been located in Thurman Munson Stadium in Canton, but as with so many teams throughout the United States, location was the key factor in the team's failure. Up until the mid-1990s, it was common for ballparks to be located in the middle of nowhere—which was the case with Thurman Munson Stadium, which was effectively obsolete the day after it was built.

Canal Park was a pioneer of a new breed of stadium not only because of its look, but because of its location right in the middle of the business district. The downside was the cost of real estate—$31 million, quite a bit for a Double-A franchise—the upside was the 500,000 fans a year the team drew for the first three seasons. The Aeros were no longer hidden from view: they were where the people of Akron worked, ate, and spent their evenings. In one season, the Akron Aeros went from a fledgling franchise to setting all-time Eastern League attendance records. It quickly set off a "downtown ballpark" building frenzy. Within a matter of three years, there were similar ballparks built in Toledo, Dayton, and then throughout the United States.

Named for the waterway that runs outside, Canal Park is a very roomy 8,500-seat ballpark which boasts twenty-five luxury boxes. Double-A standards require 6,000 seating minimum: this 9,500-seat stadium is expandable to 12,500, which gives the Aeros the option to go Triple-A, if the possibility ever arises. Canal Park also boasts the largest free-standing scoreboard in all of minor-league baseball. It measures 56 feet x 68 feet and has the capabilities for full color animation as well as a four-color matrix display.

THIS PAGE: Canal Park is spacious and roomy with good views of downtown Akron.

Location: 602 Jamestown Avenue, San Francisco, CA

Aka: 3Com Park at Candlestick Point (1995–2002); San Francisco Stadium at Candlestick Point (2002–2004); Monster Park (2004–2008)

Status: NFL football field

Architect: John Bolles

Opened: April 12, 1960

Last MLB game: September 30, 1999

Capacity: 43,765 (original), 58,000 (final, for baseball)

Dimensions:

Left Field 330 ft (1960), 335 ft (1968)

Left Center 397 ft (1960), 365 ft (1961)

Center Field 420 ft (1960), 410 ft (1961), 400 ft (1982)

Right Center 397 ft (1960), 365 ft (1961)

Right Field 330 ft (1965), 335 ft (1968), 330 ft (1991), 328 ft (1993)

World Series: 1962, 1989

All-Star Game: 1961, 1984

ABOVE: Exterior view.

BELOW: 1960s postcard showing a bird's-eye view of Candlestick Park and the surrounding area. The proximity to the Pacific Ocean made the wind in the stadium unpredictable.

Overlooking San Francisco Bay in the Bayview Heights area, Candlestick was a beautiful place to watch baseball on a warm, sunny day; unfortunately, that was a relative rarity. More often the stadium's exposed location and semicircular double-deck grandstand would subject spectators to some of the worst weather in baseball—it was cold, damp, windy, and sometimes foggy. A box holder even sued the stadium owners because his box was too cold ... and won. "The Stick" acquired the reputation of being the coldest and windiest in the majors, and that was when it wasn't fog-bound.

Candlestick Park can claim to be the first modern baseball stadium as it was constructed entirely of reinforced concrete. But in such an open location, the park started to fall apart within years of opening, and needed substantial dollars for refurbishment: having cost $15 million to build in 1960, the city of San Francisco contributed $16.1 million to modify and enlarge the park as part of its welcome to the NFL's 49ers for the 1972 season. The double-decking seating was extended over winter 1971–1972 to fully enclose the stadium and was predicted (by some) to improve the experience for baseball fans. It didn't: instead the cold, damp winds swirled unpredictably around the stadium rather than howling straight into the ballpark. To add insult to injury, the view of the bay was cut off completely. Nevertheless, the San Francisco Giants played at Candlestick for almost four decades before moving to a new stadium at Pacific Bell Park.

In an attempt to reduce the clouds of dust that swirled around the playing area on hot days, in 1970 artificial turf was laid down on the playing field in place of the natural

bluegrass. The ploy worked but was tough on the players around the pits, so for the following season dirt cut-outs were made around the bases as sliding pits: this lasted until the end of the 1978 season when the artificial turf was replaced by grass.

During their 1989 World Series against the Oakland A's, the Bay Area was struck by the huge Loma Prieta earthquake just minutes before the start of game three. Candlestick Park took some minor damage but amazingly nobody was hurt—Candlestick's solid structure possibly saved many lives that day. The World Series was stalled for ten days while structural engineers assessed the damage.

The Giants played (and lost) their last game at Candlestick Park against the Dodgers. In 2000 they moved to Pacific Bell Park, then called AT&T Park and now SBC Park.

BELOW: Aerial view of Candlestick Park configured for baseball; now home field of the San Francisco 49ers NFL team.

Location: 4601 Ontario Street, Vancouver, British Columbia, Canada
Aka: "The Nat"; later Scotiabank Field at Nat Bailey Stadium
Status: Home of the Vancouver Indians
Opened: July 1, 1951
Capacity: 6,500
Dimensions:
Left Field 335 ft
Center Field 395 ft
Right Field 335 ft

BELOW: Footprint of Capilano Stadium.

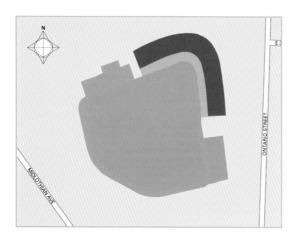

TOP and BELOW: A classic 1950s ballpark. External and internal views of the stadium before renaming as Scotiabank Field.

Nat Bailey Stadium was built at a cost of $550,000 in 1951 and named Capilano Stadium. It replaced the aging Athletic Park, which had been home to baseball in Vancouver since 1913. The new concrete-and-steel ballpark was the jewel of the city and its sturdy, classically beautiful construction was hard to ignore. Before long, the ballpark was promoted from Single-A baseball to the Triple-A Pacific Coast League. With a capacity of 6,500 (7,000 people squeeze in on Canada Day) and a stunning location, it has always been a popular venue.

It immediately became home to the Vancouver Capilanos, a highly successful team in 1951 with a 94–51 record. With the opening of the new ballpark, attendance at Capilano games rocketed from just under 100,000 fans in 1950 to 165,000 the following year. By the end of the decade, however, Capilano, like every stadium in America, began to suffer from the effects of the introduction of television. Attendance declined so much that just five years after opening, Capilano went dark for a year as the Northwestern League cut teams.

In 1956 the Oakland Oaks arrived, changed the team name to the Vancouver Mounties, and made Capilano a Triple-A facility. They remained until 1969, when the team was sold to Salt Lake City.

The stadium was dark for seven years from 1970 to 1977, but when baseball returned in 1978, the ballpark was renamed in honor of Nat Bailey, the restaurateur who had done so much to popularize baseball in Vancouver. The Oakland Athletics announced that they would make the stadium their Triple-A home, but they remained for just one season before they were succeeded by the Milwaukee Brewers. The Vancouver Canadians, the Northwest League affiliates of the Toronto Blue Jays, have played home games at Nat Bailey since 2000.

The City of Vancouver, which owns the stadium, is keen to modernize the facilities, while retaining as much of its 1950s' character as possible. In 2010 the naming rights were sold to Scotiabank and the stadium became Scotiabank Field at Nat Bailey Stadium.

The Capitoline Grounds ballpark, also known as Capitoline Skating Lake and Base Ball Ground, was built to match nearby Union Grounds. The park was, at first, the temporary home of several local teams but it soon became the full-time home of the Atlantic Base Ball Club of Brooklyn, a team that had been founded in 1855 and was in the National Association of Base Ball Players.

Many of organized baseball's first memorable events took place at the ballpark during the 1860s and early 1870s. The perhaps most noteworthy came on July 14, 1870, when a large crowd (estimated at 20,000) watched the Atlantics end the Cincinnati Red Stockings' eighty-four-game winning streak with a come-from-behind 8–7 victory in the bottom of the eleventh inning. The Reds' captain, Harry Wright, had turned down a proposal to draw the game at 5–5 at the end of the ninth inning.

The Atlantics won their last game at the ballpark in 1872 but left for the Union Grounds the following year. The Capitoline Grounds continued to host lesser matches, but John B. Day, who owned the New York Metropolitans in 1880, was frustrated about having to play in then-isolated Brooklyn. Happily, his shoeshine boy suggested a site in much more convenient Manhattan, a piece of land that would become renowned as the Polo Grounds.

Location: Brooklyn, New York, NY
Opened: 1864
Closed: 1880
Capacity: 5,000

Capitoline Grounds

TOP: View of the grandstand of Capilano Stadium.

RIGHT: Few images remain of the Capitoline Grounds, which was closed in 1880. This view shows a game in 1866

Cashman Field

Location: 850 North Las Vegas Boulevard, Las Vegas, NV

Status: Home of the Las Vegas 51s

Opened: 1983

Capacity: 9,334 (12,500 with standing room and berm)

Dimensions:

Left Field 328 ft

Center Field 433 ft

Right Field 323 ft

World Series: Home to the Triple-A World Series 1998–2000

All Star Game: Triple-A All-Star Game on July 11, 1990

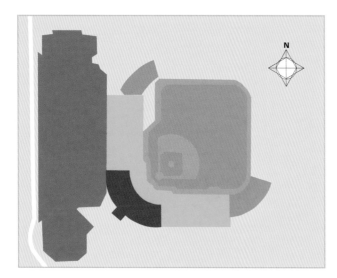

ABOVE, TOP to BOTTOM: View from right field with mountains in the distance; view of the main grandstand from left field; footprint of Cashman Field with Cashman Center alongside.

Cashman Field is a ballpark with a problem: location. Situated in one of the great leisure cities of the world, the attractions of Las Vegas lure visitors and inhabitants alike away from the ball games to the bright lights, the glitter, and the rustle of money.

Built in 1983, Cashman Field was originally home to the San Diego Padres and the Las Vegas Stars, from 1983 until 2000. From 2001 to 2008, it was the Triple-A home of the 51s, the Stars renamed as the minor league affiliates of the Los Angeles Dodgers, who utilized the region's alien connections for the team name and logo. (Area 51 is a desert location in Nevada infamous for UFO sightings.) Since then, they have been affiliated to the Toronto Blue Jays and play in the Pacific Coast League (PCL). In 1996, the Oakland A's played the first six games of the regular season at Cashman due to construction delays in their home stadium.

Cashman Field usually draws 335,000 fans per year and since it opened in 1983 the stadium has never broken the 400,000 mark. However, attendance has never sunk as low as 200,000 either. While this level of consistency might be a general manager's dream, in a way it's not, because while the population of Las Vegas has tripled since 1983, attendance has remained static. On April 1, 1983, when the San Diego Padres faced the Seattle Mariners, 13,878 crammed into the ground, a figure surpassed easily on April 3, 1993, when a record 15,025 watched the Chicago White Sox play the Cubs.

Cashman Field is a perfect desert ballpark. With its dark reds and beige highlights, the colors mimic the local scenery. Helping to create this atmosphere are unusual light towers. Fans of major league baseball can still get their dose right here; every spring training at least one major league exhibition game is played.

The Stratosphere peeks from just past the light tower, and the Vegas Strip beckons fans to join all the action after the game. Cashman Field does not get enough respect as a unique and exciting place to see a ball game.

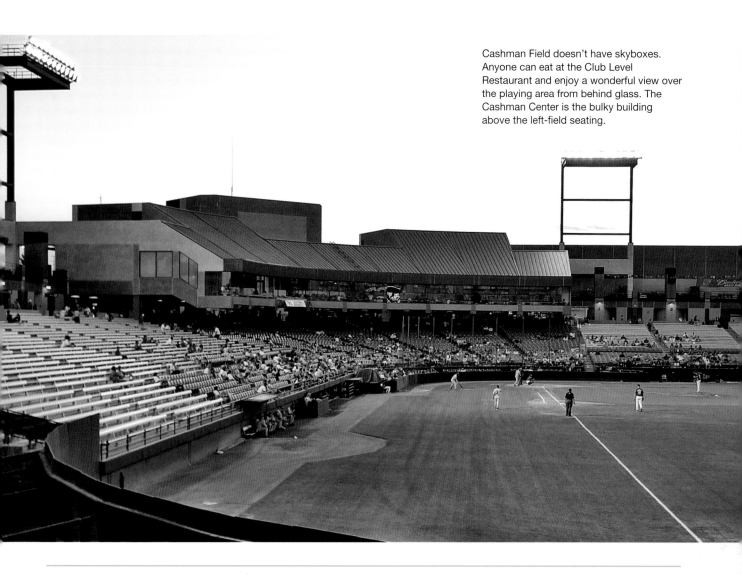

Cashman Field doesn't have skyboxes. Anyone can eat at the Club Level Restaurant and enjoy a wonderful view over the playing area from behind glass. The Cashman Center is the bulky building above the left-field seating.

Casino Park was a ballpark in the Negro League that was home to the Monroe Monarchs, a team that played from the late 1920s until 1935. Unusually in the segregation era, the team was created and owned by a white Texan oil millionaire, Fred Stovall, and was keenly followed by both black and white fans.

The Monarchs initially played in the semi-pro Dixie League, until Stovall founded the Negro Southern League. The Monarchs won the league title in 1932, and went on to challenge the Pittsburgh Crawfords in the Negro League World Series. This match brought some of the great Negro players to Casino Park, such as Satchel Paige, Cool Papa Bell, and Josh Gibson (then known as "the black Babe Ruth"). According to one story, Gibson hit a home run that landed on a passing train, and the Crawfords claimed that the shot carried on to the next town.

Casino Park was situated on Stovall's plantation, at the junction of what became 29th Street and Hope, and the area is now a park with recreational facilities. The ballpark's facilities were widely admired, particularly as it was unusual for a Negro League team to have its own ballpark. The Monarchs not only had a ballpark, but Stovall also provided accommodation, a cook, and three cars for the team's travel.

All that remains of Casino Park today is a marker which reads:

"One half mile North. The Monroe Monarchs played Negro League baseball in what was known as Casino Park. Owned by local oil and machine works businessman Fred A. Stovall, the Monarchs became champions of the Negro Southern League in 1932 and played in the Negro League World Series, losing to the Pittsburgh Crawfords. Despite their success, the Monarchs were excluded from the Negro League realignment in 1933. During their short time though, the Monarchs launched the Hall of Fame careers of Hilton Smith and Willard Brown."

Location: 29th and Hope, Monroe, LA
Status: Demolished
Capacity: 3,000
Dimensions:
Left Field 360 ft
Center Field 450 ft
Right Field 330 ft
World Series: 1932 (Negro League)

Casino Park

Location: University Road, Burlington, VT

Aka: Centennial Field II

Status: Home to the Vermont Lake Monsters

Opened: April 17, 1906; renovated 1922; expanded 1995

Capacity: 4,400

Dimensions:

Left Field 330 ft

Center Field 404 ft

Right Field 325 ft

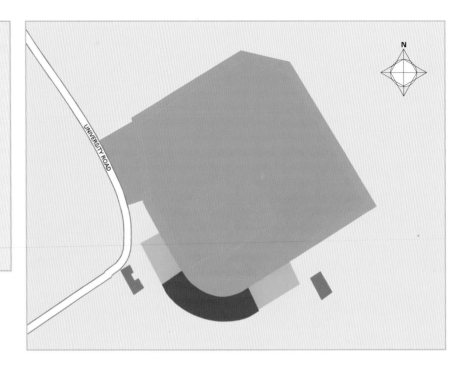

RIGHT: Footprint of Centennial Field.

OPPOSITE, BELOW: Interior and exterior of Hawkins Field in the late 1940s. (Photos courtesy of Chris Hunter)

BELOW: The sylvan setting of Centennial Field. It is home to the minor league Vermont Lake Monsters. The team plays in the short-season A classification New York-Penn League.

The former home of the Vermont Expos, Centennial Field was built to honor the hundredth graduating class of the University of Vermont, and baseball has been played at this location since 1906.

A beautiful wooden grandstand was built for the college and play began with a 10–4 defeat of the University of Maine. Unfortunately, just eight years later, the wooden ballpark burned down.

Centennial Field II was erected using wooden bleachers as a temporary structure, but it outlived the first ballpark, lasting for an entire decade, from 1913 to 1922.

In 1922 a new ballpark was constructed out of steel and concrete. Centennial Field III was created with the expectation that there would be no need for a Centennial IV: eight decades later, very little has changed within these friendly confines. Professional affiliated baseball teams continue to utilize its beautiful turf and tranquil Vermont surroundings, year in and year out. Today, this quintessential Vermont ballpark stands as the oldest professional stadium still being utilized by affiliated minor league baseball.

Centennial Field's first taste of baseball outside the collegiate arena was in the mid-1930s, when the semi-pro Northern League began playing at the ballpark. (This should not be confused with the minor league Northern League based in Minnesota.) Pro baseball arrived in 1955 when Kansas City moved its short-lived Class C affiliation to Burlington, renaming the team the Burlington A's.

After a twenty-year break, baseball returned in 1984, when the Cincinnati Reds installed their Double-A franchise, the Burlington Reds, at Centennial Field. In 1988 the Seattle Mariners took over, with the Burlington Mariners playing for one very successful year. The stadium was renovated in 1993 and the Montreal Expos began their long association with the ballpark, which lasted until 2004. The home team is now the Vermont Lake Monsters, recently affiliated with the Oakland Athletics.

BELOW: The home of UVM athletics since 1906 and a field that saw use by the Negro Leagues, Centennial's grandstand was erected in 1927 and is one of the earliest in the country.

Chadwick Stadium was home to the Albany Senators who played in the New York State League, the original Eastern League, the International League, the New York-Pennsylvania League, and the modern Eastern League. The Senators played a memorable doubleheader at their home ballpark against the Pittsfield Hillies on May 30, 1924—the first game lasted nine innings but the second went to twenty, and it thus remains one of the longest doubleheaders by its number of innings in professional baseball.

Chadwick Stadium was rebuilt in 1928 and renamed Hawkins Stadium the following year. Lights were installed for night games in 1930. The Senators folded in 1959 and their home ballpark was demolished to make way for commercial and administrative buildings.

Location: Albany, NY
Aka: Hawkins Stadium (after 1928)
Status: Demolished 1960
Opened: 1915, rebuilt 1928
Capacity: 6,500 (1915), 10,000 (1928), 8,650 (1944)
Dimensions:
Left Field 300 ft
Center Field 425 ft
Right Field 352 ft

Chadwick Stadium

Chain of Lakes Park

Location: 500 Cletus Allen Drive, Winter Haven, FL

Status: Home of the GCL Indians

Opened: 1966; renovated 1993

Capacity: 7,000

Dimensions:

Left Field 340 ft

Center Field 425 ft

Right Field 340 ft

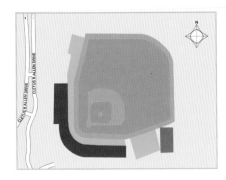

ABOVE: The footprint of Chain of Lakes Park.

THIS PAGE: Chain of Lakes Park benefited from Homestead Stadium's misfortune and became home of the Indians 1993–2009.

Built in 1968, Chain of Lakes Park is the perfect setting for a spring afternoon of baseball and is spring training home to the Cleveland Indians. In 1993 Chain of Lakes Park was renovated, and the capacity increased to over 7,000 seats, a reflection of the team's immense popularity.

Perhaps the most interesting fact about this stadium is that the Indians aren't really supposed to be here. Chain of Lakes Park has been the home base of the Indians since 1993, but they should have been training in a suburb of Miami. In 1992, the Indians commissioned HOK to build them a state-of-the-art spring training facility in Homestead, just south of Miami, complete with six major/minor league practice fields, a 6,500-seat stadium, a 1,000-seat stadium, a dormitory for 200 players, mess halls, and entertainment centers. It was supposed to rival the best of the new Arizona spring training complexes.

Finished in 1992, the entire Homestead Stadium was destroyed by Hurricane Andrew, which swept through on August 24, 1992. With the 1993 spring training season looming, the Indians had nowhere to go. Fortunately, Chain of Lakes Park had recently been vacated by the Red Sox and was ready for use. The only catch was that the Indians needed a few improvements, and in order to persuade the town of Winter Haven to fund them, they agreed to sign a ten-year lease to use the facility. A year or so later, Homestead Stadium had been rebuilt, but it remained empty.

Chain of Lakes has developed into one of Florida's most beautiful ballparks, with an original amphitheater design. From the player's point of view, however, it lacks many of the innovatory features of more modern ballparks and in 2009 the Indians moved out to the $75 million Goodyear Ballpark in Phoenix, Arizona.

Location: 2300 El Jobean Road, Port Charlotte, FL

Status: Home of the Charlotte Stone Crabs and GCL Rays

Opened: 1987; renovated 2008–2009

Capacity: 7,000

Dimensions:

Left Field 338 ft

Center Field 402 ft

Right Field 338 ft

BELOW: The footprint of Charlotte County Stadium.

Charlotte County Stadium was built in 1987, at a cost of $5 million, to be the new spring home of the Texas Rangers, and the summer home of the Florida State League's Charlotte Rangers. It was the successor to the Rangers' venerable and much-loved Pompano Beach Stadium, where they had trained for many years. By the mid-1980s, they had outgrown the facility and struck a deal with the town of Port Charlotte, Florida, to build a modern new ballpark.

The new stadium, located just north of Fort Myers, was a modern facility with training fields, batting tunnels, and seating for 6,000 fans. It featured a large concrete-block press box behind the plate. Long lines of seating went down each side of the stadium, made up of bench seating. Chair seating took up the front five rows. The Rangers moved into the stadium in 1987, but in the early 1990s, baseball stadium designs suddenly became more sophisticated.

With the opening of the Twins' Hammond Stadium (Lee County Stadium) in Fort Myers in 1991, the whole attitude to stadiums changed. It was no longer sufficient to build a big concrete block with the team's insignia on the exterior. Teams now demanded dramatic tropical scenes with fountains and a breathtaking facade. The construction of Palms Park for the Red Sox in 1992, also in Fort Myers, provided a stadium that combined good looks with great atmosphere, and these two stadiums would set a new benchmark for spring training ballpark design.

These new "super ballparks" were great news for ballpark fans, but bad news for the group of ballparks that had just been built from 1985 to 1990. Although only five or so years old, many of the new Florida ballparks were considered obsolete. In 2002 the Texas Rangers and the Kansas City Royals both left their relatively new Florida facilities, to share a new super stadium in Surprise, Arizona.

Charlotte County Stadium's finest hour finally arrived in 2004, when its massive concrete structure survived Hurricane Charlie, which devastated the rest of the city. Although the grandstand and field were seriously damaged, the press box served as a staging area for the emergency services.

Charlotte County Stadium was rebuilt in 2005 and in 2009 the Tampa Bay Rays began their spring training after a $27 million investment to upgrade the facilities.

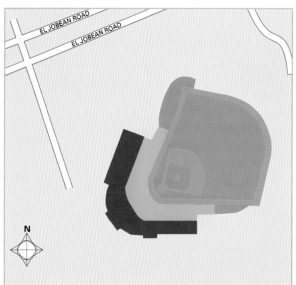

TOP and ABOVE: Charlotte County Stadium was renovated in 2008–2009. The dominant feature is the concrete-block press box.

Location: 401 E. Jefferson Street, Phoenix, AZ

Aka: Bank One Ballpark (1998–2005), the BOB

Status: Home of the Arizona Diamondbacks

Architect: Ellerbe Becket

Opened: March 31, 1998

Capacity: 49,033

Dimensions:

Left Field 330 ft

Left Center 374 ft

Center Field 407 ft

Right Center 374 ft

Right Field 334 ft

World Series: 2001

All-Star Game: 2011

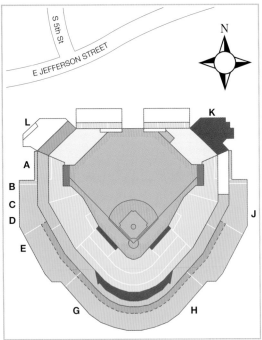

ABOVE: Footprint and entrances of Chase Field, renamed from Bank One Ballpark in 2005.

Bank One Ballpark was named after Bank One of Chicago and has been the home of the Arizona Diamondbacks since their arrival as an expansion team in 1998. The exterior of the stadium is of red brick and green structural steel, with huge baseball murals along the sides. It has been compared to an aircraft hangar but the architects insist it blends seamlessly into the surrounding utilitarian warehouse district of Phoenix.

Arizona in the spring is lovely, but Phoenix in the summer is hot, really hot with average high temperatures of over 100 degrees for three consecutive months. So, to make things bearable for players and spectators alike, the architects installed 8,000 tons of air-conditioning equipment, enough to create cold air for 2,500 homes and cool the temperature down by thirty degrees in three hours before the fans arrive to take their seats.

To prevent the unremitting heat literally cooking the spectators, Bank One Ballpark has a unique retractable domed roof—the first retractable stadium roof in the U.S.—that allows sunlight to shine on the grass playing field. It can fully open and close in five minutes and also has a variety of partially open positions, depending on conditions: this is achieved by using nine million pounds of structural steel and old-fashioned drawbridge technology. On game day, if the roof needs closing, it is left open so that the grass can grow until three hours

RIGHT: Chase Field is rectangular, which is not a normal shape for a baseball stadium. The field is set into the middle of the long part of the rectangle.

before game time; then it is shut and the air conditioning put to work so the ambient temperature drops and the stadium is cooled for the spectators.

Despite all the high-tech equipment—accounting for the $354 million price tag—the park nevertheless has something of a classic feel with its natural grass and old-fashioned dirt strip connecting the pitcher's mound to home plate (only Comerica Park shares this feature). For the spectators, more than 80 percent of the seats are positioned between the foul poles, but there is no upper deck in the outfield. For fans who really want to cool down, there is a swimming pool located just beyond the right field fence, although they run the slight risk of being surprised by a ball flying in 415 feet from home plate, as has happened dozens of times.

In late 2005, Bank One of Chicago merged with New York–based Chase and the ballpark was renamed Chase Field. In 2008 the scoreboard was replaced by a monster 136-foot wide, 46-foot-high high definition scoreboard, costing $14 million: only Kauffman Stadium has a bigger board.

Location: 2502 South Tyler Street, Tacoma, WA

Status: Home to the Tacoma Rainiers

Architect: City of Tacoma, the Triple-A Tacoma Rainiers, and the Cheney Foundation

Opened: 1960

Capacity: 9,600 (current); 20,000 (post-renovations)

Dimensions:

Left Field 325 ft

Center Field 425 ft

Right Field 325 ft

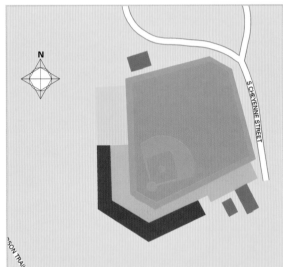

THIS PAGE and OPPOSITE TOP: Footprint and views of Cheney Stadium.

Cheney Stadium is one of the older ballparks of the Pacific Coast League. Built in 1960, this stadium has seen almost every one of the Pacific Coast League brethren move toward the newest and most advanced in ballpark technology. When the Portland Beavers move out of PGE Park to a new ballpark in 2011, Cheney Stadium will be become the oldest ballpark in the league.

The stadium's existence is down to the hard work and investment of one man: lumber magnate and sports fan Ben B. Cheney. The man credited with inventing the "2 by 4" piece of building material had a sharp eye for a good business opportunity. In 1958 the New York Giants were looking for a new stadium after their move to San Francisco, and Cheney persuaded the Tacoma city authorities to build a new home for the team, stumping up $100,000 of his own money to do so. Incredibly, the stadium was built in just forty-two days in time for the Giants' opening game of the 1960 season. Many of the fixtures and fittings were taken from the old San Francisco Seals Stadium, and the wooden seats and lighting are still in place fifty years later.

In 1960 the new Tacoma Giants played at Cheney Stadium for the first time, just as the Rainiers still do today. It was the first time that Tacoma had been a part of the Pacific Coast League since 1905. They took to the field behind future Hall of Fame pitcher Juan Marichal, who would go down in history not only as one of the greatest pitchers in baseball, but also as the first pitcher to win a game at Cheney Stadium. In 1961 the Tacoma Giants would go 97–57, winning the PCL championship, and Ben Cheney couldn't have been more proud.

Since then, Cheney Stadium has been home to seven teams and many great players have played there: Jose Cardenal, Jim Ray Hart, Tito Fuentes, and catcher Randy Hundley of the Tacoma Giants; Tony Phillips and Kelvin Moore, the hitting stars on the early 1980s Tacoma Tigers; and Luis Polonia, Mike Gallego, and Mark McGwire from the late 1980s. Attendance figures soared to over 300,000 per game in the 1989 season.

Home to the Tacoma Rainiers since 1995, the stadium is scheduled for renovation in 2011 and the fruitful association between the Rainiers and Cheney contracted to continue for twenty years.

Chukchansi Park, formerly known as Grizzlies Stadium, is a city-owned baseball stadium and the home of the Pacific Coast League's Fresno Grizzlies since 2002 and the Fresno Fuego of the USL Premier Development League since 2007. Located in downtown Fresno, it is a key component in the rehabilitation of the area.

The dramatic views of the downtown skyline and nearby Sierra Mountains, the incredible sight lines from every seat, the thirty-three luxury suites, two party decks, the spacious Tecate Cantina used for group picnics and special events, and the pool and spa perched just above the left-center fence did not come cheaply: construction cost $46 million—but anyone who has watched a game at the ballpark will agree it was money well spent.

In September 2006, Chukchansi Gold Resort and Casino, a business closely tied to the Chukchansi Native American tribe, announced it would be the premier corporate sponsor for Grizzlies Stadium in a valuable fifteen-year deal. The multipurpose stadium is also used for soccer matches, music concerts, motocross, and high school football games.

Location: 1800 Tulare Street, Fresno, CA
Aka: Formerly Grizzlies Stadium
Status: Current home of the Fresno Grizzlies
Architect: HOK Sport (now Populous)
Opened: May 1, 2002
Capacity: 12,500
Dimensions:
Left Field 324 ft
Center Field 402 ft
Right Field 335 ft

Chukchansi Park

LEFT: Grizzlies Stadium has fine views of Fresno from the grandstand.

BELOW: The tight urban confines are highlighted in this footprint of Grizzlies Stadium.

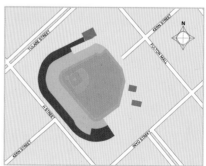

Citi Field

Location: 126th Street and Roosevelt Avenue, Flushing, NY

Status: Home of the New York Mets

Architect: HOK Sport (now Populous)

Opened: March 29, 2009

Capacity: 41,800

Dimensions:

Left Field 335 ft

Left Center 379 ft

Center Field 408 ft

Right Center 383 ft

Right Field 330 ft

RIGHT: Citi has a capacity of 41,800— over 15,000 fewer seats than Shea Stadium.

BELOW: The dramatic exterior of Citi Field is built from red bricks, mimicking Ebbets Field. The front of the building allows access through the Jackie Robinson Rotunda.

After forty-four years the New York Mets said a fond farewell to Shea Stadium at the end of the 2008 season and moved into nearby Citi, built at a cost of $900 million. The new ballpark is designed in the popular retro style by HOK Sport and is a dedicated baseball-only stadium. Named for the global financing services company that bought naming rights for twenty years at $20 million a year, the stadium opened to the public for the first time in 2009. The first game was in April 2009, an exhibition game against the Red Sox.

The impressive arched facade is clad in traditional red brick (a careful color match for the bricks at Ebbets Field), cast stone, granite, and limestone over a robust steel and reinforced concrete interior. The main grandstand runs from the right-field pole to home plate, then to the left-field foul pole and on into left center field. The ballpark has a seating capacity of around 42,000 spectators, all of whom sit on green seats—in homage to the Polo

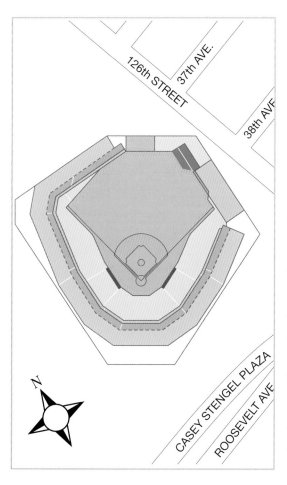

Grounds' color scheme—in three main seating levels, all enjoying excellent sight lines with very few obstructed-vision seats. The fans almost unanimously miss Shea but love their new ground with its modern facilities; it seats about 15,000 fewer spectators than Shea did and claims a more intimate atmosphere partly because of this.

In a nod to the past, the popular Home Run Apple from Shea has been replicated—but four times bigger—and sited beyond the outfield walls where it pops up every time the Mets hit a home run. Another reminder of Shea is the unique orange foul poles, and the famous skyline from the top of the scoreboard that now sits on top of the restaurant in center field.

LEFT: Footprint of Citi Field. A year after moving into its sparkling new $800 million stadium, the *New York Times* reported that while the Mets have the most home victories in the major leagues, attendances were dropping badly—because of the weather and the economic downturn, and—probably the most important—the lack of the immediate success their crosstown rivals enjoyed. As on-field results picked up—the Mets became the first team in baseball to win twenty home games in 2011—no doubt sunshine will breed success.

BELOW: Panorama showing off the Citi Field scoreboard: Daktronics installed 12,000 square feet of scoring and video boards throughout the stadium. In front of the batter's eye is the famous Mets apple that rises when a home run is hit. However, many would say that Citi's spacious outfield ensures that there are fewer of these than at Shea.

Location: Pattison Avenue, Philadelphia, PA

Status: Home of the Philadelphia Phillies

Opened: April 12, 2004

Capacity: 43,000

Dimensions:

Left Field 329 ft

Left Center 370 ft

Center Field: 401 ft

Right Center: 370 ft

Right Field: 330 ft

World Series: 2008, 2009

ABOVE: Entrance to Citizens Bank Park, where the crowd is always ready to "root, root, root for the home team."

BELOW: Memory Lane reminds you of the history of the Phillies, their great players, and great occasions.

Citizens Bank Park is located across the street from Veterans Stadium, the unlamented old cookie-cutter park where the Phillies held court for thirty years. The new baseball-only ballpark opened in time for the 2004 season and is designed to be reminiscent of the original Baker Bowl, where the Phillies first started playing, and of World War I–era grand old Shibe Park.

The classical exterior of Citizens Bank Park is composed of red brick, stone, and steel, and, to add to the impact, the principal entrances are framed by huge standard light. Inside the stadium above first, home, and third are fifty-foot-high glass towers that light up at night.

In order to make the most of the views of downtown Philadelphia over the center field wall, the ballpark is tilted 45 degrees clockwise. The outfield is reminiscent of Shibe Park and much to many Phillies' relief, the infield is natural grass with dirt basepaths. The field itself is quite distinctive with a small lip in left field that can produce eccentric bounces. As part of the design process, the architects conducted extensive wind studies and analysis to measure wind velocities and ball trajectories and concluded that the conditions would not unduly favor either hitters or pitchers: however, time has proved different and Citizens is regarded as being one of the most hitter-friendly parks in MLB.

With a capacity of some 43,000, Citizens Bank Park accommodates 20,000 fewer spectators than Veterans; however, in compensation, it has Ashburn Alley, 625 feet long and

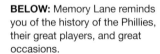

Location: 2077 Willamette Street, Eugene, OR
Aka: Willamette Stadium
Status: Home to South Eugene High School
Architect: Works Progress Administration
Opened: October 27, 1938
Capacity: 6,800

Civic Stadium (or Willamette Stadium) in Eugene, Oregon, is the former home of the Eugene Emeralds (aka Eugene Ems). Civic Stadium was built in 1938 at a cost of $18,000, and until 2009 it was one of the only remaining wooden ballparks still in use in affiliated professional baseball. It has been used for both short-season Single-A baseball and Triple-A Pacific Coast League baseball, and more unusually, has hosted rodeos, football, and just about every other sport. This is why the ballpark was built in an "L" form. The smaller curve in the L is meant more for baseball, while the long first base line is intended for football and soccer.

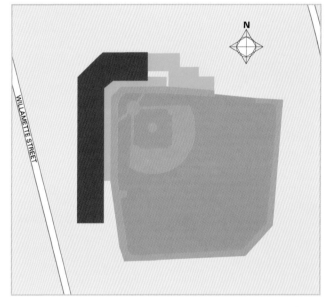

The 5,000-seat stadium began life as an open air ballpark, but was topped off before World War II. Even after the arrival of pro baseball in 1969, the third base line was never built upon, and it still serves as one of the two main picnic areas in the stadium.

The stadium's glory years were arguably 1969–73 when the Eugene Emeralds played here as the Triple-A affiliates of the Phillies. The Phillies were renowned at the time for having one of the most fertile systems in minor league baseball and that impact was felt immediately in Eugene, as several future Phillies stars came to town, including one future Hall of Famer.

Larry Bowa, Oscar Gamble, Willie Montanez, Greg Luzinski, and Larry Hisle all went on to great futures in the major leagues, but the finest player to grace Civic Stadium was undoubtedly Mike Schmidt. Schmidt was more than just a superstar—he would go on to be considered by many as the best third baseman ever to play the game. He made the All-Star team twelve times in his career, won ten Gold Glove awards, and was inducted into the Hall of Fame in Cooperstown in 1995.

The Ems have played their last season at Civic Stadium and have moved to the University of Oregon's new facility at PK Park, citing costs of renovating Civic Stadium as a reason for the move.

Today there is doubt that the stadium will survive without the Ems, and it is possible that this historic ballpark will disappear.

THIS PAGE: Willamette Stadium was the first professional home of future Hall of Famer Mike Schmidt as well as future MLB All-Stars Greg Luzinski, Larry Hisle, Mario Soto, Larry Bowa, Eric Davis, Jeff Russell, Tom "Flash" Gordon, Kevin Appier, Mike Sweeney, Jon Lieber, Lance Carter, Odalis Perez, and Jason Bartlett.

Clark Griffith Park

Location: 400 Magnolia Avenue, Charlotte, NC

Aka: Jim Crockett Sr. Memorial Park from 1971

Status: Burned down on March 16, 1985

Opened: 1940

Capacity: 6,500

Dimensions:
Left Field 320 ft
Center Field 390 ft
Right Field 320 ft

There were very few stadiums in the world that could compare with the colorful wooden ballpark that went by two different names, Clark Griffith Park from 1940, and from 1971 onward, Jim Crockett Park. The beautiful wooden grandstand, interwoven with steel beams, was a marvel when it was completed in 1940 and it became home to the Charlotte Hornets, the Charlotte Orioles, the Charlotte Twins, and three future major league baseball Hall of Fame ballplayers.

There is some discrepancy as to when Crockett Park first hosted professional baseball. The Hornets had been playing in the Piedmont League at Hayman Park when this ballpark was completed in 1940 and did not play at Clark Griffith Park until 1941. Some books state that they remained at Hayman Park until 1946, but the reality was probably a little of both. The Hornets probably began playing here in 1941 while still maintaining Hayman Park as its main base.

Part of the Washington Senators organization, the Hornets enjoyed great success at the end of the 1940s, dominating the Tri-State League and winning the championship in 1946 and 1948. Attendance at Clark Griffith Park rocketed, as 111,000 fans came through the gates. Even though the team failed to make the playoffs in 1948, record numbers of spectators turned out, rising to 122,000 in the 1948 season.

Charlotte's fruitful relationship with the Washington Senators continued even after the franchise moved to Minnesota and became the Minnesota Twins in 1961. The Twins began sending major talent to Charlotte, such as Tony Oliva and Graig Nettles, who both became major league All-Stars.

In 1973 the Twins and Charlotte parted company, and baseball was not revived in the city until 1976, when the stadium became Jim Crockett Memorial Park and the Baltimore Orioles moved their Double-A Southern League franchise, the Charlotte Os, into Crockett Park for the 1976 season.

Just four years after the debut of another Hall of Famer, Cal Ripken Jr., at Crockett Park, the stadium was burned down by juvenile arsonists and an icon of baseball history disappeared forever.

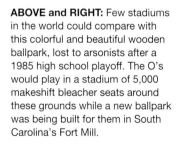

ABOVE and RIGHT: Few stadiums in the world could compare with this colorful and beautiful wooden ballpark, lost to arsonists after a 1985 high school playoff. The O's would play in a stadium of 5,000 makeshift bleacher seats around these grounds while a new ballpark was being built for them in South Carolina's Fort Mill.

Clearwater Athletic Field was one of the great spring training facilities in Florida from 1922 to 1955, when it was replaced by Jack Russell Stadium. During the Brooklyn Dodgers' tenure (1923–1932 and 1936–1941), it was known as Brooklyn Field, and between 1935 and 1938 it was renamed Ray Green Field in honor of Clearwater's mayor. The site is now the parking lot for Jack Russell Stadium.

Built in 1922, the 2,000-seat stadium was first used for professional baseball in 1923, when the Brooklyn Dodgers arrived for spring training. More than 4,000 fans turned out for the first game, when the Dodgers defeated the Boston Braves 12–7. The small wooden ballpark served them well and they remained incredibly loyal to the city of Clearwater, remaining for just over a decade.

The Newark Bears (1933–1935) stepped in for a short period, and after the Dodgers finally left in 1941, the Cleveland Indians used the stadium in 1942 and 1946, before the Philadelphia Phillies began their long relationship with the city.

The Clearwater Pelicans used the park during the main season, in 1924, and from 1945 to 1954 the Clearwater Bombers, the champions of the Amateur Softball Association, played their home games here. One comment from a softball veteran perhaps explained why the Phillies eventually rebuilt their spring training facility. "The bleachers would seat 300 to 400 people, but the nails stuck through and, if you weren't careful, you'd rip your fanny."

Eventually the Phillies decided that they needed more spacious facilities and replaced Green Field with a new concrete ballpark. Jack Russell Stadium quickly became an iconic feature of the Clearwater landscape and the Phillies remained there until 2004.

Location: Clearwater, FL
Aka: Formerly Brooklyn Field (1923–1932 and 1936–1941); Ray Green Field (1935–1938)
Status: Demolished 1956
Opened: March 15, 1923
Closed: 1954
Capacity: 2,000 seats plus 1,000 bleachers
Dimensions:
Left Field 340 ft
Center Field 400 ft
Right Field 290 ft

Clearwater Athletic Field

Professional baseball has a long but sketchy history in the Lehigh Valley. Several minor league teams have made Allentown and the surrounding valley their home, but none of them had any sense of longevity. Pro baseball in Allentown has enjoyed mixed fortunes over the years, with attendance at games veering wildly from 85,000 per game in the 1940s, to 40,000 for an entire season in 2004. In 1964 the Breadon Field ballpark was demolished to make way for a shopping mall, and baseball did not return to the area until 1997. So the introduction of a new ballpark in 2008 was viewed with skepticism by many.

In 2007 the Philadelphia Phillies began to look for a new home for their minor league franchise the Triple-A Phillies, who were then based in Ottawa. They wanted their new Triple-A team to represent the steel factories that were responsible for Allentown's highs and lows. The team was named the Lehigh Valley Iron Pigs, pig iron being one of the tools of the trade in making steel. Along with the historical significance, the name also provided

Location: 1050 Iron Pigs Way, Allentown, PA
Status: Home of the Lehigh Valley Iron Pigs
Architect: Populous
Opened: March 30, 2008
Capacity: 10,000
Dimensions:
Left Field 334 ft
Left Center 374 ft
Center Field 400 ft
Right Center 369 ft
Right Field 325 ft
All-Star Game: 2010 Triple-A All-Star Game

Coca-Cola Park

LEFT: A colorful sunset over a packed Coca-Cola Park.

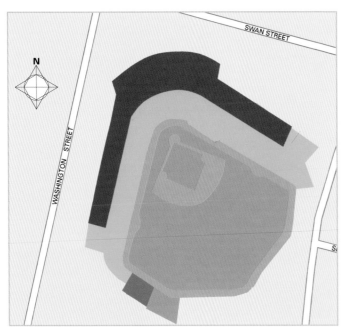

a wealth of possibilities for various marketing mascots and team logos. Most surprising was the budget—a huge $50 million, which enabled the construction of a minor league field built to major league standards.

The Lehigh Valley Iron Pigs drew 602,000 fans to the new 10,000-seat ballpark in 2008, more than any Allentown team had drawn in their entire history. The new team's performance on the field was mediocre, but this did not deter the fans, and with improved play, attendance rose in 2009 and 2010. In 2010 the Lehigh Valley Iron Pigs drew 645,000 fans to see their team finish nowhere near playoff contention, putting them as the top draw in all of minor league baseball from Triple-A to every level below it.

LEFT: Footprint of Coca-Cola Park.

BELOW and BOTTOM: The Lehigh Valley Iron Pigs have a big fan base that ensures great attendance at the massive Coca-Cola Park.

Location: 500 Friday Road, Cocoa, FL

Status: Amateur and training field

Opened: 1964

Capacity: 5,200

Dimensions:

Left Field 360 ft

Center Field 400 ft

Right Field 340 ft

LEFT and BOTTOM: The other end of the scale: Cocoa Expo Stadium—last used as a major league spring training park in 1993 and today showing its age.

Last used as a major league spring training park in 1993 by the Florida Marlins, the Cocoa Expo Stadium was originally built for the Houston Astros (formerly known as the Colt 45s), who left Arizona and trained in Florida for twenty-one years, from 1964 until 1985.

The Astros shared the ground with the Cocoa Astros from 1964, a rookie minor league team in the Florida State League, and affiliated to the Houston Astros from 1965 until 1972. The Florida State League went on to use the stadium for Single A ball games.

The Florida Marlins' inaugural spring training game in 1993 drew 6,696 fans to Cocoa Expo Stadium. Out of that dugout came Jeff Conine to hit the first home run in Marlins history. The Marlins went on to beat the Expos 12–8. Although the Marlins only used Cocoa Expo for a couple of years, the stadium is still painted teal, the color of the Marlins.

Today, Cocoa Expo Center is owned and operated privately. Alongside the original 5,000-seat stadium are six baseball fields, four athletic fields, and basketball and volleyball courts. Since 1984 it has been used for tournaments and competitions for various amateur and semi-pro teams across the country. It is also used by NCAA collegiate teams as a spring training facility to prepare their players for the upcoming season. Since this was a former spring training complex, Cocoa Expo Stadium has many minor league practice fields, as well as a large soccer stadium. While most Florida ballparks wind up on the scrap heap, investors saw a gold mine here in Cocoa. Thanks to private enterprise, this former major league facility will continue to exist for a long time.

It's not hard to see why this ballpark has been retired. Compared to modern spring training facilities, it's surprising that it was still being utilized as late as 1993. However, it still plays a valuable role in the world of college baseball and has a proud history as the former home of the Astros and the Marlins.

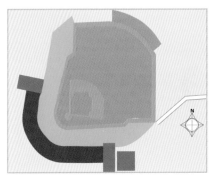

ABOVE: Footprint of Cocoa Expo Stadium.

Location: 22nd Avenue North and First Street North, St. Petersburg, FL
Aka: Sunshine Park
Status: Demolished 1928
Opened: 1914
Capacity: 850

Coffee Pot Park was a small ballpark, but it shot to center stage in 1914 when mayor Al Lang persuaded the St. Louis Browns to travel to Florida for their spring training. It was the beginning of the lucrative arrangement between cities of the Sunshine State and the major league teams that needed warm-weather training facilities every spring.

It offered plain and simple facilities, with one cold shower and a wooden grandstand with a capacity of 500, "if 400 of them were thin," as writer John C. Skipper noted in his book *Wicked Curve*. Situated near Coffee Pot Bayou, the park was also used by local high school teams and softball amateurs during the main season.

For the first game in 1914, the Chicago Cubs sailed across Tampa Bay to beat the Browns 3–2 in front of 4,000 fans. The Browns remained for just one season, but the Philadelphia Phillies took their place in 1915, remaining for three years. Part of their training was the daily two-mile walk from their hotel along the bayou to the ballpark.

Several minor league clubs used the park for their training. The St. Petersburg Saints played at Coffee Pot Park from 1914 and were part of the Florida State League from 1920 to 1928. The Double-A Indianapolis Indians trained here during the 1921 season.

The location of the ballpark was never really very satisfactory, situated as it was on a bayou two miles north of the city. In 1916 a game against Tampa ended early, "in order that the visitors could catch the boat back to Tampa," according to the local newspaper. Coffee Pot Park met its end in 1928 and has been replaced by the Snell Isle Golf Club.

Location: Houston, TX
Aka: Colts Stadium
Status: Dismantled and shipped to Mexico
Opened: 1962
Capacity: 33,000
Dimensions:
Left Field 360 ft
Left Center 395 ft
Center Field 420 ft
Right Center 395 ft
Right Field 360 ft

Houston was without a major league team until 1962 when the city persuaded MLB to grant them a franchise; their decision was swayed by an impressive model of a domed stadium, the very first of its kind, though it only existed on paper. Baseball arrived in Houston, in the form of the Colt .45s, but while their new venue was being built they made their home at Colt Stadium as a stopgap.

The temporary ballpark cost $2 million, with a capacity for 33,000 spectators, and was ready by the start of the 1962 season in April. The spectators could sit in open, single-tiered stands that ran either side of home plate down left and right fields to the foul poles. The scoreboard was located in the center and was flanked by bleachers in right and left field.

Unfortunately, the very open aspect of the ballpark left spectators roasting in the heat of the Texas climate during daytime, with little respite during evening games from the blistering temperatures. At one particularly notorious Sunday game some hundred Colt fans had to be given first aid for heat-related problems. The other problem was the mosquitoes that appeared in the humid weather and ate players and fans alike alive—one of the problems that the Astrodome solved.

The Colts stayed at Colt Stadium for just over two years until 1964, when the Astrodome was ready and the Colt .45s moved in, becoming in the process the Houston

BELOW: The Houston Astrodome was built in the shadow of Colt Stadium.

RIGHT: The scoreboard during the game between the Houston Colts and the Los Angeles Dodgers at Colt Stadium, April 29, 1964.

ABOVE: Colt Stadium was hot. Rusty Staub said, "I don't care what ballpark they ever talk about as being the hottest place on the face of the earth, Colt Stadium was it." Even at night it was hot—and the mosquitoes were terrible. I guess that's why you build a dome!

BELOW: 1962 seating guide to the main stands at Colt Stadium. Note the ticket prices—now those *were* the days.

Astros. Colt Stadium was left mainly as a storage facility during which time its owner, Roy Hofheinz, had it painted gray so that it wouldn't show up on aerial shots and blemish the view. The stadium was occasionally used by the Astros before away games to acclimatize them to outdoor conditions, although the rattlesnakes basking on the field were an unwelcome hazard.

Then in the late 1960s, a minor league Mexican team bought the stadium, dismantled it, and shipped it to Gomez Palacio, Mexico, where it was reconstructed for a minor league team. The stadium has since moved again, to Tampico, Mexico, where it remains. As for the old Colts ground, it was paved over and became part of the Astrodome parking lot.

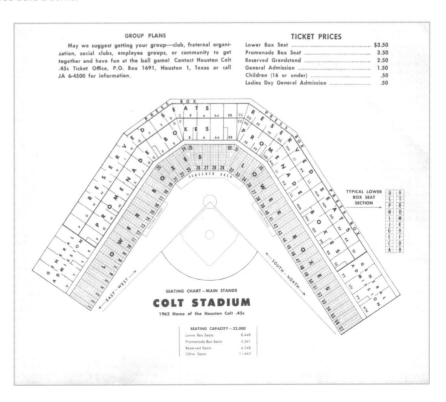

GROUP PLANS

May we suggest getting your group—club, fraternal organization, social clubs, employee groups, or community to get together and have fun at the ball game! Contact Houston Colt .45s Ticket Office, P.O. Box 1691, Houston 1, Texas or call JA 6-4500 for information.

TICKET PRICES

Lower Box Seat	$3.50
Promenade Box Seat	3.50
Reserved Grandstand	2.50
General Admission	1.50
Children (16 or under)	.50
Ladies Day General Admission	.50

SEATING CHART—MAIN STANDS

COLT STADIUM

1962 Home of the Houston Colt .45s

SEATING CAPACITY — 32,000

Lower Box Seats	8,448
Promenade Box Seats	5,541
Reserved Seats	6,348
Other Seats	11,663

Location: Philadelphia, PA

Aka: Centennial Park (1875–1883), Recreation Park (1883–1890)

Status: Demolished 1890

Opened: 1860

Capacity: 6,500

Dimensions:

Left Field 300 ft

Center Field 331 ft

Right Field 247 ft

The Philadelphia Phillies occupy a special place in baseball history, being the oldest continuous franchise that has stuck with the same name and its home city since the day of its foundation. The early parks of this legendary team are, therefore, an important part of their legacy.

Recreation Park was the team's first home. It is likely that the field was the site of the first baseball game played in Pennsylvania in 1860, but with the advent of the Civil War the field was occupied by the Union Army for the next few years.

In 1866 it became Columbia Park and was enclosed with a nine-foot-high fence, but it was barely used and by 1871, even these rudimentary facilities were looking neglected. In 1875, it was taken over by the Philadelphia Centennials of the National Association, who built a clubhouse and grandstands and attracted crowds up to 5,000 strong. Renamed Centennial Park, it survived despite the fact that the league collapsed the following year. By the late 1870s, part of the grounds had been taken over by a horse market.

Finally, in 1882 former player Alfred J. Reach purchased the land and turned it into an acceptable baseball field, despite the odd dimensions of the site. Only 79 feet from home plate to the grandstands, with a short right-field line of 247 feet, it became the home of Roach's new team, the Phillies.

With a three-section grandstand, the park had a total capacity of 6,500: 2,000 on bleachers, 2,500 standing, and 1,500 in the grandstands. For four years, the Phillies drew increasingly large crowds, until in 1886 it became clear that the team needed a new home. The Phillies moved out to the Baker Bowl and Recreation Park was retired. The land was built over, and sadly, there is no visible reminder of the Phillies' original home.

Location: 2900 Columbia Avenue, Brewerytown, PA

Aka: Columbia Park or Columbia Avenue Grounds

Status: Demolished 1912

Opened: April 26, 1901

Capacity: 9,500 (1901); 13,000 (1905)

Dimensions:

Left Field 340 ft

Left Center 392 ft

Center Field 396 ft

Right Center 323 ft

Right Field 280 ft

World Series: 1905

Columbia Park has long since disappeared, but its legacy endures in the world of baseball. It may only have lasted eight years, but in that short time this major league stadium hosted a World Series, was the home of a new league, and was the ballpark in which many Hall of Famers launched their careers.

Built in 1901 at a cost of $35,000, it was a small ballpark, originally with a capacity of 9,500. A covered wooden grandstand extended from home plate to first and third bases, while bleacher seating extended down the foul lines. In the early days, overflow crowds would watch ballgames from the roofs of the surrounding houses. It was built for the Philadelphia Athletics and was the first American League stadium in Philadelphia under the guidance of Connie Mack and his partner Benjamin F. Shibe, who took a ten-year lease on the site. By 1905, seating capacity was increased to 13,600 with the addition of bleachers in the outfield.

The Philadelphia Athletics lost 5–1 to the Washington Senators in their first game in April 1901 before a sell-out crowd, but public enthusiasm did not last the season, with attendance averaging just 3,300 during that first year. Fortunately, as it became clear that Connie Mack's Athletics really were worth watching, the crowds returned. They won the American League title in 1902 and 1905 and finished second twice.

In 1905 the World Series between the Athletics and the New York Giants was held at Columbia Park. Even though seating capacity had been increased, it was still inadequate for the huge numbers that came to watch a magnificent series of ballgames. The Athletics lost, but were rewarded by a huge parade along Broad Street before 300,000 fans who lined the route.

The team's popularity and the fact that the gates of Columbia Park were regularly shut in the faces of clamoring fans convinced Connie Mack that the Athletics needed larger premises, and in 1908 the sod from Columbia was transplanted to a new stadium at Shibe Park.

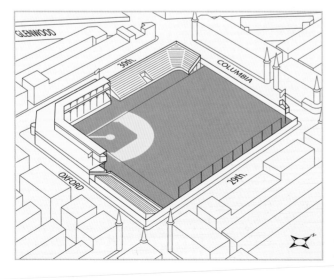

LEFT: Artist's impression of Columbia Park.

Location: 2100 Woodward Avenue, Detroit, MI
Status: Home of the Detroit Tigers
Architect: HOK Sports
Opened: April 11, 2000
Capacity: 40,120
Dimensions:
Left Field 346 ft
Left Center 402 ft
Center Field 422 ft
Right Center 379 ft
Right Field 330 ft
World Series: 2006
All-Star Game: 2005

There is no doubting that the Tigers play at Comerica Park—huge tiger statues greet visitors outside the stadium and the perimeter is lined with tigers holding baseball bats in their mouths (they are actually lights). Inside, two more enormous tigers guard either side of the scoreboard and roar when the home team hits a home run. Further evidence of predators are the tiger claw marks scratched into the pillars around the park and along the first base side, even the kids' merry-go-round features thirty hand-painted tigers. State-of-the-art modern is the ambience here, as evidenced by the multicolored water fountain shooting "liquid fireworks," the air-conditioned bar, the enormous scoreboard, and the lack of a single pillar to block spectators' view. It also frames a spectacular view of downtown Detroit, which has worked so hard to keep baseball in the city.

Constructed at a cost of $300 million of brick and steel in asymmetric dimensions, Comerica Park mimics historic ballparks of old, especially where the dirt patch stretches from the pitcher's mound to home plate. Originally, just like Tiger Field, the center-field flagpole was in play, but after the fences were moved in, it now lives outside the fence.

THIS PAGE: Comerica Park is a fine place to watch baseball, with great views of downtown Detroit.

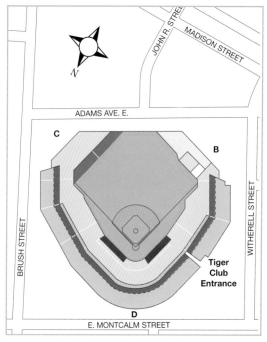

Comerica Park also celebrates Detroit's rich baseball heritage in other ways. Six oversized statues cast in stainless steel along the center field wall show legendary Tigers in classic poses: Ty Cobb sliding spikes up, Willie Horton swinging, along with Charlie Gehringer, Hank Greenberg, and Hal Newhouser. Al Kaline is shown making a one-arm grab with his glove positioned in a way that one day, some shot to deep center might just get caught.

LEFT: In case you didn't realize it—this is the home of the Tigers!

BELOW: Comerica panorama.

Comiskey Park

Location: 35th Street & Shields Avenue, Chicago, IL
Aka: White Sox Park; Old Comiskey
Status: Demolished in 1991
Architect: Zachary Taylor Davis (original park); the Osborn Co. (expansion)
Opened: July 1, 1910
Last MLB game: September 30, 1990
Capacity: 28,800; 52,000 (final)
Dimensions:

	Initial 1910	Final 1990
Left Field	363 ft	347 ft
Left Center	382 ft	382 ft
Center Field	420 ft	409 ft
Right Center	382 ft	382 ft
Right Field	363 ft	347 ft

World Series: 1917, 1918, 1919, 1959
All-Star Game: 1933, 1950, 1983; also frequent home to the Negro League East-West All-Star Game from 1933 to 1960

Comiskey Park has a history that stretches back to the turn of the twentieth century. The White Sox started playing at South Side Park (aka 39th Street Grounds) in 1901. It had a capacity of only 15,000 and few facilities but still proved a popular draw—Chicago's cricket team had previously used the grounds in the late 1800s—and to cater to the public, White Sox owner Charles Comiskey built a wooden grandstand there.

Comiskey's stated ambition was to give Chicago the "baseball palace of the world" and accordingly work started February 1, 1910, on a new ballpark: the cornerstone was laid on St. Patrick's Day. The White Sox were able to move in only five months later. At first called White Sox Park, it was soon renamed Comiskey Park and it cost $750,000 to build. It was a spacious and symmetrical field almost entirely surrounded by double-deck stands. However, opening day on July 1, 1910, saw the home team lose to the St. Louis Browns 2–0 in front of a capacity crowd. During the first year 583,208 fans went through the turnstiles. The million was reached in 1951 (1,328,234) and 1984, the ground record year, saw a total attendance of 2,136,988.

The White Sox proved a remarkable team; in 1906 and 1917 the White Sox won the World Series, beating the Chicago Cubs 4–2 and the New York Giants 4–2 respectively. However, in the 1919 season they lost to the Cincinnati Reds. A year later it was discovered that eight members of the White Sox had agreed to throw the series in what became dubbed "the Black Sox Scandal." Even though they admitted their guilt, the accused players were acquitted, but they were not allowed into the Baseball Hall of Fame.

In 1933 Comiskey Park hosted the first-ever All-Star Game and the crowd was thrilled by Babe Ruth's performance as he steered the American League to victory. The venue was used twice more for All-Star Games, 1950 and 1983.

In 1969 Astroturf was installed in the infield; it was removed in 1976. One of the great features of the stadium was the exploding scoreboard with pinwheels.

The White Sox were in the doldrums for many years after the scandal until in they made

the World Series in 1959 but failed to win against the Los Angeles Dodgers. They did not reappear in the World Series until 2005.

By the late 1980s the ballpark was really showing its age, so the then-chairman of the White Sox, Jerry Reinsdorf, threatened to take his team to St. Petersburg, Florida, if the city did not build a new ballpark. The city contributed over $200 million for the new ballpark next door: New Comiskey Park (now U.S. Cellular Field) opened in April 1991. The first Comiskey Park was demolished over summer 1991, at which time it was the oldest ballpark in the majors. The site became the parking lot for the new ballpark. The old home plate is marked by a marble plaque on the sidewalk and the foul lines are painted across the lot.

TOP, LEFT and RIGHT: 1990 interior views (New Comiskey in background). (Both courtesy Jerry Reuss, Jerryreuss.com)

ABOVE AND ABOVE LEFT: Interior of Comiskey Park in its final years. (Both courtesy of Robert K. Shoop)

BELOW: 1986 view of Comiskey Park from the parking lot.

Location: 1425 W. Ocotillo Road, Chandler, AZ

Status: As of 2009, unused and in a state of disrepair

Opened: 1986

Capacity: 5,000

ABOVE: New Comiskey was built next door to its namesake. This image is from 1990. Old Comiskey was demolished the next year.

BELOW: The former spring training home of the Milwaukee Brewers, Compadre Stadium sits abandoned, awaiting the wrecking ball.

Located in Chandler, Arizona, Compadre Stadium was formerly the spring training home of the Milwaukee Brewers. Built in 1985 at a cost of $1.6 million, Compadre Stadium is now a shell of its former self.

At one time a thriving spring training ballpark that drew tremendous crowds in southeast Phoenix, Compadre Stadium now sits abandoned, awaiting the wrecking ball. It is in perfectly fine shape structurally, and with a bit of care would be a viable ballpark. The Brewers moved into Chandler in 1986, abandoning their previous spring training home in Sun City, Arizona, which was then only a decade old. Sun City was left to decay and was eventually razed in 1995. They had left their previous home, Tempe Diablo Stadium, after only five years in 1973.

Compadre Stadium appeared in the Brewers' promotional material and was touted as the next great spring training ballpark. But, true to form, the Brewers moved on. In late 1996 it was announced that a new "super stadium" would be built in Maryvale for the Brewers. Only a decade old, Chandler's Compadre Stadium was considered completely obsolete and in 1998 the Brewers moved to the new Phoenix ballpark.

Compadre would never find another suitor. Eventually the Brewer blue seats were sold, leaving behind a bare concrete grandstand. There are no plans to renovate the ballpark into something useful. Soon Compadre will meet the fate of the ballpark before it.

removed the Yankee clubhouse, replacing it with one that still stands today. The original Yankees' lockers were moved to the new clubhouse, and during more recent changes in 2003, renovators tried to retain as many original features as possible. The Mets renamed the ground again, in 1963, as the Huggins-Stengel Field, honoring their own manager alongside the Yankees' man. With the Mets' departure, the Baltimore Orioles and the Tampa Bay Devil Rays used the grounds during the 1990s. It is now used mainly for college games.

RIGHT: 1950s view of Yankee spring training.

ABOVE and ABOVE RIGHT: During the 1970s the Mets took over Huggins-Stengel from the Yankees for spring training.

Baseball is a serious business in Rochester, New York, and dates back at least to 1877, when the "Rochesters" played as part of the International Association. Many baseball historians believe the game can be traced as far back as 1825, when games were played in a meadow bordering the Genesee River.

Culver Field was built on a wooded site owned by the Culver family and was the home of the Rochester Bronchos from 1886 until the park's fiery end in 1892. The 1890 season was one of great success, and the only year in which the Bronchos played in the major leagues. In April 1890, a record-breaking crowd of 4,000 turned out to watch Rochester defeat Brooklyn 5–1. The team finished fifth in the league with a 63–63 record.

After the first Culver Field burned down, there was no baseball at all in Rochester until 1894. Finally, Culver Field was revived and a new park was rebuilt in time for the 1898 season. The Rochester Beau Brummels used it for their home games for a decade, but they were one of Rochester's less-successful teams, winning twenty-eight games and losing 105 in the 1904 season.

The current Rochester Red Wings began playing as the Rochester Bronchos at the new Culver Field in 1899, and since that first game, they haven't missed a single season in any year, even throughout the war years when cities like Buffalo and Syracuse went dark for periods of time. No other professional minor league team in baseball can claim that it has played uninterrupted for every season since 1899.

In 1906 the right field bleachers at Culver Field collapsed, injuring dozens of spectators and prompting a flurry of lawsuits from affronted fans. The park was sold in 1907 to the tool manufacturer Gleason Works, and baseball moved on to the vast Bay Street Park.

Location: Northwest corner of University and Culver, Rochester, NY
Status: Burned down in 1892; rebuilt 1898; demolished 1907
Opened: 1886
Closed: 1906

Culver Field

Location: 2400 East Capitol Street, SE, Washington, D.C.

Aka: The Robert F. Kennedy Memorial Stadium

Status: Still in use but not for baseball

Architect: Osborn Engineering

Opened: April 9, 1962

Capacity: 45,250 (opening day); 56,000 (current)

Dimensions:

Left Field 335 ft

Left Center 380 ft

Center Field 408 ft

Right Center 380 ft

Right Field 335 ft

World Series: None

All-Star Game: 1962, 1969

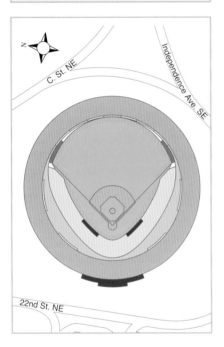

Best known as a football venue, D.C. Stadium was the first of the multipurpose "cookie-cutter" stadiums and was built specifically for the Washington Senators and the NFL's Washington Redskins. It cost $24 million to build and subsequently had a further $18.5 million spent on renovations.

The Washington Senators moved into D.C. Stadium to play their first game on April 9, 1962. They shared the facility with the Redskins for nine years until they left in 1971, while the Redskins stayed on until 1997.

The dual-purpose stadium did not really please either set of fans; the seating was arranged over five tiers around the arena of mostly covered seating. For baseball followers, the source of grief was that the only outfield seating was above a high wall, with no seating at all on the lower deck.

The stadium was lit by arc lights rather than the usual light towers because they would have visually disrupted the sight line between the U.S. Capitol and the Washington Monument. One enormous problem was the cost involved in changing the configuration of the seating: every time the stadium was changed from football to baseball or soccer, it cost a staggering $20,000 and then another $20,000 to put it back! At first this happened only a couple of times a year, but the changes later became more frequent. Much of this was in the rolling back and forth of the lower-level seats along a buried rail and for laying and removing sod from the infield dirt. Later conversions of the stadium rectified this somewhat and the costs came down.

In 1968 the stadium was renamed Robert F. Kennedy Memorial Stadium (or, more often, RFK Stadium) after the assassinated attorney general Robert F. Kennedy, who had done a lot to help racial integration in sports, particularly with the Washington Redskins.

The Senators were never a successful franchise, and their fan base dwindled through the 1960s. Their last game was played at RFK on September 30, 1971, and the franchise moved to Dallas-Fort Worth and became the Texas Rangers. Unfortunately, their last game was disrupted by crowd trouble as fans scrabbled for souvenirs and the Senators were forced to forfeit the game. After seventy-one years of continuous major league baseball, the nation's capital was without an MLB team to support.

At last, in April 2005, after a professional baseball drought lasting thirty-four years, MLB returned to RFK Stadium when the relocated Montreal Expos became the Washington Nationals, who played there until their home at the new Nationals Stadium opened in spring 2008.

LEFT: Seating plan.

LEFT: Besides the Nationals, Senators, and Redskins, RFK Stadium has hosted many other sporting and concert events. RFK's primary tenant before the Nationals was the DC United soccer team. RFK has hosted many large concerts, including the Rolling Stones, the Grateful Dead, the Eagles, Elton John, Michael Jackson, and the Cure.

TOP and ABOVE: RFK Stadium was never quite as large as you expected it to be. The stadium is really only two decks—upper and lower. Compared to the massive former doughnuts in Philadelphia, Pittsburgh, and St. Louis, this ballpark is relatively small in comparison.

Location: 2101 Ontario Street East, Montreal, Quebec, Canada
Aka: Montreal Stadium, Hector Racine Stadium, Delorimier Downs
Status: Demolished 1971
Opened: May 1928
Capacity: 20,000
Dimensions:
Right Field 293 ft

Delorimier Stadium was the home of the mighty Montreal Royals from 1928 until 1960, the Triple-A affiliates of the Brooklyn Dodgers.

Constructed in 1928 by a consortium called the Montreal Exhibition Company, which was led by former Boston Braves manager George Stallings, Delorimier Stadium had a seating capacity of 20,000. Building costs were in the region of $700,000—a considerable sum in the late 1920s. It was conceived as more than just a baseball stadium, however, with accommodation underneath the stands for exhibitions and facilities for other sports. As early as June 1928, an exhibition soccer match with the Scottish Glasgow Rangers was arranged, and in May 1939 the stadium hosted a royal visit from King George VI and Queen Elizabeth.

The Montreal Royals played thirty-three seasons at Delorimier, winning the International League pennant eight times. They were one of the most successful minor league teams in the 1940s and 1950s, and became the top farm team for the Brooklyn Dodgers in 1940, which meant that many major league stars began their careers in Montreal.

The most notable signing in the Royals' history was when the Royals recruited Jackie Robinson in 1946, in direct contravention of the (unofficial) color bar which prevented black players from playing for major league teams. There was much speculation about whether fans would support the Royals, but on the opening day of the 1946 season, not only did a sell-out crowd arrive, but Robinson spent an hour signing autographs.

Robinson's arrival coincided with some of the Royals' most successful years: they won the league in 1945 and 1946, followed by a win in the Junior World Series. Sadly, Montreal fans only seemed to support a winning team, and when the Royals' fortunes declined, attendance nose-dived too.

When the Dodgers moved to Los Angeles, they changed their affiliation, and without the Dodgers' support, the Royals' performance suffered. The team folded in 1960, ending pro baseball at Delorimier, and the stadium was finally demolished in 1971.

Location: 1300 SW Temple Street, Salt Lake City, UT
Status: Demolished 1994
Built: 1947
Capacity: 10,000

Derks Field was the home to Salt Lake City baseball for some fifty years and hosted teams from both the Triple-A Pacific Coast League and the rookie-level Pioneer League, including the Bees, the Gulls, the Trappers, and the Giants. Aside from an art deco–style entranceway and a grass playing surface, the stadium was rather plain and either very wet or very hot! Derks Field was actually a replacement for Community Park, which burned down in 1947, and the new stadium took its name from a sports editor for the *Salt Lake Tribune*, John C. Derks. It was replaced by Covey Field in 1994, which itself was renamed Spring Mobile Ballpark in 2009.

BELOW: Footprint of Derks Field.

BELOW RIGHT: The art deco entrance.

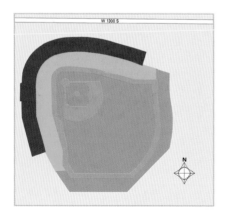

Constructed in 1969, Desert Sun Stadium was the spring training home of the San Diego Padres from 1969 until 1993, and is part of the Ray Kroc Baseball Complex, a multi-field training facility. It has hosted a succession of other teams who played in various minor leagues, notably the Yuma Bullfrogs and currently the Yuma Scorpions. It is also a training center for the Arizona Winter League and Arizona Summer League.

The facilities at Desert Sun Stadium have lasted well, given that they are now over forty years old. The stadium has a seating capacity of 10,500, with major league-standard facilities for players and visiting teams. It is completely uncovered, a roof being superfluous in the arid Arizona climate. The field is dedicated to the former owner of the Padres (and, more famously, of McDonald's), Ray Kroc.

The Padres used Desert Sun for their spring training for quarter of a century until they were lured to new facilities at Peoria near Phoenix in 1994, when the Cactus League focused its training facilities in just two cities, Peoira and Phoenix. The Padres have not forgotten their roots, however, and return every spring to play an exhibition match against the Arizona Diamondbacks. The Yakult Swallows, a Japanese team, also used the stadium for spring training for two decades.

Since the turn of the century, Desert Sun has been home field for the minor league Yuma Bullfrogs (2000–2002) and the Yuma Scorpions (2005–present). The Bullfrogs lasted only three seasons, and folded with the demise of the Western Baseball League. The Scorpions were founding members of the Golden Baseball League and are also charter members of the Arizona Winter League, an instructional league that plays from January to March.

Location: 1280 West Desert Sun Drive, Yuma, AZ
Status: Home of the Yuma Scorpions; hosts the Arizona Winter League and Arizona Summer League
Opened: 1969
Capacity: 10,500
Dimensions:
Left Field 345 ft
Center Field 420 ft
Right Field 345 ft

Desert Sun Stadium

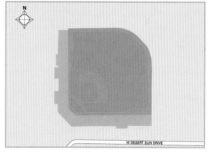

TOP LEFT and RIGHT: Derks Field with the Wasatch Mountains in the distance.

ABOVE: Footprint of Desert Sun Stadium.

LEFT: Desert Sun Stadium may seem spartan but it has major league-standard facilities.

Location: Peace Street between West Street and Capital Boulevard, Raleigh, NC

Status: Demolished 1979

Opened: 1938

Closed: 1971

Dimensions:

Left Field 324 ft

Left Center 379 ft

Center Field 488 ft

Right Center 380 ft

Right Field 313 ft

Situated in downtown Raleigh, Deveraux Meadow now conjures up a host of nostalgic memories among baseball fans. Built in 1938, it was home to the minor league Raleigh Capitals, a popular team which won the league championship in 1946 and 1947.

The field's dimensions were identical to those at Fenway Park, the home of the Boston Red Sox, and when the field was demolished in 1979, it was clear that fans remembered a typical all-American ballpark that provided entertainment for all the family during the golden age of baseball.

Major league affiliations were varied and never seemed to last long: the Cincinnati Reds (1945) were succeeded by the Boston Braves (1946), the Boston Red Sox (1958–1960), the New York Mets (1961), and the Washington Senators (1962). Legendary players included Carl Yastrzemski (1959–60), who once hit the ball out of the park and into the traffic on Downtown Boulevard. Yastrzemski went on to a long and successful career with the Boston Red Sox, then the Caps' major league affiliate.

In 1940 the Birmingham Black Barons of the Negro League used Devereaux Meadow for one season.

Attendence at Devereaux Meadow was good during the 1940s and 1950s, but it became harder to fill ballparks in the 1960s, and the Caps swapped affiliation almost annually, until finally the club became the Raleigh-Durham Mets, an independent team shared by the cities of Durham and Raleigh in 1968. From 1968 the Durham Bulls played half their home games at Devereaux, but they dropped out of the Carolina League in 1971. Devereaux Meadow went dark in 1971 and was finally torn down to make way for a waste disposal facility in 1979.

Location: 400 West Broadway, North Little Rock, AR

Status: Home of the Arkansas Travelers

Architect: HKS, Inc.

Opened: April 12, 2007

Capacity: 5,800

Dimensions:

Left Field 332 ft

Left Center 360 ft

Center Field 400 ft

Right Center 375 ft

Right Field 330 ft

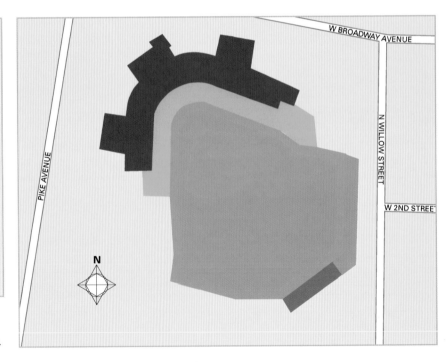

RIGHT: Footprint of Dickey-Stephens Park.

Constructed at a whopping cost of $40.4 million, Dickey-Stephens Park is a Double-A stadium that opened in April 2007. With a capacity of 5,800, it is currently home to the Arkansas Travelers, who play in the Texas League. The name ingeniously commemorates two sets of brothers: baseball-loving businessmen Jack and Witt Stephens, and players George Dickey and his brother, Baseball Hall of Fame member Bill Dickey.

The Travs are affiliated to the Los Angeles Angels, who replaced the thirty-four-year associates, the St. Louis Cardinals, in 2001. The team moved to Dickey-Stephens Park after over seventy years at the venerable Ray Winder Field, drawing 7,943 fans to their first game—who watched them lose to the Frisco RoughRiders 6–5. The Travs have broken their all-time attendance record in each year of operation since the move in 2007. The stadium commemorates the area's links to the railroad, with its low redbrick profile and a colonnaded

frontage that harks back to the train sheds of the nineteenth century. Old friends from Ray Winder Stadium have been transported to the new ballpark, including the organist who entertains fans at each game, as well as the plaques that honor the Travs' legendary associates Ray Winder, Jim Elder, and Max Moses.

Dickey-Stephens enjoys a beautiful location beside the Arkansas River in North Little Rock (a city distinct from Little Rock itself) on a site donated by businessman Warren Stephens. His donation carried two stipulations—that the site be used to build a ballpark, and that he could name it. He chose the name wisely, commemorating his father Jack and uncle Witt, as well as two of Little Rock's greatest players. Former umpire and manager of the Travs, Bill Valentine also deserves a great deal of the credit for the construction of the new park. As he said at the opening ceremony, "If you build it, they shall come. We did. You did. Let's play ball!"

ABOVE: The berm gives a great view of the grandstands and the game.

BELOW: Panorama of Dodger Stadium.

Dodger Stadium

Location: 1000 Elysian Park Avenue, Los Angeles, CA
Aka: Chavez Ravine (when used by the Angels)
Status: Home of the Los Angeles Dodgers
Architect: Captain Emil Praeger
Opened: April 10, 1962
Capacity: 56,000
Dimensions:

	Original 1962	Current
Left Field	330 ft	330 ft
Left Center	380 ft	385 ft
Center Field	410 ft	395 ft
Right Center	380 ft	385 ft
Right Field	330 ft	330 ft

World Series: 1963, 1965, 1966, 1974, 1977, 1978, 1981, 1988
All-Star Game: 1980

RIGHT and BELOW: Under the "THINK BLUE" sign on the hillside, Dodger Stadium sits in a bowl. The entrance to the upper deck "red" level (where this photograph was taken) is level with the parking lot out back. Eight million cubic yards of dirt had to be moved to make room for Chavez Ravine.

Dodger Stadium has no pretensions to be a historic ballpark—it is a five-tiered, perfectly symmetrical arena sitting proudly at the top of Chavez Ravine. Dodger Stadium proves that there is more than one way to build a great baseball park.

The site was given to Dodgers owner Walter O'Malley (who had spotted it from a helicopter) by the city of Los Angeles, which then evicted the Mexican-American residents living there—creating Latino animosity toward the Dodgers that persisted for decades.

Among the distinctive features of Dodger Stadium are its simplicity, its cleanliness, and its single-minded devotion to the game. Between 1914 (Wrigley Field) and 1995 (Coors Field), Dodger Stadium was the only National League park built exclusively for baseball. The sight

lines have no obstructed views, and every season each deck is freshly painted with its own color. The distinctive wavy roof over the bleachers gives an instantly recognizable look to the stadium that was originally designed with the ability to expand to 85,000 seats, but has remained far smaller.

The setting is spectacular and the groundskeeping is meticulous. The Chavez Ravine stadium finally opened on April 10, 1962, having cost a cool $23 million to construct. The Dodgers played there for the first time (against the Cincinnati Reds) in front of a 56,000-strong crowd. They continue to play their baseball there to the present day. Between April 17, 1962, and September 22, 1965, the Dodgers shared the stadium with the Los Angeles/California Angels, but when the American Leaguers moved out, the venue become more commonly known as Dodger Stadium.

Three thousand trees grow on the 300-acre site, including several dozen trademark palm trees down the right and left field foul lines, which along with the Elysian Hills and the distant San Gabriel Mountains give the park a distinctive Southern California look. Deep power alleys have made this a pitchers' park, and the computer-controlled Bermuda grass field, with state-of-the-art vacuum chambers to help drainage, was rated number one by baseball players in a *Sports Illustrated* survey in 2003.

Dodger Stadium has hosted many and various events, including the visit of Pope John Paul II, the Beatles, the Rolling Stones, and the Three Tenors.

The stadium has changed little over the past four decades. A video screen capable of showing instant replays, which debuted during the 1980 All-Star Game, was baseball's first. Since 2000, the Dodgers have added new field level seats and club suites, and a new state-of-the-art video screen. After the 2005 season all of the old seats were removed and replaced by new ones in yellow, light orange, turquoise, and sky blue. Ambitious plans to build a new field level concourse, with more concessions and restrooms, were completed in 2008.

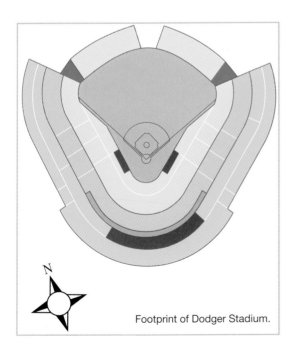

Footprint of Dodger Stadium.

117

Location: Main Street and Chestnut Street, Cooperstown, NY

Status: Hall of Fame field

Capacity: 9,791

Opened: September 26, 1920; current brick and steel structure, May 6, 1939

Dimensions:

Left Field 296 ft

Left Center 336 ft

Center Field 390 ft

Right Center 350 ft

Right Field 312 ft

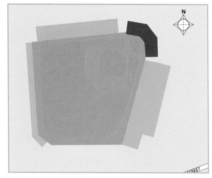

Doubleday Field is the official home of the Oneonta Tigers of the New York-Penn League, though they only play here once a season. The ground was named after Abner Doubleday, the Civil War Union general who is often wrongly credited with having invented baseball.

However, Cooperstown is in many ways an important spiritual center of baseball, for as well as this historic ballpark, two blocks away lies the home of the National Baseball Hall of Fame and Museum. Between 1940 and 2008, Doubleday Field has hosted the annual Hall of Fame Game, MLB's only in-season exhibition, and part of the Hall of Fame's induction festivities.

Baseball has been played at Doubleday Field since 1920, and between mid-April and mid-October, the ground still hosts around 350 games, ranging from youth baseball to senior leagues: any team is allowed to play so long as they pay the village fees of a few hundred dollars.

In 1924 a wooden grandstand was built for the fans; this lasted until 1939, when as part of President Franklin Roosevelt's New Deal, a Works Project Administration construction team demolished the old grandstand and replaced it with a modern steel-and-concrete building.

THIS PAGE, from TOP to BOTTOM:

TOP RIGHT: Doubleday Field still hosts major and minor league baseball— particularly during the Hall of Fame induction process. Also, throughout the year, Doubleday Field hosts scores of amateur and American Legion teams.

TOP: Footprint of Doubleday Field.

ABOVE: Entrance to the spiritual home of baseball.

RIGHT: There are no lights at Doubleday and it would be considered a sacrilege to install them now. A minor league team, however, couldn't survive without night baseball.

Location: 7725 Gaylord Parkway, Frisco, TX

Aka: Dr Pepper/Seven Up Ballpark

Status: Home of the Frisco RoughRiders

Architect: David M. Schwarz, HKS, Inc.

Opened: April 3, 2003

Capacity: 10,600

Dimensions:

Left Field 335 ft

Left Center 364 ft

Center Field 409 ft

Right Center 364 ft

Right Field 335 ft

There are no prizes for guessing which company won the naming rights to this fine Double-A stadium in Frisco, Texas. Home to the Frisco RoughRiders since it opened in 2003, Dr Pepper/Seven Up Ballpark was constructed at a cost of $22.7 million and has a capacity of 10,600. Now known simply as "Dr Pepper Ballpark," it hosts corporate and charity events as well as ball games.

Dr Pepper is without doubt a beautiful, well-designed stadium that has been highly praised by fans of both baseball and architecture, and has won numerous awards for its design. It has a unique "park-within-a-park" look, with wide walkways, landscaped areas, and balustraded pavilions. There is even a pool area behind the right field wall, which can be rented by groups of twenty-five people to cool off during the games.

The concession stands, restrooms, and boxes are housed within separate buildings to the rear of the main grandstand seating, and they are connected by a series of walkways. A concourse that surrounds the entire park enables fans to stroll around the facility and yet still retain a view of the game. There is no red brick in evidence, the whole structure being an elegant, light gray color. The most unusual feature is the bullpens, which are built into the stands and surrounded by seating, so players warm up quite close to the spectators.

When the Riders took over Dr Pepper Ballpark, they were a new team, having previously been the Shreveport Captains. Affiliated to the Texas Rangers, the Riders play in the Texas League.

When the team was purchased by Mandalay Entertainment, which also owns the stadium, they moved to Frisco and changed their name. Despite losing their inaugural game to the Tulsa Drillers, their first season was very successful and the Riders qualified for the playoffs, before losing the series to the San Antonio Missions.

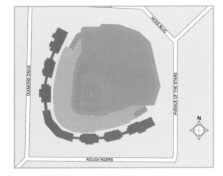

THIS PAGE: The unique Dr Pepper Ballpark has won accolades for its design and layout—and the only criticism is about its prices.

(Above right photo courtesy of Joe Mock, baseballparks.com; right photo courtesy Brian Merzbach, ballparkreviews.com.)

LEFT: Footprint of Dr Pepper Ballpark.

Dunedin Stadium

Location: 373-A Douglas Avenue #A, Dunedin, FL

Aka: Knology Park; Florida Auto Exchange Stadium

Status: Home of the Dunedin Blue Jays

Opened: 1990

Capacity: 5,510

Dimensions:

Left Field 333 ft

Center Field 400 ft

Right Field 336 ft

ABOVE: Grandstand of the original Grant Field.

ABOVE RIGHT and BELOW: Florida Auto Exchange Stadium. Ranked by *Sports Illustrated* as one of the top five places to watch a spring training game.

Dunedin Stadium at Grant Field, which was previously known as Knology Park, is the grass-surfaced spring training home of the Toronto Blue Jays, as well as home to the Dunedin Blue Jays of the Class A Florida State League and the Dunedin High School Falcons baseball team. The Blue Jays played at what was Grant Field, which had a seating capacity of 3,417, from 1977 to 1989. It had opened in 1930 and was named after a mayor of Dunedin who donated the land.

The city of Dunedin built a new stadium called Dunedin Stadium at the same location as Grant Field in 1990. It had a larger capacity, but the original playing field and team clubhouses remained in situ. However, the ballpark was substantially renovated in the first decade of this century. Work included building a new two-story building that includes a clubhouse, training room, weight room, and office space next to the stadium. The most recent renovations at Dunedin Stadium include redesigned restrooms and the replacement of grandstand seats. The upgraded ballpark was renamed Florida Auto Exchange Stadium in 2010.

Location: 546 Luce Street, Elmira, NY
Aka: Maple Leaf Park; Maple Avenue Driving Park
Status: Home of the Elmira Pioneers
Opened: 1938; renovated 1992
Capacity: 4,448
Dimensions:
Left Field 325 ft
Left Center 358 ft
Center Field 386 ft
Right Center 358 ft
Right Field 325 ft

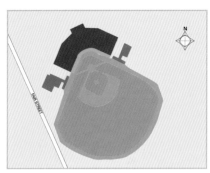

There is perhaps no ballpark standing today that more represents the grand era of the Eastern League. Though the Double-A team pulled out of here for good in 1972, Dunn Field served the Eastern League for a total of twenty-nine years from 1938 to 1955, and again from 1962 to 1972.

The ballpark was built quickly in 1938 to replace the first Dunn Field, which was just a tiny wooden facility with a small central grandstand behind the home plate and long bleachers down the lines. Dunn Field burnt to the ground in early 1938, leaving the Brooklyn Dodgers' Elmira Pioneers trying to continue playing baseball in what was left of the ballpark. All the while, construction began on a new concrete-and-steel facility situated alongside the Chemung River that it is still in excellent shape today, some seventy years later. The stadium now has a capacity of 4,448, with most of that seating under a covered grandstand.

In 1939 the stadium hosted its first full season of professional baseball for the Elmira Pioneers, then affiliated to the Brooklyn Dodgers. The Dodgers were succeeded by the Detroit Tigers in 1941, who followed the Dodgers' example of packing the Pioneers with many future major league players. The Dodgers returned in 1950, signing a six-year player development contract with the Pioneers. The Philadelphia Phillies took over from 1959 to 1961, followed by a successful stint with the Baltimore Orioles (1962–68). The Orioles packed the Pioneers with talent and they won the league in 1962. The Boston Red Sox remained in Elmira from 1973 to 1992, temporarily altering the team name for a few years.

Some great players began their careers here, including Brady Anderson, Wade Boggs, "Oil Can" Boyd, Bob Ojeda, and Curt Schilling. Attendance has been steady but has never reached that elusive 100,000 figure for any year. In 2006 the Pioneers changed leagues, leaving pro baseball for the amateur New York Collegiate Baseball League, but ensuring that baseball continues to be played at the historic Dunn Field.

TOP, ABOVE, and BELOW: Footprint, entrance, and view of main grandstand.

Location: 409 Blackwell Street, Durham, NC

Aka: DBAP, D-BAP

Status: Home of the Durham Bulls; Duke Blue Devils; Central Eagles

Architect: Populous (formerly HOK Sport)

Opened: 1995

Capacity: 10,000

Dimensions:

Left Field 305 ft

Left Center 375 ft

Center Field 400 ft

Right Center 375 ft

Right Field 325 ft

THIS PAGE: DBAP is a modern, well-proportioned baseball park.

Built in 1995, the Durham Bulls Athletic Park (DBAP) is a 10,000-seat stadium that cost $16 million to build, and is the successor to the venerable Durham Athletic Park (DAP) made famous by the Kevin Costner movie *Bull Durham*. In fact, the old ballpark became so popular after the movie's release that it couldn't handle the large crowds and a new, much larger stadium was built.

The stadium was designed by HOK and was designed to fit seamlessly into its environment, what is now called the American Tobacco Historic District. It certainly accomplishes that well, as the ballpark blends perfectly with the old Lucky Strike factory next door.

DBAP first opened its doors in 1995, three years before it became the Triple-A home of the Tampa Bay Rays. The original DAP transferred its Single-A Carolina League player development contract with the Atlanta Braves to the brand-new DBAP. Durham Bulls Athletic Park would serve as the Atlanta Braves' advanced Single-A franchise for three seasons. The new Triple-A stadium playing Single-A baseball drew 385,000 in its first season, a ridiculous number of fans for a Carolina League team (where 125,000 is considered a good year). The Durham Bulls continued to draw over 350,000 as the Atlanta Braves' farm club began producing future superstars such as Andruw Jones, Kevin Millwood, and John Rocker.

In 1997 two new teams appeared in major league baseball, the Colorado Rockies and the Tampa Bay Devil Rays. The Rays adopted the Durham Bulls as their Triple-A team, and this new affiliation drew nearly half a million fans in the 1998 season. Bubba Trammell joined the team and led the Bulls to the playoffs for three years in a row. It was Carl Crawford, however, who would turn Durham into a champion, and led Durham to their first International League title, with attendance finally breaking the magic half a million mark.

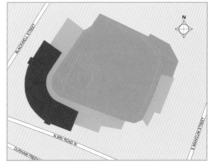

ABOVE and LEFT: Footprint of DBAP and view of left-field berm.

The Dyckman Oval at Inwood, Manhattan, was an important location for the growth of Negro League baseball throughout the 1920s and 1930s. The ground was named after the local Dyckman family, who had owned 400 acres in the area since the seventeenth century. When it first opened it was used for ice-skating, but soon the Oval became a venue for motorcycle racing, soccer, wrestling, and boxing matches as well as baseball. In 1914 the Lincoln Stars Negro League baseball team played at Dyckman and were very successful for a few seasons, but the team folded in 1917. Then for over a decade the facility was badly run and the structure began to suffer.

In 1935 Dyckman Oval became the home grounds of the formidable New York Cuban Stars after tem owner Alejandro Pompez gave the owners of the Oval $60,000 for the use of their facility. The team played in the Eastern Colored League and was composed of Cubans, Puerto Ricans, African Americans, and Dominicans. The Cuban-born, Harlem-based owner Pompez was a popular but controversial cigar store owner whose wealth came from numbers rackets but whose enthusiasm for baseball was genuine. He ran the Cubans for the duration of the Negro League and was also the Negro League vice-chairman.

When the ECL folded in 1928, the Cubans moved into the American Negro League. In 1930 Pompez installed floodlights at the Oval so that night games could be played—the first professional ballpark in New York to have lights—and the capacity was increased to 10,000. Pompez

Location: 204th Street and Nagle Avenue, New York, NY
Status: Demolished 1938
Opened: 1920
Capacity: 4,500; final 10,000

Dyckman Oval

spent considerable sums refurbishing the grounds, but thanks to his organized crime links (he eventually turned state's evidence), the Cubans had to withdraw from seasons 1937 and 1938. They returned to play on in 1939, but without their ballpark, as the City of New York had demolished the Oval and turned it into a parking lot. Later apartment blocks, called Dyckman Houses, were built over the site.

In 1943 the Cubans moved to the Polo Grounds to become a farm team for the New York Giants following the demise of the Negro Leagues. The Cubans were forced to fold in 1950 with the arrival of integrated baseball. Pompez died of natural causes in 1974 aged eighty-three, and was elected to the National Baseball Hall of Fame in 2006.

ABOVE: The Dyckman Oval was named after the family who owned 400 acres of land from the seventeenth century. It was used for the leading Negro League and semi-pro teams during the 1920s and 1930s and for boxing, wrestling, and motorcycle races.

Location: 55 Sullivan Place, Brooklyn, New York, NY

Status: Demolished February 23, 1960

Architect: Clarence Randall Van Buskirk

Opened: April 9, 1913

Capacity: 18,000 (opening); 32,000 (1932)

Dimensions:

	Original 1913	Final 1932
Left Field	419 ft	351 ft
Center Field	450 ft	389 ft
Right Field	350 ft	297 ft

World Series: 1916, 1920, 1941, 1947, 1949, 1952, 1953, 1955, 1956

All-Star Game: 1949

ABOVE: Ebbets Field was one of the most storied ballparks of them all and recognized as a classic. One of the early concrete-and-steel "jewel box" parks, it hosted nine World Series, including the Dodgers' only victory in 1955. It was also the place where Jackie Robinson opened the way for African American players to play in the major leagues.

BELOW: 1950s view of the stadium.

BELOW RIGHT: The left-field corner during the 1920 World Series shows temporary bleachers.

OPPOSITE, ABOVE: Ebbets Field under construction in 1913.

OPPOSITE, BELOW: The 1956 World Series was the Dodgers' fourth in five years. They lost to their local rivals, the Yankees.

The Los Angeles Dodgers have been through several incarnations—they were the Trolley Dodgers in 1884, then they became the Brooklyn Dodgers, and in the late twentieth century they moved and became the Los Angeles Dodgers. The Dodgers' last home in New York was at Ebbets Field, which was built by Charlie Ebbets on a former garbage dump for $750,000 and was subsequently upgraded on several occasions. It has been said that Ebbets had to buy around forty different pieces of land from various people to get control of the site. The first game was in April 1913, when 25,000 eager fans watched the Dodgers run out.

The first-ever televised baseball game was transmitted from the ballpark on August 26, 1939, when the Dodgers played the Reds. The club became the property of Walter O'Malley in the early 1950s and, within a few years, he was lobbying for a new stadium to be built, but the Brooklyn authorities were lukewarm about the idea. O'Malley responded by making the deeply resented decision to move the Dodgers to Los Angeles. Their swan song at Ebbets Field came on September 24, 1957. Three years later, the grand old stadium was destroyed and apartment blocks were built on the site. The only small reminder of the famous venue to be seen today is one of the outfield walls.

125

Location: 28th and Elliott Streets, West Louisville; 28th and Broadway; Seventh and Kentucky Streets, all in Louisville, KY

Status: All three burned down

Eclipse Park (1902)

Opened: 1902

Capacity: 8,500 (1902); 10,000 (1910)

Closed: Destroyed by fire November 20, 1922

Dimensions:

Left Field 397 ft

Center Field 389 ft

Right Field 322 ft

Eclipse Park had a sorry history as a baseball stadium, being destroyed by fire not once, but three times over the course of forty-eight years.

The first Eclipse Park was built in 1871. One of baseball's earliest teams, the Louisville Eclipse played at the first Eclipse Park from 1882 until 1884, but the arena had hosted semi-pro baseball as early as 1874. It burned down in 1892.

The second Eclipse Park (1893–99) was built across the street from the original ballpark, on land supplied by the Kentucky & Indiana Railroad, which also helped finance a new grandstand. The owners of the major league Louisville Colonels paid $35,000 for a thirteen-acre site, on which they built a ballpark, amusement arcade, bicycle paths, and picnic area. With a capacity of 3,000, the park often hosted sell-out games and, despite the installation of extra bleachers, the team owner became frustrated because he had to turn away so many fans.

The Colonels won the American Association pennant in 1890, but for much of that decade they languished around the bottom of the National League (which they joined on the demise of the American League in 1891). One of baseball's greatest players made his debut for the Colonels in 1897. Honus Wagner went on to a stellar career with the Pittsburgh Pirates and was one of the original Hall of Famers in 1936, but even his early promise could not improve the Colonels' performance. In 1899 disaster struck Louisville. Not only did Eclipse Park burn down, but in a reorganization of the National League, four teams were dropped, the Colonels being one of them.

With the departure of many of the Colonels' best players for Pittsburgh and nowhere to play, the team hit a new low. Former major league star George Tebeau forced through plans for a new ballpark, and in 1902 the third Eclipse Park opened its doors. With a capacity of 8,500, the new park also hosted football games, but it remained the Colonels' home ground until it, too, was destroyed by fire in 1922. Baseball moved on to Parkway Field, and the site lay empty and neglected until it was built over in 1938.

Location: 12th Street and Tuttle Avenue, Sarasota, FL

Status: Spring training ground of the Baltimore Orioles

Opened: 1989; renovated 2011

Capacity: 8,500

Architect: HOK Sport (original structure); David M. Schwarz Architects, Inc. (renovation)

Dimensions:

Left Field 340 ft

Left Center 375 ft

Center Field 400 ft

Right Center 375 ft

Right Field 340 ft

RIGHT: Footprint of Ed Smith Stadium.

Spring training home of the Baltimore Orioles and summer home of the Sarasota Reds of the Florida State League until 2009, Ed Smith Stadium opened in March 1989. It replaced the venerable Payne Park, which had hosted minor league baseball for over sixty years, and is now a multi-court tennis facility.

Sarasota had a proud baseball history, which was centered on Payne Park, a small ballpark built in 1924. It served the major league well for sixty years, hosting the New York Giants and the Boston Red Sox, but sadly, it was totally demolished in 1990.

Ed Smith Stadium was constructed in 1989 and the Chicago White Sox trained there for nine years until 1997, when they moved their operations to Tucson, Arizona. The vacancy in Sarasota was filled by the Cincinnati Reds, who had been playing at their facility in Plant City, Florida. They packed their bags and headed an hour south to Sarasota, where they remained until 2008, leaving their Single-A team, the Sarasota Reds, behind every summer. After their departure, the stadium remained empty for a year, before the Baltimore Orioles began spring training in 2010. They have signed a thirty-year agreement, which included a $31.2 million renovation completed prior to the 2011 season.

When the White Sox moved into the new Ed Smith Stadium, they also moved their Single-A farm team over from Tampa for summer baseball. The Sarasota White Sox played for five seasons in the Florida State League before moving to north to Woodbridge, Virginia, and playing as the Prince William Cannons. In 1994 the Boston Red Sox moved their Triple-A team to Ed Smith, renaming them the Sarasota Red Sox. They remained for eleven years, before they left the Florida State League in 2005. They were succeeded by the Sarasota Reds, affiliates of the Cincinnati Reds, who remained at Ed Smith until 2009.

TOP: The Gulf Coast League Reds are now the Arizona League Reds and have moved to the Goodyear Ballpark.

ABOVE and LEFT: Before (above) and after (left). Ed Smith Stadium enjoyed sixteen spring training games in the 2011 Cactus League. It is right across the street from the Nick Lucas Baseball Complex, the county's primary youth baseball facility. The first photograph was taken before a $31.2 million renovation that was completed before the 2011 season. The changes included refurbished seats from Camden Yards; three suites numbered 66, 70, and 83 (the years ot the Orioles' three World Series championships); a new shade system out from the roof substantially increasing the number of shaded seats; and a large video board in the outfield.

El Toro Park

Location: 428 Morris Street, Durham, NC

Aka: Durham Athletic Park (from 1934)

Status: Latest renovation allows Triple-A usage

Architect: George Watt Carr

Opened: 1926; renovated 1939–40; 1979–80; 2008–9 (Struever Bros. Eccles and Rouse)

Capacity: 5,000

Dimensions:

Left Field 330 ft

Center Field 410 ft

Right Field 305 ft

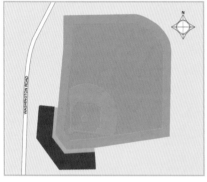

THIS PAGE: The DAP before (below right) and after renovation—not many ballparks can boast a turret! Softball leagues play on bare infields. There is no grass in an official softball diamond, hence the naked grounds.

This former home of the famed Durham Bulls and onetime set for the 1988 movie *Bull Durham* was built in 1926 and named El Toro Park. It was renamed Durham Athletic Park and had to be rebuilt in 1939 after a major fire. When it reopened, it was home to the Bulls for the next seven decades. It had 2,000 grandstand seats and portable bleachers along the first and third base lines.

The DAP has reopened after a recent renovation funded by the city of Durham ($5.5 million). Minor League Baseball agreed to help in the renovation and operate the DAP when the project was completed. The "grand opening" took place on August 15, 2009.

The Durham Bulls departed the ballpark and switched to the Durham Bulls Athletic Park. The move was largely prompted by the need to increase seating capacity and, of course, the move means that the original ballpark no longer hosts pro ball. It is now being used by semi-pro softball leagues and baseball leagues, including the summer league known as the Coastal Plain League. Indeed, many clubs have used this park for their minor league affiliations, including the Atlanta Braves, Philadelphia Phillies, New York Mets, Houston Astros, Detroit Tigers, Brooklyn Dodgers, Cincinnati Reds, and New York Yankees.

On May 10, 2010, the Durham Bulls played a regular-season game against the Toledo Mud Hens; in 2011 they played the Indians. They needed portable lighting to bring the facility up to Triple-A standards.

128

Memphis became a real baseball city in 1914 when a Memphis businessman, Russell Gardner, purchased a controlling interest in the local amateur club, which he renamed the Chickasaws, or "Chicks," after the local Native American tribe.

Originally built in 1896, the all-wooden, 3,000-seat ballpark was then named Elm Wood Park. The name changed in 1915 when Gardner wanted it to reflect his contribution; he also upped the capacity to 6,000. Russwood Park was built on a six-sided asymmetrical block, meaning that both left and right fields were considerably farther away from home plate than straightaway center. After a successful 1921 season, the seating was doubled to accommodate about 11,500.

In 1941 the Chicks became a farm club for the Chicago White Sox, but the latter pulled out of the relationship in 1956. The team remained in the Southern League until the league itself was disbanded after 1961.

One of the highlights of the old stadium's time came on July 4, 1956, when local boy Elvis Presley played a benefit gig at Russwood in front of some 14,000 overexcited fans.

The old wooden grandstand mysteriously caught fire on Easter Sunday, April 17, 1960, after a game. The fire was so fierce that windows were shattered and patients in the nearby Baptist Memorial Hospital had to be evacuated for fear of the fire spreading. For the remainder of that season the Chicks had to play elsewhere—at Hodges Field and Tobey Field—and at the end of the season the Chicks withdrew from the Southern Association and Memphis was left without a baseball team until the arrival of what had been a Texas League franchise in 1968. The Memphis Blues played at American Legion Field (renamed Tim McCarver Stadium).

The site of Russwood Park was bought by the hospital and used in an expansion program, though that too was demolished in 2005.

Location: Memphis, TN
Aka: Russwood Park (1915)
Status: Destroyed by fire in 1960
Opened: 1896
Capacity: 3,000; later 11,500; 14,000 in 1950s
Dimensions:
Left Field 400 ft
Center Field 366 ft
Right Field 302 ft

ABOVE: Russwood Park was overlooked by the Baptist Hospital, which was demolished in 2005. Note the unusual shape of the ballpark with its short center and long left and right fields.

BELOW: 1953 view. (Courtesy of J.J. Guinozzo, official scorer of the Memphis Redbirds.)

Location: 11th and Washington Streets, Hoboken, NJ

Status: Demolished in the 1870s

Opened: 1845

Last game: 1873

Capacity: 20,000

The claim of Elysian Fields to be the birthplace of baseball rivals that of Cooperstown. On June 19, 1846, an organized baseball game was played between the New York Base Ball Club and the Knickerbockers on Hoboken's Elysian Fields. The umpire was Alexander J. Cartwright of the Knickerbocker Club, and it was played according to his rules.

The Knickerbocker Club of New York City used Elysian Fields as their home field from 1845, crossing the Hudson River to play in the tree-filled park because there was no suitable field nearer home in Manhattan. The Knickerbockers were charged rental of $75 per year by the field's owner, Colonel John Stevens, and to collect the fees, Alexander Cartwright organized his players into a ball club. The players who refused to cross the river to play in Hoboken formed their own ball club, the New York Nine, conveniently providing a team for Cartwright's men to play against. Cartwright left his native New York in 1849 to join the California gold rush, and was responsible for disseminating the rules of baseball in the towns where he stopped on his travels. He ended up in Hawaii.

Meanwhile, Elysian Fields continued to host baseball games until the construction of more formal ballparks from the late 1860s. Once the ballparks were enclosed by fences, spectators could be charged to watch games, and baseball began its inexorable climb to the multimillion-dollar business it is today. Pictures of Elysian Fields show a baseball diamond scratched out according to Cartwright's specifications, with spectators standing at the treeline on the outfield to watch the game. Other fans seem perilously close to the batter.

Elysian Fields was eventually developed for housing, and nothing now remains except a small monumental marker. The last game was played here in 1873.

BELOW: A baseball game at the Elysian Fields, October 15, 1859.

BOTTOM: Photo's original caption: "The American national game of base ball. Grand match for the championship at the Elysian Fields, Hoboken, N.J."

Location: 1130 East Third Street, Chattanooga, TN
Aka: Andrews Field; the Joe
Status: Home of Tennessee Temple University and Howard High School
Architect: James G. Gauntt
Opened: 1930; renovated 1988
Capacity: 12,000 (1930); 5,997 (today)
Dimensions:
Left Field 325 ft
Center Field 471 ft
Right Field 318 ft

Built in 1930 at a cost of $150,000, Engel Stadium served the Chattanooga region for seventy years until 2000, playing a major part in the Southern League throughout its history. It was decommissioned in 2000 in favor of the new Bellsouth Park (now called AT&T Field), built in the Riverfront section of Chattanooga, and while the loss of a historic stadium is a shame, in this case, the replacement is terrific. The new ballpark with a bizarrely configured grandstand is modern, unique, and fits in perfectly with the beautiful resurgence that Chattanooga has recently undergone.

Engel Stadium is still maintained to professional standards, and although Chattanooga has embraced the future, it has not forgotten the past. Today, Engel Stadium serves as a home for baseball tournaments and collegiate playoffs. It is also home to the "Spring Fling IX-TSSAA State Baseball Championships." In 2009 the Engel Foundation was formed to preserve the stadium and ensure its continued use as a sports and entertainment venue.

Engel Stadium opened in 1930 to much fanfare. The Chattanooga Lookouts had been part of the Southern Association (a Double-A league that lasted until 1961) since 1910, and Joe Engel promised to promote his beautiful new stadium. With an exhibition game planned against Babe Ruth and the Yankees, Joe needed to have something special up his sleeve, and he did. On April 2, 1931, Jackie Mitchell stepped up to this mound and made baseball history as the first female pitcher to take out two major league legends, Babe Ruth and Lou Gehrig. Engel was a showman whose promotions included the all-girl team the Engelettes and a chance to win a house.

Attendance at the Lookouts' games was high and the team quickly attracted affiliation from the major league Washington Senators in 1932. The Phillies took over in 1960, but when they left in 1965, the stadium went dark until 1976. It was renovated in 1988 at a cost of $2,000, but a decade and a half later, repairs seemed too costly and so the Lookouts relocated to their new home.

THIS PAGE: Historic Engel Stadium was the location where, in 1931, seventeen-year-old Jackie Mitchell pitched in an exhibition game against the New York Yankees. She struck out the first batter she faced—Babe Ruth—and also struck out Lou Gehrig.

Location: One block south of Geary at Masonic, Richmond District, San Francisco, CA
Status: Destroyed by fire in 1926; demolished in 1938
Opened: May 16, 1914
Capacity: 17,000

RIGHT: J. Cal Ewing, who had owned the San Francisco Seals, had always wanted his own ballpark. He decided to invest $100,000 to build a "super stadium."

ABOVE: A panorama taken on Ewing Field's opening, May 16, 1914. By the first season's end, the San Francisco Seals had lost their entire fan base. Beautiful 17,000-seat Ewing Field was abandoned after only one year.

A state-of-the-art stadium when it was constructed in 1914, Ewing Stadium failed to live up to its architectural promise simply because of the ballpark's location.

It was the home of the San Francisco Seals, who moved there after sharing premises at Recreation Park with the Oaklands Commuters club for over a decade. The Seals' owner, J. Cal Ewing, invested an incredible $100,000 (the equivalent of some $70 million today) in a new ballpark for his team, which took it over in May 1914.

With a capacity of 17,000, the grandstand roof and structure were similar to those at the widely admired Recreation Park, but the whole ballpark was more spacious and elaborate. The stadium was filled to capacity at the inaugural games, but as the game wore on and the temperature dropped as the afternoon chilled, fog rolled in off the bay and the outfield became almost invisible. Ewing attributed this to bad spring weather, but when the same thing happened the next week, he began to realize that his new ballpark was utterly at the mercy of San Francisco's notoriously fickle weather. Ewing Field was repeatedly subject to fog, and according to one story, in one game the team mascot was sent out to find outfielder Elmer Zachar to tell him that the batters had been retired.

The Seals stuck at Ewing Park for just one season and returned to Recreation Park in 1915, where they remained until 1931 before moving to Seals Stadium.

Ewing Field never hosted professional baseball again, and was used for football, amateur baseball, rodeo, and finally a circus. During an amateur game in June 1926, a fan's cigarette butt started a fire that not only destroyed Ewing Field, but ravaged the whole area as well. Ewing Field will go down in history as the only ballpark to be abandoned because of consistently bad weather, a real shame given the stadium's fine facilities.

Location: West of downtown between Gardiner Expressway and Lake Shore Boulevard West, Toronto, Ontario, Canada

Aka: Canadian National Exhibition Stadium, CNE Stadium

Status: Demolished in 1999

Capacity: 25,303 (original, football); 43,737 (baseball)

Opened: April 7, 1987

Last MLB game: May 28, 1989

Dimensions:

Left Field 330 ft

Left Center 375 ft

Center Field 410 ft

Right Center 375 ft

Left Field 330 ft

Not far from Lake Ontario, Exhibition Stadium collected a reputation as a cold and wet venue, especially when the icy winds brought fog and rain. The first stadium was built on this site in 1879 and Canadian National Stadium was the fourth incarnation when it was built as the Canadian National Exhibition Center and football stadium in 1948. At that time, the north grandstand and the left field bleachers were put in. Built in a number of phases, the later venue was an odd horseshoe-shaped construct. In 1959 the ground was expanded to take 33,150 football fans, for which a south bleacher was built as the venue was adapted for Canadian football.

Then, in the 1970s, Exhibition Stadium was converted to become a dedicated ballpark with the hope of attracting an expansion MLB team. It worked as the Toronto Blue Jays started playing at Exhibition Stadium in April 1977. A grandstand was built down the foul lines, but the venue was never very convincing as a ballpark. The cheap seats on the left field bleachers and the seats directly behind home plate were the only positions giving a good view of play; most of the other seats faced away from the field and some of them even looked directly at each other. Many of the outfield seats were a long way from play and the farthest away were 820 feet from home plate—the farthest in the majors. Exhibition also had a huge seatless gap in right field as a legacy of its football past.

Additionally, the ground had artificial turf to counter the variable climatic conditions. Exhibition's other claim to fame is that it was the only MLB ground on which baseball was played while still covered with snow!

In 1982 the Grey Cup Canadian Football League championship game was played in driving rain at Exhibition Stadium, a game known as "the Rain Bowl." Players and fans alike were frozen and soaked and the demand for a new facility started. Tens of thousands of people demonstrated at city hall demanding a dome to protect them from the elements.

The Blue Jays stayed for twelve seasons and played their last game at Exhibition Stadium on May 28, 1989, before moving to the SkyDome. Exhibition Stadium was left mosty dormant until in January 1999. Demolition started and the site became a parking lot until 2006, when it became a soccer stadium. In 2007 BMO Field became the home of Toronto FC.

ABOVE: Aerial view of Exhibition Stadium in 1979. Note the light towers. They were 180 feet high, and you could see them from miles away while driving into Toronto from the west along the lakeshore.

BELOW: Photographs dated 1988. After 1978, this was the only completely single-decked stadium in the majors. Note, at right, the scoreboard. This sat at the far east end of the stadium, about 200 feet behind the right-field fence.
(Photos courtesy All-Star pitcher and broadcaster Jerry Reuss Jerryreuss.com.)

Location: Between current sites of PNC Park and Heinz Field, Pittsburgh, PA

Status: Demolished, date unknown

Capacity: 16,000

Opened: April 22, 1891

Last MLB game: June 29, 1909

Dimensions:

Left Field 400 ft

Center Field 450 ft

Left Center 400 ft

World Series: 1903

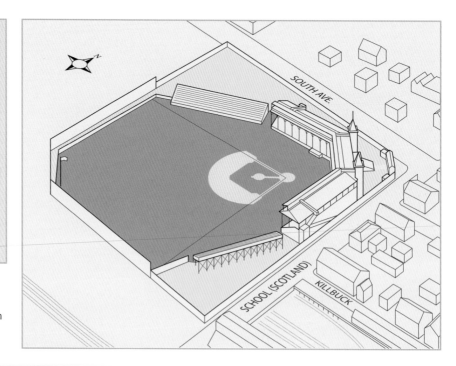

RIGHT: Artist's impression of Exposition Park, which occupied the the same site as the later Three Rivers Stadium.

TOP: Pittsburgh playing Chicago on July 2, 1908.

ABOVE: Pittsburgh vs. the Yankees in 1907.

RIGHT: Exposition Park on August 23, 1904—15,935 spectators watch the Yankees and Pirates. The year before, Pittsburgh had competed in the first World Series against Boston.

In the late 1880s, the area on the north shore of the Allegheny River, near where Three Rivers Stadium stood, saw three ballparks. They can be identified as the lower field (1882), the upper field (1883), and the best known—Exposition Park—that opened in 1891.

The American Association Alleghenys played here from 1882 to 1884 until they moved to Recreation Park after the river flooded. The flooding was not unusual: the record was in July 1902 when a foot of water covered the outfield.

The third Exposition Park was built to house the Pittsburgh Burghers of the Players' League, but the team only lasted a year, and it became the home of the Pittsburgh Pirates, who played there until 1909, when they moved to Forbes Field. The ballpark had a covered single-tier grandstand extending from first to third base and uncovered bleachers the remaining distance down the foul lines. Additional fans frequently stood in right field.

Exposition Park was the first National League ballpark to host a World Series game in 1903, and the Western University of Pennsylvania, now the University of Pittsburgh, played home football games at the stadium. The park was also home to the university baseball team.

Location: 937 Phillips Lane, Louisville, KY
Aka: Cardinal Stadium
Status: Minor league stadium
Opened: 1957
Capacity: 19,000 when set up for baseball—but 48,000 with stage setup
Dimensions:
Left Field 360 ft
Center Field 405 ft
Right Field 312 ft
All-Star Game: 1991 Triple-A All-Star Game

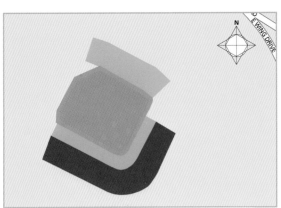

Cardinal Stadium is a huge minor league venue in Louisville, Kentucky, that is as big as a few major league stadiums. Formerly home to the Louisville Redbirds, it has a seating capacity of 33,500, which can be expanded with bleachers to accommodate 49,000 fans.

Built in 1956, Cardinal Stadium started out as an American Association ballpark, and was called Fairgrounds Stadium. In 1968 it became part of the International League until 1972. In 1982 the name was changed to Cardinal Stadium and it rejoined the American Association, remaining until the league disbanded in 1997. It rejoined the International League for just one year. It was finally decommissioned when the Redbirds moved into their new ballpark, Louisville Slugger Stadium, in 2000, which is now home to the Louisville Bats.

Cardinal Stadium replaced the smaller Parkway/Colonials Field in Louisville, which still exists, although without the grandstand. As the name implies, Fairgrounds Stadium was the home of the Kentucky State Fair, one of the biggest state fairs in the country, and is built on the site of the Kentucky Exposition Center. Underneath the stands, in the underbelly of the stadium, there are hundreds of stalls for horses and other animals, although the space is mainly used for car parking today. There is also a full-sized baseball training area, complete with warm-up mounds, batting cages, and training facilities. It is a multipurpose facility, and to solve the problem of where to site the press box most advantageously, there are actually three, one behind the home plate and two along the third base line for football games.

THIS PAGE: Views of the enormous stadium. The footprint shows the asymmetric stand and the large open stand in right field.

Until 2005 Cardinal Stadium was home to the University of Louisville's baseball team and was without doubt an amazing facility for a college baseball field. With the departure of both the university football and baseball teams, the stadium is now largely vacant.

Fenway Park

Location: 4 Yawkey Way, Boston, MA

Status: Home of the Boston Red Sox

Architect: Osborn Engineering

Capacity: 35,095 (1912); 37,493 (current)

Opened: April 20, 1912

Dimensions

	Original 1912	Current
Left Field	324 ft	310 ft
Left Center	379 ft	379 ft
Center Field	488 ft	420 ft
Right Center	380 ft	380 ft
Right Field	313.5 ft	302 ft

World Series: 1903, 1912, 1914, 1918, 1946, 1967, 1975, 1986, 2004

All-Star Game: 1946, 1961, 1999

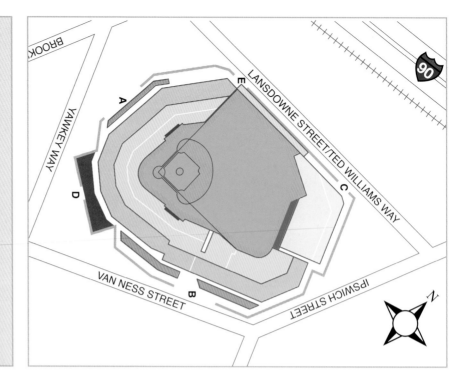

ABOVE: Fans gather on Yawkey Way—note the banners identifying honors—World Series, AL pennants, divisional titles.

BELOW: Panorama of Fenway taken on September 28, 1912. The facilities have changed considerably, but Fenway is still the ultimate example of what a ballpark should be.

Claimed to be "America's most beloved ballpark," Fenway Park is the longtime home of the Boston Red Sox as well as being many fans' favorite sports venue. It was built in 1912 at a cost of $650,000. The Red Sox arrived from their previous home of Huntington Avenue Grounds in 1912 but their first two scheduled games were postponed due to heavy rains and the Red Sox finally started their tenure at Fenway with a win over the New York Highlanders (later to become their hated rivals the Yankees) on April 20, 1912, just six days after the tragic sinking of the RMS *Titanic*.

Fenway Park has retained its character over the decades and is remarkably unchanged from the early years, and has the proud distinction of being the oldest ballpark still in use by the major leagues. The ground proved itself from the start when the Red Sox reached and won the World Series in their first season (defeating the New York Giants 4–3) there and then went on to three more World Series in 1915, 1916, and 1918. In fact, Fenway Park also hosted the 1914 World Series, but that year for the Boston Braves, whose own ballpark was under construction. However, it would be eighty-four long years before the Red Sox won another World Series in 2004 when they defeated the St. Louis Cardinals.

Most changes at Fenway Park have been forced by fire: in 1926 a small fire destroyed the left field bleachers but they were never replaced. A much more serious fire raged in 1934 during the course of a general revamp of the park by then-owner Tom Yawkey. All the stops were pulled out to rebuild the ballpark so it was able to reopen in three months. Following the fire the wooden left field was replaced by a similar metal wall 25 feet high, and in the process starting the evolution of one of Fenway Park's defining features, the Green Monster. This thirty-seven-foot wall of metal separates Lansdowne Street from the outfield and was probably originally constructed to stop nonpaying fans from watching the ball game for free. In 1934 the wall was built up to its present height and painted green; many years later in 2003 the seats built on top of it have become some of the most sought-after in baseball.

Location: Notre Dame Campus, South Bend, IN
Aka: The Eck
Status: Home of the Notre Dame Fighting Irish
Opened: 1994
Capacity: 2,500

LEFT: Frank Eck's name is etched into the home plate entrance. A 1944 graduate of Notre Dame, Eck followed in his father's footsteps, as did his own son, Frank Jr. Eck's gifts to the university total over $35 million.

BELOW and BOTTOM
Attendance is usually good at the stadium. The all-time record is 13,927 vs. West Virginia on April 21, 2007.

Home of the Notre Dame Fighting Irish, Frank Eck Baseball Stadium is located on the campus of the University of Notre Dame near downtown South Bend, Indiana. Although Notre Dame is known as football territory, the fact is, their baseball program has had almost thirty postseason appearances since 1954, and produced many well-known major league ballplayers.

This intimate grassed ballpark is located on the southeast side of the campus and seats 2,500 spectators in a simple but elegant, permanent concrete-and-steel grandstand. The stadium replaced the old Jake Kline Field, where the Fighting Irish used to play until 1988 when they started playing most of their games at the Single-A South Bend Silver Hawks' ballpark, Coveleski Regional Stadium. Frank Eck Stadium brought the Fighting Irish back home on campus.

Frank Eck Stadium was completed in 1992 at a cost of $5.7 million. Since then, it has undergone several renovations and additions. Most notably, a spacious indoor pitching and batting cage facility outfitted with clay mounds in two of the three batting tunnels that were completed prior to the 2000 season. The stadium sound system was upgraded with the latest technology while an enclosed, sound-resistant radio booth sits within the Eck Stadium press box, and a full-function message board was added in 2001.

Notre Dame's Fighting Irish have had four homes for baseball since the university began this sports program. Cartier Field, formerly located between Notre Dame Stadium and the Hesburgh Library, served the Fighting Irish for over eighty-five years. Jake Kline Field took over in 1977 and served as the primary home, until South Bend's new ballpark, Stanley Coveleski Regional Stadium, was completed in 1988.

Finally in 1994, Frank Eck Stadium was completed and the Fighting Irish came home to Notre Dame's campus.

Location: 1365 South West Temple, Salt Lake City, UT

Aka: Spring Mobile Ballpark (since 2009), Franklin Quest

Status: Home to the Salt Lake Bees and the Utah Utes

Opened: 1994

Capacity: 15,500

Dimensions:

Left Field 345 ft

Center Field 420 ft

Right Field 315 ft

All-Star Game: 1996, 2011

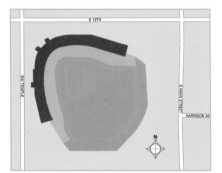

Spring Mobile Ballpark, formerly known as Franklin Covey Field, is home to Salt Lake City's minor league team, the Salt Lake Bees. When Franklin Covey opened in 1994, the Minnesota Twins moved their Triple-A team to Salt Lake City, naming them the Buzz.

Salt Lake City had been represented for decades by Derks Field, an uncovered ballpark that during its later years resembled Seals Stadium. It was a simple concrete ballpark, but one that had garnered the love and admiration of the people of Salt Lake City. It had previously served the Pacific Coast League, but the Seattle Mariners moved the team to Calgary's Foothills Stadium.

In 1992 Salt Lake City's mayor, who was keen to return the city's team to the Pacific Coast League, initiated the construction of a new ballpark on the Derks Field site, Franklin Covey Field. With magnificent views of the Wasatch Mountains, the park has a retro style of wrought iron, dark green seats, and red brick. The facility has a seating capacity of around 15,000 and is the third biggest ballpark in the Pacific Coast League. Its size gives it the air of a major league ballpark, but its huge capacity is well justified, because baseball is immensely popular in Salt Lake City. Franklin Covey Field quickly won over the fans, and they flock here consistently. In the past few years, the Bees have averaged between 450,000 and 480,000 fans per season, remarkable attendance figures given that there are two other professional baseball stadiums within a few miles of the ballpark.

The Salt Lake Buzz remained at Franklin Covey for seven successful years, promoting many future major league players. They were succeeded in 2001 by the Anaheim Angels' team, the Salt Lake Stingers, who were renamed in 2006 as the Salt Lake Bees, the traditional name of the Salt Lake team.

THIS PAGE: One of the first Triple-A double-decked stadiums, Franklin Covey Field is a comfortable place to watch a game. In 1995 some 14,596 people packed the park to watch the Salt Lake Buzz (now Bees) beat the Minnesota Twins.

Location: One Morrie Silver Way, Rochester, NY

Status: Home to the Rochester Red Wings

Architect: Ellerbe Becket

Opened: July 11, 1996

Capacity: 10,868 (up to 13,500 with standing room)

Dimensions:

Left Field 335 ft

Center Field 402 ft

Right Field 322 ft

All Star Game: 2000

The Rochester Red Wings are one of the oldest minor league baseball teams in the United States, having begun life in 1899 as the Rochester Bronchos, and have played uninterrupted for every season since then in the same city.

The team's stability owes much to the major league clubs who have sponsored Rochester. The club first gained major league affiliation in 1928, when the St. Louis Cardinals adopted them, and they remained together for a remarkable thirty-three years. In 1960 the Baltimore Orioles took over, signing the Red Wings to a player development contract lasting a whopping forty-two years. This kind of loyalty is almost unheard of in professional baseball, and the Baltimore Orioles would make Rochester their Triple-A home from 1961 until 2002, meaning they spanned the era of professional baseball from Silver Stadium and well into the opening of the new Frontier Field. In 2003 the Minnesota Twins succeeded the Orioles.

The Red Wings played for years at Silver Stadium, a stately 1920s ballpark. It was replaced in 1997 by $35.3 million Frontier Field, a beautiful stadium with a capacity of 13,700 and an unusually wide field. It was designed in this way so that the stadium could be used for professional soccer, and was home to the Rochester Rhinos for nine years.

The Red Wings initially enjoyed tremendous success in their new home, ending the 1997 season at 83–58 and beating the Columbus Clippers in the Triple-A World Series to bring home the tenth International League title to Rochester and the first to Frontier Field. The team's form declined in subsequent seasons, and although attendance dipped from the all-time high of 540,000 during the 1997 season, it has still hovered around 450,000.

The Red Wings have an amazingly loyal fan base that continues to flock through the gates of Frontier Field, which says a lot about how important this ballpark is to the traditional stability of Rochester baseball.

THIS PAGE: Despite not being a baseball-only field and being bigger than most, Frontier Field is not lacking in intimacy. This ballpark has terrific views of the downtown area, passing trains, radio towers, churches, and many of the other highlights of the city of Rochester.

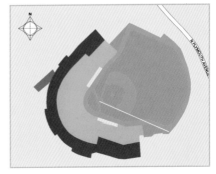

Fort Lauderdale Municipal Stadium

Location: 1401 NW 55th Street, Fort Lauderdale, FL

Aka: Fort Lauderdale Municipal Stadium

Status: Home to the Fort Lauderdale Strikers soccer team

Opened: 1962

Last MLB game: 2009

Capacity: 8,340

Dimensions:

Left Field 332 ft

Center Field 401 ft

Right Field 320 ft

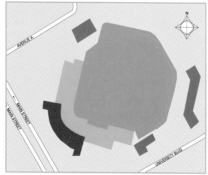

THIS PAGE and OPPOSITE, ABOVE: The Yankees organization would call Fort Lauderdale Stadium home for thirty-four long years. They trained here in 1977 and 1978 before going on to win back-to-back World Series victories. In 1996, the Yankees would move to a "mini" version of Yankee Stadium named Legend Field, saying good-bye to Fort Lauderdale Stadium.

Fort Lauderdale Municipal Stadium was built in 1962 for the New York Yankees. When the Yankees moved here for their spring training in 1962, they brought their Single-A club, the St. Petersburg Saints, who were renamed the Fort Lauderdale Yankees. For the first time in their history, the Yankees had their major league team and their Florida State League Single-A team under the same roof, and would call it home for thirty-four years.

The Fort Lauderdale Yankees were immediately impressive, winning the Florida State League in 1962, the same year that their parent club won the World Series. It was the first of seven FSL championship titles. Many of the Fort Lauderdale Yankees players went on to enjoy great careers in the majors —but not always with the New York Yankees, who had a habit of trading the talent that rose through their ranks. Names such as Jose Rijo, Bob Tewksbury, Al Leiter, Deion Sanders, Jim DeShaise, Jay Buhner, Willie McGee, and Rafael Santana could have done much to arrest the Yankees' decline in the 1970s and 1980s, but they were traded to other major league sides.

In 1993 the Yankees moved on to a new "super-stadium," Legend Field in St. Petersburg, and the Fort Lauderdale Yankees left with them. The Boston Red Sox visited for the 1993 season, but then the Baltimore Orioles, who had spent thirty-two springs in the Bobby Maduro–Miami Stadium, made Fort Lauderdale their home. It was near enough to their Miami fan base for the fans to commute up the coast with them. The Orioles remained until 2009, when they left for Sarasota, and the city of Fort Lauderdale was left to debate the fate of their stadium. It's now home to the Fort Lauderdale Strikers, a soccer team recently relocated from Miami, and sadly, for the first time in nearly fifty years, there are no baseball games at this venerable stadium.

Fuller Field was built in 1878, making it the oldest continuously used baseball diamond in the world. It is still in use for baseball and other sports, and is used by the local Clinton High School. The historic claim is based on maps of Clinton dating back to 1878, which have been authenticated and recorded as a Guinness world record.

Fuller Field today is approached past ticket booths and through a gateway guarded by a sculpture of a white lion. Inside is a multipurpose venue and more lion sculptures around the fieldhouse. Bleacher seats occupy the right side alongside a sign announcing the historic claim to be baseball's oldest diamond. However, Labatt Park in London, Ontario, contests this statement and claims their baseball field was set out a year earlier in 1877.

Location: 450 High Street, Clinton, MA
Status: Used for high school baseball
Opened: 1878

Fuller Field

Baseball came to Texas in 1888, but the first few years were erratic as teams and leagues came and went, and in 1898, play was suspended entirely because of the Spanish-American War. The original Gardner Park opened in 1919, but after this burned down in July 1924, it was replaced by a new stadium just across the road. Gardner Park was the home of pro baseball in Dallas for the next forty years. The golden age for baseball in Dallas was during the 1920s. In 1922 a group of businessmen led by George and Julius Schepps bought a controlling interest in the team and renamed it the Steers. Attendance rose sharply, and when the new stadium was built, it had a capacity of 8,000 and became known as Steer Stadium. The 1926 team won the league pennant and went on to win the Dixie Series after defeating New Orleans of the Southern Association.

Like its predecessor, Gardner Park was destroyed by fire in 1940, and a larger replacement was built on the same site in 1947 with a capacity of 9,000. It was not quite ready for the opening game of the 1941 season, and the team (by then called the Rebels) had to play in Waco for three games. Wartime shortages meant that the stadium lacked a roof until 1946. The name of the team changed again in 1947 when George Schepps sold his interest to Dick Burnett, and they became the Eagles until 1957. Burnett purchased the stadium at the same time and renamed it Burnett Field. He refurbished the facility, adding seats and increasing capacity to 10,324. Under his ownership the Eagles flew high, setting all-time highs for attendance and beating Nashville in the 1953 Dixie Series. Burnett also worked to integrate black and white players together in the Texas League. In 1958 the team became the Dallas Rangers, joining the American Association the following year. With the merger of the minor league teams in Dallas and Fort Worth in 1960, the writing was on the wall for Burnett Field, and in 1964, with the construction of Turnpike Stadium in Arlington, pro baseball left Dallas.

Location: 1500 East Jefferson Boulevard, Dallas, TX
Aka: Burnett Field (after 1947); Steers Stadium; Rebels Field; Rebels Stadium
Status: Closed 1964
Opened: 1924
Last MLB game: 1964
Capacity: 10,500
Dimensions:
Left Field 329 ft
Left Center Field 361 ft
Center Field 377 ft
Right Center Field 373 ft
Right Field 341 ft

Gardner Park

Location: 2301 Grizzlie Bear Boulevard, Sauget, IL

Aka: GMC Stadium

Status: Home of the Gateway Grizzlies

Architect: Kuhlmann Design Group

Capacity: 6,000

Dimensions:

Left Field 318 ft

Center Field 385 ft

Right Field 301 ft

Winner of the 2005 Digitalballparks Ballpark of the Year Award

THIS PAGE: This stadium broke new ground in baseball architecture... both for its price and its aesthetics. The ballpark was relatively cheap compared to the huge brick-and-concrete monsters being constructed, but wound up being far more attractive than those monsters as well.

GCS Ballpark is an open-air ballpark with huge concourses that prevent that claustrophobic feel you get from other stadiums; even on a sold-out day, you don't feel crammed in. There are lots of berms and picnic areas and not much in the way of permanent seating, which offers certain freedoms. Even the roofed upper deck is open on all sides, giving the ballpark a very roomy feel.

GCS Ballpark marked a major change in direction for the Frontier League. The league had previously been a true "frontier league," playing in small cities all over mid-America, many of which had small ballparks forgotten by Minor League Baseball after many years.

Then, under league president Bill Lee the Frontier League went from small-town semi-pro league, to suburban big-time baseball. Since the league is completely unaffiliated with Major or Minor League Baseball, it can do anything it wants and not worry about the fact that the Cardinals have a protected jurisdiction of seventy-five miles around the St. Louis area. Bill Lee decided to take full advantage of the freedoms of being an independent system and began moving all of his struggling ballclubs into the suburbs of major cities, usually well within the boundaries of major league clubs.

This ballpark was built in the shadows of the St. Louis Arch (on the Illinois side of the bridge) and only five miles away from Busch Stadium. The new expansion team, the Gateway Grizzlies, played their first season at Sauget Field, probably the worst ballpark ever to be called a professional home. Then, like a phoenix rising from the ashes, GCS Ballpark was built in Sauget. The stadium broke new ground in baseball architecture both for price and aesthetics.

The Grizzlies' new ballpark was an instant hit. Over 92,000 fans came out to see the ballpark in its first season and by 2003 season's end, the Grizzlies had broken the all-time league record by bringing in 168,000 fans—a record that they would soon beat over again. The Grizzlies became the first league team to break the 200,000 mark at the gate.

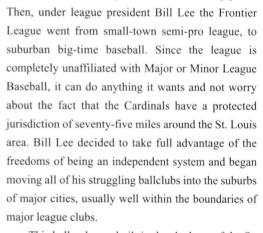

Location: 100 Joe Nuxhall Way, Cincinnati, OH

Capacity: 42,059

Status: Home to the Cincinnati Reds

Architect: HOK Sports

Opened: March 31, 2003

Capacity: 42,271

Dimensions:

Left Field 328 ft

Left Center 379 ft

Center Field 404 ft

Right Center 370 ft

Right Field 325 ft

Great American Ball Park replaced Cinergy Field (formerly Riverfront Stadium) as the home of the Cincinnati Reds in 2003 and sits on almost the same site as the old stadium. The $290 million complex was funded by a half-percent sales tax increase in Hamilton County started in 1996 to raise funds for new venues for the Reds and the NFL's Bengals. The ballpark is named for the Great American Insurance Company, which bought thirty years of naming rights for $75 million.

The facade of Great American Ball Park is built of cast stone and painted steel in homage to vernacular Cincinnati architecture and in particular of the nearby Roebling

LEFT: Great American Ball Park is designed to reflect the local architecture, especially that of nearby Roebling Suspension Bridge.

BELOW: With its Ohio River backdrop, the Great American Paddleboat pays homage to the many old-time steamboats that stream past the ballpark every day. The paddleboat's double decks serve for functions and corporate parties and can be rented out for a unique game-day experience. For every home run that is slugged by one of the Reds, fireworks explode from the smokestacks—a relatively common occurrence in this hitter's park.

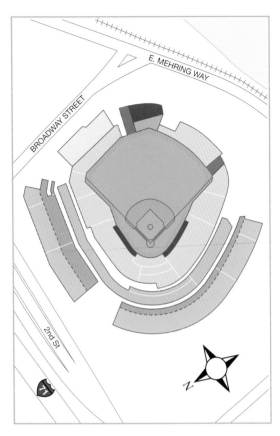

ABOVE: Footprint of Great American Ball Park.

BELOW: The best part of the left-field section is the view. While you may not be watching the paddleboats floating by on the river, you have a dramatic view of the ballfield and the game.

Suspension Bridge, which crosses over the Ohio River into Kentucky. Although the park has state-of-the-art amenities and comforts, there is an emphasis on baseball tradition: the main gateway and seats are designed to resemble the old park, and the scoreboard, although huge, is distinctly reminiscent of the one that graced Crosley Field. And in a nod to one of their greatest players, a rose garden has been planted outside the stadium on the spot where Pete Rose's record 4,192nd hit landed in the old Riverfront Stadium.

However, the single greatest feature of Great American Ball Park is "the Gap" down the first base line (see photo on page 159). This unique break in the seating allows for better vision as well as proximity to the field for seats down the line, and opens up views of downtown Cincinnati—and allows Cincinnati to look back inside.

After decades of being totally enclosed in the Riverfront/Cinergy cookie-cutter, Great American Ball Park doesn't keep the outside world hidden from the spectator. In fact, it flaunts it. The entire right and center field grandstand is one level high. The Ohio River and the state of Kentucky provide a dramatic backdrop. Also, the upper level of the left-field grandstand provides a cheaper alternative by providing bench seats, not individual chairs as in the rest of the ballpark.

A scoreboard is just above the bi-level left-field grandstand. A long data board keeps fans updated with lineups, scores, balls, strikes, as well as trivia. The entire left-field wall contains a constantly updating out-of-town scoreboard.

It was in 1869 that the Cincinnati Red Stockings took the field as America's first professional baseball team. Many teams talk about tradition and history, but the Cincinnati Reds are the oldest major league team playing today. They have played in eight different ballparks before this, but many would say that Great American Ball Park is the best.

ABOVE: A giant notch was cut out of the ballpark past home plate on the left field line. The notch not only brought the outside world into the new ballpark, it also added a lot of character to Great American, and another design element. Notice how the single upper-deck level changes to a bi-level after the cut.

Greenlee Field in Pittsburgh had a short but brilliant life and was the first stadium to be owned and built by the black baseball community. Built in 1932 for the Crawfords Negro League team at a cost of $100,000, it was situated in the heart of the black community in Pittsburgh.

Like many other black teams in the first half of the twentieth century, the Crawfords played at any stadium which would host them, but in the segregation era the players were banned from the dressing rooms at white-owned fields. In 1931 Gus Greenlee purchased a plot of land from the Entress Brick Company and built the first ballpark specifically for black players in the United States.

An attractive building of brick, concrete, and steel, Greenlee Field had a capacity of 7,500 and opened with a game between the Crawfords and the New York Black Yankees on April 29, 1932. Satchel Paige pitched for the Crawfords, but they lost 1–0 to the Yankees. Greenlee had made shrewd calculations when opening the park. He calculated that over 80 percent of fans would be able to walk to the stadium, and he was proved right—over 69,000 fans came to watch the Crawfords during their first season in their new home.

Greenlee also ensured that the Crawfords employed the bast players in the Negro League such as Satchel Paige, Josh Gibson, and James "Cool Papa" Bell. The 1935 team fielded five Hall of Fame players and won the Negro National League title in both 1935 and 1936.

The demise of Greenlee Field was largely due to segregation politics, when the white members of the board of directors forced Greenlee to bar black workers from ballpark jobs, such as ticket sales, during the 1938 season. Fans reacted angrily by staying away, and this, combined with financial troubles, prompted Greenlee to sell the Crawfords and demolish Greenlee Field.

Location: 2500 Bedford Avenue, Pittsburgh, PA
Status: Demolished 1938; Pennsylvania historical marker identifies location
Architect: Bellinger
Opened: April 30, 1932
Last game: 1938
Capacity: 7,500
Dimensions:
Left Field 360 ft
Center Field 442 ft
Right Field 376 ft

Greenlee Field

Location: Corner of College and Cumberland, University of Saskatchewan, Saskatoon, Canada
Aka: Griffiths Stadium at Potash Corp Park (since 2006)
Status: Used by the University of Saskatchewan
Opened: 1967; renovated 1988 and 2006
Capacity: 4,997

From 1913 to 1936, Cairns Field was the home of professional baseball in Saskatoon. It had a capacity of nearly 5,000, but at the height of the Depression in 1935, the University of Saskatchewan worked to build a new stadium. Griffiths Stadium was built for the university as a multipurpose stadium for baseball, football, and athletics. It was designed free of charge by the faculty of the College of Engineering for an initial price of $25,000. The chosen site was the corner of College and Cumberland, and as it was at the height of the Depression, it was decided after much debate that to help students earn some money they would provide the labor force. Work started on May 17, 1936, under the supervision of the superintendent of buildings, Professor A.R. Greig.

The official opening of Griffiths Stadium was on October 3, 1936, when 2,000 fans watched the University of Saskatchewan Huskies beat the Alberta Golden Bears 5–3.

In June 1967 the new Griffiths Stadium was built a few hundred yards east of the original site to allow the widening of College Drive. The first stage officially opened on June 2, 1967. The stadium was renovated and improved in 1988 for the Jeux Canada Games and then again in 2006 for the Vanier Cup university football championship, when a $5 million donation was received from Potash Corp. The name changed, too, as a result. Further donations will see a new clubhouse built in 2011.

LEFT: Money from Potash Corp. and donations will lead to a new clubhouse.

Location: East Orange, NJ
Aka: Monte Irvin Field
Status: Amateur
Opened: 1908
Capacity: 1,800
Dimensions:
Left Field 240 ft
Center Field 360 ft
Right Field 280 ft

Home to the New York Cubans from 1941 until 1947, Grove Street Oval was commissioned as a ballpark in 1908, and the 6.5-acre site also included tennis courts and an athletic track. The original wooden grandstand had a capacity of 1,800 and was built at a cost of $70,000. In 1923 the original shelter house was replaced with a more elaborate structure, which included a decorative Spanish-tiled roof, and at the same time a clubhouse was erected behind center field. One quirk of the ballpark was the four-foot-high water fountain in center field, which remained in play.

Like other Negro League teams, the New York Cubans lacked a permanent home and had played at a succession of stadiums, including Recreation Park and the Polo Grounds in New York City. The popular Cubans and the New York Black Yankees competed for the affection of New York fans, and although the Cubans fielded consistently good teams, they did not win a league title until 1947. They went on to defeat the Cleveland Buckeyes of the Negro American League 4–1 to win the Negro World Series that same year.

Their finest player was probably Martin Dihigo, who began his career playing for Havana in the Cuban League, played his finest season in the Mexican League in 1938, and is the only player to be inducted into the American, Cuban and Mexican Halls of Fame. Known as "El Maestro," he went on to become the Cuban minister of sport after the 1959 revolution.

An unlikely amateur baseball player at Grove Street Oval was singer Dionne Warwick, who grew up in the area and recalls playing baseball with her friends. Grove Street Oval still exists, and is a slightly shabby inner-city ballpark, home to amateur softball games.

Location: Lee County Sports Complex, 14100 Six Mile Cypress Parkway, Fort Myers, FL
Status: Home to the Fort Myers Miracles
Architect: Lescher & Mahoney
Opened: 1991; some renovations in 2007
Capacity: 7,500
Dimensions:
Left Field 330 ft
Center Field 405 ft
Right Field 330 ft
All-Star Game: 48th Florida State League 2009

Hammond Stadium is the spring training home of the Minnesota Twins and also houses their advanced Single-A affiliate, the Fort Myers Miracles, who play in the Florida State League. The Twins' rookie league affiliate, the Gulf Coast League Twins, play in the same sports complex but not at Hammond Stadium itself.

The stadium was built at a cost of $14 million and is named in honor of former Lee County commissioner Bill Hammond, who was a key figure in getting the facility built and thus drawing the Twins away from their former spring home in Orlando, Florida.

Hammond Stadium's outer facade was designed with Churchill Downs in mind, and its parking zones feature street signs named after former Twins greats, including Bert Blyleven, Kirby Puckett, and Kent Hrbek. Inside the stadium, in 2007, there were some changes that included creating a small berm that can seat 230, changes to the party deck and drink-rail seats, and relocating the visiting team's bullpen to the right-field corner.

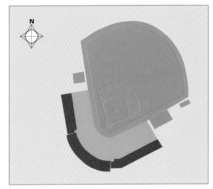

ABOVE: It is said that the stadium's exterior was designed to evoke comparisons to Churchill Downs: certainly it is striking and, with its water, palms, and tower, more interesting than many other facilities.

LEFT: The Twins won the World Series following their first spring training in Hammond Stadium, so something worked well. Unlike the exterior, the interior of the stadium is straightforward and a little lackluster.

Hammons Field

Location: 955 East Trafficway, Springfield, MO

Aka: John Q. Hammons Field

Status: Home of Double-A Springfield Cardinals

Opened: 2004

Capacity: 7,986 seats, plus 2,500

Dimensions:

Left Field 315 ft

Center Field 400 ft

Right Field 330 ft

THIS PAGE: Hammons Field is a superb facility. It has every amenity of a major league park, just a bit smaller. It has proved successful, too. Through the end of the 2010 season, a total of thirty-two former Springfield Cardinals have made their big league debut with the St. Louis Cardinals.

The Springfield Cardinals, the Double-A Texas League affiliate of the St. Louis Cardinals, and the Missouri State University Bears play in Hammons Field. The $32 million ballpark was built by local businessman John Q. Hammons, as a leap of faith before he had secured a minor league team to the city. Hammons succeeded when he persuaded the St. Louis Cardinals to buy the El Paso Diablos franchise and relocate them to Springfield as the Springfield Cardinals. The field is made up of a Bermuda and rye grass mix: when the weather warms up, the groundskeepers kill off the latter to allow the Bermuda grass to take over. The venue includes a large fully furnished indoor practice facility complete with AstroTurf, batting cages, and a small diamond for drills. Hammons Field has one of the largest electronic scoreboards in the country—used for on-field replays, between-innings entertainment, and recaps from MLB games. On top of the screen are the flags of all of the Texas League teams and their current standings on game day. Hammons has also twice hosted the Missouri Valley Conference baseball tournament, in 2004 and 2007.

Hawkins Field combines the best of modern facilities encapsulated within a classic ballpark. It is located on the Vanderbilt University campus, alongside the Vanderbilt Football Stadium and Memorial Gym. The redbrick frontage and brick and rod-iron fence design give way to 2,000 chair-back seats, with additional bleacher seating that brings total capacity to 3,700. The thirty-five-foot wall on left field is reminiscent of the Green Monster at Fenway Park and adds to the excitement of games.

The Commodores won the NCAA championship in 2007. The Outlaws were founded in 2010 by three former executives of the city's minor league team, the Nashville Sounds, and share that team's colors.

The Commodores' success has meant that money has been available for improvements to Hawkins Field. A $4.5 million renovation program in 2006 added more bleacher seating and a two-story locker room, offices, and a hall of fame. A new pitchers' training area is situated next door in the football stadium, while a new indoor batting cage is housed in the Memorial Gym. In 2009 the dugouts were renovated and a new trainers' room was installed along with more seating along the first base line.

BELOW: Hawkins Field with Vanderbilt Stadium dominant behind left field.

Home to two early New York teams, the Troy Haymakers (1871–72) and the Troy Trojans (1881–82), Haymakers Grounds was located on Green Island, Albany County, New York (also known as Central Island, because of its position in the middle of the Hudson River). Today it is a rather bleak-looking industrial area of fuel tanks, and the only record of the park's existence is a few miles down the road at Knickerbocker Park in Troy itself.

The Troy Haymakers were more formally known as the Unions of Lansingburgh and were one of the first professional baseball teams in the United States, having been founded in 1861. When they defeated the New York Mutuals in 1867, the urban club was shocked that it had lost to a team of rural "haymakers," and the nickname stuck.

In 1871 the National Association of Professional Base Ball Players was founded in New York City and the Haymakers were one of nine teams who paid $10 to join the league. Home games were played at Haymakers Grounds and the Haymakers were reasonably successful, with a 15–10 record in 1872. Sadly, however, they were forced to disband midway through the season. "The Haymaker Base Ball Club of Troy has disbanded on account of an empty treasury," reported the local newspaper.

The National League, which remains the oldest professional league still in existence, emerged in 1876 to replace the ailing National Association. In 1878 the Lansingburgh Haymakers were admitted and became known as the Troy Trojans. Despite an initially enthusiastic local following, the Trojans did not cover themselves in glory, and during the four years of their existence, they won 134 games and lost 191. They set a new record for low attendance in September 1881 when just twelve fans came to Green Island to watch them play the Chicago White Stockings.

The Trojans folded in 1882, but the rights to the team were purchased by John B. Day, who distributed the players among his two other teams, the New York Metropolitans and the New York Gothams (later the Giants). So the Trojans have a key place in the history of one of baseball's greatest franchises, the Giants.

Location: Green Island, Albany County, New York, NY
Status: Closed September 30, 1881
Opened: May 9, 1871

Haymakers Grounds

Location: 534 Chestnut Street, Nashville, TN

Aka: Greer Stadium

Status: Home to the Nashville Sounds

Architect: Stoll-Reed Architects Inc.

Opened: April 26, 1978; renovated 1984 and 2008–2009

Capacity: 7,200 (1978); 18,000 (1984); 25,000 (current)

Dimensions:

Left Field 327 ft

Center Field 400 ft

Right Field 327 ft

All-Star Game: Southern League 1979, 1983; Triple-A 1994

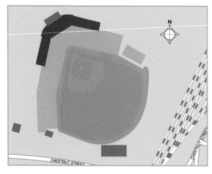

ABOVE: Footprint of Herschel Greer Stadium.

TOP and BELOW: Herschel Greer Stadium is typical of the ballparks built in the late 1970s and early 1980s. While there aren't many to be found in Triple-A, there are plenty to be found in the Grapefruit League. Florida is filled with spring training parks from this era that have a similar size, look, and construction as Hershel Greer.

Built in 1978 at a cost of $1 million, Herschel Greer Stadium has hosted seven affiliated teams in three different leagues and is now the home of the Nashville Sounds, the Triple-A team of the Milwaukee Brewers.

Nashville is best known as being the center of country music, and Herschel Greer Stadium has certainly capitalized on that by naming their baseball team the Nashville Sounds. It's the gigantic guitar-shaped scoreboard, however, that has made this stadium famous, and is perhaps the most photographed scoreboard in the entire world.

The construction of Herschel Greer brought baseball back to Nashville after a fifteen-year drought, after Greer's predecessor Sulphur Dell was demolished in the mid-1960s. Herschel Greer first served as the Double-A home for the Southern League and the Cincinnati Reds. The Reds were succeeded by the Yankees, who placed some great future ballplayers at Greer Stadium, and remained in Nashville for five years.

In 1985 the Detroit Tigers took over and brought promotion to the stadium by placing their Triple-A team in Nashville. Although they stayed only two years, Greer was established as a Triple-A ballpark, and in 1987 the Cincinnati Reds returned as Triple-A associates.

When they left five years later, Greer somehow acquired two new teams who shared the facilities. The White Sox' Triple-A team took over the Sounds name, and when they were away, the Minnesota Twins' Double-A team, the Nashville Xpress, used the stadium. It was a treat for baseball fans, and both teams performed well during the 1993 and 1994 seasons, but it was only ever a temporary arrangement.

The White Sox remained until 1997, when the American Association was dissolved and the Triple-A teams divided between the eastern International League and the western Pacific League. Nashville wound up in the Pacific League and the Pittsburgh Pirates took over the franchise from 1998 until 2004, followed by the Milwaukee Brewers from 2005.

ABOVE and BELOW: The gigantic guitar-shaped scoreboard made its debut in 1993. Its unique look was perfect for this stadium and its connection to the country music world.

Opened in 1914, Hilldale Park, near Philadelphia, was one of the great ballparks of the Negro Leagues. It was home to the Hilldale Athletic Club, the team founded in 1910 and also known as the Hilldale Daisies or the Darby Daisies.

With a capacity of 8,000, it was a compact ballfield with a left foul line of only 315 feet. A tree stood in center field and any ball caught in its branches was considered to be in play.

Philadelphia post office clerk Ed Bolden founded the Hilldale Athletic Club in 1910 as an amateur sports club. Bolden was more than just a casual manager, however, and had ambitions for his new team. In 1916 he turned the team pro, naming them the Hilldale Baseball and Exhibition Co. The Daisies played as associates of the western Negro National League in 1920 and 1921, defeating the Chicago American Giants to win the title in 1921.

Bolden was a founder of the Eastern League in 1923, which was formed to compete with the National Negro League. Hilldale won the league championship for three successive years (1923–25), and won a place in the final of the inaugural Colored World Series in 1924, losing to the Kansas City Monarchs. In 1925, they defeated the Monarchs to win the World Series at Hilldale Park.

By now known as the Hilldale Giants, the team attracted the best players in the Negro Leagues, such as Biz Mackey, future Hall of Famer Judy Johnson, and outfielder Clint Thomas. Bolden withdrew the club from the Eastern League in 1927 and was later forced out of management. The impact of the Depression on poor black communities affected attendance and the Hilldale Giants folded in 1932.

Location: Corner of Chester and Cedar Avenues, Darby, PA
Status: Demolished; Pennsylvania historical marker identifies location
Opened: 1914
Last game: 1932
Capacity: 8,000
Dimensions:
Left Field 315 ft
Center Field 400 ft
Right Field 370 ft

Hilldale Park

In 2006, Hilldale Park was commemorated with a Pennsylvania historical marker entitled "The Hilldale Athletic Club (The Darby Daisies)." It identifies that the team won the Eastern Colored League championship three times and the 1925 Negro League World Series, and remembers Hall of Famers Pop Lloyd, Judy Johnson, Martin Dihigo, Joe Williams, Oscar Charleston, Ben Taylor, Biz Mackey, and Louis Santop. It finished by identifying owner Ed Bolden as one of the people who helped set up the Eastern Colored League.

Location: In Manhattan, west of Broadway between 165th and 168th Streets, New York, NY
Aka: American League Park
Status: Demolished in 1914
Capacity: 15,000 (seated)
Opened: April 3, 1903
Last game: October 5, 1912
Dimensions:
Left Field 365 ft
Center Field 542 ft
Right Field 400 ft

The New York Yankees have had several homes in New York. When they started out, they played as the New York Highlanders in the American League at Hilltop Park in the Washington Heights neighborhood of New York. They stayed there from 1903 until 1912. Officially named American League Park, the venue was built within six weeks at a cost of $300,000 and comprised a single-deck roofed grandstand stretching from first to third base, with bleachers on either side down the left and right field lines. More bleachers were built in center field in 1912. The location gave the Highlanders the nickname "Hilltoppers," although as early as 1905 the newspapers started dubbing them the Yankees.

Hilltop Park could officially seat 15,000 people but the capacity could almost double when needed, as there was sufficient standing room for at least a further 10,000 people in the outfield.

Near neighbors New York Giants shared Hilltop Park for two months with the Highlanders after their Polo Grounds burned down at the start of the 1911 season. The Giants soon returned to their rebuilt home and graciously allowed the Yankees to sublet part of Polo Grounds II between 1913 and 1923, when Yankee Stadium opened. By the start of the 1913 season the Highlanders were universally known as the Yankees.

Hilltop Park was demolished in 1914 and is the current site of the Columbia-Presbyterian Medical Center.

BELOW: Panoramic view of Hilltop Park, circa 1910.

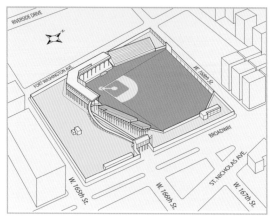

ABOVE: Artist's impression of Hilltop Park, New York's last wooden ballpark.

RIGHT: Women, children, and cigar-smoking gentlemen queuing to get into American League Park.

Formerly home to the New York Black Yankees, the grand oval of Hinchliffe Stadium still stands proudly in Paterson, New Jersey, even though it has seen better days.

Most Negro League teams did not have their own stadiums and were forced to barnstorm and play in other ballparks, often miles from their home. Most of the few Negro League stadiums, like storied Greenlee Field in Pittsburgh, are now gone. Only a handful of dedicated Negro League stadiums still exist today.

When the stadium faced demolition, it was saved by a remarkable community group, the Friends of Hinchliffe, who have spent the last few years stopping the wrecking crews and chopping down the trees that had overgrown the stadium.

Built in 1932, Hinchliffe has hosted semipro football, soccer, track and field, boxing, concerts, and even auto racing. Its biggest claim to fame, however, came in 1933 when the New York Black Yankees first began playing at this stadium. They would go to the Negro National League Championships versus the Philadelphia Stars that season, and all of their championship home games would be played at Hinchliffe. Although they lost to the Stars, they were thrilled by the ballpark and by 1934 it had become their regular home. In 1936 they were joined by the New York Cubans, who also played in the Negro League.

In 1938 the Black Yankees moved out to Triborough Stadium on Randalls Island, later known as Downing Stadium, but they missed the loyal fans of Paterson and moved "home" to Hinchliffe in 1939. From 1939 to 1948 the Black Yankees played almost all of their home games here. Local boy Larry Doby, while never a member of the Black Yankees, played on the field for Paterson High School. Doby was only the second black player to join a major league team when he signed with the Cleveland Indians in 1947.

With the ending of segregation in baseball from 1948, the Negro League gradually lost players and teams, and Hinchliffe, like other Negro League stadiums, was left empty.

Location: Maple and Liberty Streets, Paterson, NJ
Aka: City Stadium
Status: Abandoned Negro League stadium
Architect: Olmsted Brothers
Opened: 1932
World Series Games: 1933

BELOW and BOTTOM: An important relic—one of the few Negro League ballparks still in existence.

Location: Franklin Delano Avenue, Hato Rey, Puerto Rico

Status: Home to the San Juan Senators

Opened: 1962

Capacity: 17,000; increased to 18,000 with additional bleachers

Dimensions:

Left Field 325 ft

Center Field 404 ft

Right Field 325 ft

The name of Hiram Bithorn Stadium honors the first Puerto Rican to appear in the major leagues, Hiram Bithorn, who made his debut with the Chicago Cubs in 1942. The stadium is now home to the San Juan Senators and was home to the Santurce Crabbers of the Puerto Rico Baseball League until 2009.

The stadium hosted Major League Baseball's opening day game in 2001, when the Toronto Blue Jays faced the Texas Rangers, and was the part-time home of the Montreal Expos in 2003 and 2004 prior to their move to Washington, D.C. The ballpark is FieldTurfed and has hosted a number of games for the World Baseball Classic. Puerto Rico is a hotbed of baseball, but too many of their best players move to the U.S. The home league was forced to cancel the 2007–2008 season and was reconstituted as the Puerto Rico Baseball League.

THIS PAGE: The Hiram Bithorn Stadium's first regular season major league game was between the Expos and the Mets on April 11, 2003: the Expos won 10–0.

BELOW: The footprint of Hiram Bithorn Stadium.

Major League Baseball returned to the stadium in 2010, when the Florida Marlins faced the New York Mets in a three-game series.

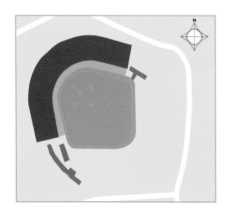

Location: 1201 S. Mellonville Avenue, Sanford, FL

Status: Home to the Sanford Babe Ruth League and the Sanford River Rats

Opened: 1926; rebuilt 1951; renovated 2001

Capacity: 2,015

Dimensions:
Left Field 330 ft
Center Field 385 ft
Right Field 330 ft

Formerly the spring training home of the Atlanta Braves and the "split squad" New York Giants, this beautifully renovated jewel was built in 1926. This ballpark has undergone massive renovations twice, in 1951 and 2001. The seating was replaced; the termite-infested wooden flooring was gutted; and the press box was rebuilt, which cost over $2 million. This not only brought this ballpark back to life, but it may now be the most beautiful historic ballpark in all of Florida.

The New York Giants used this ballpark as a secondary home to their main spring training facilities. In 1942 the Boston Braves made Sanford their primary facility. Inside the stadium is the Dugout Lounge, which incorporates the full history of Historic Sanford Memorial Stadium, including scorecards, baseball cards, and game-day memorabilia. The Giants rebuilt the stadium in 1951 on the site of the original building.

Sanford really owes its place in baseball history to the era of segregation. The legendary Jackie Robinson took to the field in 1946 to play an exhibition game, and although it was not uncommon for black teams to play white teams, black players were never part of the white teams. On this occasion Robinson was playing for the white side, and by the time he reached first base the uproar was tremendous. Robinson was escorted off the field, and not surprisingly, never returned to Sanford. Two years later, he became the first black player to join a major league team.

The $2 million makeover in 2001 provided facilities worthy of a major league team, and the stadium is currently home to two collegiate teams, the Sanford Babe Ruth League, and the Sanford River Rats of the Florida Collegiate League. With capacity at just over 2,000, the refurbished stadium now offers modern amenities alongside the classic architecture of the original building.

THIS PAGE: The ballpark was in poor repair in the 1970s (above right) and brought back to life with $2 million in renovations, producing what may be the most beautiful historic ballpark in Florida.

Location: 1235 North Center Street, Mesa, AZ

Aka: Dwight W. Patterson Field

Status: Home to the Mesa Solar Sox; Chicago Cubs spring training facility

Architect: HOK Sport

Opened: 1997

Capacity: 12,632

Dimensions:

Left Field 340 ft

Left Center 390 ft

Center Field 410 ft

Right Center 390 ft

Right Field 350 ft

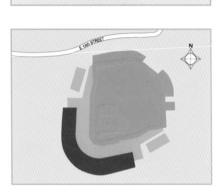

TOP: The bullpens are in the right field of this expansive stadium.

ABOVE: Footprint of HoHoKam Park.

RIGHT: HoHoKam Park is becoming more and more popular. In 2010 it enjoyed the single-game record of 13,462 visitors.

BELOW: In 2009 the home attendance was 203,105—breaking the home attendance record the Cubs had set in the same stadium in 2005.

HoHoKam Park has been the spring training facility for the Chicago Cubs since 1997. HoHoKam means "those who vanished" but the name has less to do with local Native Americans than Mesa rancher and builder Dwight Patterson and his friends—the HoHoKams, today a charity—who put up a $22,000 guarantee and lured the Cubs to Mesa's Rendezvous Park in 1952 from Catalina Island, its spring home for thirty years.

The second-largest stadium in the Cactus League, the grassed stadium also boasts the largest scoreboard, which measures 12 feet by 16 feet—rather smaller than the iconic scoreboard at Wrigley Field in Chicago. The Mesa Solar Sox, who play in the Arizona Fall League, also call the ballpark home and have done so since 1997; so do the Mesa Cubs in the Arizona Rookie League. The stadium is also the scene of the Western Athletic Conference college baseball tournament.

174

Location: 4001 26th Street, Vero Beach, FL
Aka: Dodgertown
Status: Vero Beach Sports Village
Architect: Norman Bel Geddes
Opened: 1953
Capacity: 6,500
Dimensions:
Left Field 340 ft
Center Field 400 ft
Right Field 340 ft

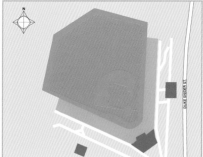

Dodgertown's Holman Stadium, located in Vero Beach, Florida, was the spring training home of the Los Angeles Dodgers and former ground of the Florida State League's Vero Beach Devil Rays. Adrift in a sea of "super stadiums," Holman Stadium is the last holdout of an earlier time, and is barely even a stadium although it cost some $117 million.

The grandstand is nothing more than a simple set of single-level concrete stands that reach out deep into the outfield from its central point at home plate. There is nothing ornate, or encased in brick, or anything even remotely unique about them. That is in fact what makes them so different. If it wasn't for this little house sitting behind home plate, there wouldn't be anything here at all but this simple grandstand. The little house holds the majority of the concession stands, press box, and bathrooms just like a local high school field would have a little all-in-one structure behind the plate.

This ball field harks back to a simpler time. Constructed in 1953 as part of a complex called Dodgertown, it is simple and offers fans a "pure" baseball experience, uncluttered by the modern concessions and on-field distractions between innings. The open-air dugouts are unique and put players virtually within touching distance of fans.

The ballplayers, of course, loved the fact that Dodgertown is really one huge country club golf course with a baseball stadium located on the eighteenth hole. After a day of training in the hot sun, players would take a shower and hit the links. This was the case in 1953, and it was still the case nearly sixty years later. It is probably why this little ballpark has lasted so long.

Minor league baseball first came to Dodgertown in 1980 when the Dodgers returned to the Florida State League. Over the years, many future Dodger superstars would make their first pro appearances for the Single-A Vero Beach team, such as John Franco, Sid Fernandez, and Paul Lo Duca.

With the departure of the Dodgers in 2008, Dodgertown became the Vero Beach Sports Village in 2010. A complex run by Minor League Baseball, there are two half fields, four full fields, as well as Holman Stadium.

THIS PAGE: A classic, intimate spring training park that is well worth a visit. It's not the same since the Dodgers left in 2008, but it's still a brilliant ballpark.

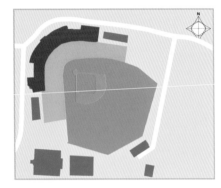

Homestead Sports Complex

Location: 1601 SE 28th Avenue, Homestead, FL

Status: Used for college games

Opened: 1991

Capacity: 6,500; can expand to 9,000

Dimensions:

Left Field 322 ft

Center Field 400 ft

Right Field 322 ft

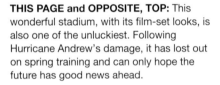

THIS PAGE and OPPOSITE, TOP: This wonderful stadium, with its film-set looks, is also one of the unluckiest. Following Hurricane Andrew's damage, it has lost out on spring training and can only hope the future has good news ahead.

Located in Homestead, Florida, just south of Miami and the last major city before you enter the Florida Keys, lies perhaps the saddest baseball stadium story. Homestead Sports Complex was commissioned by the Cleveland Indians in 1991. The Indians wanted a new spring training complex, with all the facilities required by a major league team. More than that, they wanted the best stadium ever constructed, and Homestead started the trend for "super stadiums."

The ballpark turned out to be more ornate, especially on the exterior, than any ballpark anyone had ever seen. It was the perfect Florida paradise. The Indians were excited about the new facility and managed to play a few games at the new ballpark before announcing that they would officially be moving to Homestead in 1993, leaving behind Tucson's Hi Corbett Field where they had been loyally training for forty-five years since 1947.

Unfortunately before they could move in, Hurricane Andrew, one of the worst hurricanes in history, made landfall on Homestead on August 24, 1992, demolishing everything in its path. The brand-new $12 million Homestead Sports Complex was destroyed (along with most of the city of Homestead) and the Indians were terrified that it would not be rebuilt in time for the 1993 spring training season.

The Indians approached Chain of Lakes Park in Winter Haven, which had recently been vacated by the Boston Red Sox, and negotiated a deal whereby they could use the stadium for 1993, as long as they signed a ten-year deal to remain there. The insurance payout covered the reconstruction of the stadium in Homestead, but the Indians never used it, and the city needed to find a new major league team to utilize it.

The new stadium was exactly the same as the original, and it was still one of the most attractive ballparks in the spring training circuit. Twenty years on, it has never had a major league resident, and although it has hosted the odd ball game and appeared in a couple of movies, it has never been regularly used and is slowly falling into disrepair, and local taxpayers have had to pay more than $6 million to maintain it.

This elegant ballpark, built in 1988, is the home of the Birmingham Barons, a Double-A minor league team in the Southern League, and hosts the annual Southeastern Conference baseball tournament. Regions Park hosts numerous events during the year, including the football and baseball games of Hoover High School, as well as other collegiate sporting events and entertainment.

Owned by the city of Hoover, it was constructed at a cost of $14.5 million and provides seating for 10,800 fans, which can be expanded to 16,000 when the patio, banquet, and grassy side areas are opened up. One of the largest stadiums in the Southern League, it was designed by HOK, one of the United States' premier designers of sporting complexes, and has state-of-the-art banqueting suites, dressing rooms, and training rooms.

The naming rights of the stadium were sold in 2007 to the Regions Financial Corporation, although it is still affectionately known as "the Met." At the same time, a $4.5 million renovation program upgraded facilities, replacing the chairs, revamping the press boxes, and improving the ticketing facilities.

The Barons have a loyal local following and have been affiliated to the Chicago White Sox since 1986. They have reached the Southern League playoffs twelve times since 1983 and have won the league title five times, most recently in 2002, but their real moment in the sun came in 1994 when Michael Jordan joined the team on his first retirement from basketball. One of the stadium meeting rooms is named after Jordan, and they recorded their highest ever attendance figure of 16,247 during his last game as a Baron in 1994.

In November 2010, the Barons announced that they would be leaving the Met for a new ballpark under construction in downtown Hoover, leaving Regions Park to college baseball for the immediate future.

Location: 101 Ben Chapman Drive, Hoover, AL
Aka: The Met, the Hoover Met, Regions Park (from 2007)
Status: Home to the Birmingham Barons
Architect: Gresham, Smith and Partners, HOK Sport
Opened: 1988
Capacity: 10,800; can expand to 16,000
Dimensions:
Left Field 340 ft
Left Center 385 ft
Center Field 405 ft
Right Center 385 ft
Right Field 340 ft

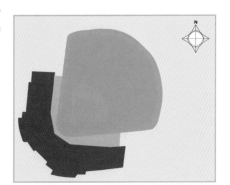

RIGHT: Footprint of the Met, which has been home to the SEC baseball tournament since 1977.

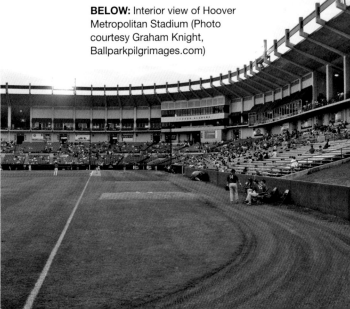

BELOW: Interior view of Hoover Metropolitan Stadium (Photo courtesy Graham Knight, Ballparkpilgrimages.com)

Location: 1648 North Memorial Drive, Racine, WI
Aka: Horlick Field, North Side City League Park, City League Park, League Park
Status: Home of the Racine Raiders
Architect: Walter Dick
Opened: 1907
Capacity: 8,500

BELOW: As the plaques show, Horlick Field was once the home of women's professional baseball.

Horlick Field is both a football stadium and a baseball park, one enclosed within stone walls and chain fences. The land for the field was donated by William Horlick, the inventor of malted milk. Football has been a part of Horlick Field's history since 1919, and today the Racine Raiders, a minor league team in the Elite MCFL, call the stadium home. Teams from high schools and local leagues play their regular season games in the grassed baseball diamond, which is the site for local tournaments and championship games. In 2006–2007, the bleachers were given a $250,000 upgrade.

The park has been the home of the Old Timer's Athletic Club Softball Tournament for over three decades, and the Racine Belles, who were portrayed in the 1992 movie *A League of Their Own*, played there when the Girls Professional Baseball League was in existence.

BELOW: Sophie Kurys, star of the Racine Belles of the All-American Girls Professional Baseball League, slides into the bag as a player from the South Bend Blue Sox looks on, June 27, 1947.

Location: Borderline Road, South Williamsport, PA
Status: Home to the Little League World Series
Opened: 1959; renovated 1992
Capacity: 40,000 (15,000 in stands)
Dimensions:
Left Field 225 ft
Center Field 225 ft
Right Field 225 ft

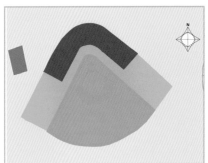

Howard J. Lamade Stadium joint-hosts the Little League World Series together with the Little League Volunteer Stadium every year. The series is one of the few sports events where children take center stage. The World Series takes place in the last week of August.

The stadium was upgraded in 1992 when lights were added so that night games could be played as part of the expansion of the series. The fences were moved back 20 feet to 225 feet to all fields in 2006 as home runs were becoming far too common. Other improvements at the time included the extension of the roofs to the end of the grandstands, and some of the bleacher seating was replaced by backed seating. And if you don't have a ticket to the big event, it doesn't matter: the Little League World Series is always free to those with blankets. Berm seating doesn't require a ticket, even for the big game.

The last ten years show the international nature of the sport, as the tournament has seen winners from Venezuela, Japan, Curacao, as well as Kentucky, Hawaii, Georgia, and California.

THIS PAGE: This stadium gives the Little League a feel of the majors. The grandstand alone will sit 10,000 fans. Over 20,000 fans can join in, among the rolling berms over the outfield fences.

Location: 400 Huntington Avenue, Boston, MA

Status: Demolished in 1912

Opened: 1901

Closed: 1911

Capacity: Seating capacity 9,000, plus 2,500 standing

Dimensions:

Left Field 350 ft

Left Center 440 ft

Center Field 530 ft (635 ft in 1908)

Right Field 280 ft (320 ft in 1908)

World Series Games: 1903

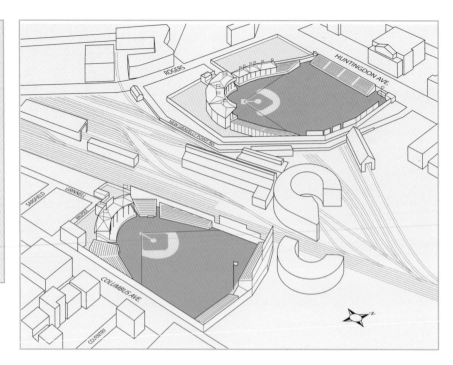

RIGHT: Huntington Avenue Grounds is at the top of this artist's impression; South End Grounds lower down.

ABOVE: Game three of the first World Series was played in 1903 at Huntington Avenue between the Boston Pilgrims and the Pittsburgh Pirates. Over 18,000 attended and watched Pittsburgh take a 2–1 lead.

BELOW: This October 8, 1904, game between Boston and New York had a massive 28,040 attendance.

The Boston Americans were founding members of the American League and played their fixtures at the wooden-framed Huntington Avenue Grounds that sat at the intersection of Huntington Avenue and Rogers (now Forsyth) Street and was built for a reported $35,000 in 1901. In 1903 the ballpark held the first-ever World Series in October, between the Boston Americans and the Pittsburgh Pirates with Boston winning five games to three. Their owner, John I. Taylor, renamed his team the Boston Red Sox in 1907 and Huntington Avenue Grounds remained their home until they moved to a new ballpark called Fenway Park only one and a half miles away.

Huntington Avenue Grounds was only used for eleven years between 1901 and 1911 before the Boston Red Sox left. They played their last game here on October 7, 1911, when they beat Washington 8–1.

The old baseball ground was demolished in 1912 and has now completely disappeared; its footprint forms part of the campus of Northeastern University. The only memento of the ballpark is a bronze statue of Cy Young (dated September 1993) near where the pitcher's mound was; it reads: "*At this site in October 1903 baseball's winningest pitcher led Boston to victory in the first World Series.*"

Another plaque reads, "*The site of the former Huntington Avenue American League Baseball Grounds, on which in 1903 four games of the first World Series were played. The Boston Americans defeated the Pittsburgh Nationals five games to three. This plaque is located approximately on what was then the left field foul line.*"

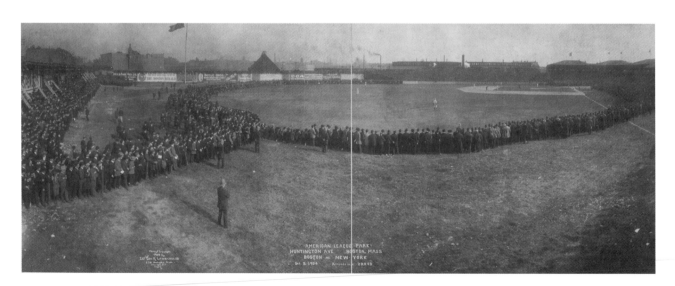

Location: 330 Huntington Park Lane, Columbus, OH
Status: Home to the Columbus Clippers
Architect: 360 Architecture
Opened: April 18, 2009
Capacity: 10,100
Dimensions:
Left Field 325 ft
Left Center 360 ft
Center Field 400 ft
Right Center 365 ft
Right Field 318 ft

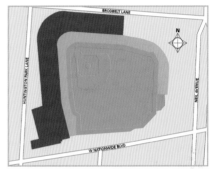

Huntington Park replaced one of the most historic ballparks in the United States, Cooper Stadium, which opened in 1931 and was the Triple-A home to the Pittsburgh Pirates, Cleveland Indians, Washington Nationals, Kansas City A's and, for twenty-eight years, the New York Yankees.

Completed in 2009 for a cost of $56 million, Huntington Park is a beautifully designed ballpark, produced with care and imagination by 360 Architecture from Kansas City, and incorporates touches simply not seen in minor league stadiums. The bars, for example, are styled to match the lofty local warehouse spaces that have been transformed into trendy watering holes. The walls are covered with baseball memorabilia and photographs, which fills every available space of the interior concourses.

Underneath the double-decked Home Run Porch is what looks like a third field-level deck, with five windows looking out onto right field. This is indeed a field-level area to watch the ballgame from, but you can't get to it from inside the ballpark. It pays homage to the old knothole gang, when kids used to try to watch the game for free through knotholes in the outfield fence. Anyone passing by can stop and spend as long as they like watching the game with an amazingly great view—and it is absolutely free.

The Columbus Clippers of 2010 should bode well for the future of their parent club, as they claimed that season's Triple-A national championship.

The Coop was a great vintage ballpark, but Huntington Park is a worthy successor, and looks set to become one of the great American ballparks.

THIS PAGE: Footprint, view over home plate, and internal views of Huntington Park—winner of the 2009 Digitalballparks.com Ballpark of the Year Award.

Location: Intersection of Avenida
Cesar Chavez and University
Boulevard, Albuquerque, NM
Aka: The Lab
Status: Home to the Albuquerque
Isotopes
Architect: HOK Sport
Opened: 2003
Capacity: 13,279
Dimensions:
Left Field 340 ft
Left Center 428 ft
Center Field 400 ft
Right Center 428 ft
Right Field 340 ft
All Star Games: 2007

Home to the Albuquerque Isotopes, Isotope Park was constructed in 2003 for $25 million and has a playful, almost whimsical design that reflects its desert setting. The name of both the team and the park are rooted in the popular cartoon *The Simpsons*. In one episode, Homer struggles manfully to prevent the relocation of the Springfield Isotopes to Albuquerque. Life really does imitate art, because in 2002, the Calgary Cannons were lured to Albuquerque after twenty years in Calgary, and displaying a keen sense of humor, the ownership named the team the Isotopes in honor of *The Simpsons*. In addition, Albuquerque's position in the New Mexico desert, in an area known for its atomic tests, made the name even more appropriate.

Triple-A Pacific Coast League baseball had been played in Albuquerque for decades until 2000. The Albuquerque Dukes (part of the Dodgers franchise) played at the Albuquerque Sports Stadium, which was the predecessor to Isotopes Park. Built in 1969, it featured a unique drive-in facility, whereby cars could park on a tiered space in the outfield, allowing drivers to watch the game from their automobiles. In 2000 the Albuquerque Dukes moved out to a more modern facility and the city of Albuquerque renovated and rebuilt the stadium on the same site. Sadly, security concerns meant that the drive-in feature was scrapped. Capacity is now just over 12,000.

With an imaginative design and striking desert colors, the structure of this stadium does not seem to have many straight lines. The new stadium attracted over half a million fans in its first year, an amazing total for any minor league stadium. The Isotopes are a popular team and although many fans would have liked to retain the old Dukes moniker, this was not possible for copyright reasons. Once a year, the Isotopes wear the old Dukes uniforms, tying in historic memories with more recent successes.

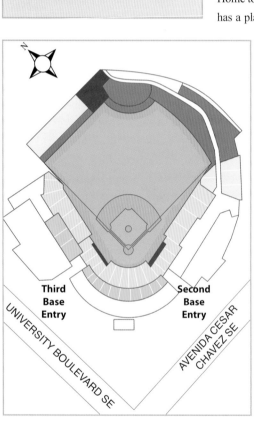

ABOVE: Footprint of Isotopes Park showing entrances.

BELOW: Beyond the right-field fence is the Creamland Berm, a popular place for families to stretch out.

TOP: While there is no direct link with *The Simpsons*, there are statues of Homer and Marge in the park.

BELOW: The stands at Isotopes seat 12,215.

Location: 800 Phillies Drive, Clearwater, FL

Aka: Jack Russell Stadium

Status: Partially demolished 2007; still used by high school and college teams

Architect: Marr and Holliman

Opened: March 10, 1955

Capacity: 4,744 (1955); 6,942 (2003)

Last pro game: August 23, 2003

Dimensions:

Left Field 340 ft

Center Field 400 ft

Right Field 340 ft

Built in 1955 at a cost of $317,653, Jack Russell Stadium was the spring training home of the Philadelphia Phillies from the day it opened its doors. The Phillies' links to Clearwater stretch back to 1947, when they utilized Green Field (which became the site of the parking lot for Jack Russell).

Jack Russell himself was a major league player who settled in Clearwater, becoming a city commissioner and a leading advocate for a new ballpark in the early 1950s. The Phillies played their first game in March 1955, beating the Detroit Tigers before a 4,000-strong crowd. Jack Russell Memorial Stadium became their home for spring training for nearly fifty years, and during the summer, the amateur softball team the Clearwater Bombers used the stadium from 1955 until 1984.

In the early 1980s, the city of Clearwater asked the Phillies to consider locating a minor league affiliate at Jack Russell. After a few alterations to the clubhouse and the provision of additional seating, the Clearwater Phillies played their first game in April 1985 as part of the Florida State League. The capacity of the stadium was increased again in 1989, raising the capacity from 5,300 to nearly 7,000.

By the early 2000s, the Phillies wanted to consolidate their entire affiliated family within one complex and began plans for a new stadium, which was built four miles to the east, at Bright House Networks Field next to their spring training camp. In a nice touch, Robin Roberts, who threw out the first pitch at Jack Russell Stadium on March 10, 1955, also threw out the first pitch at the last Clearwater Phillies game on August 23, 2003. A crowd of 6,472 watched the game, the second largest ever at Jack Russell.

Jack Russell Stadium was partially demolished in 2007, although the field, dugout bleachers, and offices were spared and the stadium is now used by high school and college teams.

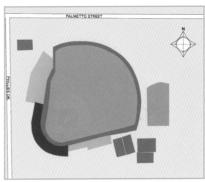

TOP: Taken during the Phillies' residence, the wall next to the home plate entrance proclaims the Phillies' 1980 world championship. This, the main grandstand, and roof have all since been demolished.

ABOVE: Footprint of Jack Russell Stadium.

RIGHT: The Phillies had a long, uninterrupted stretch at Clearwater from 1947 to 2003.

Jacksonville Baseball Park

Location: Jacksonville, FL

Aka: Sam W. Wolfson Baseball Park (from 1963)

Status: Demolished 2002

Opened: 1954

Capacity: 8,200

Dimensions:

Left Field 323 ft

Center Field 401 ft

Right Field 325 ft

THIS PAGE: An absolutely classic facility, some great players learned their trade in Wolfson Park: a pretty decent prospect in a young Tom Seaver, a phenomenon named Alex Rodriguez, a very tall and rather imposing Randy Johnson, and a guy with a pretty good fastball for a kid, Nolan Ryan. This great national treasure was demolished in September 2002, just after completion of its final game on Labor Day.

Jacksonville Baseball Park was constructed in 1954 at a cost of $400,000 to replace the venerable Durkee Field, and became home to the Jacksonville Tars, who were renamed the Braves when they moved to their new home. It was renamed Sam W. Wolfson Park in 1963 after Sam Wolfson, local businessman, civic leader, and owner of the Jacksonville Tars, who had worked hard to improve baseball facilities in the city.

Jacksonville Baseball Park was a showcase facility when it opened in March 1955, with the first game played between the Cincinnati Redlegs and the Washington Senators. In the 1950s many major league teams stopped off in Jacksonville on their way home after spring training, and it hosted many great exhibition games. Some of baseball's legendary names graced the field just two weeks after the park opened, when an exhibition match between the Brooklyn Dodgers and the Milwaukee Braves attracted a crowd of over 8,000 fans. Jackie Robinson, Hank Aaron, and Pee Wee Reese were among nine future Hall of Famers who played that day.

In July of the same year a young singer by the name of Elvis Presley had to hide in a bathroom to escape hordes of female fans, and was so exhausted by his concert at the baseball stadium that he spent three days recovering in a Jacksonville hospital.

The Jacksonville Braves, a minor league team affiliated to the Milwaukee Braves, played in the South Atlantic League from 1953 until 1960, and moved to the new baseball park when it opened in 1955. The Jacksonville Suns became residents at Wolfson Park from 1962 and remained there until the park's demolition forty years later in 2002. There was a slight break between 1969 and 1972, when the team's major league affiliate, the New York Mets, moved the team north, and they became the Tides. In 1970, a new Suns team was launched, which was affiliated to the Kansas City Royals from 1972 until 1984.

Location: 285 Rue Faillon West, Montreal, Quebec, Canada
Aka: Parc Jarry, Du Maurier Stadium, Stade Uniprix
Status: Mostly demolished in 1995 and rebuilt as a professional tennis venue
Capacity: 28,456
Opened: April 14, 1969
Last MLB game: September 26, 1976
Dimensions:
Left Field 340 ft
Left Center 368 ft
Center Field 420 ft
Right Center 368 ft
Right Field 340 ft

Situated in the Villeray neighborhood of Montreal, Jarry Park was located in an urban park created in 1925 and was home for the Montreal Expos (Les Expos de Montréal) between 1969 and 1976; the Expos were the first MLB Canadian franchise. This multipurpose open-air park provided facilities for a wide variety of amateur sports ranging from baseball to basketball, tennis, and almost everything in between. The park itself was named after Raoul Jarry, a late nineteenth-century Montreal politician.

Once the Expos were awarded the franchise, they needed to find a suitable home. The only realistic possibility was Jarry Park, but it needed serious upgrading to get anywhere near league standards for the four years or so that it was needed while a permanent ballpark was constructed. The original small grandstand was open to the elements and seated around 3,000 specatators. For the Expos, the existing open stand was hastily extended to the left and right field corners, a scoreboard was constructed behind the right field fence, and a huge bleacher built across left field with the clubhouses behind. All this work boosted seating capacity to a more acceptable 28,500, but the short Montreal summers and the open seating meant early and late-season games were sometimes postponed because of the weather. Also, the Expos did not enjoy stellar performances very often.

The Expos played their last games at Jarry on September 26, 1976, in a doubleheader against the Phillies; they lost 4–1 and 2–1. The Expos then moved into the Montreal Olympic Stadium. Jarry Park was left for occasional civic events and the venue was gradually altered to become a tennis stadium and has undergone numerous name changes: in September 1984 it was renamed to mark the visit of Pope John Paul II, then changed again to become Du Maurier Stadium (after the cigarettes) in 1987, and yet again to become Stade Uniprix (after a local pharmacy chain) in 1993.

THIS PAGE: While Jarry Park was hardly big enough for major-league baseball when chosen, it was certainly something to build on. It was, after all, only supposed to support the Montreal Expos for four years until a new domed stadium could be completed. Jarry could be expanded very quickly with 12,000 bleacher seats down each line and a few in the outfield. More than a million fans came to see the Montreal Expos in this little 29,000-seat ballpark in the Expos' first full season.

RIGHT: View of Jarry Park from center field.

Jefferson Grounds

Location: In a block bounded by Jefferson Street, 25th Street, Master Street, and 27th Street, Philadelphia, PA

Aka: Athletics Park, Jefferson Park, Centennial Park

Status: Demolished

Opened: May 15, 1871

Closed: October 11, 1890

Capacity: 5,000

Dimensions:

Center Field 500 ft

Now occupied by the Daniel Boone Public School, Jefferson Grounds was once one of the great ballparks of the late nineteenth century. Opened in May 1871, it was home to the Philadelphia Athletics (1871–76) and, for two years, to the Philadelphia White Stockings (1873–75).

Jefferson Grounds was the first enclosed ballpark in Philadelphia and had a capacity of 5,000. Unusually for the time, it also included a swimming pool just behind the right field fence. More importantly for the players, the park was apparently so well-groomed that the teams boasted, "it was as level as a billiards table."

The Philadelphia Athletics were founder members of the National Association of Professional Base Ball Players (NA) in 1871 and had a good record, winning 165 games and losing only 86 during their five-season life in the NA. When the league was reorganized, the Athletics joined the new National League in 1876, and on April 22 hosted what is regarded as the first game in the history of professional baseball at Jefferson Grounds. They lost 6–5 to the Boston Red Caps, and this seemed to be a hint of games to come, as the team's performance faltered in the new league and they were expelled at the end of the season.

The Philadelphia Athletics were revived in 1882 as part of the American Association and returned to Jefferson Street Grounds for their home games. They won the league pennant in 1883, beating the St. Louis Brown Stockings by one game. In the same year, however, the rival National League established a new team in Philadelphia, the Philadelphia Quakers, who went on to become the city's greatest and most enduring team, the Phillies. The Athletics lasted until 1890, when many players left for the newer and better-paid Players' League. After the final game at Jefferson Street Grounds on October 11, 1890, when they finished at the bottom of the league, the Athletics were expelled and were replaced by a new Athletics team, previously the Philadelphia Quakers.

Jerry Uht Park

Location: 110 E. 10th Street, Erie, PA

Status: Home of the Erie SeaWolves

Opened: 1995; renovated 2006

Capacity: 6,000 (1999); 6,952 (2006)

Dimensions:

Left Field 312 ft

Center Field 400 ft

Right Field 328 ft

RIGHT: Part of the 2006 improvements was a two-level picnic area known as "the Gardens" located down the right-field line.

Erie professional baseball had been played at Ainsworth Field since the ballpark was built in 1938. The little concrete-based and fully roofed facility still stands today on Washington Place. The ballpark was used professionally all the way up to 1994 when the Frontier League placed a team there. It was clear, however, that the team couldn't survive without a new ballpark, and if Erie was going to keep professional baseball in its city, a new (preferably downtown) ballpark needed to be built.

The resulting Jerry Uht Park (completed in 1995) is a combination of two completely separate grandstands that look nothing alike and share no common architectural bond. The left side of the stadium contains a large, sweeping, one-level gray-and-red grandstand with a small overhang that covers a luxury box area. The right side of the stadium meanwhile contains a bi-level grandstand, which has a small roof covering the upper-level walkway. The bottom part of the grandstand is, of course, completely covered by this upper deck, which bends a third of the way out toward right field. Behind home plate is a large open concourse that divides the two grandstands.

Jerry Uht Park is bounded on all sides by something: in right field, just past the fence are residential homes that overlook the outfield. In left field, the stadium is bordered by the Louis J. Tullio Arena, a 5,600-seat indoor stadium that is home to the Erie Freeze arena football team and the Erie Otters ice hockey team. The entire first and third base lines,

meanwhile, are bordered by downtown Erie's bustling business sector, with large office buildings, the Warner Theater, and the Bayfront Convention Center. The downtown setting was key when the SeaWolves were looking to move from their previous home at Ainsworth Field. Designed by the DLR Group, Jerry Uht is considered to be one of the most exciting and innovative stadium designs in all of baseball.

ABOVE: As a part of the $4 million renovation project, a brand-new, state-of-the-art video scoreboard was located in right field. An additional scoreboard was added to the Tullio Arena measuring 40 feet across and providing fans with out-of-town scores.

"The Joe" is home to Alabama's Double-A team, the Huntsville Stars, who play in the Southern League. Built in 1984 and owned by the city of Huntsville, it is a large multipurpose facility with a capacity of 10,200. It was named after Joe Davis, the mayor of Huntsville who is credited with bringing minor league baseball to the city.

Some baseball fans complain that the ballpark is a little large and lacking in character, with the seating configuration better suited to football, which was played there until 2010. Known as the "Crown Jewel of the Southern League" when it was first opened, the Joe is now the oldest stadium in the Southern League and has recently undergone renovations. The stadium's rather lackluster appearance has not changed and many spectators comment that the whole place needs more decoration. However, the seating has been improved, the lighting has been brought up to Double-A standards, and a new video board installed, but the consensus is that the Joe needs a major overhaul to attract more spectators.

The Huntsville Stars are affiliated to the Milwaukee Brewers and the team name is drawn from the area's connections to the space industry—the town is known as "Rocket City" and NASA employs a large number of local people. The Brewers are highly regarded for their excellent minor league farm system, and their input won the Stars their third

Location: 3125 Leeman Ferry Road, Huntsville, AL
Aka: The Joe
Status: Home to the Hunstville Stars
Opened: 1985
Capacity: 10,200
Dimensions:
Left Field 345 ft
Center Field 405 ft
Right Field 330 ft

Joe W. Davis Municipal Stadium

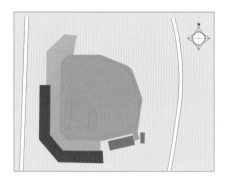

Southern League title in 2001. The team has won a succession of divisional titles, most recently in 2007.

In more recent years, attendance at Joe Davis Municipal Stadium has dropped off, but the Stars have a lease until 2015 and are committed to remain. The Stars' owner has made it clear that his team needs better facilities, whether that be a completely new ballpark (rather than a stadium) for Huntsville, or a remodeled Joe.

LEFT: The footprint of Joe W. Davis Stadium.

BELOW and BOTTOM: The Joe's left-field seating shows a football configuration.

Location: 235 Montage Mountain Road, Moosic, PA

Aka: PNC Field from 2006

Status: Home to the Scranton/Wilkes-Barre Red Barons

Opened: April 26, 1989

Capacity: 10,380

All-Star Game: 1995

Dimensions:

Left Field 330 ft

Left Center 371 ft

Center Field 408 ft

Right Center 371 ft

Right Field 330 ft

Home of the Scranton/Wilkes-Barre Red Barons, and built into the side of Montage Mountain, Lackawanna County Stadium became the home of the Triple-A Phillies in 1989. The Triple-A Phillies had previously been playing in Maine at the Ballpark at Old Orchard Beach, which, by the late 1980s, did not measure up to Triple-A standards. It was determined that Triple-A stadiums should be mini major league fields, with at least 10,000 seats.

The Phillies decided to bring their "Phuture Phillies" home to Pennsylvania. They built a new ballpark for $25 million, within driving distance of Veterans Stadium, in Lackawanna County. To make their Triple-A players feel as much at home as possible, the Phillies set out to design a new stadium that replicates as closely as possible the play, dimensions, and overall aura of Veterans Stadium.

With its large double-decked grandstand, bright orange seats, and artificial surface, Lackawanna County Stadium really was like a baby Vet, and this worked well until Veterans Stadium was demolished in 2004. However, Lackawanna County Stadium finally gave the Phillies a real home for their Triple-A team, which had moved countless times since they joined the International League in 1948, from Toronto, to Baltimore, Miami, San Diego, Toledo—and elsewhere.

In 2007, the eighteen-year agreement with the Phillies ended, and the Scranton/Wilkes-Barre Red Barons became affiliated to the New York Yankees. The contract called for a few alterations to the ballpark, notably the conversion of the playing surface to natural grass. In 2010 the stadium was renamed, as the Yankees sold the naming rights of the stadium to PNC Bank. Even more change is on the horizon, as the Yankees announced a $40 million renovation in 2010, which will alter considerably the layout of the ballpark.

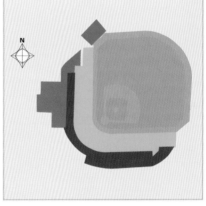

TOP: Exterior of Lackawanna County Stadium before renaming.

ABOVE: Footprint of the stadium.

RIGHT: Lackawanna was designed to be as close to the play and dimensions and overall aura of Veterans Stadium as possible.

Location: 1085 West Third Street, Cleveland, OH

Aka: Lakefront Stadium, Cleveland Municipal Stadium, the Mistake by the Lake

Status: Demolished 1996

Architect: Walker and Weeks, the Osborn Co.

Opened: July 31, 1932

Last MLB game: October 3, 1993

Capacity: 78,000 (1932); 74,483 (1993)

Dimensions:

	Original 1932	Final 1993
Left Field	322 ft	320 ft
Left Center	430 ft	395 ft
Center Field	470 ft	404 ft
Right Center	430 ft	395 ft
Right Field	322 ft	320 ft

World Series: 1948, 1954

All-Star Game: 1935, 1954, 1963, 1981

ABOVE: Sitting on Lake Erie, the ballpark was dubbed the "Mistake by the Lake."

BELOW: Aerial of Cleveland Municipal showing its huge horseshoe shape.

The Cleveland Indians initially played at League Park until the late 1920s when the city decided to build a new $3 million multipurpose stadium on a landfill site near Lake Erie. Many locals thought it a plot to bring the 1932 Summer Olympics to Cleveland, not knowing that Los Angeles had already been chosen: it was the first stadium to be funded by public money.

When Lakefront Stadium opened, it had a running track and could accommodate baseball and football. The NFL's Cleveland Browns settled in happily but after being there for a year the Indians opted to only play night and weekend games until 1947, instead preferring to share League Park even though it didn't have any floodlights.

By the 1930s the ballpark was better known as Cleveland Municipal Stadium, although widely dubbed the "Mistake by the Lake." In winter spectators literally froze in the arctic winds blowing across Lake Erie, and even in summer the cold could be chilling, but then when the sun blazed the stadium was notorious for attracting swarms of flying insects. Other complaints were that thanks to its 78,000 seats, the stadium could feel empty even with a crowd of 20,000 (the average Indians pull), although the Browns often filled the stadium.

In 1947 team owner Bill Veeck moved the Indians to Cleveland Stadium permanently and League Park was abandoned and demolished four years later. The following year the Indians won the World Series 4–2 against the Boston Braves and contested the series the following year, but this time they lost to the New York Giants 4–0. That same year the stadium hosted the All-Star Game (won by the AL) and then again hosted the game in 1963 and 1981 with victory for the NL.

By the mid-1970s the joint occupation of baseball and football made the financing of the stadium difficult, with much of the revenue going to the Browns even though a lot was generated by the Indians. The stadium itself was starting to show its age with a general aura of disrepair as large blocks of concrete started to drop off. The Indians finally got the voters and local government to agree to build a new stadium, Jacobs Field, which they moved into at the end of the 1993 season.

The Browns stayed another year, but without the bolster of baseball revenue and the city declining to build them a new stadium, the owner decided to move the franchise to Baltimore. In 1996 Lakefront/Cleveland Stadium was demolished and the rubble deposited into Lake Erie to create an artificial reef for divers and fishermen. By 1999 the new Cleveland Browns Stadium opened on the site after the NFL granted Cleveland a new franchise.

TOP: Construction of Cleveland Municipal Stadium in 1931.

ABOVE and BELOW: The Indians spent sixty years at the Muni before moving to Jacobs Field. The cavernous stadium (the biggest ever used for baseball at the time) often attracted fewer than 10,000 fans per game for whole seasons at a time. This made the ballpark look even more empty. (Photo above courtesy Robert K. Shoop; below courtesy Michael Collins.)

Location: San Diego, CA

Status: Closed 1957

Opened: March 31, 1936

Dimensions:

Left Field 339 ft

Center Field 480 ft

Right Field 355 ft

The San Diego Padres played at Lane Field from 1936 until 1958, when the aging stadium was replaced by Westgate Park. The only physical reminder of its existence between the sea, the railroad, and the Pacific Coast Highway is a bronze plaque dedicated in 2003 where the ballpark once stood:

Hurriedly built in two months by the Works Progress Administration (WPA) for $25,000 in 1936, the wooden, green-painted and later termite-infested ballpark was the original home of the Pacific Coast League (PCL) San Diego Padres. The breeze that once carried baseballs from Lane Field onto Pacific Highway still blows in from San Diego Bay. Legend goes that left-hand hitting Ted Williams. . . or Max West, Jack Graham, Luke Easter . . . or George McDonald hit a home run that bounced in to an open boxcar. The ball was later found 120 miles away in Los Angeles. This was the longest home run ever hit.

When Bill Lane agreed to move his baseball franchise to San Diego in 1936, the Works Progress Administration was spurred into action to erect a ballpark in record time. They chose a site that was already used by the Navy for sporting events, and the city paid only $4,000 of the upgrade cost. Partly because it was constructed so quickly, the park had a temporary feel to it, lacking a roof, lights, and a backstop. But it could hold between 9,000 and 12,000 spectators and they flocked in to see the Padres win the Shaughnessy Cup in the PCL playoffs in 1937. The most famous player of the team was undoubtedly Ted Williams, who played for the Padres for a year before embarking on his legendary major league career with the Boston Red Sox.

The Padres won the league again in 1954, but by then the wooden ballpark was suffering from exposure to the salty spray of the Pacific and the team was looking for a new home. The Padres left Lane Field after the 1957 season and the site is now a parking lot.

Location: Robin Roberts Stadium at Lanphier Park, Springfield, IL

Aka: Reservoir Park, Lanphier Park, Robin Roberts Stadium

Status: Home of the Springfield Capitals

Opened: 1978

Capacity: 5,000

Dimensions:

Left Field 320 ft

Center Field 415 ft

Right Field 320 ft

A small and simple ballpark, Lanphier Park was built in 1925 on land donated by Robert Lanphier, president of Sangamo Electric. Also known as Robin Roberts Stadium, the stadium was renamed in 1977 after the Philles' star pitcher and Hall of Famer who was born in Springfield.

Springfield has a long history of baseball, dating back as far as 1880. When the new Reservoir Park was opened in 1925, 12,000 people came to witness the occasion. The earliest teams to play at Reservoir Park were the Senators, who played in the Three-I League from 1925 until 1932. In 1938 the team became the Class B Three-I affiliate of the St. Louis Browns, and was renamed the Springfield Browns. They remained with St. Louis until 1949, when the city lost their minor league team until the arrival of the Springfield RedBirds in 1978.

After the departure of the RedBirds in 1981, the St. Louis Cardinals revived their connection with Lanphier Park, and their Triple-A team the Springfield Cardinals played home games at Robin Roberts Stadium from 1982 until 1993. They were succeeded by the

RIGHT: The pennant proclaims the Sliders as 2008 league champions—the Central Illinois Collegiate League was disbanded at the end of that season and the Sliders are now part of the Prospect League.

Class A Sultans of Springfield (1994–95) and then by the Capitals, who played in the Frontier League from 1995 to 2001, when the stadium went dark. Pro ball did not return until 2007.

When the Redbirds arrived, the stadium was renovated in 1977 at a cost of some $200,000 and consists of a small covered grandstand with extensive bleacher seating, and a total capacity of 5,200. Although it has hosted minor league teams during its long life, it is now badly in need of updating and many Springfield fans are hoping that a new baseball park will be constructed soon. The playing field is kept in good order by the Benedictine University of Springfield, whose team, the Benedictine Bulls, use the field every year. But the ancillary facilities, such as the scoreboard, the bleachers, and the lights, need replacing.

Since 2007 the Springfield Sliders, a collegiate team in the Prospect League, have done a great deal to revive local interest in baseball, playing a season from June until August.

ABOVE and BELOW: The Sliders play over fifty games a season in the Western Division of the Prospect League.

Akron claims a long and distinguished history in the world of baseball. League Park opened in 1906, a year after Akron had won a new baseball franchise in the Ohio and Pennsylvania League.

During the inaugural season, the Akron Tip-Tops finished as runner-up in the league, a feat they repeated in 1906. League champions for three years from 1908 to 1911, the Tip-Tops folded when the league collapsed, and for a time, there was no pro baseball at League Park, although it did host college and high school games.

In 1920 a team of Akron investors purchased a franchise in the International League—just one step away from the major leagues. The Numatics (named after the newly invented pneumatic tire) attracted a crowd of 11,000 for their victorious opening game against Jersey City. Sadly, despite an incredibly successful season, the Numatics were ousted from the league at the end of the season simply because of the city's geographical position in relation to other league members on the East Coast.

While the park was unused by pro baseball, the New York Yankees played an exhibition game against the Firestone team, and on July 22, 1921, the great Babe Ruth obligingly hit one of his trademark home runs over the right field fence. The Yankees returned in September that same year, and played what was likely the last baseball game at League Park. The Babe was mobbed and was forced to escape using his tried and tested method of lobbing a signed ball into the air and running off while the fans scrambled for the ball.

League Park was auctioned the following year and briefly used by the Akron Pros football team. By December 1922 the site had been sold to the Summit Growers Association, the grandstand and bleachers auctioned for scrap, and the ballpark transformed into a farmers' market.

Location: 101-155 Beaver Street, Akron, OH
Status: Demolished c. 1922
Team: Akron Yankees
Opened: May 6, 1906
Last MLB game: September 1921
Capacity: 5,000

League Park, Akron

Location: Lexington Avenue and E 66th Street, Cleveland, OH

Aka: Dunn Field (1916–1927)

Status: Largely demolished 1951

Architect: Osborn Engineering Company

Opened: May 1, 1891

Capacity: 9,000; 21,414 (final)

Dimensions:

Left Field 375 ft

Left Center 415 ft

Center Field 420 ft

Right Field 290 ft

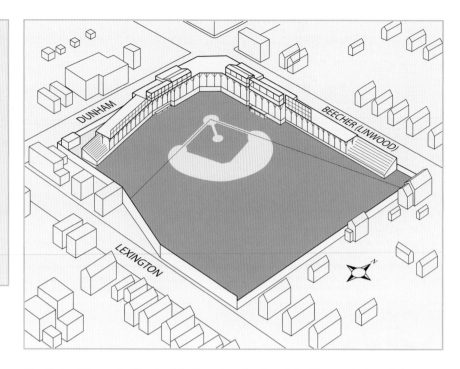

ABOVE: Artist's impression of League Park I (1891–1901) built around houses on Lexington. When League Park II was built, these houses were purchased and the whole site used.

BELOW: Interior of League Park in 1914—the double-deck main grandstand.

The National League's Cleveland Spiders played at the original League Park until they went out of business in 1899, but were replaced the next year by the Cleveland Lake Shores. The renamed Cleveland Bluebirds were a charter member in the new American League, which became a major league in 1901. The park was rebuilt for the 1910 season as a concrete-and-steel stadium. A new team owner renamed it Dunn Field, but his widow sold the franchise in 1927 and the ballpark's name reverted back to League Park. From July 1932 through the 1933 season, the Indians played at the new and far larger Municipal Stadium but moved most of their games back to League Park in 1934.

They split their schedule between the two parks from 1936 and, beginning in 1938, they also played at Cleveland Stadium. The Indians were playing most of their home games at Municipal Stadium by 1940 and left League Park for good after the 1946 season. Following the demise of the Negro American League Cleveland Buckeyes at the end of the 1950 season, League Park was no longer used as a regular sports venue. Most of the structure was demolished the next year and the area is now a public park.

LEFT: Postcard of League Park showing the impressive exterior on Linwood Avenue and E 66th Street (which runs from left to right).

BELOW: 1910 view of Cleveland's League Park, just after being rebuilt. The building on the corner of Lexington Avenue and E 66th Street, as well as the brick wall and part of the facade on E 66th Street, can still be seen today.

Home to professional baseball in Fort Wayne from 1883 until 1935, League Park was located on the northern edge of the downtown business district, in an area known as Jailhouse Flats because of its proximity to the old Allen County Jail.

The new park was built for the 1883 Northwestern League season. The wooden grandstand had a twenty-foot-high roof and this was extended in 1908, while the bleachers were moved further down the foul lines to provide more seating. The first game on June 2, 1883, between the Quincy Professionals from Illinois and the local Methodist College attracted a capacity crowd of 2,000. Those who had been turned away gouged holes in the fence to watch the game, or clambered aboard wagons in the nearby street to peer over the fence. This was also the first recorded night baseball game.

Fort Wayne has hosted only twelve major league games in its long history, and the last two were played at League Park in 1902. On June 22, the Cleveland Bronchos defeated the Washington Senators 6–4, and a few weeks later on August 31, the Boston Americans beat the Bronchos 3–1.

Capacity figures are a little sketchy, but in 1902 around 3,500 fans watched the last Cleveland Bronchos game, and in the 1920s, 5,000 spectators regularly attended Fort Wayne's minor league games. The wooden grandstand was destroyed by fire on July 22, 1930, but remarkably, was rebuilt just ten days later, albeit on a smaller scale with just 2,000 seats.

By 1939 the park was no longer used for baseball, having been turned into an open area and used for other sports and entertainment.

Location: In a block enclosed by the St. Marys River, South Calhoun Street, and South Clinton Street, Fort Wayne, IN
Aka: Jailhouse Flats
Status: Closed 1935
Opened: 1883
Capacity: 3,500
Dimensions:
Left Field 300 ft
Center Field 425 ft
Right Field 300 ft

League Park, Fort Wayne

Location: 3802 West Dr. Martin Luther King Boulevard, Tampa, FL
Aka: George M. Steinbrenner Field (since 2008)
Status: Home to the Tampa Yankees and spring training for the New York Yankees
Architect: Lescher & Mahoney
Opened: 1996; added to in 2007
Capacity: 11,000
Dimensions:
Left Field 318 ft
Left Center 399 ft
Center Field 408 ft
Right Center 385 ft
Right Field 314 ft

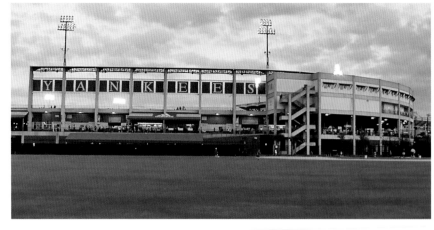

George M. Steinbrenner Field actually began life as Legends Field, a name that it was known by from its opening in 1996 until it was renamed in 2008 in honor of the New York Yankees' former owner and long-time Tampa resident. The thirty-one-acre facility is owned by the local Tampa Sports Authority and is the spring training home of the New York Yankees and the full-time home of the Florida State League's Single-A Tampa Yankees. The stadium has also hosted FC Tampa Bay of the North American Soccer League since 2010 and is also home to the Hillsborough Community College Hawks baseball team.

It may not be Yankee Stadium, but it displays all the grandeur of its parent park. Opened in 1996 and with a capacity a little over 10,000, this stadium is comparable to the best Triple-A ballparks in the country in size, facilities, and appearance.

Legends Field was designed by Lescher Mahoney/DLR Group, which also designed nearby Plant City Stadium. In 2011, just six months after Steinbrenner's death, a life-sized bronze statue of him was erected at the stadium.

Although the Yankees had trained in Fort Lauderdale for many years from the 1960s, they moved north to Tampa in the 1980s, utilizing Al Lopez Field for spring training in 1988. Al Lopez Field was demolished in 1989. It is now the parking lot that serves Legends Field and Raymond James Stadium, the new football stadium for the Tampa Bay Buccaneers.

Legends Field deliberately shares the same outfield dimensions as Yankee Stadium with its left field power alleys, so every spring the Yankees arrive for training, and since the Tampa Yankees have to train for a career at Yankee Stadium, Legends Field gives them practice. The roof of the grandstands incorporates a decorative frieze similar to that in the original Yankee home. It also celebrates the history of this great club in Monument Park, which honors some of the Yankees' greatest players. Besides Yankee Stadium itself, there are no other ballparks like it.

After the Tampa Tarpons were sold in 1988, the city of Tampa lacked a baseball team to call its own. Founded in 1994, the Tampa Yankees filled the gap and have won the Florida State League several times, in 1994, 2001, 2004, 2009, and 2010. They moved to Legends Field in 1996 and several future Yankees began their careers in Tampa.

THIS PAGE: Interior and exterior views of George M. Steinbrenner Field.

Location: Fifth Street, Lake Charles, LA
Aka: Alvin Dark Stadium (from 2010)
Status: Used by local schools
Architect: Renovations by Kal Ripkin and Associates
Opened: 1934; renovated 2010
Capacity: 4,500
Dimensions:
Left Field 307 ft
Center Field 415 ft
Right Field 304 ft

When it opened in 1934, Legion Field was regarded as a great opportunity for the town of Lake Charles, Louisiana, and the Lake Charles Explorers began their inaugural season with high hopes. Unfortunately, the ballpark burned down just two months into the season, and the Explorers retreated rather ignominiously to Jeanerette High School Stadium while Legion Field was rebuilt.

The Explorers signed a short-lived contract with Cincinnati in 1935, and were renamed the Skippers. Despite their appalling record, they acquired a second contract with the Detroit Tigers in 1937, and somehow turned their game around, reaching the playoffs that year. In 1939 they became the Evangeline League champions and in 1941 they were signed by the Chicago Cubs.

After World War II, there was no baseball at Lake Charles until 1950, when the Lake Charles Lakers played in the new Gulf Coast League until its demise in 1953, when they returned to the Evangeline League. In 1956, the team signed with the New York Giants and became their Class C franchise. The Lakers would officially change their name to the Lake Charles Giants. The Giants themselves were grooming a new outfielder named Felipe Alou, whom they placed in their new Class C Lake Charles franchise. Alou wouldn't stay too long, as he was quickly promoted. He did, however, have his first professional at bats at Legion Field. The New York Giants were a very strong team who (along with Felipe Alou, as it would turn out), put Lake Charles permanently on the minor league baseball history map.

By the end of 1957, the Evangeline League called it quits and the Lake Charles Giants were no more. The Kansas City Monarchs Negro League baseball team began playing many of their home games at Lake Charles and continued to use Legion Field until 1962.

Lake Charles' Legion Field is still maintained and is in fantastic shape. It is used by the school board for events and amateur baseball. In 2010 the stadium benifited from $360,000 worth of renovations and the stadium was renamed Alvin Dark Stadium, in honor of the former pro baseball player and manager Alvin Dark.

THIS PAGE: Legion Field before the renovations and renaming to Alvin Dark Stadium. The renovations have made an enormous difference in the quality of the field and have remedied problems with the playing conditions that have plagued the field for years.

Location: W. University Avenue and N. Dunlap, St. Paul, MN

Status: Demolished 1957

Opened: 1897; rebuilt 1915

Capacity: 6,000 (1897); 10,000 (1915)

Dimensions:

Left Field 315 ft

Center Field 470 ft

Right Field 365 ft

ABOVE: 1954 aerial view of Lexington Park. It was commissioned by Charlie Comiskey for his St. Paul Saints Western League baseball franchise.

ABOVE RIGHT and BELOW: Lights were installed in Lexington Park in 1937.

(All three photos courtesy Matthew Coulliard.)

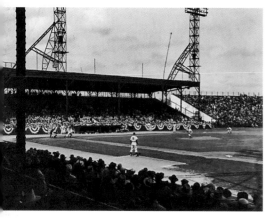

At the start of the twentieth century, Triple-A American Association baseball was played in beautiful vintage ballparks built during the late 1800s: Borchert Field (1888) in Milwaukee, St. Paul's rival Nicollet Park (1886) in nearby Minneapolis; and Lexington Park, built in 1897. These ballparks would serve for over fifty years until they all came down between 1956 and 1957. In all three cases the reasoning behind their demise was the same: each city wanted a major league team, and all three built new stadiums to attract an MLB franchise. Minneapolis built Metropolitan Stadium, which attracted the Washington Senators. Milwaukee built County Stadium, which attracted the Braves to move out of Boston and to the Brew City. St. Paul built Midway Stadium, which was—at best—utilitarian. True, it could be easily expanded, but it had only 7,000 seats. Needless to say, the gamble didn't work out. The Saints played for only three more years and then had to give up the franchise when the Twins moved in.

Lexington Park was completed in 1897, but stood relatively unused until 1909, as the St. Paul Apostles played most of their games at the "Pill Box" and moved permanently into Lexington Park only when the Pill Box was deemed inadequate for professional baseball. In 1914, to complete their new identity, the team changed its name to the St. Paul Saints. Lexington Park was built of wood. As with so many ballparks of that era, it had to rebuild sections after fires. Two were particularly damaging—in 1908 and in 1915, the latter necessitating a major rebuild, including turning the entire ballfield ninety degrees.

In 1935, the Saints signed with the Chicago White Sox. In 1944, they signed with the Brooklyn Dodgers, a contract that would outlast the Dodgers' move to Los Angeles. The payoff was that from 1944 to 1952 the Saints, who hadn't seen a playoff game since 1931, found themselves in the playoffs every year except 1947. In 1948, they won yet another title.

In 1957, the Saints moved to their new home at Midway Stadium. Within a few years, the Dodgers pulled out of the American Association and baseball in St. Paul was no more. Lexington Park became a Red Owl grocery store, and is now a local bank.

Location: Hopkins & McLean Avenue, Cincinnati, OH

Aka: Union Cricket Club Grounds, the Grand Duchess

Status: Demolished c. 1875

Opened: May 4, 1869

Capacity: 4,000

Better known as Union Grounds, Lincoln Park was home to the nation's first professional baseball team, the Cincinnati Red Stockings, from 1866 until 1870. Located near the Union Railway terminus, Union Grounds was an eight-acre fenced area behind the popular Lincoln Park, and was originally known as the Union Cricket Club Grounds.

In 1867 the president of the new Cincinnati baseball club, Aaron Champion, ordered $10,000 of improvements, including the construction of a new grandstand and clubhouse and the turfing of the field. The grandstand was a splendid affair, topped with a cupola that was nicknamed the "Grand Duchess," and incorporated a high platform which acted as a bandstand. It seated approximately 4,000 spectators. The entrance was equally grand, with a double gate where the teams' horse-drawn buggies could pull up.

Harry Wright was hired in 1865 as the club's professional manager and he began the business of organizing and hiring team members. By 1868 about half the team were imports from the Eastern Seaboard and in 1869 the team was fully professional, with ten men on salary for eight months. Wright's younger brother George, the most talented player on the team, rightly commanded the highest salary of $1,400, which was $200 more than his player-manager brother. In 1868 Union Grounds was fully enclosed and admission was charged from this season on.

Wright's skills resulted in the Red Stockings delivering the first—and so far only—perfect season in baseball history, as the team produced a 57–0 record. In 1869 the team traveled all over the United States, incurring travel costs alongside the players' salaries, which they hoped to recoup in the winter of 1869–70 by hiring out Union Grounds as an ice rink. Unfortunately, the weather did not oblige and in 1871 the team was forced to disband.

When the Pocatello Posse moved from Halliwell Field in Pocatello, Idaho, to Ogden, Utah, they weren't sure what to expect. A temporary ballpark had been quickly erected for them at Serge Simmons Field and featured a few sets of indistinguishable stands erected around a local men's league ballfield. It did have one thing, however—spectacular views of Ogden's mountain range, the western slopes of the Rocky Mountains. For three long years construction continued on Lindquist. When it finally opened in 1997 everyone was speechless: the view was incredible, the ballpark itself was unique, exciting, and filled with little details everywhere, including raptors with glowing red eyes that are built into the walls throughout the ballpark. In 2003, the Milwaukee Brewers moved their operations out of Lindquist Field to Helena, Montana (which they had moved their other Pioneer League team out of two years earlier). The vacancy was quickly filled by the Los Angeles Dodgers, who moved out of Legion Park in Great Falls, Montana (an unbelievable stadium in its own right) after a twenty-year relationship.

The Dodgers brought with them their successful farm system. Attendance has steadily risen over the years. An interesting fact: the mountain range looks familiar because it's the view Paramount shows before each of its movies. The Raptors offer their ballpark (when the Raptors are on the road, of course) for companies to use for whatever they like—softball games right on the professional playing field, picnics on the grass—free! The only catch is you have to agree to use the Raptors' own catering service instead of bringing in your own. That's it. Just use the Raptors' concession services and you can have this entire ballpark all to yourself.

Location: 2330 Lincoln Avenue, Ogden, UT
Status: Home of the Ogden Raptors
Opened: 1997
Capacity: 5,000 (2005); 8,000 (2008)
Dimensions:
Left Field 335 ft
Center Field 390 ft
Right Center 350 ft
Right Field 335 ft
Winner of Digitalballparks' 2007 Ballpark of the Year Award

RIGHT: Lindquist Field has fabulous views over to the Rockies.

BELOW: Seating capacity is 6,700 after the 2008 improvements.

Location: N 18th Street & W Lloyd Street up to W North Avenue, Milwaukee, WI
Aka: Milwaukee Park
Status: Closed 1903
Opened: 1895

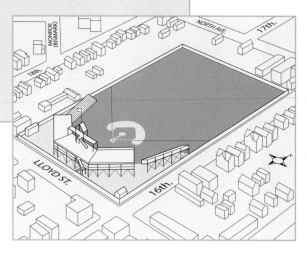

ABOVE: Artist's impression of Lloyd Street Grounds.

The ballpark at Milwaukee's Lloyd Street Grounds was constructed in 1895 after the owners of the Milwaukee Brewers decided that the rent on the city's Athletic Park was too expensive. A park was urgently needed for the 1895 season of the Western League and the high, flat plot of land at Lloyd Street Grounds, about a mile northeast of the city center, seemed perfect.

It was constructed quickly but carefully for a cost of $7,400 from February 1895. The semicircular wooden grandstand was two stories high with a steel frame, and had a capacity of 4,000. The bleachers, which were also arranged in a semicircle around the park, seated an additional 2,500 people and provided an excellent view of the game. There are few surviving pictures of the stadium, but one line drawing shows an elegant building, and the only complaint on opening was that the stairways were too narrow.

The new stadium was also known as Milwaukee Park and the first game was played on May 1, 1895, before a crowd of 6,000 fans. In 1897 Connie Mack arrived to manage the team, but left in 1900 just as the club joined the new American League. The Brewers played their first major league game at Lloyd Street on May 3, 1901, but they failed to shine during that first season, coming last in the league.

The biggest crowd at Lloyd Street was, ironically, for the Brewers' former boss Connie Mack, when he returned with the Philadelphia Athletics to play the Brewers before a crowd of some 10,000 fans on May 26, 1901. Unfortunately, low attendance for the rest of the season prompted the American League to shift the franchise, and the minor league Milwaukee Creams took over at Lloyd Park for the 1902 season. With the collapse of the (revived) Western League, the Creams folded and Lloyd Street Grounds was torn down in 1904.

Location: 1915 Scott Street, Lafayette, IN
Aka: Columbian Park Recreational Center (1940–1971)
Status: Hosts tournaments and league championship games
Opened: 1940
Capacity: 3,500

Located in Lafayette, Indiana, Loeb Stadium is the former home of the Lafayette Leopards and part-time home to the Ohio Valley Redcoats. Built in 1940, Loeb Stadium—aka the Columbian Park Recreational Center—is located next to the Columbian Park Zoo.

Usually there is a good explanation as to why a well-built and vintage ballpark has been overlooked by professional baseball—sometimes, it's the quality of the neighborhood. Other times, it's the fact that the ballpark was built only for amateur baseball, but here it seems, despite numerous attempts, the location and city just aren't big enough to support a professional team.

The Chiefs lasted only the one season before giving way to the Red Sox. The new Lafayette Red Sox played two seasons at Loeb Stadium. In 1958, the Lafayette Red Sox announced that they were moving to Waterloo, Iowa. There was no replacement team for the Red Sox, so the Columbian Park Recreational Center sat dormant to professional baseball for thirty-six years.

Then the Northern League appeared in 1993, as a rebirth of the Class A Northern League that had played throughout the northwoods of the United States until 1971. The abandoned ballparks of the region were turned into thriving professional facilities again, without any affiliation to the majors. The league was a tremendous success, and by 1994 indy leagues began to spring up everywhere in North America. Indy franchises came and went at Loeb: in all, Loeb Stadium has seen nine seasons of professional play, three as an affiliate of the Red Sox and Indians. Today, Loeb Stadium continues to host tournaments and league championship games such as the Colt World Series.

RIGHT: Loeb Stadium press box.

Location: 1500 Sugar Bowl Drive, New Orleans, LA
Aka: New Orleans Superdome, the Dome
Status: Current multipurpose stadium
Architect: Curtis and Davis
Opened: 1975
Capacity: 55,670
Dimensions
Left Field 325 ft
Center Field 421 ft
Right Field 325 ft

Louisiana Superdome

The Louisiana Superdome is about as far away from the homely family ballpark as you can get, and cost $134 million to construct. Nevertheless, it is an outstanding sports facility, although its very size means that it has failed to attract a long-term baseball franchise. Many baseball fans admit that the venue is better suited to football games, but it has hosted many major league exhibition games.

New Orleans has a strong minor league and collegiate tradition, but has never attracted a major league franchise and so there has been no demand for a top-class baseball facility in the city.

Opened in 1975, the Superdome was conceived as a multipurpose facility. In addition to football, basketball, and baseball, it has hosted the Rolling Stones and 87,000 of their fans, Pope John Paul II, and George H.W. Bush. The first baseball game was a major league exhibition between the Minnesota Twins and the Houston Astros in 1976, and during the 1977 season the Triple-A Pelicans used the Superdome for home games. The pursuit of a permanent baseball tenant has proved fruitless, and over the years officials have tried to lure the Oakland Athletics and the Pittsburgh Pirates to the city, without success. The Yankees, Orioles, Phillies, Cardinals, and Blue Jays have all played exhibition games in the stadium.

As a baseball venue the Superdome has serious drawbacks. First, it is a covered venue and therefore every game is played under lights and has the appearance of a night game. Second, and more seriously, the sightlines from the upper decks are very poor. The Superdome has a total capacity of 63,525 for baseball games and the lower decks are retracted along the sidelines to accommodate the field more efficiently. In 2005, after the devastating Hurricane Katrina, the Superdome was renovated at a cost of $193 million.

ABOVE and BELOW: The Louisiana Superdome is forever synonymous with Hurricane Katrina.

OPPOSITE: The entrance to Loeb Stadium proclaims the ballpark's original name: the Columbian Park Recreational Center.

Location: 401 E Main Street, Louisville, KY

Aka: Slugger Field, LSF

Status: Home to the Louisville Bats

Architect: HNTB

Opened: April 12, 2000

Capacity: 13,131

Dimensions:

Left Field 325 ft

Center Field 405 ft

Right Field 340 ft

All-Star Game: 2008

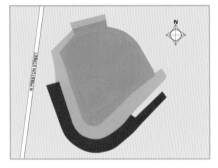

ABOVE: Footprint of Louisville Slugger Field.

TOP: There is plenty of berm seating and standing room, especially since the concourse rounds the entire playing field for overflow crowds.

BELOW: Interior views.

OPPOSITE, ABOVE: The Louisville Colonels (their name comes from the Kentucky Colonels) played in the American Association during its ten-year existence from 1882 until 1891, and then in the National League until 1899.

Home of the Louisville Bats, Louisville Slugger Field was built in 2000 for $27.8 million and succeeded Cardinal Stadium as the largest minor league stadium. While most remember the Louisville Redbirds as a Cardinals franchise, the Milwaukee Brewers actually took over in 1998, changing the team name to the RiverBats in 1999. Just as the stadium was due to be completed, the Brewers moved on to Indianapolis, and the nearby Cincinnati Reds took over. The team continued to play as the new RiverBats for two more seasons until 2002, when they became known simply as the Bats.

Louisville Slugger Stadium seats over 13,000 and is a huge facility with plenty of berm seating and standing room (especially since the concourse rounds the entire playing field) for overflow crowds. Built on the site of Louisville's old train yard, the stadium incorporates the old buildings into its design. Entrance into the ballpark is actually through the old train shed that once protected Louisville's locomotives from the elements. Designed with imagination and respect for the area's heritage, its age and historic significance is definitely the best thing about this ballpark. The outfield view features the I-65 bridge, which spans the Ohio River and reaches into Indiana. The scoreboards mimic their background with a little wire bridge of their own to fit seamlessly into their environment.

The naming rights of the stadium went to Hillerich and Bradsby, the manufacturers of the legendary Louisville Slugger baseball bat. Louisville is justifiably proud of its new facility and the ballpark sells out consistently. This team can draw upward of 700,000 fans a year. Every season since it has opened, Louisville Slugger Field has been in the top five in the country for attendance, and that includes all minor league systems.

Once home to the Toledo Mud Hens, Lucas County Stadium opened in 1965, replacing the venerable Swayne Field, which had been demolished ten years earlier.

The loss of the Mud Hens franchise in 1955 was a serious blow to the city's baseball fans, and local politician Ned Skeldon worked to revive the team in the early 1960s. Part of his plan involved converting the racetrack of the Lucas County fairground in the Toledo suburb of Maumee. In 1965 the Toledo Mud Hens were reborn as the Triple-A affiliate of the New York Yankees and played in the International League.

The racetrack stands at Lucas County were converted into third-base seating and total capacity was 10,000, much of it under a large cantilevered roof. Press boxes and luxury boxes, known as the "Diamond Club," jut out directly behind home plate. The conversion was carried out quickly and in many ways the facilities were a little less than luxurious. There was no running water in the dugouts, for example, and the locker and training rooms were poorly equipped for a Triple-A facility. Despite this, the Mud Hens called it home for nearly forty years, relocating in 2002 to the new Fifth Third Field in downtown Toledo. Lucas County Stadium was renamed in honor of Ned Skeldon, the man who worked so hard to bring the Mud Hens home, just three months before his death in 1988. Unlike many other ballparks of this vintage that have been bulldozed, Ned Skeldon is still in use, although it becomes a little more dilapidated with each passing year. Bowling Green State University now uses it for home games and the Lake Erie Monarchs use it for weekday home games. It also hosts the Great Lakes Summer League and other amateur games.

Location: 2901 Ket Street, Maume, OH
Aka: Ned Skeldon Stadium, Lucas County Stadium
Status: Home of Bowling Green State University
Opened: 1965
Capacity: 10,197
Dimensions:
Left Field 325 ft
Center Field 410 ft
Right Field 325 ft

Lucas County Stadium

BELOW: Ned Skeldon Stadium was built in 1965 to replace Swayne Field, which was demolished ten years earlier.

Luther Williams Field

Location: Central City Park, Macon, GA

Aka: Macon Baseball Park

Status: Home to the Macon Pinetoppers

Opened: 1929

Capacity: 3,500

Dimensions:

Left Field 388 ft

Center Field 402 ft

Right Field 338 ft

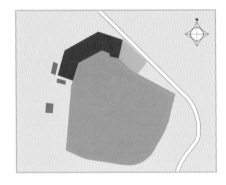

TOP: Home plate entrance: note the black iron fence surrounding the ballpark and the modern roof. Lights were installed in 1936.

ABOVE: Footprint of Luther Williams Field.

BELOW: An atmospheric view that shows what it's like to watch a game in the second-oldest minor league park.

Luther Williams Field is a historic ballpark built in 1929, originally for the Southern League. The ballpark has been the home to Single-A, Double-A, and independent baseball and is now the second-oldest minor league stadium in the country. Originally known as the Macon Baseball Park, it was built at a cost of $60,000. It was named Luther Williams Field in honor of the mayor of Macon at the time of construction.

The Macon Peaches were the first team to play here in 1930, as part of the Southern League. Unaffiliated to a major league team (like all the teams in the league), their first full season at Luther Williams Field was an excellent one, with the team finishing in first place with an 87–52 record. They would lose in the finals, but the Peaches had certainly made an immediate mark in their new ballpark.

The Peaches won their first league championship in 1938, which attracted affiliation from the Brooklyn Dodgers, who were succeeded by the Chicago Cubs in 1941. They won a second championship in 1942, before play was suspended for the war.

In 1949 Jackie Robinson broke the major league color bar when he played as part of a Dodgers team during a preseason exhibition, which attracted Luther Williams Field's biggest crowd ever at 6,400 fans. Both the Dodgers and the Red Sox stopped off at Macon to play exhibition games after spring training in Florida, and the field hosted stars such as Ted Williams, Pee Wee Reese, and Roy Campanella.

In 1962 the Southern League folded and the Cincinnati Reds moved their Triple-A team to the city, which was packed with exciting players who drew record crowds to Luther Williams Field. After some lean years in the 1970s when the park was unused, the return of professional baseball in 1980 and then the arrival of the Atlanta Braves in 1991 revitalized baseball in Macon.

Incredibly, over eighty years after it was opened, Luther Williams Field is still in use as part of the Peach State League.

Location: 300 Coventry Road, Ottawa, Ontario, Canada
Aka: Jetform Park (1993–2002), Stade d'Ottawa, Ottawa Rapidz Stadium (2008)
Status: Used for amateur games
Opened: April 17, 1993
Capacity: 10,332
Dimensions:
Left Field 325 ft
Left Center 380 ft
Center Field 404 ft
Right Center 380 ft
Right Field 325 ft

Lynx Stadium's grand opening in 1993 signaled a triumphant return of the International League to Ottawa. Also known as Stade d'Ottawa or Ottawa Stadium, it was home to the Ottawa Lynx from 1993 until 2007. They were the Triple-A affiliate of the Montreal Expos (1993–2002), the Baltimore Orioles (2003–2006), and finally the Philadelphia Phillies.

Lynx Stadium is located right off of Route 417, and in the middle of several office complexes and some residential housing. One of the most intriguing parts of the stadium is a building just over the outfield wall. The giant mirrored frontage that seems to turn all sorts of colors with the setting of the sun is the home of the Royal Canadian Mounted Police.

In 1993 the new Lynx team was part of the Montreal Expos' excellent farm system. While many of their players would go elsewhere to become stars, fans of the new Ottawa Lynx got to see them as rookies firsthand. The first Lynx team would produce almost thirty major leaguers, such as Cliff Floyd, Kirk Rueter, Gil Heredia, Matt Stairs, and Rondell White. They proved immensely popular, drawing 693,000 fans to the 10,000-seat stadium, and shattering a sixty-three-year-old International League record.

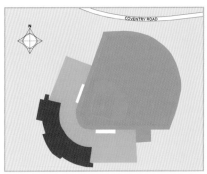

THIS PAGE: Footprint, exterior, and interior view of Lynx Stadium.

In 2002 the Expos pulled out of Lynx Stadium after ten years of great memories, and were replaced by the Baltimore Orioles, who shocked the baseball world when they announced they were leaving Rochester, New York, after forty-one years. The Lynx, however, were glad to welcome them to Canada and it didn't take long for the Lynx to see some future impact players. Future All-Star Brian Roberts played for the new Baltimore Triple-A affiliate in 2003.

When the Lynx club was sold in 2006 and the new owners entered a legal dispute with the city of Ottawa, professional baseball died in Ottawa. Efforts to revive it with the short-lived Rapidz have left Lynx Stadium empty and awaiting a new tenant.

Location: Corner of Mack Avenue and Fairview Street Detroit, MI
Status: Demolished 1960s
Opened: 1914
Capacity: 6,000

Mack Park was home to one of the Negro League's most successful teams, the Detroit Stars, from 1920 until 1929. The ballpark was constructed in 1914 by Joe Roesink, a haberdasher of German-Jewish descent.

It was a substantial ballpark that could seat 6,000 fans, with a wooden single-decked structure topped by a tin roof. For the first few years it hosted unofficial games by passing teams such as the Boston Braves, the Phillies, and the New York Giants, who often played exhibitions to generate extra income on their off days. In 1918 Roesink accepted an offer from the Chicago sports promoter Rube Foster to place a Negro National League franchise at Mack Field.

Established in 1919, the Detroit Stars were one of the most powerful teams in the west, and were both popular and successful. Among their players were star catcher and pitcher Ted "Double-Duty" Radcliffe and future Hall of Famers left-handed pitcher and right-handed batter Andy Cooper, and Norman "Turkey" Stearnes, one of the greatest batters in the Negro Leagues. Despite this, they never managed to win the league, finishing no higher than second during their twelve seasons with the league. With the demise of the Negro National League in 1931, the Stars became independent and moved away to Hamtramck Stadium in 1933.

Mack Park barely survived a serious fire in 1929, when gasoline, which had been spread on the field after heavy rain, ignited and destroyed the wooden stands. Even worse, 200 spectators were injured and Roesink not only refused to refund the money of fans, but also declined to offer condolences to those injured. Mack Park was rebuilt, but its glory days had passed. The Stars moved on and Roesink ran into financial difficulties. The ballpark was used by high school baseball teams until the 1960s, when the site was razed for a housing complex.

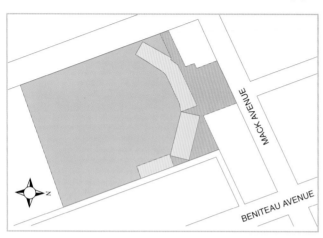

ABOVE: Footprint of Mack Park.

Location: Madison Avenue, Baltimore, MD
Aka: Monumental Park
Status: Defunct
Opened: April 28, 1860

Madison Avenue Grounds was one of the earliest formal baseball grounds (and certainly the first in Baltimore), hosting its first game in September 1860 between the Baltimore Excelsiors and the Brooklyn Excelsiors.

The city of Baltimore purchased land on Druid Hill from the Rogers and Gardener families, and this became only the third municipal park in the United States after Central Park in New York and Fairmont Park in Philadelphia. Used as Union army camp for part of the Civil War, the park incorporated several sports fields. None of the new baseball fields got any form of permanent seating until 1866—in 1865, spectators reportedly sat in their carriages surrounding the diamond.

Sources differ as to the number of games played at Madison Avenue Grounds, or indeed of the precise names of the various clubs on Druid Hill. The Waverly Club was later known as the Past Time Club after it joined with the Excelsior Club in 1861, and it was on their ground that the first inter-city ballgame was played on September 15, 1860. About 1,000 people turned out to watch this highly anticipated game.

The *Baltimore American and Commercial Advertiser* reported of one early game, "Both bowling and batting were performed in such a manner as to show considerable skillfulness, while the physical and mental exercise, which the game calls for cannot but prove highly beneficial to young men, especially those of sedimentary habits."

The ground was enclosed in 1866 and admission was charged, initially of 15 cents, although ladies were admitted for free. At some point after 1869 permanent stands were erected, including a ladies-only stand. The Baltimore Railroad did not extend as far as Druid Hill until 1864, so the ballpark was not easily accessible by large crowds. Madison Avenue Grounds became home to the Maryland Club of the National Association during its brief life in 1873, but it appears to have fallen out of use after that.

This Connecticut ballpark, also known as Fort Hill Grounds, was built for the Middletown Mansfields, who became members of the National Association in 1872. They were Middeltown's only baseball team, and remain the only major league team to hail from Connecticut. The Mansfields were organized by Ben Douglas Jr. in 1866, who named the team after his late uncle, a hero of both the Mexican-American War and the Civil War, who was killed at the battle of Antietam.

By 1870, the Mansfields were amateur champions of Connecticut and became more serious about their future. They realized that they needed an enclosed field, which would enable them to charge admission to their games. Just before the start of the 1871 season, local brick factory owner Dewitt Clinton Sage donated a plot of land, "near the shirt factory, five minutes walk from the McDonough House [a famous hotel on Main Street], for their free use as a base ball ground for five years." It was an incredibly generous offer and the team wasted no time in grading and leveling the bare cow pasture, and erecting boards to fence off the ball field. It was a big task and they were forced to delay the start of their season until June 9, when they lost to the Brooklyn Atlantics before a crowd of 650.

It was a respectable start. The new stands held 800 and the field's hillside position provided wonderful views of Middletown and the river.

By now, they were also good enough to play some of the best professional teams in the country, although they hadn't actually beaten any of them. In 1872 Harry Wright, the owner of the Boston Red Sox, advised them that if they were really serious about playing professionally, they should invest $10 and join the new National Association. The Mansfields did so and fulfilled the only criterion necessary to play alongside teams from New York, Boston, and Philadelphia. Sadly, the whole venture folded at the end of the 1872 season, as the team from a small town could not attract the same sort of crowds as those from the big cities. [Drawn from David Arcidiacono's book, *Middletown's Season in the Sun —The Story of Connecticut's First Professional Baseball Team.*]

The site is now covered by a residential development.

Location: Middletown, CT
Aka: Fort Hill Grounds
Status: Closed July 4, 1872
Opened: May 2, 1872
Capacity: 800

Maple Leaf Stadium was built by Lol Solman for his Toronto Maple Leafs baseball team of the International League on the site of a stadium that had been built in 1907. Previously, the Maple Leafs had played at Hanlan's Point Stadium. The opening game was held on April 29, 1926, and it was the team's home for forty-two seasons until they left following the 1967 season. In the early 1960s their owner, Jack Kent Cooke, tried to persuade the Toronto city council that a new stadium was needed to attract a major league team, but the city was unwilling to shoulder the costs. After the Maple Leafs left, the stadium was considered to be a safety hazard and demolition began within a few months. The site is currently occupied by apartments shaped like the old ballpark.

Location: Bathurst Street and Lake Shore Boulevard West, Toronto, Ontario, Canada
Status: Demolished 1968
Architect: Chapman, Oxley & Bishop
Opened: 1929
Capacity: 13,000

LEFT: Maple Leaf Stadium in 1934, the year that floodlights were put in. (Photo courtesy Chris Hunter and the Schenectady Museum and Science Center.)

ABOVE: View inside the stadium in 1961.

Location: Putnam Avenue & Ontario Street, Zanesville, OH
Aka: Mark Park Farm Diamond, Mark Grays Athletics Club
Status: Demolished 1939
Opened: 1919
Capacity: 1,600 (1919); 3,000 (1920)
Dimensions:
Left Field 304 ft
Center Field 386 ft
Right Field 265 ft

In 1919 the Mark Manufacturing Company of Zanesville, Ohio, bought a parcel of land and laid out a baseball diamond for use by the factory workers. Known as the Mark Grays Athletics Club, the ballpark initially had bleachers with seating for 1,600 people.

As the use of the ballpark spread beyond the factory staff and more fans arrived to watch games, a new grandstand and clubhouse were built in 1920. With additional bleachers, capacity expanded to 3,000. It was clearly an amateur concern to start with—not only did it lack a Fenway Park–style wall, but right field was so short that several feet of chicken wire was added to the top of the fence to retain big home run hits. In later years, several feet of chicken wire was also added to the top of the left field fence.

With the establishment of the Eastern Ohio League, Mark Park was used for games by the Zanesville team, but the most famous game at Mark Park did not involve the local team. Mark Park was used by barnstorming Negro League teams who lacked a permanent base, and on July 28, 1938, hosted a game between the Homestead Grays and the Memphis Red Sox. Legendary player (and later Hall of Famer) Josh Gibson played right field for the Homestead Grays and hit a remarkable four home runs, including two in one inning. This was the only time such an achievement was accomplished in a Negro League game and not for nothing was Gibson known as the "Black Babe Ruth." (Famously, Babe Ruth said he would be honored to be called the "White Josh Gibson."

Just a year after Gibson cleared the chicken wire in Mack Park, the stadium was torn down and today the site is a residential development.

Location: 3600 N. 51st Avenue, Phoenix, AZ
Status: Home of Arizona League Brewers, and spring training facility for the Milwaukee Brewers
Opened: January 1998
Capacity: 10,000
Dimensions:
Left Field 350 ft
Center Field 400 ft
Right Field 340 ft

RIGHT: The ballpark has a recessed playing field and shaded concourse. As well as 7,000 seats it has an outfield berm that increases capacity by 3,000.

Maryvale Baseball Park is a stadium that is owned and operated by the city of Phoenix Parks and Recreation Department. It has been the home stadium of the Arizona League Brewers rookie league baseball team since 1998 and has also been the spring training home of the Milwaukee Brewers since it opened. The evolution of the facilities owed much to a local developer, John F. Long, who gifted the fifty-one-acre site to the city authorities and assisted in financing the project. Aside from the main stadium, it contains seven practice fields, clubhouses, administrative buildings, and press facilities.

LEFT: The Maryvale complex has seven practice fields and other facilities.

Location: 30 Buchanan Place, Asheville, NC
Status: Home to the Asheville Tourists
Opened: 1924; renovated 1959; rebuilt in concrete 1992
Capacity: 4,000
Dimensions:
Left Field 300 ft
Center Field 390 ft
Right Field 300 ft

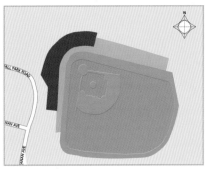

ABOVE: The footprint of McCormick Field.

TOP: McCormick Field is one of the few places where the visitors don't play the home team but the Tourists.

BELOW: Lights were installed in time for the 1930 season.

In 1992 the original wooden grandstand of McCormick Field, once regarded as one of the top classic facilities in the United States, was beginning to show its age. Almost seventy years old, it was becoming a safety hazard and the decision was taken to rebuild it. Officials promised that the new ballpark would echo the sentiment of the former facility, but many fans wondered whether baseball would ever be the same in this town.

What rose up out of the ashes surprised many because the town eschewed a huge modern facility, building instead a small, intimate 4,000-seat ballpark with a covered roof. Asheville had replaced its classic little ballpark with a classic little ballpark.

McCormick Field has been a wonderful attraction for Asheville's residents since the original wooden ballpark was built in 1924. The original was home to five different minor league systems throughout its lifetime: the Piedmont League, the South Atlantic League, the Tri-State League, the Carolina League, and the Southern League. The local team was generally known as the Tourists and has been affiliated to over a dozen major league teams. The Asheville Tourists continue to be a thriving minor league team who are the Single-A affiliates of the Colorado Rockies. They have sent hundreds of their ballplayers to the major leagues, most recently Bobby Abreu, Ed Lynch, Dave Tomlin, and Jamie Wright.

"My, my, what a beautiful place to play. Delightful. Damned delightful place!" said Babe Ruth while playing the outfield during an exhibition game in 1926. Unfortunately, he almost didn't make it there. The season before, an intestinal abscess turned nasty on the train ride in from Knoxville, and he fell off the train into teammate Steve O'Neill's arms on the platform. Rumors spread all over that the mighty Babe had died. Fortunately, after a seven-week stay in an Asheville hospital he recovered, but the "bellyache heard round the word" remains one of the great baseball legends and helped put Asheville on the map.

McCoy Stadium

Location: One Columbus Avenue, Pawtucket, RI

Status: Home of the Pawtucket Red Sox

Opened: June 6, 1946; renovated and reopened April 14, 1999

Capacity: 10,031

Dimensions:

Left Field 325 ft

Center Field 400 ft

Right Field 325 ft

All Star Games: 2004

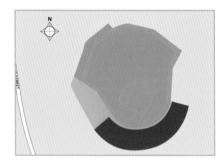

TOP: Within two years of reopening, McCoy could boast its highest ever attendances: 647,928 in 2001, 615,540 in 2002, and in 2005 a remarkable 688,421 watched baseball here.

ABOVE: Footprint of the stadium.

BELOW: There's no doubt the new stadium has brought success, but no repeat of the longest game—in 1981 the Red Sox beat the Rochester Red Wings 3–2 in 33 innings.

Built during World War II, this classic minor league stadium has almost the same richness and history as its big league parent ballpark. While this isn't Fenway Park, it is certainly its eldest son. McCoy Stadium is located in Pawtucket, Rhode Island, a suburb of Providence, and is the home of the Triple-A Pawtucket Red Sox (also known as the PawSox).

McCoy Stadium first began hosting affiliated minor league baseball in 1946, serving the Boston Braves. The Pawtucket Slaters would play for four seasons in the New England League as the Braves' affiliates. Professional baseball disappeared from Pawtucket for eighteen years, before returning in 1966 as a part of the Eastern League. After two years as Double-A affiliates of the Cleveland Indians, McCoy was taken on by the Boston Red Sox in 1970. The Pawtucket Red Sox spent three years in the Double-A Eastern League before being promoted to the Triple-A International League, and the Red Sox have remained there ever since.

When there were whispers in the late 1990s that McCoy was not quite being up to Triple-A standard, fans of ballparks were worried that this could mean the beginning of the end for McCoy Stadium. Fortunately, the owners decided not only to renovate this great facility, but also to preserve the historical integrity of the building.

The renovations began in 1999 and included a new terraced berm in the outfield, which provides great views of the action, and gives families on a budget an inexpensive way to enjoy the ballpark. Above the berms are walkways, providing 360-degree views of the ballpark. New seating was added to the stadium and was made to match perfectly the rest of the grandstand. It's almost impossible to tell where the old section ends and the new section begins. This classic 10,000-seat ballpark is now one of the best in Triple-A. It has gone from vintage to exciting, and continues to draw fans in their thousands.

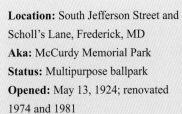

Location: South Jefferson Street and Scholl's Lane, Frederick, MD
Aka: McCurdy Memorial Park
Status: Multipurpose ballpark
Opened: May 13, 1924; renovated 1974 and 1981
Capacity: 2,500
Dimensions:
Left Field 348 ft
Center Field 600 ft
Right Field 506 ft

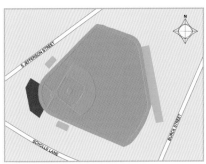

ABOVE: The footprint of McCurdy Field.

TOP and BELOW: McCurdy Field's grandstands were condemned because the beams holding up the roof were rotten. A $150,000 state and federal grant ensured they were rebuilt by 1974. More improvements, including a roof, were made in the early 1980s.

Between 1920 and 1990 (when Harry Grove Stadium was built for the Frederick Keys), McCurdy Field was the home of all professional baseball in Frederick. It cost $15,000 to build in 1924 and was the spring training home of the Philadelphia A's, as well as the Hustlers of the Blue Ridge League. Most recently, McCurdy Field was home to the Frederick Keys, a Carolina League team that began play in 1989.

McCurdy's heyday was probably during World War II, when travel restrictions prevented major league clubs from traveling farther south than the Potomac River for their spring training. Instead they utilized grounds nearer home, and McCurdy hosted the Syracuse Chiefs in 1943, followed by the Philadelphia Athletics in 1944 and 1945.

The Frederick Hustlers were McCurdy's main tenants from 1924, but after they were disbanded in 1950, McCurdy was used mainly by youth teams, notably the Babe Ruth League.

The current stadium structure, which is mainly aluminum, was constructed in 1981 and replaced the 1924 original, which had long since deteriorated. In fact, by 1971, the only thing left was the actual baseball field as the wooden stands and grandstands were condemned as unsafe. The new stadium was built with money raised from donations. It is a small ball field that was most recently home to the Frederick Keys, a Carolina League team that began playing here in 1989. The Keys added a dugout and press boxes up the first and third base lines, complete with electricity and plumbing. It's great that the Keys were able to take this great little ballpark out of retirement and once again make it a useful facility. It has professional-level facilities and is now a multipurpose ballpark that includes a small bleacher section, as well as a scoreboard for football usage.

Location: 1611 Ninth Street, Bradenton, FL

Status: Home of the Bradenton Marauders and spring training facility for the Pittsburgh Pirates

Opened: 1923; renovated 1993

Architect: (Renovation) L.D. Astorino

Capacity: 4,200 (1923); 6,602 (1993)

Dimensions:

Left Field 335 ft

Left Center 375 ft

Center Field 400 ft

Right Center 375 ft

Right Field 335 ft

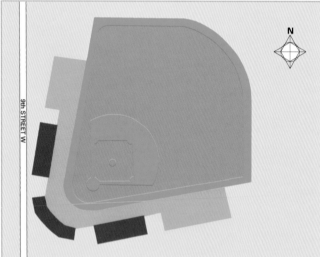

TOP: The Spanish Mission architecture with its white stucco facade was part of the renovations of 1993.

ABOVE: Bradenton is the "Friendly City," and the ballpark is decidedly old-fashioned, without lights and in a neighborhood environment.

Built in 1923, Bradenton Field has seen its share of history. It has been used as a spring training field for major league baseball by five different teams, and currently hosts the Pittsburgh Pirates every March.

McKechnie Field's first tenant was the St. Louis Cardinals, who moved in for the inaugural 1923 season, and stayed till the following season. The Philadelphia Phillies then took over, staying from 1925 until 1927. After the Phillies moved to Winter Haven, the Boston Red Sox came in from 1928 to 1929. The Cardinals made a second appearance in 1930, this time staying seven years until 1936. The Boston Braves (Bees) made their first appearance from 1938 to 1940, and returned again in 1948, remaining until 1962. The Oakland A's then came in for six years, from 1963 to 1968. Finally, the Pirates arrived in 1969, and have remained ever since.

McKechnie Field was completely refurbished in 1993 at a cost of $30 million. New aluminum bleachers were added to hold overflow spring training crowds. The large old-style press box was created and placed behind home plate. Unlike many spring training complexes, the minor league practice fields, dormitories, batting/pitching cages, and recreational facilities are located off-site a mile away at Pirate City. There are four spring training practice facilities there, in the form of a cloverleaf. Scouts, coaches, and fans can watch the game from a centrally located tower. All the Pirates' minor league teams hold their spring training exercises and games at that facility.

Pirate City also hosts Gulf Coast League baseball, the lowest rung of the minor leagues. While baseball fans aren't restricted from these games, GCL baseball isn't publicized and fan attendance is not encouraged. McKechnie Field lies vacant after March 30, not opening up the doors to pro baseball till March 1 of the following season.

In 1993 McKechnie Field was renovated in the Spanish Mission style, which has preserved a wonderful retro baseball look that has been highly praised by baseball fans.

The Met hosted the 1965 All-Star Game that was won by the NL. Over time the stadium started to show its age until in 1982 both the Twins and Vikings moved over to the Metrodome, leaving the old Met at the mercy of vandals. After three years the old stadium was demolished in the early months of 1985. Seven years later the site had become the Mall of America, and in its far northwest corner a brass plaque is embedded in the floor where home plate sat for twenty-eight years.

BELOW: When the Twins and Vikings left Metropolitan in 1982 only the vandals were still interested in the venue. It was demolished three years later and its footprint has disappeared under a vast shopping mall.

The world's most famous Art Deco baseball stadium—Miami Stadium, later to become Bobby Maduro Stadium—opened in 1949. Costing $2,200,000 to build, it became home to many future minor league baseball teams, as well as many future major league teams as a spring training facility, particularly the Dodgers. When the Dodgers moved from Brooklyn to Los Angeles in 1958, they would play their first game ever as the "Los Angeles Dodgers" here in Miami Stadium in a spring training exhibition.

The first team to call this home was the Florida International League's 1949 entry, the Miami Sun Sox. The Sun Sox were christened the new Class B entry of the Brooklyn Dodgers, and were managed by Pepper Martin. The team began the season at Miami Field (now the parking lot of the Orange Bowl) as Miami Stadium's construction was pushed back significantly. They finally moved into this new ballpark near the end of the 1949 season. On August 31, the Miami Sun Sox officially made Miami Stadium (soon to be renamed Bobby Maduro Stadium) their full-time home.

The stadium had a high-arched roof over the grandstand that protected the spectators from the elements without any stanchons to block the view.

When the Florida Marlins left in 1993 (they went on to win the World Series in 1997 and 2003) the stadium lost its main tenant and the City of Miami offered the complex for $1.6 million plus demolition costs for warehousing, but nobody wanted to develop the site at that price. Accordingly, the city changed the zoning allocation to allow residential use and a large housing complex was built instead, called the Miami Stadium Apartments.

Miami Stadium (1949)

Location: 2301 Northwest Tenth Avenue, Miami, FL
Aka: Bobby Maduro Stadium
Status: Demolished 2001
Opened: August 31, 1949
Capacity: Almost 14,000
Opened: 1949
Dimensions:
Left Field 330 ft
Center Field 400 ft
Right Field 330 ft

ABOVE: The classic Art Deco frontage of Miami Stadium.

LEFT: Interior view of Miami Stadium.

(Photos courtesy Kurt Schweizer.)

Location: 1501 NW Third Street, Miami FL
Status: Under construction
Architect: HOK Sport
Opened: Projected for start of 2012 season

The new home of the Florida Marlins is designed by HOK Sport and scheduled to be completed for the start of the 2012 season. Being built at a projected cost of about $515 million, it occupies the site of the former Miami Orange Bowl. Oriented south to east, it features a retractable roof that should open in about fourteen minutes (and weighs as much as the Eiffel Tower) and a grass playing surface. However, the venue will only have a seating capacity of 37,000, the smallest in MLB. The inside temperature when the roof is closed is expected to be 75°F.

Calls for a new ballpark for the Florida Marlins started in the late 1990s, and after much debate over funding and location, the ground was broken on the site in Little Havana in July 2009. The new venue will retain some of the dimensions of the Marlins' former home, Sun Life Stadium, and on opening the team will become the Miami Marlins. A huge plaza will surround the stadium and be filled with retail outfits, restaurants, a hotel, and entertainment facilities.

Location: Along Eliot Street on a site now partially occupied by Invesco Field
Aka: Bears Stadium
Status: Demolished in 2002
Capacity: 76,098 (baseball)
Opened: 1948
First MLB game: April 9, 1993
Last MLB game: August 7, 1994
Dimensions:
Left Field 333 ft
Left Center 366 ft
Center Field 423 ft
Right Center 420 ft
Right Field 400 ft

RIGHT: Mile High Stadium during an MLB game between the Philadelphia Phillies and the Colorado Rockies in May 1993. How to squash a ballpark into a football stadium!

In fifty-three years, Bears Stadium, later Mile High Stadium, only hosted two years of Major League Baseball. The venue was built in 1948 to house 17,000 seated spectators and the minor league team the Denver Bears, all funded by the Howsams, a local family. Originally playing in the Western League, the Bears moved on to join the Triple-A American Association and enjoy one of the most successful legacies in all minor league history.

However, owner Bob Howsam was far from satisfied: he wanted bigger, much bigger, and he wanted a major league team to grace his stadium. In the late 1950s he believed it would happen and rejuvenated the venue and increased capacity to almost 35,000 seats. However, MLB told him he would have to wait, and to his immense frustration he was left with a large and impressive stadium but only minor league baseball.

In 1960 Denver was awarded a franchise from the newly formed NFL and a few years later Howsam sold the stadium to Denver. In 1968 they added another tier of seating so 50,000 fans could attend the games. Additionally, the stadium was renamed Mile High Stadium to celebrate the fact that Denver, at 5,000 feet above sea level, is known as the Mile High City. On the twentieth row of the upper deck the seats become purple, to indicate that the level there is 5,280 feet, exactly a mile above sea level. And here in the thinner air the balls fly farther and curveballs break less sharply—two defining features of Mile High.

Trains are a motif throughout the stadium, starting with the main entrance through the 1911 vintage Union Station. The scoreboard is the biggest in MLB and explodes in celebration of every Astros home run, but the signature feature of Minute Maid Park is a huge 57-foot, 24-ton, 1860s steam locomotive, which chugs down an 800-foot track along the length of the left field roof when the Astros hit a home run or win a game. The tender is filled with giant oranges in tribute to Minute Maid's most celebrated product, orange juice.

In April 1999 the Houston-based energy conglomerate Enron Corporation paid over $100 million phased over thirty years for the naming rights to the field and changed the name to Enron Field. At the park's opener, with soon-to-be president George W. Bush on hand, Enron president Ken Lay threw out the ceremonial first pitch. Two years later the energy conglomerate had gone bankrupt amid scandal. The large Enron sign remained on the park until the Astros bought back the naming rights in February 2002 and temporarily named the venue Astros Field, then in June they sold the rights to Minute Maid (a local subsidiary of the Coca-Cola Company), which agreed to pay an estimated $170 million for a twenty eight-year deal.

BELOW LEFT: The scoreboard has changed since this this photograph was taken. During the 2010–2011 offseason, the Astros installed two new, high-definition video boards with the new primary video board in right field. Now the fourth-largest of its kind in the major leagues, it measures 54 feet high and 124 feet wide.

BELOW: Tal's Hill in center field is named after Tal Smith, a baseball executive who has spent most of his career with the Astros. He received the lifetime achievement award in 2005.

Multnomah Stadium

Location: 1955 SW Morrison, Portland, OR

Aka: Civic Stadium (1966–2001), PGE Park (2001–2010), Jeld-Wen Field (from 2010)

Status: Home to the Portland Timbers and Portland State University Vikings

Architect: A.E. Doyle

Opened: 1926; renovated 2001

Capacity: 20,000

Dimensions:

Left Field 307 ft

Center Field 407 ft

Right Field 348 ft

All-Star Game: 2009

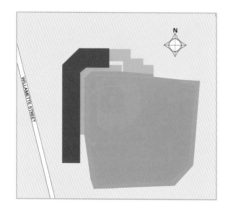

THIS PAGE: In 2001 there was a whopping $38.5 million renovation. The most noticeable difference was the set of luxury and press boxes behind home plate (top). The "new" stadium was renamed PGE Park and the renovations also helped to secure the San Diego Padres' Triple-A franchise from Cashman Field in Las Vegas.

This magnificent facility originated as Multnomah Stadium in 1926, when it was built to serve all sporting events in the Portland area, although originally, baseball wasn't one of them. In fact, dog racing proved to be the most popular draw for many years.

The first baseball team to play at Multnomah was the Portland Beavers, who arrived in 1956 and were the Brooklyn Dodgers' Triple-A farm club. The Dodgers were succeeded by the Cubs from 1957 to 1959, who gave way to the Kansas City Athletics, 1960 to 1961, the St. Louis Cardinals (1961), the Athletics again (1962–64), and finally the Cleveland Indians, who offered some stability to the Beavers by staying for five years until 1969.

The Beavers have been affiliated to sixteen major league clubs over the years, but enjoyed their greatest success under the mantle of the Philadelphia Phillies (1983–86), when they won the Pacific Coast League title in 1983.

In 1966, the Multnomah Club sold the stadium to Portland and the city renamed the ballpark Civic Stadium. While the stadium began to go through renovations, some things remained the same, including the awesome manual scoreboard.

When Triple-A baseball deserted Portland between 1973 and 1977, and again from 1995 to 2000, the Single-A teams the Portland Mavericks and Portland Rockies kept interest alive. The stadium also hosted soccer matches.

The venerable stadium was renovated in 2001 and the naming rights were sold to Portland General Electric (PGE). The city of Portland lavished millions of dollars on the stadium in the hope of attracting a major league franchise, but they were to be disappointed, although Major League Soccer began to show an interest. In 2011, the process was repeated, and after a $31 million renovation, the name was sold to the window manufacturer Jeld-Wen. The Beavers played their last game there in 2010, to be replaced by the professional soccer team the Portland Timbers.

ABOVE: Attendance improved with the 2001 refurbishment: to a staggering (for Portland) 436,000, and then topped out at 452,000 in 2002. The stadium did attract a major team—the Portland Timbers soccer team—and so the Beavers will move to a new stadium because the MLS demands "soccer-only" stadiums.

Connie Mack Field was originally known as Municipal Athletic Field and was the spring training home of the Philadelphia Athletics for many years. The stadium hosted its first event, a football game, in October 1924 and the inaugural baseball game was played the following December. It was renamed Wright Field in 1927 after the West Palm Beach city manager, George C. Wright, but was renamed for the second time as Connie Mack Field in 1952 to honor the renowned long-time Philadelphia Athletics manager and owner. It was superseded by the West Palm Beach Municipal Stadium in 1962, although the stadium's original grandstand remained standing until 1973. The field itself was in use until 1992, but it was then razed to make way for a garage.

Location: West Palm Beach, FL
Aka: Wright Field (1927–1952), Connie Mack Field (since 1952), Mack Field
Status: Demolished in February 1992
Opened: October 1924
First MLB game: December 1925
Capacity: 3,500

LEFT: Cornelius McGillicuddy Sr. (1862–1956)—better known as Connie Mack—seen in 1913, the year he managed the Athletics to their third pennant and third World Series in four years. In 1914 they would win the pennant again, but lose the World Series to the Braves.

Municipal Stadium, Colorado Springs

Location: 4385 Tutt Boulevard, Colorado Springs, CO
Aka: Sky Sox Stadium, Security Service Field
Status: Home to the Colorado Spring Sky Sox
Opened: 1988
Capacity: 8,400
Dimensions:
Left Field 350 ft
Left Center 385 ft
Center Field 410 ft
Right Center 385 ft
Right Field 350 ft

Fortunately for the residents of Colorado Springs, they were the recipients of a fantastic $3,700,000 ballpark in the late 1980s. Originally called Municipal Stadium, it became Sky Sox Stadium, and then Security Service Field but all the while remained the home field of the Colorado Springs Sky Sox, the Triple-A affiliate of the Colorado Rockies, since it opened.

Sky Sox Stadium was home to the Sky Sox for seventeen seasons and, during that time, they won two Pacific Coast League championships, in 1992 and 1995. However, declining crowds and a multitude of problems with the ballpark itself forced the owners to opt for a major renovation program. Construction is continuing and, along with these various changes, the naming rights went to a long-term sponsor of the Sox, Security Service Federal Credit Union, which changed the name of the venue to Security Service Field in 2004.

Municipal Stadium, East Hagerstown

Location: 274 Memorial Boulevard, East Hagerstown, MD
Status: Home of the Hagerstown Suns
Opened: 1930; renovated 1981 and 1995
Capacity: 4,600
Dimensions:
Left Field 335 ft
Center Field 400 ft
Right Field 330 ft

This is the home of the Hagerstown Suns, members of the South Atlantic League. Though based in the Carolinas, this league has been moving steadily northward, gathering teams along the way.

Municipal Stadium was built in 1929–30 and has been a part of many different leagues throughout the years, including the Eastern League, Carolina League, Piedmont League, and the Interstate League. With its wooden plank bleachers and 1940s-style grandstand, this is simply a grand old ballpark!

It's fantastic to have a ballpark like this still operating in this day and age. There's not many like it left anymore, as they are being torn down with alarming regularity. This is baseball from another era.

Hagerstown Municipal Stadium is the site of one of the greatest historical moments in baseball history . . . though no one at the time knew it. Willie Mays, one of baseball's greatest legends, made his professional baseball debut right on this field as a member of the visiting Trenton team in 1950. The Hagerstown Braves were part of the Class B Interstate League at that time.

The aluminum grandstand soaks up much of the heat, and it's actually very comfortable under the roof, even during the hottest months of summer. One of the great things about old parks like this is the closeness to the field. Players are accessible to the fans, and this helps to make the audience feel like they are part of the game. The players are actually close enough that you could practically touch them. This is pure 1930s baseball being played in the twenty-first century.

The stadium has had two major renovations—the first in 1981, when minor league baseball returned. About $546,000 was spent and the overhaul included the installation of a PA system, lights, and new seats and bleachers. The 1995 improvements included new seats and the addition of the Sunset Grille and bar area.

ABOVE: With other, newer parks in the South Atlantic League, Hagerstown's Municipal Stadium looks a little worn and it's likely to be replaced.

RIGHT: The playing surface was renovated after the 2010 season.

The first ballpark in Kansas City was Muehlebach Field, which opened in 1923 when it was home to the minor league Kansas City Blues. It had cost $400,000 to construct and could seat 16,000 fans in a one-tiered, mostly covered grandstand. The Blues were bought as a farm team in 1937 by the New York Yankees, at which time the stadium was renamed Ruppert Stadium after the Yankees owner; four years after he died the stadium was renamed again to become Blues Stadium.

The other tenants of Muehlebach Field since opening day were the Kansas City Monarchs, who played there since the start; they were the Negro Leagues' equivalent to the New York Yankees and were the longest-running Negro National League franchise. In 1924 and 1925 they appeared in back-to-back Negro League World Series—both against the Hilldale Daisies, winning the first in 1924 but losing the following year. They left the stadium in 1955.

Location: Intersection of 22nd Street and Brooklyn Avenue, Kansas City, MO

Aka: Muehlebach Field (1923–1937), Ruppert Stadium (1938–1942), Blues Stadium (1943–1954)

Status: Demolished in 1976

Architect: Osborn Engineering

Opened: July 3, 1923

First MLB game: April 12, 1955

Last MLB game: October 4, 1972

Capacity: 16,000 (1923); 35,561 (1969)

Dimensions:

	Original 1923	Final 1969
Left Field	350 ft	369 ft
Left Center		408 ft
Center Field	450 ft	421 ft
Right Center		382 ft
Right Field	350 ft	338 ft

All-Star Game: 1960

World Series: 1924, 1925 (Negro Leagues)

Municipal Stadium, Kansas City

ABOVE: Lineup for the opening game of the first Negro League World Series, October 11, 1924.

Late in 1954 Kansas City got the news they were waiting for—major league baseball was coming to town. The relocating Philadelphia Athletics were due to arrive for the 1955 season, and in preparation for the event the ballpark's grandstand was enlarged so that ground capacity was upped to 30,000. To accompany the changes the ballpark was renamed Municipal Stadium in time for the arrival of the Kansas City A's. The A's had a controversial owner, Charlie Finley, who aggravated the league by continually playing to the edge of the rules: one notorious time he created an area of bleachers known as the "Pennant Porch," which considerably shortened right field, making home runs much easier—the league quickly asked him to revise it.

Other features of Municipal Stadium were the picnic area behind right field and a small zoo which housed the A's mascot, Charlie O the mule. During the period of two All-Star Games per year, the ballpark held the first game in 1960, with the NL coming out on top 5–3.

In 1962 the AFL's Kansas City Chiefs moved in to share the facility and stayed until 1971. And in 1964 the Beatles played a sell-out concert at Municipal during their first U.S. tour.

In the mid-1960s Kansas City offered to build a new stadium for their teams, but Finley got a better offer from Oakland, California, and moved the A's there. Luckily for the citizens of Kansas City, MLB was looking to expand and so they were happy to award them a new AL franchise—the Kansas City Royals were created and played at Municipal until 1973.

TOP: 1965 aerial view with two-tier grandstand but without the bleachers added in the 1969 upgrade.

RIGHT: The two-tier grandstand under construction.

ABOVE and BELOW: Two early views of the single-tier ballpark.

Location: 18th Avenue at Eighth Street Northeast, Pompano Beach, FL

Status: Demolished 2008

Opened: March 22, 1957

Last MLB game: 1990

Capacity: 4,500

Dimensions:

Left Field 350 ft

Center Field 410 ft

Right Field 350 ft

Municipal Stadium, Pompano Beach

LEFT and BELOW: Two contrasting photographs. The first (left) shows the ballpark in its latter years without the central grandstand. The second (below) in its heydey, when the Senators used it with the central grandstand in place.

Opened in 1957, Pompano Beach was a small and simple hodgepodge of bleachers and grandstands, but became spring training home to the Washington Senators and the Texas Rangers. It also hosted the minor league Pompano Beach Cubs from 1976 to 1978.

Pompano Municipal Stadium in its final years was a rickety old ballpark with a small capacity, but it had historic roots, despite being a pretty ordinary ballpark. Two separate and totally different grandstands made up most of the seating at this stadium—particularly after the press box and the roofed grandstand had been demolished. It seemed as if the stadium was gradually allowed to decay. It was not used for professional play after 1990 and it was battered in a number of hurricanes. In all, Pompano hosted two major league teams over twenty-six spring training seasons, four minor league teams lasting eleven seasons, and one senior circuit team—not bad for a small stadium with limited facilities.

In 1954 the Washington Senators settled on the little Municipal Stadium in Pompano Beach, a ballpark that had never before hosted a major league game, and remained there for their spring training for eleven years. In 1972, the Senators became the Texas Rangers, and although one might imagine the new team would want new training facilities, nothing could be further from the truth. The Rangers remained for fifteen years, finally moving out in 1987.

Pompano Beach found it difficult to get new tenants and the Rangers were not replaced by another major league team. In 1989 a new professional league was established, the Senior Professional Baseball Association, which was made up of players over the age of 35 who attempted to create their own "senior circuit." The Gold Coast Suns split their time between Pompano Beach and Bobby Maduro Stadium in Miami. Sadly, it was a short-lived venture and Municipal Stadium in Pompano Beach did not host a professional game after this. It was finally demolished in 2008.

BELOW LEFT and BELOW: Demolished in 2008, it hadn't been used for professional play since 1990. It is always sad when an historic ballpark is demolished—particularly when it has served as a major league spring training stadium for twenty-six years.

Municipal Stadium, Savannah

Location: 1401 East Victory Drive, Savannah, GA

Aka: Grayson Stadium

Status: Home of the Savannah Sand Gnats

Opened: 1927; refurbished 1995 and 2007

Capacity: 8,500

Dimensions:

Left Field 322 ft

Center Field 400 ft

Right Field 310 ft

Opened in 1926 and with a capacity of 8,000, Grayson Stadium is home to the Savannah Sand Gnats, the Single-A affiliate of the New York Mets. It is the oldest working minor league ballpark in the United States and, with its brick facade shadowed by weeping trees, one of the most picturesque stadiums, too.

When it was built in 1926, Municipal Stadium (as it was known) was home to the Savannah Indians for just two years before the team folded. In the spring of 1927 it hosted an exhibition game between the defending World Series champion St. Louis Cardinals and the New York Yankees, starring Babe Ruth and Lou Gehrig. Major league play returned in 1932 when the Boston Red Sox used Municipal Stadium for spring training. During the Depression of the 1930s there was no professional baseball at the stadium until the Indians were revived in 1936 and 99,000 fans came to watch their first season. The Indians went on to win their fourth league championship the following year.

A hurricane destroyed both their winning streak and the entire wooden stadium apart from two sections of bleachers in 1940. Led by Spanish-American War veteran General William L. Grayson, the city of Savannah rebuilt the stadium and renamed it in honor of the man who had done so much to reconstruct it.

Baseball resumed in earnest after the war to sellout crowds and the team has undergone several name changes according to their major league affiliation. The Sand Gnats have called Grayson Stadium home since 1996, and despite four changes of affiliation, the name seems to be as tenacious as the pesky insect.

Seventy years on, it is still a lovely ballpark, with most of the seating under a large covered stadium, in addition to bleachers along the third base side and in left field. It was refurbished in 1995 and again in 2007, but while modern facilities were installed, care was taken to retain the historic features.

Municipal Stadium, Syracuse

Location: Syracuse, NY

Aka: MacArthur Stadium (1942–1996)

Status: Demolished 1996

Opened: 1934

Capacity: 8,500 (1934); 10,000 (1942)

Dimensions:

Left Field 320 ft

Center Field 434 ft

Right Field 320 ft

RIGHT: Municipal Stadium, by then named MacArthur Stadium, was razed to make way for the new Alliance Bank Stadium (now renamed P&C Stadium). (Photo courtesy Gary Jarvis, minorleagueballparks.com)

Opened in 1934, Municipal Stadium in Syracuse hosted minor league baseball from 1937 until 1996, when the ballpark was demolished to make way for the new Alliance Bank Stadium. It was renamed in 1942 in honor of General Douglas MacArthur.

When MacArthur Stadium opened in 1934, the Boston Red Sox were the first team to make this their International League home. Then, with the exception of seasons 1956 and 1957, when MacArthur served the Double-A Eastern League, this ballpark had always been a Triple-A facility and hosted the International League for six decades.

The Red Sox remained at MacArthur for three seasons until 1937, when they gave way to the Cincinnati Reds. The Reds remained with the Syracuse Chiefs for two years until

1939, when the Chiefs played for the International League as an unaffiliated ball club. The Pittsburgh Pirates came in for one season in 1940, then left the following year. Again, the Chiefs were unaffiliated, but that would only last one season.

In 1942, the Cincinnati Reds came back to Syracuse, and this time stayed for nine years until 1950. After two seasons as an unaffiliated team, the Chiefs joined up with the Yankees for a year in 1953. The Yankees left in 1954 but came back to stay for a decade in the late 1960s. Dormant for three seasons after the departure of the Eastern League in 1958, MacArthur returned to pro baseball with the arrival of the Minnesota Twins' Triple-A team in 1961.

The Syracuse Chiefs played uninterrupted at MacArthur from 1961 until 1996, when they moved to the new Alliance Bank Stadium. They were affiliated to the Detroit Tigers, the New York Yankees, and the Toronto Blue Jays in this period. The Yankees were an especially welcome addition to Syracuse, as it was the first time that a local team called MacArthur Stadium home. Ron Guidry is probably the one player who every Syracuse fan remembers from this era.

Sadly, this classic stadium was demolished in 1996 and replaced with a new Triple-A facility, the Alliance Bank Stadium.

ABOVE: In 1942 the ballpark was renamed MacArthur Stadium for the general who had just won a Medal of Honor for his defense of the Philippines. (Photo courtesy Gary Jarvis, minorleagueballparks.com)

LEFT: The Yankees were welcomed to Syracuse and stayed for eleven years. (Photo courtesy Gary Jarvis, minorleagueballparks.com)

The first professional baseball league was founded in the United States in March 1871: the National Association of Professional Base Ball Players, or simply the National Association, is regarded by some baseball historians as the first major league.

There were twenty-five original members of the league, which included most of the professional clubs then in existence. The Cleveland Forest Citys were founder members and the league's first game—and the first professional game ever—took place in Fort Wayne between the Forest Citys and the Fort Wayne Kekiongas on May 4, 1871. The crowd numbered 200 and Fort Wayne won. The *New York Times* reported breathlessly that it was the "finest game of base-ball ever witnessed in this country."

The Forest Citys were the first fully salaried team in Cleveland and their home ground was the National Association Grounds, a new field located at Wilson and Garden. As more than half the teams in the National Association were on the East Coast, the Forest Citys embarked on an extensive tour on May 11, 1872, and it is uncertain how many games they actually played at home in Cleveland. They were not a particularly successful team, finishing seventh out of nine teams in 1871. After improving their performance only slightly in 1872, when they finished sixth, the team folded at the end of the season.

Location: Wilson Avenue, Cleveland, OH
Status: Defunct
Opened: May 11, 1871
Closed: August 19, 1872

National Association Grounds

National League Park

Location: In an area bounded by West Lehigh Avenue, North 15th Street, West Huntingdon Street, and North Broad Street, Philadelphia, PA

Aka: Philadelphia Base Ball Grounds (1887–1895); Baker Bowl; Huntingdon Street Grounds

Status: Demolished 1950

Architect: John D. Allen; Al Reach (rebuild)

Opened: April 30, 1887; rebuilt 1894

Last MLB game: June 30, 1938

Capacity: 18,000 (1887); 18,800 (1894)

Dimensions:
Left Field 341 ft
Center Field 408 ft
Right Center 300 ft
Right Field 272 ft

World Series: 1915; 1924–1926 (Negro Leagues)

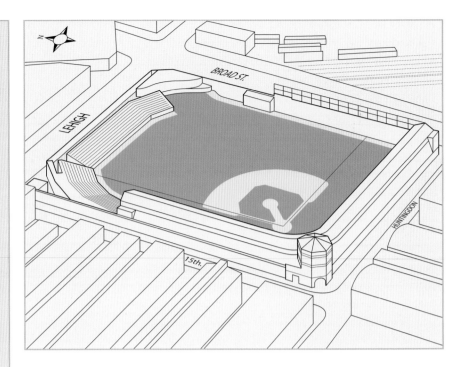

The Philadelphia Phillies have been in the National League, under one name or another, since 1883, when they were known as the Quakers. The first Baker Bowl, though it was called National League Park at the time, was built in 1887 and could hold 18,000 seated spectators and was encircled by a fairly low brick wall. In these early years the ballpark shook to the sounds of the railroad tracks located behind center field. Many years later, the railroad was substantially lowered and fed through a tunnel while the field above was extended over the top; this area became known as "the Hump" after the raised area it created. Also, the once four-foot-high wall was incrementally raised until the right field wall became an immense sixty feet high.

The pavilion could hold 5,000 seated spectators and the grandstands along the left and right field lines a further 7,500 fans. On August 6, 1894, a devastating fire started and by the time it had burned out almost the entire ballpark was destroyed with the exception of part of the exterior outfield wall (this solitary remainder was later incorporated into the stadium that became Baker Bowl II). The estimated $80,000 worth of damage was covered by insurance. Temporary stands were hastily erected for the game on August 18 and used for the rest of that season.

ABOVE: Baker Bowl's bleachers in 1915.

RIGHT: Aerial photograph dated around 1931. Note Shibe Park at left and Baker Bowl at right.

The National League Grounds opened on May 2, 1895. It was notable for being the first ballpark built predominantly of steel and brick and was the first sports stadium to have cantilevered upper decks. Because of this, it has been acclaimed as the "first modern ballpark." The spectators were seated in a grandstand that, thanks to the new concept of cantilevered concrete supports, had far fewer obstructed vision seats than its predecessor or, for that matter, any other contemporary ballpark.

The ballpark became known for its right-field wall that would resonate with a distinctive noise whenever it was hit. The original wall—only 280 feet from home plate—had been brick-built, but after criticism that it made home runs too easy, it was raised to 60 feet using a mixture of metal pipes, wood, metal, and wire. But the rough lower surface frequently skinned fielders, so a layer of steel was placed all over the wall except for the very top. As if to make the wall even more dominant, a huge sign for Lifeboy Soap was painted there.

Between 1913 and 1930 the owner of the Philadelphia Phillies was William F. Baker, and the ballpark became increasingly referred to as Baker Bowl in deference to him. However, for much of their first ninety-three years, the Phillies were underachievers, managing only two pennants, in 1915 and 1950, and no World Series titles.

Located on a tight city grid plot, the ballpark was known for its constraints (hence its nicknames of the "Band Box" and the "Cigar Box"). The short right field was 279 feet down the line and only partly offset by the tall wall.

The Baker Bowl was heavily criticized in its later years—and Baker was seen as being penny pinching. The Phillies abandoned it after the 1938 season in favor of sharing Shibe Park.

In the 1920s and 1930s the Baker Bowl was a frequent home of The Negro League's Hilldale Daisies. Then, between 1933 and 1935, Baker Bowl was home ground for the newly franchised Philadelphia Eagles NFL team, making the venue the first dual-use professional ground in Pennsylvania.

Location: 1500 South Capitol Street SE, Washington, D.C.

Status: Home of the Washington Nationals

Architect: HOK Sports (now Populous)

Capacity: 41,546

Opened: March 22, 2008

Dimensions:

Left Field 336 ft

Left Center 377 ft

Center Field 402 ft

Right Center 370 ft

Right Field 335 ft

ABOVE: Home plate entrance. Twenty percent of the park is constructed from recycled materials. The dates highlight important moments in Nationals history—1859 was the year that the Nationals, the first club in Washington, D.C., were organized.

BELOW and OPPOSITE, BELOW LEFT: These views inside the stadium show the great sightlines enjoyed by fans around the ballpark.

Washington was without professional baseball for three decades until April 2005 when the Montreal Expos moved south to become the Washington Nationals and play in the National League.

In anticipation, the city invested over $18.5 million to upgrade RFK Stadium for baseball and also pledged to build a modern state-of-the-art $535 million dedicated baseball stadium to be called Nationals Park, which opened in time for the 2008 season. Politicians and locals alike got involved in the long and heated discussions as to where the ballpark should be sited: eventually a site was selected in southeast D.C. at South Capitol and N Streets.

The ground was broken in early 2006 and construction went along quickly to adhere to the ambitious two-year building plan: it was built to schedule using 20 percent recycled materials and opened on time after a cost of $611 million. The exterior is an innovative design of glass and white precast concrete covering a steel structure in keeping with Washington's impressive environs. The playing field was constructed twenty-four feet below street level, meaning a little over half the fans don't have to climb stairs or use elevators to get to their seat.

The Washington Monument and the Capitol are visible from parts of the upper deck on the left side of the field. The ballpark features the statues of three historic Washington ballplayers: Walter Johnson of the original Washington Senators, Frank Howard of the expansion Senators, and Josh Gibson of the Negro League Homestead Grays. The main high-definition scoreboard is five times bigger than the old board at RFK at 101 feet long by 47 feet high. Also, in the right field wall is an out-of-town scoreboard.

Nationals Park is the first sports facility in the United States to be Leadership in Energy and Environmental Design (LEED) certified. The ballpark was designed to be energy efficient and minimize water pollution into the nearby Anacostia River. Nationals has a contemporary design with half of its seats on the lower deck nearer the action. In all there are some 41,000 seats around the infield all angled so each has a great view of the playing field, plus seventy-nine luxury suites. From the main concourse almost the entire playing field is visible, so fans need not miss out on any of the action or entertainment while buying food. In addition to numerous food and retail outlets, there is a popular interactive kids zone which opens three hours before every game.

ABOVE: Aerial view of Nationals Park looking over the home plate entrance.

BELOW: Footprint of Nationals Park.

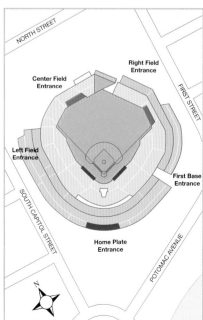

Navin Field

Location: 2121 Trumbull Avenue, Detroit, MI

Aka: Briggs Stadium (1938–1959); Tiger Stadium (1959–1999)

Status: Demolished 2008–2009

Architect: Osborn Engineering

Capacity: 23,000 (1912); 52,416 (1938)

Opened: April 20, 1912

Last MLB game: September 27, 1999

Dimensions:

	Original 1926	Final 1938
Left Field	341 ft	340 ft
Left Center	365 ft	
Center Field	467 ft	440 ft
Right Center	370 ft	
Right Field	371 ft	325 ft

World Series: 1934, 1935, 1940, 1945, 1968, 1984

All-Star Game: 1941, 1951, 1971

Navin Field was built for the Detroit Tigers by Frank Navin over winter 1911. It was a concrete-and-steel venue built to house 23,000 spectators and opened on April 20, 1912 (the same day as Fenway Park in Boston). In 1924 a second tier was added to the stands behind home plate to bring the capacity up to 30,000.

Navin Field became the well-worn intersection of Michigan and Trumbull, and a corner where baseball was played for more than a century. The unique feature of Navin was the 125-foot flagpole standing in play in center field, making it the tallest in-play obstacle in major league history!

In 1934 the World Series came to Navin Field but the Tigers lost in seven games to the St. Louis Cardinals; however, the following year the Tigers triumphed with a 4–2 margin against the Chicago Cubs.

Frank Navin died in 1935 and the new owner, Walter Briggs, decided to update the ballpark; capacity was upped to 36,000 immediately and by 1938 after double tier stands were built in the outfield the stadium could accommodate 53,000 fans. Furthermore, the ballpark had taken on its distinctive shape and changed its name to Briggs Stadium. To help finance the changes the NFL's Detroit Lions made the stadium their home and stayed until 1974.

TOP and ABOVE: 1950s postcard and 1951 aerial view of the then Briggs Stadium.

BELOW: 1920 view looking toward left field—there are said to be 100,000 people in this crowd.

In 1940 the Tigers hosted the Cincinnati Reds in the World Series at Briggs only to narrowly lose 4–3. The following year the All-Star Game came to Briggs despite it being one of the few major league parks not to possess floodlights; these were installed in 1948, making the Tigers the last team in the AL to outfit their stadium for night baseball. In 1945

the Tigers again appeared in the World Series, and beat the Cubs. A few years later in 1951 Briggs Stadium hosted the All-Star Game, with the NL triumphing in what would be Joe DiMaggio's last midsummer classic.

John Fetzer became the new owner of the Tigers in 1961 and Briggs Stadium was renamed to become Tiger Stadium. No more major changes occurred until an extensive refurbishment program in the 1980s, and then blatant commercialization with huge exterior beer signs in the 1990s. The World Series again came to Detroit in 1968 (victory against St. Louis) and in 1984 (victory over San Diego), and another All-Star Game in 1971. Then in September 1999 the Detroit Tigers moved to Comerica Park.

ABOVE: 1935 left-field bleachers under construction.

LEFT and BELOW: Interior images taken shortly before demolition. Tiger Stadium was rusting away and the city gave preservationists a deadline to raise funds. When they weren't forthcoming, demolition began in July 2008. There was a further pause, but officials lost patience so the demolition was finished in 2009.

Neil Park

Location: 512 Cleveland Avenue, Columbus, OH

Status: Demolished 1937

Opened: April 15, 1900; rebuilt 1905

Capacity: 4,500 (1905); 6,500 (1910)

Completed at a cost of $64,000 in 1905, Neil Park was an extraordinary structure, not just because it was the first concrete-and-steel baseball stadium, but because the building it replaced on the same site had been dismantled and moved across town.

The Columbus Senators joined the Interstate League in 1900 and it seemed to the management that they were not drawing many fans at their home games at Athletic Park on the outskirts of Columbus. Instead of simply constructing a new stadium elsewhere, the team moved their existing stadium via the Columbus Street Railway System to a new site, 512 Cleveland Avenue. The wooden structure was rebuilt and renamed after Robert Neil, the owner of the land.

Three years later, and with the Senators by now a successful minor league team in the American Association, a new stadium was built. Neil Park was initially a 4,500-seat stadium, its concrete-and- steel construction announcing to the world that the Senators could afford a top-quality ballpark that was far more permanent than the old wooden structure. In 1909 America's second concrete-and-steel stadium was constructed at Forbes Field in Pittsburgh, and gradually other clubs followed the example of Columbus.

"Despite the cold weather," reported the *New York Times* on April 6, 1905, "over 4,000 shivering baseball fans turned out today to witness the dedicatory game at Neil Park," when New York beat Columbus 9–4.

The Senators repaid the investment by winning the league in 1905, 1906, and 1907, but their later performance never recaptured their early glory. Capacity was increased by 2,000 in 1910 when a new grandstand section was added.

After the Senators became the Red Birds and part of the St. Louis Cardinals' franchise, they remained at Neil Park until June 1932, when they moved to the new Red Bird Stadium.

Neil Park was also used by the Negro National League's Columbus Buckeyes, the team run by John Henry Lloyd and Sol White in 1921.

ABOVE: Footprint of Neil Park in 1921.

New Britain Stadium

Location: 230 John Karbonic Way, New Britain, CT

Status: Home to the New Britain Rock Cats

Architect: Kaestle Boos Associates

Opened: April 12, 1996

Capacity: 6,100; record 8,790 on June 18, 2010

Dimensions:

Left Field 330 ft

Center Field 400 ft

Right Field 330 ft

All-Star Game: Eastern League, July 16, 2003

Home of the New Britain Rock Cats, New Britain Stadium was built in 1995 as a permanent replacement for Beehive Field. The latter was an aluminum stadium that had housed minor league baseball since 1983 and although only a little over a decade old, it was obsolete by the mid-1990s after a whirlwind of design changes altered the thinking behind ballparks. Old and even recent stadiums were quickly being scrapped in favor of beautiful ornamental ballparks with a retro feel.

The Boston Red Sox originally held their Double-A camp at Beehive Field, having moved there from beautiful vintage Muzzy Field in nearby Bristol. By the early 1990s, there was much talk about replacing the relatively new Beehive Field with one of these "super retro" ballparks. It wasn't easy, trying to explain why a nine-year-old ballpark was completely outdated. The Red Sox gave up the fight, and instead moved into one of those "super retro" ballparks in Trenton, New Jersey. The Minnesota Twins picked up the torch and continued the fight. Within two years, they had proven that Beehive Field was no longer a viable ballpark.

RIGHT and OPPOSITE: New Britain Stadium was built in Willowbrook Park, a sports complex which now includes two professional baseball stadiums, the other being the Rock Cats' earlier venue, the Beehive (opposite, bottom left).

New Britain Stadium was built to hold 6,100 fans in Willowbrook Park, a sports complex which now includes two professional baseball stadiums (the former Red Sox facility, Beehive Field, and the new Twins ballpark), and the Veterans Stadium football/soccer venue.

With New Britain Stadium completed, the Twins settled in and use this ballpark as their Double-A home. New Britain Stadium is a welcome respite from old Beehive Field, perhaps the worst ballpark in the Eastern League—and New Britain is perhaps one of best.

BELOW: New Britain Stadium is visible over right field in this photograph of the Beehive, a 4,000-capacity ballpark that opened in 1983. The Rock Cats played there until New Britain opened.

Newark Schools Stadium was a striking landmark in the Roseville suburb of Newark, New Jersey. Nicknamed "the Old Lady of Bloomfield Avenue," the stadium was used for a variety of sports, primarily football, although when it opened in 1926, it was also home to the Newark Stars of the Negro League.

Built by Thomas J. Scully, the same man who constructed Rupperts Stadium, it was a reinforced-concrete horseshoe-shaped stadium and had a capacity of 15,000. It hosted NFL games, concerts, athletics, and hundreds of school sports events. The great Jesse Owens ran here before he hit his Olympic stride. It was an iconic fixture in Newark, a traditional stadium that resembled the Colosseum—in more ways than one by the time of its demise in 2006, when the facade had deteriorated and it was deemed unsafe for players and spectators.

The Newark Stars were the only pro baseball team to use the facility, but eighty years after their demise, school baseball teams played there regularly. The Stars were Newark's first major Negro League team and played in the Eastern Colored League for just one year, 1926–27, shutting down halfway through the season after a solitary win against ten losses.

The decision to condemn the stadium in 2006 outraged sports fans, but was inevitable after decades of neglect. However, in 2011 a new stadium will open, reconstructed at a cost of $24 million, from the shell of the old building, but featuring state-of-the-art sporting facilities. There will be two baseball fields, an eight-lane running track, a field marked for football, soccer, and lacrosse, as well as ample locker rooms, a community center, and associated facilities. Capacity will be about 5,000 and it is expected to be used entirely for school sporting events.

Location: 450 Bloomfield Avenue, Roseville, Newark, NJ
Aka: The Old Lady of Bloomfield Avenue
Status: Demolished 2009
Opened: 1925
Capacity: 15,000

Newark Schools Stadium

Location: San Antonio, TX

Aka: San Antonio Municipal Stadium, the Wolff, "the Jewel of the Texas League"

Status: Home of the San Antonio Missions

Opened: 1995

Capacity: 9,200

Dimensions:

Left Field 310 ft

Center Field 402 ft

Right Field 340 ft

Located almost ten miles west of the Alamo and downtown San Antonio, opened in May 1995 and is used primarily for baseball. A concourse surrounds the playing field and gives fans varied views of the game. It is the home of the (TL) San Antonio Missions, Double-A affiliate of the San Diego Padres. The University of Texas–San Antonio Roadrunners baseball team also plays some home games here. The $10 million venue has official seating for 6,200 but can hold a further 3,000 on the berm in left field. Lackland Air Force Base is just behind the outfield wall.

RIGHT and BELOW: The stadium has seating for 6,200.

Location: In a block from Nicollet Avenue, 31st Street, Blaisdell Avenue, and Lake Street, Minneapolis, MN

Aka: Wright Field

Status: Demolished in 1955

Opened: June 19, 1896; renovated 1909 and 1911

Last game: 1955

Capacity: 4,000 (1896); 10,000 (1911); 10,500 (final)

Dimensions:

Left Field 334 ft

Center Field 432 ft

Right Field 280 ft

Nicollet Park, a ballpark from the mid-1890s, stood well into the mid-1950s, serving the Triple-A American Association Minneapolis Millers, although it would need constant maintenance due to fires and rotten wood. Originally built for a cost of $4,000, the new ballpark, which was briefly known as Wright Field, was spacious compared to the one the Millers had left, but soon became known for its modest dimensions, particularly the short distance to the right-field fence. Home plate was in the southwest corner, with a grandstand that extended down the third-base line along Blaisdell Avenue and down the first-base line, along West 31st Street, which separated the ballpark from the garages of the local transit company.

Over the following years, the ballpark was renovated. The main grandstand was rebuilt prior to the 1909 season with a tier of box seats put in front of the regular seats, necessitating the moving of the players' benches as well as the press box. In addition, repairs were made to the third-base bleachers, and the first-base bleachers were converted into a roofed grandstand. The main entrance was also moved to the 31st Street side of the ballpark. Greater changes took place after the 1911 season: for $30,000 these included a new grandstand and bleachers. The main entry remained at the corner of 31st and Nicollet, with a walkway running underneath the grandstand to the seats on the third-base side and an inclined walk, replacing stairs, taking fans into the stands on the first-base side of the field.

The winds of change were starting to blow through the Twin Cities during the 1950s. While both local teams were focused on beating each other, they were also dead set on landing a major league team. In order to do so the two teams came to the same conclusion. The only way to win a major league franchise was to demolish their vintage ballparks and build modern facilities. The ballparks were demolished within a year of each other and replaced by major league stadiums. The Millers played their final season at Nicollet Park in 1955 and then moved to the huge Metropolitan Stadium. In 1983 a historical marker was put up on 31st and Nicollet, on the site of Nicollet Park, today the Northwood Bank Building.

BELOW LEFT to RIGHT: Nicollet Park's distinctive home plate entrance; looking out over home plate from the grandstand; watching from the left-field grandstand. The Millers played their final season at Nicollet Park in 1955, winning ninety-two games and an American Association championship.

Oakdale Park, a long-gone ballpark, was used for amateur baseball from around the time of the Civil War and very briefly served as the Philadelphia Athletics' home in 1882, their first year in the American Association. The ballpark was situated at the junction of Huntingdon Street to the north, 11th Street to the east, Cumberland Street to the south, and 12th Street to the west. Oakdale Park was abandoned at the end of the 1882 season and the Athletics moved to Jefferson Street Grounds for the 1883 season. The old ballpark was sold shortly thereafter and then demolished. Baker Bowl was built a few blocks west of the old stadium site five years later.

Location: In a block formed by Huntingdon Street, 11th Street, Cumberland Street, and 12th Street, Philadelphia, PA
Status: Demolished in 1883
Opened: May 2, 1882
Closed: Fall 1882

Oakdale Park

Oaks Park, which was also known as Oakland Baseball Park and nicknamed Emeryville Park, was home to the Pacific Coast League's Oakland Oaks from 1913 until 1955. It was located in Emeryville between Oakland and Berkeley and the stadium was bounded by 45th Street to the north, San Pablo Avenue to the east, Park Avenue to the south, and Watts Street to the west. The Oaks had been playing most of their home games at Recreation Park in San Francisco, once that new ballpark opened in 1907. Even after moving back to Oakland in 1913, the Oaks still played a number of games in San Francisco during each season as the Pacific Coast League's founder, J. Cal Ewing, owned both the Oaks and the San Francisco Seals from 1903 until the 1920s. The Oaks played all their games in Oakland from 1922.

Lights were installed in 1931, although players complained that they created shadows, particularly in the outfield. Brick Laws and Joe Blumenfeld purchased the club from Cookie Devincenzi at the close of the 1943 season and they spent $250,000 upgrading the park. However, the team was soon to face declining attendance and, having had enough of playing in an aging ballpark, decided to move to Vancouver in 1956. This was two years before Major League Baseball came to the Bay Area and twelve years before the arrival of the Oakland Athletics. Oaks Park, which had never been suitable for hosting major league games, was long demolished by then. Today the site is part of a Pixar Studios expansion plan and will become a parking lot with a public bicycle path and park.

Location: San Pablo and Park Avenue, Emeryville, CA
Aka: Oaks Park; Emeryville Park
Status: Demolished
Opened: 1879
Capacity: 7,000 (1879); 14,000 (final)

Oakland Baseball Grounds

Location: 7000 Coliseum Way, Oakland, CA

Aka: Oakland-Almeda County Coliseum (1966–1998, 2008-2011); UMAX Coliseum (1997); Network Associates Coliseum (1998–2004); McAfee Coliseum (2004–2008); Overstock.com Coliseum (May 2011); Oakland Coliseum, the Mausoleum

Status: Current home of the Oakland A's

Architect: Skidmore, Owings & Merrill

Capacity: 43,662 (1968); 35,067 (2006)

Opened: April 17, 1968

Dimensions:

	Original 1968	Final 1996
Left Field	330 ft	330 ft
Left Center	378 ft	362 ft
Center Field	410 ft	400 ft
Right Center	378 ft	362 ft
Right Field	330 ft	330 ft

World Series: 1972, 1973, 1974, 1988, 1989, 1990

All-Star Game: 1987

Determined not to live in the shadow of their more glamorous neighbor San Francisco, the politicians and businessmen of Oakland decided to construct their own professional sports venue to attract their own MLB and NFL franchises. After much consideration Oakland Coliseum was built for $25.5 million beside the newly built Nimitz Freeway in East Oakland on 120 acres of land.

The American League stated in 1961 that they would be interested in including an Oakland-based team in their West Coast expansion plans. Accordingly, construction started in spring 1962 although it was delayed for two years by legal issues and cost difficulties. The resulting building was circular, with the interior containing an almost complete three-tiered grandstand, and opened on September 18, 1966, with an NFL game.

The building is partially sunk into the ground, which in turn gives the illusion that it is much smaller than it really is. Internally this means that the playing surface is twenty-one feet below sea level, so when fans enter the venue they walk into the main concourse at the top level of seats.

They had the venue, but Oakland still needed an MLB team. However, over in Kansas, the owner of the Kansas City A's wanted a move away; and, impressed with Oakland's new Coliseum, agreed to move his franchise. The Oakland Athletics played their first game on April 17, 1968.

The Coliseum quickly established a reputation as a pitcher's park, with the largest foul territory in MLB. The massive center field grandstand was added for the football crowd. As a venue for the Oakland Athletics, it was considered to be a reasonable if rather unexciting ballpark, but by the early 1970s it was beginning to look a little run-down and earned itself the soubriquet of "the Oakland Mausoleum" even when the play was exciting and the Athletics were regularly winning pennants. On one notable occasion in April 1979, only 653 paying spectators attended a game against the Seattle Mariners.

The Oakland Raiders left in 1981 when they moved to Los Angeles, leaving the A's as the only full-time tenants of the Coliseum, although the venue was frequently used for live music concerts. Then, in July 1995, the Raiders agreed to return to what was now called the Oakland-Alameda County Coliseum, provided a number of changes were made using an investment of $200 million: More seats for football meant removing the outfield bleachers and replacing them with a four-tier grandstand. Luxury seats were added and two giant video boards installed, as well as other football-related improvements. During this time, the A's had to play some of their home games away in Las Vegas.

To pay for the renovations, the naming rights were sold, first to become the UMAX Coliseum in 1997, then after a legal tussle the original name was restored after only a year. In 1998 the rights were sold again, this time to Network Associates, which in 2004 changed their name and that of the Coliseum to McAfee. Since then, a six-year naming deal has been struck with Utah-based Overstock.com. The deal states that the company will pay $1.2 million the first year. That cost increases by three percent in each subsequent year.

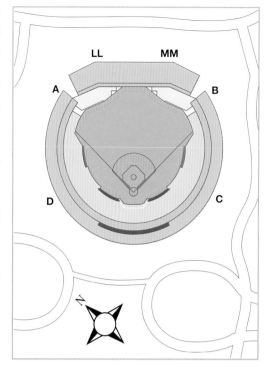

ABOVE: Footprint of the Coliseum.

LEFT: Oakland Athletics during the game against the Chicago White Sox on May 15, 2011. Note the empty upper tier that reduces capacity to 35,000 and the two giant video boards.

BELOW: The stadium has rung the changes when it comes to names—here it is the Network Associates Coliseum.

ABOVE: 1988-vintage photograph looking over home plate. A large grandstand would have filled this view from 1995. (Photo courtesy Jerry Reuss.)

Location: Oakville, MD
Status: Dilapidated
Opened: 1945

RIGHT and BELOW: Back during the 1940s, Maryland had a thriving baseball league called the Eastern Shore League that served as a Class D minor league system. All of the large local towns in the Chesapeake Bay area had a team to call their own. Segregation was still in full swing, and black ballplayers were not allowed to play on white teams. In response, the Delmarva Peninsula also had a thriving Negro League of its own, playing at many of the smaller towns throughout the area. Oakville Stadium fell into disrepair (as above right) and seemed likely to be lost, but recent work has made a substantial improvement.

In the era of segregation, Negro League Park, located in Oakville in St. Mary's County, Maryland, was the home of Oakville's Negro League ballclub. The Delmarva Peninsula, down the backroads of the Chesapeake Peninsula, had a popular Negro League of its own, which attracted a large number of fans, both black and white.

Few Negro League teams had their own ballparks, and of those stadiums, only a handful survive today. Oakville is one, along with three in New Jersey, all of which were specifically for Negro League use. Interestingly, although black players were barred from the major and minor leagues, the Negro League welcomed white players.

Today, the stadium is a shadow of its former self, with a rusting roof and a battered seating area, but its very existence and survival is cause enough for celebration. This may have been considered a modest ballpark by the standards of the day, but it's obviously one of the truest classics today. Oakville's ballclub was also one of the most talented in the league and won many Negro League championships. Oakville's Negro League Park is a national treasure long forgotten. Perhaps that's a good thing, because it's still here today and has been overlooked by progress, searching for the bigger and better.

Located in Burbank, California, and once the spring training home of the St. Louis Browns, Olive Avenue Park Stadium (soon to be renamed Olive Memorial Stadium) was built in 1947 at a cost of $64,425, for youth and recreational baseball. For a short period of four years, the ballpark shone in the spotlight of the preseason. It was apparently packed with fans, often 2,500 deep, to see spring training games—something that had not yet happened for regular season baseball. It was 1949 and the St. Louis Browns were enjoying the postwar boost that baseball received.

After moving from one ballpark to another, the Browns settled at Olive Memorial Stadium for four years from 1949. It was also the longest they would remain in one place for the rest of their tenure in St. Louis, before they moved to Baltimore to become the Orioles.

Olive Memorial Stadium came alive each March with a huge fan base, but as this was Burbank and central to Hollywood, the fans included Bing Crosby, Bob Hope, Dinah Shore, and Nat King Cole. Even Marilyn Monroe stopped by for a game to mingle with the players for publicity photos.

Despite the celebrity endorsement, the Browns were not a great team in this era. In fact, they weren't very good at all, losing between ninety and 102 games a year during their tenure in Burbank. Nevertheless, they still managed to draw crowds of 2,500 for their spring training games.

One exception to the generally mediocre levels of play was the arrival in 1951 of Satchel Paige, who spent the bulk of his career in the Negro League, but still retained the flashes of brilliance in the early 1950s that made him one of baseball's greatest pitchers.

With the departure of the Browns in 1953, major league spring training never returned to Burbank, and the stadium's final swan song was in the 1992 movie *The Babe*. In 1995 the stadium was demolished following earthquake damage, as the cost of renovation was considered too high.

Location: 1111 W. Olive Avenue, Burbank, CA
Aka: Olive Avenue Park Stadium
Status: Demolished in 1995
Opened: 1947
Closed: 1989
Capacity: 1,000
World Series: 1944

BELOW: After the Browns left town at the end of the 1952 campaign, Olive Memorial Stadium never saw professional baseball again.

BELOW: Olive Stadium's swan song came in 1992 when Babe Ruth was portrayed by John Goodman in the Universal Studios release *The Babe*.

Location: College Station, TX

Status: Home to the Texas A&M Aggies

Opened: March 21, 1978

Capacity: 7,053

Dimensions:

Left Field 330 ft

Center Field 400 ft

Right Field 330 ft

RIGHT: Olsen Field is usually packed on game days. Behind the left field wall (out of frame on the right of picture) in the Student Recreation Center parking lot is the area known as Aggie Alley, where tailgating parties take place—and opposing left fielders bear the brunt. In 2000 a new LED scoreboard was unveiled and it was moved to the left-field wall.

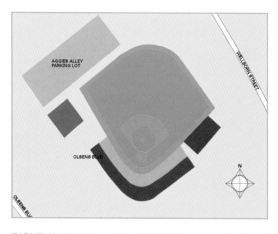

RIGHT: Having been expanded in 1994, Olsen Field has a permanent seating capacity of 7,053, although against Texas the stadium has recorded attendance of over 8,800. This rises to over 11,000 if one includes the 2,500 in Aggie Alley.

Olsen Field is the home of baseball at Texas A&M University and the ballpark was officially opened on March 21, 1978. It was named in honor of Pat Olsen, a 1923 graduate of the university who went on to play with the New York Yankees. The playing surface is Tifway bermuda grass.

Since opening, Olsen Field has served often as an NCAA regional site and its regional attendance was ranked second, recording an impressive 53,287 visitors in 1999. The first NCAA regional tournament was held at the ballpark in 1989 and *Sports Illustrated on Campus* ranked Olsen Field "the best college baseball venue" in 2004.

The Texas A&M University's athletics department is in the preliminary stages of preparing improvements and upgrades for Olsen Field that have been estimated at around $16 million. The plans include a student athletic center, extending seating nearer to the field, and updating the Aggie Alley parking lot.

Location: In a block within 16th Street NW, 17th Street NW, and S. Street NW, Washington, D.C.

Aka: National Grounds

Status: Demolished

Opened: 1870

Last MLB game: June 8, 1875

Capacity: 500

Olympic Grounds was home to the National Association's Olympic Club of Washington D.C., or Washington Olympics, during 1871 and 1872, and then to the short-lived Washington clubs of 1873 and 1875, including the Washington Blue Legs in 1875. It is generally considered a major league ballpark by those who believe that the National Association qualifies as such. The ballpark was situated between 16th Street NW to the east, 17th Street NW to the west, and S. Street NW to the south in an area about a mile from the site of the later Griffith Stadium. The old ballpark was demolished long ago and the land is now a mixture of homes and commercial properties.

Olympic Park was briefly the home of the National League's Buffalo Bisons from 1884 to 1885. Buffalo's baseball teams actually played at an unnamed park known today as Riverside Park from 1878 to 1884, but the owner of the site, Alexander Culbert, then decided to redevelop the stadium and the team therefore left for Olympic Park.

The Bisons' new ballpark was located on the northeast corner of Richmond Avenue and Summer Street and bounded by Norwood Avenue. Professional baseball in the shape of the International League continued to be played there until the lease expired in 1888. After the conclusion of that season the team temporarily settled at a stadium located on East Ferry and Michigan Avenue, but the last professional game was played there in September of the same year, when the Buffalo Bisons took on the Cuban Giants. The wooden stands were then packed up and taken to Woodlawn Avenue, where they were used until rebuilt in 1924 as Offermann Stadium. An outlaw Buffalo Bisons franchise played just one season at Olympic Park in 1890 but the ballpark was eventually demolished. The land is now a residential neighborhood.

Location: Corner of Richmond Avenue and Summer Street, bounded by Norwood Avenue, Buffalo, NY
Status: Demolished in the 1890s
Opened: 1884
Last official game: September 1888

The former home of the Grays Harbor Gulls, Loggers, Ports, Rain, and Mets, Olympic Stadium is the largest wooden ballpark existing today. The short season Single-A Northwest League called this home for a period of time, as did the Western League, although its pro ball history is less impressive. There was talk of the stadium being past its best and its future was being discussed by the city fathers. Luckily, one contacted digitalballparks.com and together they were able to prove the stadium's historical status, so it was placed on the National Register of Historic Places in 2006, the year it was also renovated.

Despite serving amateur baseball and football for decades, it wasn't until the late 1970s that professional baseball arrived. The first team, the Northwest League's Grays Harbor Ports, arrived in 1976 and were an expansion franchise that served as a co-op team, independent of Major League Baseball. The Grays Harbor Ports were gone by 1977 and replaced by the Grays Harbor Loggers, who again were an independent co-op team also playing in the Northwest League. This team did well, winning the Northwest League championship, the only time that any Grays Harbor team has won a title. Their excellent play finally brought Grays Harbor a major league affiliation when the New York Mets made the Loggers their Single-A franchise.

Some record books have the team listed as the Grays Harbor Loggers while others as the Grays Harbor Mets. Either way, the Mets were awful. Olympic Stadium would lose professional baseball for fifteen years, returning to amateur and scholastic baseball and football. It wasn't until the new Western Baseball League (WBL) was established that it would be in the spotlight again. The WBL comprised two divisions and the "North" featured four teams from the Pacific Northwest, including the Grays Harbor Gulls. They would play the majority of their games at Olympic Stadium and the rest at Pioneer Park in Aberdeen.

A month into the season, the Gulls' ownership said they could no longer play in Hoquiam, as attendance was too low to keep the franchise afloat. The league office took over the club while the team was on the road, and they would never go home again. As it became clear the Grays Harbor Gulls were no more, the league changed their name mid-season to the Western Warriors. When the league finally disbanded in 2005, many of the better baseball clubs went on to join the Golden Baseball League, an independent professional minor league that still thrives throughout Mexico, the U.S., and Canada. Olympic Stadium, however, has never again been a venue for professional baseball.

Location: 101 28th Street, Hoquiam, WA
Status: Used for amateur games
Architect: Works Progress Administration
Opened: November 24, 1938
First professinal game: 1976
Capacity: 9,000; 10,000 with overflow

THIS PAGE and OVERLEAF: Hoquiam boasts the largest wooden ballpark around today, much of which is found in its unusual right-field biased grandstand, which also runs alongside the football field. Shingle-backed and roofed, it helps protect the spectators from the vicious weather that comes in off the Pacific.

Location: 4549 Avenue Pierre de Coubertin, Montreal, Quebec, Canada

Status: Still standing, but not used by MLB

Architect: Roger Taillibert

Opened: April 15, 1977; renovated 1992

Last MLB game: September 29, 2004

Capacity: 43,739

Dimensions:

Left Field 325 ft

Left Center 375 ft

Center Field 404 ft

Right Center 375 ft

Right Field 325 ft

All-Star Game: 1982

ABOVE: The distinctive exterior of Montreal's Olympic Stadium.

RIGHT: Aerial view of the futuristic Olympic Stadium. The roof was supposed to be retractable. In reality it didn't work, and remained closed.

OPPOSITE: After being utilized for the 1976 Olympic Games, La Stade Olympique was transformed for the Montreal Expos. Attendance could be good—59,057 watched the All-Star Game in 1982—but fell away and the Expos played many games during the 2003 and 2004 seasons in Puerto Rico's Estadio Hiram Bithorn, before eventually moving to Washington, D.C. (Opposite, center left courtesy Jerry Reuss.)

In 1977 the Montreal Expos moved into the 1976 Montreal Summer Games Olympic Stadium, which was then modified for baseball. Unfortunately, Olympic Stadium earned the reputation of being one of the worst MLB stadiums ever, despite its exorbitant construction cost, along with a continual roster of problems.

The supposedly retractable roof is suspended from a 522-foot leaning tower, but that wasn't finished until 1988, so the roof never worked the way it was supposed to. After 1992 it remained closed, and was then removed for the 1998 season to be replaced by a permanently closed roof.

The team itself never enjoyed much luck: the only year they were doing well, 1994, the players' strike called off the playoffs and World Series. Then in 1991 a 55-ton roof beam fell onto the playing field, forcing the Expos to play some of their "home" games on the road. In late 2004 it was announced that the Expos franchise was moving to Washington, D.C., for the 2005 season, and they became the Washington Nationals.

Location: 1202 Bert Murphy, Omaha, NE

Aka: Johnny Rosenblatt Stadium (since 1964), the Blatt

Status: Slated for demolition

Opened: 1948

Capacity: 12,000 (1949); 25,500 (2011)

Dimensions:

Left Field 335 ft

Left Center 375 ft

Center Field 408 ft

Right Center 375 ft

Right Field 335 ft

World Series: College World Series, 1950–2010

ABOVE RIGHT and OPPOSITE, TOP: This pair of photographs shows the growth of the stadium as it went from success to success. Today, however, it seems likely that it will be torn down.

BELOW and RIGHT: Over the years the CWS has become a major event, and the city has spent over $35 million in upgrades to keep the stadium up to scratch. It created the largest ballpark in the minor leagues. Media interest in the CWS led to the unusual luxury/press box suite on stilts and the large glassed-in auxiliary press box behind the first-base grandstand—the changes are highlighted in this pair of photos—1980s (right) and today (below).

Built in 1949, Omaha's Rosenblatt Stadium is the home of minor league baseball in Omaha. When the Omaha Cardinals first joined the Western League in 1947, Omaha Municipal Stadium wasn't quite finished, so the Cardinals actually played their first two seasons in Council Bluffs, Iowa, at the American Legion Ballpark.

The move to Omaha in 1949 was very welcome. The new stadium had a traditional look to it, with a roof and a press box hanging over the top. Omaha was able to maintain their affiliation with the St. Louis Cardinals during the move to the new ballpark, and St. Louis remained affiliated with the team for the eight years that it served in the Western League.

In 1950 Rosenblatt Stadium hosted its first College World Series (CWS), which had previously been played in Kalamazoo, Michigan, but moved to Omaha after the stadium was completed. Over sixty years later, more than five million fans have passed through the gates of Rosenblatt Stadium for the CWS. The CWS has grown in popularity and Rosenblatt Stadium (it was renamed in 1964, in honor of Omaha mayor Johnny Rosenblatt) has grown with it. Capacity has increased from 12,000 in 1959 to 14,000 in 1980, when the cable network ESPN began broadcasting CWS games. By the 1990s, over 23,000 fans could be accommodated, making Rosenblatt the largest ballpark in the minor leagues.

Omaha's home team since 1969, the Royals have been affiliated to the Kansas City Royals for thirty-five loyal years, surviving two changes of name and finally, in 2010, a change of stadium, when the team moved to Werner Park as the Omaha Storm Chasers.

Rosenblatt Stadium was a fantastically well-equipped facility and was one of the best-used ballparks in the United States. Sadly, pro baseball has moved on, leaving it to the Omaha Nighthawks soccer team, and an uncertain future. In March 2011 it was sold to the Henry Doorly Zoo next door, and is likely to be demolished.

BELOW: By 1980, further expansion had increased capacity to over 14,000. The grandstand itself began to look more like the stadium that it is today. The outfield also began to feature its first set of stands. The popularity of the CWS, however, was just beginning. Within a decade of the photo above, the seating capacity of Rosenblatt would double from its original 12,000 in 1959. Note the expansion of the right and left field bleachers. In its final form, the Blatt was too large for the Royals and too small for the CWS. The final CWS game was played on June 29, 2010 (the South Carolina Gamecocks defeated the UCLA Bruins). The final game for the Royals was played on September 2, 2010, with the Royals defeating the Round Rock Express.

Oriole Park (1882–1889)

Aka: Huntington Avenue Park, American Association Park

Opened: 1882

Last MLB game: 1889

Oriole Park (1890–1891)

Opened: 1890

Last MLB game: 1891

Oriole Park (1891–1899)

Aka: Union Park

Opened: Spring 1891

Closed: 1899

Capacity: 30,000 (1891); 11,000 (1897)

Dimensions:

Left Field 300 ft

Right Field 350 ft

Oriole Park (1901–1915)

Aka: American League Park

Opened: 1901

Last MLB game: 1902

Closed: 1915

Dimensions:

Left Field 360 ft

Center Field 435 ft

Right Field 281 ft

The first field called Oriole Park, also known as Huntington Avenue Park and American Association Park, was the first home of the American Association's Baltimore Orioles from 1882 to 1889. The Orioles moved four blocks north in 1890 and opened a new Oriole Park, now commonly known as Oriole Park II. This field briefly served as the team's home during 1890 and January 1891 but the club next opened Union Park—also called Oriole Park or Oriole Park III—in early 1891 and called it home for the remainder of the decade, switching to the National League when the American Association imploded. Despite their successes of the 1890s, the Orioles were dropped when the league was reduced from twelve to eight teams in 1900.

The newly formed American League arrived the next year and the reinvigorated team opened a new Oriole Park, sometimes known as American League Park. It was located on the same site as the second park, but the Orioles played for just two seasons before they became the team now known as the New York Yankees. Baltimore was reduced to minor league status, with a team in the Eastern League (later the International League) playing at the fourth Oriole Park.

ABOVE: Union Park was the third version of Oriole Park and would stay in use until 1899.

BELOW: The ticket count for the first game at Union Park in May 1891 was 10,412, but the *Baltimore Sun* reckoned that as a serious undercount of the number who saw the game since many more watched from "house tops, fences and trees." A similar crowd has assembled here on October 11, 1897. In the distance, the deciding run of the final game for the Temple Cup is being scored.

This wooden ballpark was the home of the Federal League's Baltimore Terrapins for two seasons, 1914 and 1915. It was built on a block bounded by 11th Street, York Road, 10th Street, and the diagonal slash of Vineyard Park, and was directly across the street from the existing Oriole Park IV. Terrapin Park was built especially to stage games for the new Federal League. Construction started on February 1, 1914, and was complete for opening day on April 13, 1914. These days the site is hidden under a cluster of buildings a little north of its contemporary Oriole Park. After the 1915 season, the venue was bought by the International League's Baltimore Orioles, who renamed the venue Oriole Park.

The Baltimore Orioles stayed for twenty-eight and a half seasons, during which time they were a very successful franchise, winning seven straight International League pennants. Because of the old park's wooden structure, it was carefully hosed down after games, but on July 3, 1944, the inevitable happened. Possibly started by a carelessly left glowing cigarette stub, a fire broke out and completely consumed everything at the ballpark.

The Orioles had to move to Municipal Stadium for the rest of the season, where they attracted a much bigger crowd than could fit into Oriole Park. The large postseason crowds at that stadium, which had a far greater capacity than Oriole Park, were soon noted by the MLB. Thanks to the Orioles' on-field success and those large crowds, the city chose to rebuild Municipal Stadium as a multipurpose major league facility and renamed it Memorial Stadium. Baltimore became a major league city again in 1954.

Location: 10th Street, York Road, 11th Street, and Vineyard Lane, Baltimore, MD
Aka: Terrapin Park
Status: Destroyed by fire, July 3, 1944
Opened: 1914
Capacity: 14,000 (1944)
Dimensions:
Left Field 300 ft
Center Field 450 ft
Right Field 335 ft

LEFT: Baltimore's most famous son. Babe Ruth was born in Baltimore in 1895 and signed for the Baltimore Orioles on February 14, 1914. Babe Ruth is second from the left in the lineup.

BELOW: Terrapin Park had lights installed in September 1930. It would eventually burn down in 1944.

Oriole Park at Camden Yards

Location: 333 West Camden Street, Baltimore, MD

Status: Home of the Baltimore Orioles

Architect: HOK Sports

Capacity: 48,876 (1992); 45,971 (2010)

Opened: April 1992

Dimensions:

Left Field 333 ft

Left Center 364 ft

Center Field 410 ft

Right Center 373 ft

Right Field 318 ft

All-Star Game: 1993

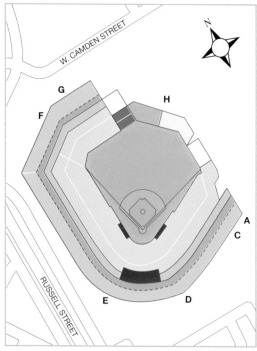

Design-wise, Oriole Park at Camden Yards was a leader in baseball venue design. Gone were the anodyne cookie-cutter coliseums in favor of modern style, but with distinct heritage overtones. The site lay between the train tracks, which led to the busy inner harbor area. Called "the Yard," it had a brick facade, an asymmetric outfield, views of downtown Baltimore, and the massive bulk of the B&O warehouse: all features reminiscent of the days of Babe Ruth, who was born just two blocks away—his father even owned a tavern in the area now occupied by center field. This nostalgic atmosphere cost $110 million to construct and was much admired and imitated within a decade by ballparks across the U.S.

Money was raised for the construction by the sale of lottery tickets, endorsed by the local legislature in part for the revival of downtown Baltimore by the construction of such a prestigious project. Maryland governor William Donald Schaefer called Oriole Park "the largest single economic development opportunity we have had in the last decade."

The architects, HOK Sports, had cleverly incorporated the best features of other ballparks (such as Shibe Park, Forbes Field, Wrigley Field, and the Polo Grounds): retro steel trusses, cozy seating arrangements, and the rustic clock on the center field scoreboard. The ballpark was an instant classic. Modern amenities include the lucrative luxury boxes, a family picnic area, and microbreweries.

TOP: Aerial view of Camden Yards. Note the long line of the redbrick B&O warehouse. The first of the so-called retro classics, Oriole Park is recognized as being the best of the recent crop of MLB stadiums.

ABOVE: Footprint of and entrances to Oriole Park.

RIGHT: The brick exterior blends in with the B&O warehouse and gives a strong retro feel.

Outside along Eutaw Street, which runs between the B&O warehouse and the outfield bleachers, shiny bronze baseballs are embedded into the walkway.

Oriole Park is overshadowed only 432 feet away by the eight-story, redbrick 1895 B&O warehouse, which at over 1,000 feet long was said to be the longest building on the East Coast and built to accommodate long railroad cars. Other features are: double-deck bullpens built one above the other, allowing both teams to warm up and have full sight of the game while doing so; and a statue of Babe Ruth entitled "Babe's Dream," by sculptor Susan Luery. Before the 2011 season, all the seats in the lower seating bowl were replaced and a number of skyboxes were eliminated to allow more party suites and luxury boxes, reducing capacity by about 300.

ABOVE: Opening day 2011: note the double-deck bullpens to the left of the batter's eye and the HD video display and scoreboard installed above the right-field bleachers in 2008.

BELOW LEFT: Eutaw Street, with its shops and concessions, is usually busy on game days.

BELOW: Two of the seats are orange to commemorate the landing of home runs by Hall of Famers Cal Ripken Jr. and Eddie Murray.

Osceola County Stadium

Location: 631 Heritage Park Way, Kissimmee, FL

Status: Home of the Gulf Coast League Astros and spring training for the Houston Astros

Opened: 1984

Capacity: 5,300

Dimensions:

Left Field 325 ft

Center Field 405 ft

Right Field 325 ft

RIGHT: View from right field toward the clubhouse.

BELOW: Footprint of the stadium; aerial view of the complex showing practice fields alongside; and front entrance and gandstand building. The Astros are guaranteed tenants until at least 2016.

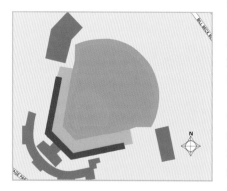

Built in 1985, Osceola County Stadium was designed to be the newest and most innovative facility of its day. With a modern design and new amenities, Kissimmee was able to lure the Houston Astros out of Cocoa Beach to be their first tenants, and the team remains there today. One of the most innovative ideas was the introduction of the cloverleaf design of four training fields, in which the home plates meet at a central point. This means that scouts, managers, front office staff, and medical teams can stand in the middle and watch four practice fields and four games simultaneously. Many spring training facilities built since Osceola was finished have used the design as a blueprint.

The stadium has a capacity of 5,300, which is the smallest of any stadium in the Grapefruit League. In 2003 it underwent an extensive $18.4 million renovation in order to maintain its reputation as one of the best major league spring training ballparks. One of the largest and most noticeable improvements is the clubhouse in left field, which houses the training and dressing facilities of the Astros. The seating was also upgraded to all-armchair seating. In return for the $18 million in renovations, Osceola County received some serious loyalty: the Astros have signed a long-term contract that guarantees they will continue to play in this ballpark until 2016.

The Osceola Astros were Kissimmee's first professional baseball team and played in the Florida State League from 1985 to 1994, having been moved from Daytona Beach. After several years of disappointing performances, their name was changed to the Kissimmee Cobras in 1995, and they played at Osceola until 2000, winning the FSL championship in 1999. In 2009 the Gulf Coast League Astros filled the minor league gap in Osceola. The team is composed almost entirely of rookies.

The stadium is also home to the national headquarters for the United States Specialty Sports Association (USSSA) and the USSSA Hall of Fame and Sports Museum.

Location: 1 Tex Simone Drive, Syracuse, NY
Aka: Alliance Bank Stadium (from 2005)
Status: Home to the Syracuse Chiefs
Architect: Klepper, Hahn & Hyatt
Opened: April 10, 1997
Capacity: 12,000
Dimensions
Left Field 330 ft
Center Field 400 ft
Right Field 330 ft

LEFT: Looking over to right field, the white building is the Hank Sauer banqueting suite. It pays tribute to the only player in Syracuse franchise history to have his uniform number retired.

BELOW: Footprint, external view, and main grandstand of the stadium.

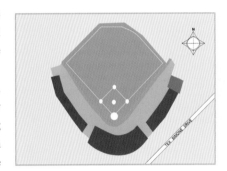

Alliance Bank Stadium is the home of the minor league Syracuse Sky Chiefs and is a first-class Triple-A facility. It originally had an artificial AstroTurf surface because of the team's onetime affiliation with the Toronto Blue Jays (1978–2008), who play on an artificial surface. This has been replaced by natural grass, and the team is now affiliated with the Washington Nationals.

Known as the P&C Stadium from 1997 until 2005 when P&C Foods sponsored it, Alliance Bank replaced the fabled MacArthur Stadium, a true classic that was beloved by baseball fans from 1934 till 1996, when it was demolished (and the new stadium parking lot now covers the site). With its Blue Jay blue seats, the new P&C Stadium, constructed in 1997 and costing $16 million, is a pleasant change from Camden Yards clones that litter the American landscape with red bricks and green seats. Alliance Bank Stadium, however, is itself a clone—there is an almost identical ballpark built for the Mets' Triple-A team at Harbor Park in Norfolk, Virginia.

It has a capacity of 12,000, and is within a short drive along the New York Thruway of two other Triple-A stadiums, Dunn Tire in Buffalo and Frontier Field in Rochester. Since 1998 the Chiefs have competed every year with local rivals the Rochester Red Wings and the Buffalo Bisons for the minor league Thruway Cup.

Location: Richmond, VA

Status: Demolished in 1985; replaced by the Diamond

Opened: 1934; renovated 1954

Architect: L.D. Astorino (renovation)

Capacity: 9,500

Dimensions:

Left Field 335 ft

Left Center 375 ft

Center Field 400 ft

Right Center 375 ft

Right Field 335 ft

courtesy Bill Mountjoy
www.digitalballparks.com

Parker Field was a multi-use stadium in Richmond, Virginia, with a capacity of 9,500. The field had been built in 1934, as part of the fairgrounds. It was named after Dr. William H. Parker, who helped with the construction of the field, and was converted for baseball in 1954, replacing Mooers Field. It was, initially, the stadium of the Richmond Virginians (1954–1964) and later housed the Triple-A Richmond Braves of the International League (1966–1984). It had two separate grandstands: a longer section which ran down third base and then around home plate, and a separate section down the first base line. Both sections were covered with a roof and were known for huge lighting banks which stood on top of them. Parker Field was replaced by the Diamond in 1985.

ABOVE and TOP: Internal and external views of Parker Field. Note the huge lights. (Photos courtesy Bill Mountjoy.)

Location: Eastern Parkway and South Brook Street, Louisville, KY

Aka: Colonels Field

Status: Defunct

Opened: May 1, 1923

Capacity: 13,242

Dimensions:

	Original 1939	Final 1949
Left Field	331 ft	329 ft
Center Field	512 ft	485 ft
Right Field	350 ft	345 ft

RIGHT: Several star major leaguers played at Parkway Field, including Babe Ruth in 1924, 1928, and 1932, and Jackie Robinson in 1946.

Parkway Field was a minor league baseball and college stadium. It was home to the Louisville Colonels of the American Association from 1923 until 1956, and then to the University of Louisville team for several decades until they abandoned it in 1998 and moved to Cardinal Stadium.

The ballpark, which was sometimes known as Colonels Field, was built by William F. Knebelkamp in 1923 for $100,000, but the locals were not greatly impressed with the project to begin with, as baseball did not have a large following in Louisville. However, once the

large concrete-and-steel stadium with its impressively large grandstand had been unveiled, most changed their minds as nothing on its scale had been built in Louisville before. The left-field wall was especially tall to protect passersby on the road beyond and the large, hand-operated scoreboard was certainly impressive. The grandstand was torn down in 1961, but some brick walls remained for a time.

Location: Andrew Avenue, Sarasota, FL

Status: Demolished in 1990

Opened: February 1, 1924

Capacity: 4,000 (1951)

Dimensions:

	Original 1924	Final 1963
Left Field	375 ft	352 ft
Center Field	500 ft	415 ft
Right Field	375 ft	352 ft

LEFT and BELOW: Baseball has been a tradition in Sarasota since 1924 when the New York Giants were the first team to train at Payne Park. These aerial views were taken before (left) and after (below) the press box was added.

BELOW CENTER: This shot was also taken before the park's trademark press box topped the grandstand.

Payne Park hosted some of baseball's greatest teams for spring training from 1923 until 1988. The facility cost $18,000 to construct. The New York Giants arrived at Payne Park in 1923, when the park featured a very simple wooden grandstand with five arches in the back and a two-section pointed and slightly slanted overhang. It also featured a long running bleacher section down the first base line. The Giants would remain at the original Payne Park for four seasons, from 1924 to 1927.

The ballpark was altered significantly in 1933, when the grandstand became deeper and acquired a covered back. It was still a very modest ballpark, however, as most of the seating was bleacher-type down the lines. The changes were a direct result of the arrival of the Boston Red Sox, who played here from 1933 until 1942, when they were forced to remain closer to home for their spring training because of wartime travel restrictions. After the war the Red Sox returned for another thirteen years, from 1946 until 1959.

Payne Park was upgraded again in 1951, with the addition of a larger grandstand behind the plate, whose sides were now closer to home plate. The bleachers were now made of aluminum and were a little "deeper" around first and third base, with some extra sets pushing further down the lines. Capacity was now just over 4,000.

During its time as the spring training facility of the Red Sox, this stadium was home to such greats as Ted Williams, Joe Cronin, Lefty Grove, and Jimmie Foxx. They were succeeded in 1960 by the Chicago White Sox, who were accompanied by the Kansas City Athletics' minor league affiliate, the Sarasota Sun Sox. The White Sox introduced their own Single-A team in 1962, who also played as the Sarasota Sun Sox until 1965.

The White Sox remained at Payne Park until 1988, installing a press box in the early 1960s, but otherwise leaving the ballpark unchanged. In 1989 the city of Sarasota began building a modern ballpark and the White Sox moved their operations to the new Ed Smith Stadium that year. Payne Park was leveled and turned into a tennis facility, and is now a public park space.

RIGHT: It was during the early 1960s that Payne Park's final configuration was completed, with a press box that ran across the top of the grandstand. This press box wasn't always used as the main radio/TV booth. The smaller press box to the left of the grandstand at the top of the first set of bleachers (behind the light pole) served as a radio/TV booth to many broadcasters.

Pendleton Park

Location: Ridgeley Street, Humbert Street, Babby Alley, and Watson Street, Cincinnati, OH
Aka: Pendleton Grounds, East End Park
Status: Demolished c1891
Architect: Al Marcus
Opened: April 25, 1891
Capacity: 5,000

Pendleton Park, which was later known as East End Park, was very briefly home to the American Association's Cincinnati Reds, a team more commonly known as "Kelly's Killers" after flamboyant Mike "King" Kelly, during the 1891 season. These east side Reds have no links with the Cincinnati Reds team that switched from the American Association to the National League in 1890. This decision led the association to field a team of its own in Cincinnati for the next year. This decision thus gave the city two major league teams in the same year and with the same nickname. Adding to the confusion was the presence of another Reds team in the association, the Boston Reds. All of these Reds teams derived their nicknames from the original Cincinnati Red Stockings of 1869–1870. Kelly's search for a suitable field led him to what was at the time the east end of the city, to a picturesque location on the banks of the Ohio River that was known as either Pendleton Park or Pendleton Grounds. He leased part of the area and built a small ballpark in 1891, which the newspapers soon named East End Park.

Penmar Park

Location: Philadelphia, PA
Status: Demolished
Aka: Parkside Bowl, Bolden Bowl, 44th and Parkside Ballpark
Opened: 1920s
Capacity: 6,000
Dimensions:
Left Field 330 ft
Center Field 410 ft
Right Field 310 ft

Originally built in 1903 for football and athletics and named the Athletic Field of the Pennsylvania Railroad Y.M.C.A., Penmar Park at 44th and Parkside was modified for baseball in the 1920s, and lights for night games were added in 1933. It became the home of the Philadelphia Stars from 1936, after they moved from their former ballpark, Passon Field, until the team disbanded in 1952. Although it was their main ballpark, they also played many of their Monday night games at Shibe Park, which was the home of the Philadelphia Athletics and Phillies at the time. During this period Negro League World Series games were often played at neutral ballparks to attract larger crowds. The Cleveland Buckeyes beat the Homestead Grays in the fourth game of the 1945 series at 44th and Parkside Ballpark, and the third game of the 1947 series was also played at the stadium, with the Buckeyes taking on the New York Cubans.

Peoria Sports Complex

Location: 8131 West Paradise Lane, Peoria, AZ
Architect: HOK Sport (now Populous)
Opened: 1994
Capacity: 12,882
Dimensions:
Left Field 310 ft
Center Field 410 ft
Right Field 310 ft

The facilities at the complex are extensive and include twelve full-size practice fields, of which several are lit by floodlights. Four half fields, eight covered major league hitting tunnels, twelve minor league hitting tunnels, and thirty practice mound galleries are also available. Each of the two clubhouses covers some 40,000 square feet and there are more than 400 lockers.

Several sports teams call the facility home. The San Diego Padres and the Seattle Marines have had their spring training at the 145-acre complex since 1994. The Peoria Javelinas and the Peoria Saguaros of the AFL have also been based at the stadium since it opened.

BELOW LEFT: Peoria seats over 12,000 comfortably.

BELOW: As well as the main stadium, the Padres and Mariners have six practice grounds each in the complex.

One of the finest early minor league parks in America was built in Indianapolis in the 1930s on the site of the former Washington Park ballpark. Opening as Perry Stadium in 1931, it was the home of the Indianapolis Indians and could accommodate 15,000 seated spectators. Perry Stadium was also an important location for the development of Negro League baseball and provided the venue for the Indianapolis ABCs and Clowns throughout the 1930s and 1940s. The Clowns lived up to their name by using humor—much in the style of the Harlem Globetrotters—to entertain the crowd while at the same time fielding a solid baseball side.

To show support for U.S. forces fighting in World War II, the stadium was renamed Victory Stadium in 1942—not, as is often assumed, to celebrate a notable on-field victory.

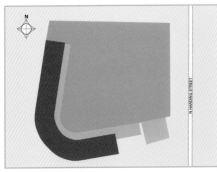

The name survived until 1967 when it was changed to Bush Stadium to honor Indianapolis native and major league player Owen Bush—in time he became the Indians' president.

The Indianapolis Indians moved out of Bush Stadium in 1996, at which time the venue was converted to become a dirt auto-racing track. The stadium is now abandoned.

Location: 1501 West 16th Street, Indianapolis, IN
Aka: Victory Field (1942–1967), Owen J "Donie" Bush Stadium (1967)
Status: Abandoned 1996; used as a speedway track
Architect: Pierre & Wright; Osborn Engineering Company
Opened: 1931
Capacity: 15,000 (1942); 12,000 (1996)
Dimensions:

	Original 1942	Final 1996
Left Field	350 ft	335 ft
Center Field	500 ft	395 ft
Right Field	350 ft	335 ft

LEFT: Footprint of Bush Stadium.

BELOW: Panoramas of the stadium today.

Location: 19 Tony Gwynn Way, San Diego, CA

Status: Home of the San Diego Padres

Architect: HOK Sports

Capacity: 46,000

Opened: April 8, 2004

Dimensions:

Left Field 336 ft

Left Center 357 ft

Center Field 396 ft

Right Center 382 ft

Right Field 322 ft

RIGHT: Downtown San Diego makes an exciting backdrop for PETCO Park. Locals claim it has the best sight lines in the game, surrounded as it is by stunning high-rise buildings.

PETCO Park claims to have the best sight lines in baseball combined with spectacular views of sunny downtown San Diego and the surrounding mountains. Built in retro style for $449 million, this open-air ballpark is unmistakably Southern Californian, being surrounded by jacaranda trees and beautifully maintained natural landscaping. The exterior is of natural stone and stucco with exposed white-painted steel. The stadium is named for the San Diego–based retailer of pet foods and supplies, which bought naming rights for a reported but unconfirmed $60 million for twenty-two years. PETCO is a baseball-only park and remarkably intimate considering its 42,000 seats (20,000 fewer than Qualcomm), all covered

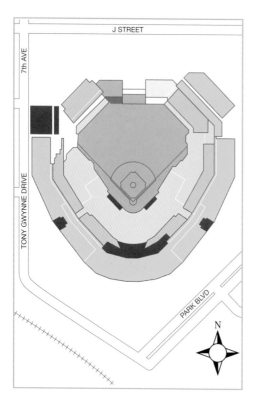

ABOVE: Footprint of PETCO Park.

RIGHT: Aerial of the newly opened PETCO with the convention center over the railway lines on the harbor.

in dark blue and arranged across three decks instead of the old stadium's four. There is also provision for a further 4,000 standing spectators at various terraces and porches around the field as well as the main concourse and a "Park at the Park" grass and picnic area capable of holding 2,500 fans behind the outfield fence. All the restaurants, offices, and amenities are located behind the seating area, leaving the playing field to the game itself and its stunning surrounds.

Consequently, the seats are all much closer to the field and all are angled for the best view of the pitcher's mound. The grandstands face due south over the pitcher's head towards San Diego Bay. Unusually, the home bullpen for the Padres is behind the left center-field wall and the bullpen for visitors is in foul territory on the first base side.

A unique feature of PETCO is the 1909-vintage four-story Western Metal Supply warehouse building that juts onto the playing field and makes a tempting target for right-hand sluggers. The building had been scheduled for demolition but it was declared a historic landmark and saved—and incorporated into the design of PETCO—so it contains rooftop seating, a restaurant, private suites, and the team store. Lucky visitors can enjoy the ballgame and stunning views from its four floors of outdoor seating. At the corner of the building is the left field "foul pole," which is actually a bright yellow strip of iron.

The first game here was delayed by two years but eventually took place on March 11, 2004, an invitational tournament hosted by San Diego State University.

Whenever the Padres hit a home run, a foghorn recording of the San Diego–based USS *Ronald Reagan* sounds and fireworks shoot out from center field.

ABOVE: South exterior, with palm trees.

BELOW: The historic Western Metal Supply Company Building—center left, next to the scoreboard—was incorporated into the stadium design. Its corner is painted yellow and serves as the left foul pole.

Location: 5999 East Van Buren Street, Phoenix, AZ

Aka: The Phoenix Muni, the Muni

Status: Home to the Phoenix Desert Dogs and spring training facility for the Oakland Athletics

Opened: March 8, 1964; renovated 2004

Capacity: 8,775

Dimensions:

Left Field 345 ft

Center Field 410 ft

Right Field 345 ft

RIGHT: Spectators on the right side of the stadium look out toward the stunning vista of Papago State Park. Those on the other side see the Phoenix airport.

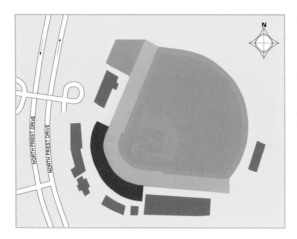

ABOVE: Footprint of Phoenix Municipal Stadium

BELOW and BELOW RIGHT: The original construction cost for the stadium was $891,380, and the 2004 renovation cost $8 million. The light poles are from the Polo Grounds in New York.

Spring training home of the Oakland Athletics and former home of the Triple-A Phoenix Firebirds, Phoenix Municipal Stadium was built in 1964 to replace its aging original namesake. The second Municipal Stadium was a step into the modern age of the early 1960s. Almost as if to complement the surrounding arid Martian landscape of Arizona, this stadium incorporates classic 1960s space-age style, which remains refreshing in the era of the many "cookie-cutter" baseball facilities that have taken over Arizona.

Phoenix's new Municipal Stadium opened to a crowd of over 8,500 on March 8, 1964, who came to see their San Francisco Giants (who had trained at Phoenix Municipal Stadium I since 1947) take on the Cleveland Indians. The Giants moved their Triple-A Pacific Coast League team from Tacoma's Cheney Stadium to Phoenix Muni in 1966, where they were known as the Phoenix Giants, before changing their name to the Phoenix Firebirds in 1986.

In 1984 the Giants swapped spring training grounds with their Bay Area neighbors, the Oakland A's. The Giants moved to Scottsdale and the A's moved to Phoenix Muni, although the Giants maintained their links with Phoenix. In 1992 the Firebirds moved to Scottsdale after the stadium was renovated, so that they could carry out training with their parent club.

During the early 1990s, Municipal Stadium was earmarked for expansion when the city of Phoenix hoped to attract a new major league team to the area. However, when that finally happened in 1998, the new Arizona Diamondbacks played in a purpose-built ballpark at Chase Field.

The Oakland A's continue to use Phoenix for their spring training, and renovated the stadium in 2004, improving, among other things, the press box which for many years was the only open-air facility in the Cactus League. The Arizona Fall League uses the stadium for games, and the Phoenix Desert Dogs have used the stadium as their home since 1992.

Location: 275 Washington Street, Buffalo, NY

Aka: Downtown Ballpark (1994), North AmeriCare Park (1995–1998), Dunn Tire Park (1998–2008), Coca-Cola Field (since 2009)

Status: Home to the Buffalo Bisons

Architect: Populous (formerly HOK Sport)

Opened: April 14, 1988

Capacity: 18,025

Dimensions:

Left Field 325 ft

Center Field 404 ft

Right Field 325 ft

All-Star Games: 1988; scheduled for 2012

The home of the Buffalo Bisons has had more names than anyone cares to remember, but it has drawn more fans to its benches than any other. Although it is a minor league baseball park, it has been built to major league standards by the world-renowned HOK architectural team, and since 2009 has been known as Coca-Cola Field.

When the new stadium was commissioned in 1986 to replace the old Rockpile (also known as the War Memorial Stadium), Buffalo expected to graduate to the major leagues, and wanted a stadium that could accommodate a crowd of 40,000. Although the Bisons never quite made it into the major leagues, their beautiful stadium, with its distinctive red seats, has hosted sellout game after sellout game, and attendance has shattered all records for minor league games year after year. It is now the largest of the minor league baseball stadiums.

Buffalo has had several chances to make the leap into the major leagues, but it has been rejected, partly because of its notoriously long winters and chilly springs, not to mention the complex negotiations between owners, TV channels, and the league administrators. As a minor league facility, however, Coca-Cola Field has served Buffalo very proudly as a Triple-A home. Over 1.18 million fans came out to the ballpark during the 1988 inaugural season, only the second time in history that any minor league team had broken the one million mark. In fact, Coca-Cola Field registered over a million fans through the gates for six years in succession until 1993.

In 1990, with the new stadium still under construction, Coca-Cola Field (now known as Pilot Field) was upgraded with 5,000 square feet of standing room only, as well as an additional 1,400 new bleacher seats. The crowds may not flock to Buffalo in quite such numbers, but the Bisons at Coca-Cola Field still outdraw 90 percent of minor league teams, and the list of major league stars who began their careers at Buffalo is impressive and includes Moises Alou, Tim Wakefield, Richie Sexson, Bartolo Colon, Sean Casey, Jake Westbrook, Victor Martinez, Fausto Carmona, and Cliff Lee.

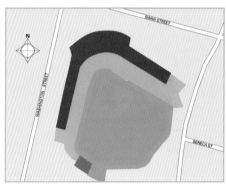

TOP: HOK created its sports group in 1983 and was commissioned in 1986 to design Coca-Cola Field.

ABOVE: Footprint of the stadium.

BELOW: With its trademark red seats, as of 2011 Coca-Cola Field is now the largest minor league baseball stadium.

Location: 350 SW First Street, Des Moines, IA

Aka: Sec Taylor Stadium (1959–1991)

Status: Demolished in 1991

Opened: 1947

Capacity: 5,000 (1947); 7,600 (1991)

Dimensions:

Left Field 335 ft

Center Field 400 ft

Right Field 335 ft

RIGHT: The Oakland Athletics tabbed Sec Taylor to be their new Triple-A home as Oakland's Iowa Oaks took the field for the first time.

BELOW and BELOW RIGHT: Views of the main grandstand. (Below images courtesy Larry A. Woolis.)

Pioneer Memorial Stadium was home of the Des Moines Bruins of the Class A Western League from 1947 to 1958, the Des Moines Demons of the Class B Three-I League from 1959 to 1961, and became the home of the Triple-A Iowa Cubs of the Pacific Coast League in 1969.

The ballpark was renamed in honor of the long-standing *Des Moines Register* sports editor Will Garner Taylor, also known as Garner W. Taylor, in 1959. His nickname "Sec" was short for "secretary." By the late 1980s the stadium was run-down and local voters backed a bond issue to rebuild it in 1990. Most of the original ballpark was demolished after the 1991 season and construction work on the new stadium began the next year, designed by Populous. It retained the Sec Taylor name and now had a capacity of 11,500. In 2004 it was renamed Principal Park. (See Sec Taylor Stadium on page 324.)

Location: 49-1 Roosevelt Boulevard, Johnstown, PA
Status: Demolished in 2005 and rebuilt
Opened: 1926 (old); 2006 (new)
Capacity: 17,000; reduced to 10,000 (old); 7,500 (new)
Dimensions:

	Original 1926	Final 2006
Left Field	262 ft	290 ft
Center Field	385 ft	409 ft
Right Field	251 ft	290 ft

LEFT: The new stadium before being turfed. Note the new seating arrangement and lack of roof.

Point Stadium has been the name of two stadiums located on the same site, and the name refers to its location, one where the Little Conemaugh, Stonycreek, and Conemaugh Rivers meet. The original stadium featured an upper deck on top of the grandstand but this was removed, reducing the ballpark's capacity to 7,000. High school football games were played at the stadium but it was also called home by numerous minor league baseball teams and hosted the All-American Amateur Baseball Association (AAABA) World Series baseball tournament.

The original grass field Point Stadium was demolished in 2005 so that a new $8 million venue could be built. This opened in August 2006 and featured Sportexe artificial turf. The opener was a game between Johnstown and Chicago in the annual AAABA National Tournament. Bishop McCort High School currently plays its home football games there and artificial turf was installed before the 2007 AAABA National Tournament. Point Stadium is also used by the University of Pittsburgh at Johnstown for selected home games. The university has hosted the West Virginia Intercollegiate Athletic Conference baseball championships at the stadium since 2008.

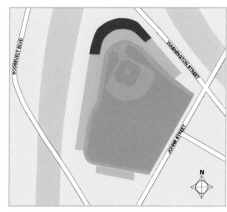

BELOW: Point Stadium was a quirky park. It had a huge center field and perhaps the shortest power alleys and foul poles in pro baseball.

Polo Grounds (1880)

Location: 110th Street between Fifth and Sixth Avenues, New York, NY
Status: Demolished in 1889
Opened: September 1880
First MLB game: 1883
Capacity: 20,709
Dimensions:
Center Field 500 ft

The original Polo Grounds were—as the name suggests—a venue for polo set up in 1876. In September 1880 they were converted to become a ballpark, with a single-story grandstand, by John B. Day and Jim Mutrie, who owned the New York Metropolitans. They organized a new team, the New York Gothams, and built a second grandstand and diamond, giving the eastern field to the Gothams and the western to the Metropolitans, separating the two with a canvas divider. The Gothams' first National League game was held on May 1, 1883, and the first by the Mets in the American Association on July 17, 1884. However, it quickly became apparent that the surface of the western diamond was unplayable, so both teams used the eastern field.

By 1885 the Gothams had changed their name to become the New York Giants, and the following year the Metropolitans moved out of the Polo Grounds to Staten Island. In 1889 the Giants were forced out of their home when the governor of New York ordered his men to cut through the park in order to lay out part of New York's street grid plan. Despite howls of protest, the work went ahead, forcing the Giants to look for an alternative home.

Polo Grounds (1889)

Location: South Coogan's Hollow, 155th–157th Street, New York, NY
Aka: Manhattan Field
Status: Demolished
Opened: July 8, 1889
Closed: September 13, 1890
Capacity: 14,000
Dimensions:
Center Field 360 ft

ABOVE: The original Polo Grounds in 1887. The deepest part of center field was 500 feet from home plate. Soft, underweighted baseballs made the home run a rare event in nineteenth-century baseball.

After playing at various temporary homes, the New York Giants arrived in 1889 at Coogan's Bluff, where there were two ballparks: the northern Brotherhood Park was the home of the New York Giants of the Players' League; the southern Manhattan Field, which we know today as Polo Grounds II, became the home of the Giants of the National League. The northern Giants team went bankrupt and the other Giants team moved into Brotherhood Park because it was bigger and renamed it the Polo Grounds (III). Manhattan Field would eventually become a parking lot for the Polo Grounds.

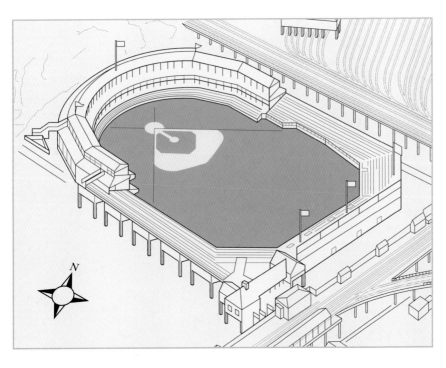

Location: Northern half of Coogan's Hollow between 157th and 159th Streets
Aka: Brotherhood Park
Status: Destroyed by fire in 1911
Architect: Henry B. Herts
Opened: April 19, 1890
Capacity: 38,000
Dimensions:
Left Field 277 ft
Center Field 500 ft (until 1909; 433 ft after)
Right Field 258 ft

By 1890 the third and final location of the Polo Grounds was occupied by the New York Giants of the Players' League, though at the time it was still called Brotherhood Park. At first it had a totally open outfield with just an outer perimeter fence, then gradually bleachers were built in and the stadium started to take shape. The huge outfield was roped off for parking carriages and early automobiles.

On April 14, 1911, the curved grandstand burned down, leaving only the steel uprights in place. Luckily, the gaps between the seating saved the clubhouse and some of the stands.

With their home in ashes, the New York Giants moved in with their bitter rivals the Highlanders (soon to become the Yankees) at Hilltop Park for two months while their stadium was rebuilt.

ABOVE and BELOW: The Polo Grounds in 1909—compare the longer grandstand with the picture below dated 1905. Manhattan Field is to the left in the artist's impression.

BOTTOM: Looking over the Polo Grounds in 1909 toward the outfield bleachers from Coogan's Bluff.

Location: West 155th Street and Eighth Avenue, New York, NY

Aka: Brush Stadium (1911–1919)

Status: Demolished in 1964

Architect: Osborn Engineering

Capacity: 16,000 (1911); 39,000 (1917); 64,417 (1936); 56,000 (final)

Opened: June 28, 1911

Last MLB game: September 18, 1963

Dimensions:

	Original 1911	Final 1963
Left Field	277 ft	279 ft
Left Center	447 ft	455 ft
Center Field	433 ft	483 ft
Right Center	440 ft	449ft
Right Field	256 ft	258 ft

World Series: 1905, 1911, 1912, 1913, 1917, 1921, 1922, 1923, 1924, 1933, 1936, 1937, 1951, 1954

All-Star Game: 1934, 1942

ABOVE: 1937 aerial view of the Polo Grounds showing proximity of railroad tracks and the entryway "nook" in dead center field.

BELOW: Opening day 1923—center field looks very different to the image opposite.

The fourth Polo Grounds became one of the legendary ballparks. On opening day, June 28, 1911, the park was still under construction and there was seating for only 16,000 fans. Construction continued as the summer progressed and by the time the season ended, double-decked concrete-and-steel grandstands lined most of the playing field and capacity had reached 34,000. The result was a horseshoe-shaped arena (though some likened it to a bathtub) that was loved by the public and hitters alike for its short measurements down the foul lines and the overhanging left field upper deck that was especially susceptible to home runs. The downside was the distant center-field fence that was virtually unreachable. The cost of the build was $300,000.

The old bleachers, which survived the fire and were incorporated into the new build, were removed in 1923 when the permanent double deck was extended to cover most of the perimeter. At the same time, new bleachers and a new clubhouse were built across center field.

The first night game was played at the Polo Grounds on May 24, 1940, but from that date onward the stadium suffered from poor maintenance, partly because while the Giants owned the stadium, they did not own the land on which it stood. Ticket sales declined even when they won the World Series in 1954. Another stadium in New York couldn't be found and in August 1957 the Giants announced they were moving to San Francisco.

The Polo Grounds remained substantially the same right up to the day that the Giants left. The stadium was virtually abandoned for three years until the new Mets and Titans teams used it while Shea Stadium was built. After much argument between the city and the landowners, the stadium was demolished in 1964 and the Polo Grounds Towers public housing project was built on the site.

ABOVE: Looking toward Coogan's Bluff in the 1930s.

BELOW: May 14, 1962: note the lights (the first night game was in 1940) and the two-tier grandstand extensions.

Location: 650 Ponce de Leon Avenue, Atlanta, GA

Aka: Spiller Park, Spiller Field

Status: Demolished in 1965

Opened: 1907; rebuilt 1923

Capacity: 20,000

Dimensions:

Left Field 365 ft

Center Field 462 ft

Right Field 321 ft

RIGHT: The left side featured some tall signage and the scoreboard, which had to be topped in order to hit a homer, while the right side featured more signage. In between, there was a steep hill with two trees, the closest a magnolia tree. This was all in play. There was no fence in center field at all.

BELOW: The 1907 ballpark featured a mostly wooden grandstand as seen here.

(Both photos courtesy Ted Jones.)

ABOVE: In 1924, a new ballpark was constructed almost entirely of steel. The white arches were gone and replaced by a roofed grandstand that covered the entire first base line. Looming over the stadium in this 1950 photograph is Atlanta's Sears & Roebuck department store building. (Photo courtesy Dean Davis.)

Ponce de Leon Park was built in 1907 and was home to the minor league Atlanta Crackers, as well as the Atlanta Black Crackers of the Negro League. It was an unusual ballpark in that it incorporated a magnolia tree in center field 450 feet from home plate, although only two players ever hit the landmark— Babe Ruth being one of them. Since the park's demolition in 1965, the magnolia tree is the only surviving feature.

Ponce de Leon Park was mainly home to minor league baseball during its near sixty-year existence. In addition to the magnolia tree, early players had to contend with the railroad tracks behind the outfield that belonged to the Southern Railway. Constructed in 1907, the original wooden stands were destroyed by fire in 1923. The club owner, Tell J. Spiller, rebuilt the structure in concrete and steel, and for ten years the 20,000-capacity stadium was known as Spiller Park.

The Atlanta Crackers made Ponce de Leon/Spiller Park their home from 1907 until 1964. They enjoyed great success, and became known as the "Yankees of the South" because of their consistent winning during the 1930s. While Atlanta nurtured some future Hall of Famers, major league players stopped by for a few games on the way from spring training to New York, such as Babe Ruth and Lou Gehrig, as well as Eddie Matthews, the only other player to hit a home run into the magnolia tree.

The Negro League team, the Atlanta Black Crackers, used Ponce de Leon Park from 1919 until they were disbanded in 1952, winning the Negro American League championship in 1938 (by default, when the series was canceled). Nat Peeples, Roy Welmaker, and James "Red" Moore were the top players on the winning 1938 team.

The Atlanta Crackers won their first major league affiliation in 1950 with the Boston Braves and were consistently successful, regularly attracting large crowds of loyal fans. Their success finally ended Ponce de Leon's career as a ballpark, when the city of Atlanta constructed the gigantic Atlanta–Fulton County Stadium for the 1965 season.

Location: 4101 Crain Highway, Bowie, MD
Status: Home of the Bowie Baysox
Opened: July 16, 1994
Capacity: 10,000
Dimensions:
Left Field 309 ft
Center Field 405 ft
Right Field 309 ft

This stadium is a multipurpose sports venue but one primarily used for baseball. It is home of the Baltimore Orioles' Double-A affiliate, the Eastern League's Bowie Baysox, a team that emerged in 1993. The stadium was built as the result of a joint venture between the Maryland Baseball Limited Partnership and the Maryland-National Capital Park and Planning Commission.

Prince George's Stadium was originally planned to open at the beginning of the 1994 season, but the ballpark did not open until July 16 because of construction delays brought on by inclement weather. While the stadium was being finished, the Baysox played one full season—1993—at Baltimore's Memorial Stadium and a few games at the start of the next season at other fields. Despite the size of their new ballpark, one with facilities more usually associated with Triple-A teams, the Baysox have done much to maintain an intimate ambience. Prince George's Stadium has been host to the Double-A All-Star Game twice, the United States Congressional Baseball Game, the yearly Allen Iverson charity softball game, a lacrosse tournament, the U.S.A. Softball team, as well as hosting non-sporting events such as yard sales, movie nights, and concerts.

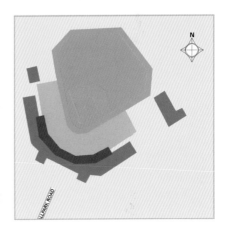

THIS PAGE: Footprint and views of Prince George's Stadium.

Privateer Park

Location: 6801 Franklin Avenue, New Orleans, LA

Status: Home to the University of New Orleans Privateers

Opened: 1979

Capacity: 4,200 (1979); 5,200 (2011)

Dimensions:

Left Field 330 ft

Center Field 400 ft

Right Field 330 ft

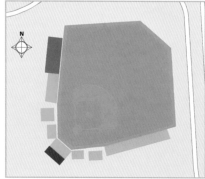

THIS PAGE : Footprint and views of Privateer Park.

Privateer Park lies on the east campus of the University of New Orleans and was a temporary home to the New Orleans Zephyrs from 1993 to 1996 while the team was waiting for their 11,000-seat Zephyr Field to be constructed. Today, Privateer Park is used only by the college's baseball team, the University of New Orleans Privateers, and consists of mostly metal bleachers with just a few chair seats. Although this small venue is perfectly suited to college baseball games, it is still a bit surprising that a Triple-A affiliate of the New York Mets once played here for four years.

Location: 2401 Ontario Street, Cleveland, OH
Aka: Jacobs Field (1994–2005), the Jake, Progressive Field (from 2008)
Status: Home of the Cleveland Indians
Architect: HOK Sports
Capacity: 43,368
Opened: April 4, 1994
Dimensions:
Left Field 325 ft
Left Center 370 ft
Center Field 405 ft
Right Center 375 ft
Right Field 325 ft
World Series: 1995, 1997
All-Star Game: 1997

The Cleveland Indians left crumbling Lakefront Stadium for Jacobs Field at the end of the 1993 season. Often described as a boutique ballpark, the new Jacobs Field was carefully designed to marry the Indians' Cleveland roots into the city's industrial heritage, blending the old and the new seamlessly into a wonderful modern ballpark, all at a cost of $175 million.

Accordingly, the stadium is built in traditional Cleveland brick and stone vernacular with exterior latticework echoing the reflections on the water created by the bridges crossing

ABOVE LEFT and LEFT: After building, Jacobs Field set attendance records after selling out 455 consecutive games between June 12, 1995, and April 4, 2001. Demand for tickets was so great that all eighty-one home games were sold out before opening day on three separate occasions— assisted by the success of the Indians in this period.

LEFT: What a difference success makes. Up till 2001 Jacobs Field boasted annual attendances of over three million. Since then the figures have plummeted: in 2009 Progressive Field could muster only 1,766,242—over 500,000 down on the AL average.

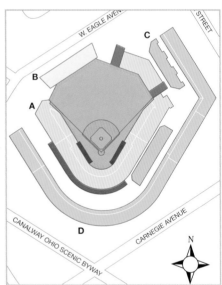

ABOVE: Footprint of Progressive Park.

the Cuyahoga River. Furthermore, all the seats are angled to face home plate and the light standards mimic Cleveland's industrial chimneys, and the design as a whole provides direct views from the park to two street-level plazas into the city. The ballpark has been the vital spark that triggered Cleveland's downtown renaissance and was named after the Indians' owner Richard Jacobs, who bought the franchise in 1985 and paid for stadium naming rights.

Spectators enjoy views over the outfield of downtown Cleveland and across the largest freestanding scoreboard in the majors at 120 feet tall and 222 feet wide. The home plate was brought from the old Municipal Stadium, and the asymmetric playing field is deepest at center left. The nineteen-foot-tall left field fence is affectionately referred to as the "Mini Green Monster," while the bleachers recall those at Wrigley Field.

In 2008 a local insurance company bought the stadium naming rights and the venue became known as Progressive Field. The same year, readers of *Sports Illustrated* voted Progressive Field the most beautiful ballpark in the majors.

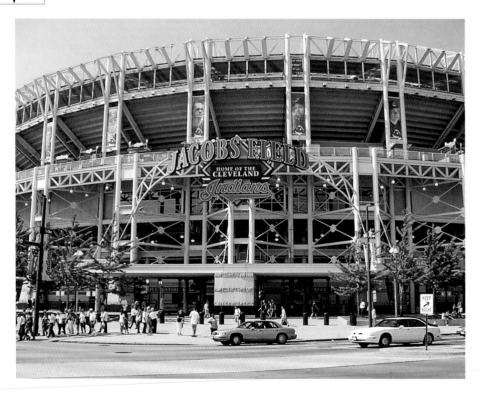

RIGHT: The home plate entrance when it was still called Jacobs Field.

Putnam Grounds is a former ballpark that was very briefly home to the Troy Trojans baseball club from late May 1879 to September 20, 1879.

Putnam Grounds is in what is now the neighborhood of Bedford-Stuyvesant in Brooklyn and it was at this baseball park in 1860 that the championship game was called a tie as a result of fan conduct. The Brooklyn Atlantics were the team to beat, but the Brooklyn Excelsiors were winning. The failure of the Atlantics to acknowledge a loss resulted in continuing tension between the two teams.

Location: Near Bedford-Stuyvesant, Brooklyn, Troy, NY
Status: Closed September 20, 1879
Opened: May 28, 1879

This minor league ballpark, just south of Vancouver, has housed two teams, the New Westminster Frasers and the Vancouver Mounties.

Built in 1950, the silver-gray grandstand of Queens Park Stadium seems to shine under a deep blue sky. Tall pine trees encircle the ballpark, reminding you that you are in the Pacific Northwest. The main grandstand behind home plate is a covered grandstand made of concrete and steel, and its right side stretches out, uncovered, well past the first base line, in the shape of a J. The third base line, meanwhile, is also covered, but it is an old-style wooden structure with its own unique beauty that seems to pay homage to the old wooden ballparks of yesteryear.

Professional baseball at Queens Park Stadium can trace its roots back to 1961 and 1962 when the Triple-A Pacific Coast League's Vancouver Mounties began using this ballpark as a secondary stadium to Nat Bailey Stadium. With doubleheaders scheduled for most Saturdays, the Mounties used these games as an opportunity to explore the eastern fringes of Vancouver. Instead of playing both of their doubleheader games at Nat Bailey Stadium, they split the games into a day-night doubleheader, with the 1:30 afternoon game being played here at Queens Park Stadium, and the night game being played at 8:00 at Nat Bailey Stadium.

The 1961 Vancouver Mounties were members of the Milwaukee Braves organization, and served as their Triple-A Pacific Coast League franchise.

The Mounties transferred to the Minnesota Twins in 1962, who moved their Triple-A team to Dallas for three seasons. When the Mounties returned in 1965, they were under new management and did not use Queens Park. In 1974 the New Westminster Frasers played at Queen's Park as part of the Northwest League.

Location: First Street and Third Avenue, New Westminster, BC, Canada
Status: Used for minor league games and tournaments
Opened: 1950

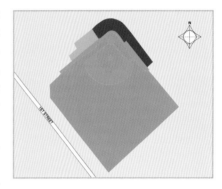

ABOVE: Footprint of Queens Park.

OVERLEAF: Queens Park grandstand. Inside at third is an old-style wooden structure, reminiscent of times past.

BELOW: Interior of Queens Park.

Location: University of Hawaii at Manoa, Honolulu, HI

Aka: Les Murakami Stadium (from 2002), the House That Les Built

Status: Home to the Hawaii Island Movers, and the University of Hawaii

Opened: February 17, 1984

Capacity: 4,300

Dimensions:

Left Field 325 ft

Center Field 385 ft

Right Field 325 ft

RIGHT: Footprint of Les Murakami Stadium.

BELOW: The stadium in 2006.

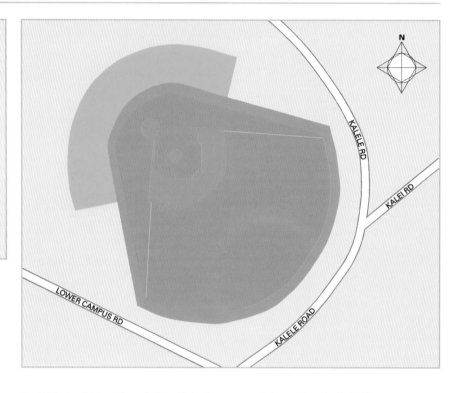

In 1983 the University of Hawaii built a state-of-the-art baseball facility on-campus. Rainbow Stadium cost $12.2 million by the time it was completed in 1985—the roof was extended from its original 1984 position down the first- and third-base lines. In 2002 the stadium was renamed after the successful late 1970s and early 1980s head coach, Les Murakami. At the same time, the outfield fences were moved and lowered to make the stadium more hitter-friendly and a new scoreboard was added.

Since then there have been further renovations: the turf (AstroTurf was replaced by new Domo Turf surface), seats (changing from red, orange, and blue seats to all green seats to give the stands a fresh, new look), roof, and speakers were replaced by the end of 2010. With a successful Rainbow team, Hawaii finished the season in the top twenty in average attendance (3,090 per game). It was the first time since 1996 that UH averaged over 3,000 per game.

Location: 400 Ballpark Drive, West Sacramento, CA
Status: Home of the Sacramento River Cats
Opened: 2000
Capacity: 25,107
Dimensions:
Left Field 330 ft
Center Field 403 ft
Right Field 325 ft
All-Star Game: 2005

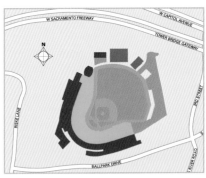

Raley Field is home to the Sacramento River Cats of the Triple-A Pacific Coast League. This new ballpark, which cost around $42 million to construct, is located on the site of old warehouses and railyards just across the Sacramento River from the California state capitol. The naming rights were bought by Raley's, a regional chain of supermarkets based in West Sacramento. The stadium was not designed with expansion in mind, so if a major league team ever decided to relocate here, there will be a need for significant upgrade work on the stadium.

THIS PAGE: Footprint, external, and internal views of Raley Field.

Ramona Park stood on the corner of Lake and Lakeside Drive until 1946, and Babe Ruth, Lou Gehrig, and the New York Yankees supposedly played in the park, according to local historical records, in the 1920s.

"Ramona" was the name of the last of the Reeds Lake steamboats and the captain of the SS *Ramona*, William Poisson, campaigned to name what is now known as John A. Collins Park as Ramona Park. According to a news story in the *Almanac* in August 1966, his wife Grace said, "When he heard about the plan to name the park after Collins [the East Grand Rapids mayor from 1933 to 1955], he said, 'There goes Ramona.' He really wanted to keep the history and he wasn't going to let it be." Thus the park was given its rather convoluted name.

Location: Grand Rapids, MI
Aka: Ramona Park, John A. Collins Park
Status: Demolished in 1946
Opened: 1920s

Location: 3400 East Camino Campestre, Tucson, AZ

Aka: Hi Corbett Field (since 1951)

Status: Home of the Tucson Toros

Opened: 1937; remodeled 1972; renovated in 1992, 1997, and 1999

Capacity: 9,500

Dimensions:

Left Field 366 ft

Center Field 392 ft

Right Field 348 ft

RIGHT: Hi Corbett Field is the Cactus League's oldest ballpark. Seventy-four Hall of Famers have played here and their names are listed on the Wall of Fame on the concourse behind home plate.

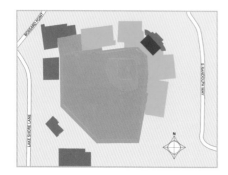

This ballpark, home to the Tucson Toros, was built for the Class D Tucson Lizards in 1937 but was renamed in honor of Hiram Stevens Corbett, who helped bring spring training to Tucson ten years later in the form of the Cleveland Indians. Hi Corbett was subsequently remodeled in 1972 and upgraded three times in the 1990s. The ballpark served as the spring training home of the Cleveland Indians until 1992 and then the Colorado Rockies until 2010. The stadium also has close ties with minor league baseball. Aside from the Lizards, the Tucson Cowboys played there on and off from the late 1930s until 1958, while the original Tucson Toros played there from 1969 until 1997. Thereafter, they played elsewhere under different names but returned in 2009.

USA Baseball was headquartered at Hi Corbett from 1997 to 2003, and it was home to the Arizona Heat women's professional softball team from 2004 to 2007. It has hosted exhibition games featuring the likes of the Colorado Silver Bullets, Houston Astros, and the University of Arizona. Parts of the 1989 movie *Major League* were filmed at Hi Corbett Field, and members of the University of Arizona baseball team acted as extras.

BELOW and BOTTOM: On a sunny day, this is an unforgiving stadium—the only shaded seats are directly under the press boxes.

Rangers Ballpark in Arlington has corners—lots of them thanks to its asymmetrical outfield. It has a retro feel to it, enhanced by the outfield nooks and crannies. The architect also incorporated several features from the old Arlington Stadium, which used to stand about 400 yards away. These include the home plate, foul poles, and bleachers. However, the ballpark is the only one of the retro type to be fully enclosed due to the positioning of a four-story office block in center field.

Yet as this is Texas, there are idiosyncrasies: cast-iron lone stars adorn aisle seats, replicating those on the building's facade. Large steer skulls and murals depicting the state's history decorate the walls, and a brick "Walk of Fame," celebrating Rangers history, surrounds the park. The grass in the batter's line of vision in dead center is named Greene's Hill after former Arlington mayor Richard Greene. There is a Texas-sized dimension to the entire stadium complex, which includes a twelve-acre, man-made lake (named for late Rangers broadcaster Mark Holtz), a 17,000-square-foot baseball museum said to be the largest outside Cooperstown, a 225-seat auditorium, a children's learning center, a four-story office building, and a kid-sized park with seats for 650 just outside.

To battle the Texas elements, the stadium is sunken, out of the wind, and enclosed by the office building, home to the Rangers front office, just beyond center field. This is one of the signature features: a four-story office building that encloses the structure from left center to right center field. A giant windscreen, 42 feet high and 430 feet long, was installed on the roof to further reduce wind. Overhead fans in the upper and lower deck porches help keep patrons cool.

Two men—Tom Vandergriff and Nolan Ryan—who played enormous roles in the history of the Texas Rangers franchise are honored with full-size bronze statues in Vandergriff Plaza. The statues were produced by noted sculptor Toby Mendez of Washington County, Maryland.

The $191 million park was paid for largely through a sales tax increase, pushed through by the team's managing partner in the early 1990s, George W. Bush. In 2010 significant renovations were announced for the 2011 season, particularly improvements in the video, technology, and audio systems. The club has partnered with Daktronics Inc. and the Sony Corporation to deliver HD digital content throughout the ballpark in a number of different formats. On the roof of Home Run Porch a new video board measures 42 by 120 feet. In addition, a new video board that is 25 by 29 feet has replaced the Coca-Cola matrix board on top of the office building in center field.

Location: 1000 Ballpark Way, Arlington, TX
Aka: Ameriquest Field in Arlington (2004–2007); Rangers Ballpark in Arlington (since 2007)
Status: Home of the Texas Rangers
Architect: David M. Schwarz Architectural Services, Inc.
Opened: April 11, 1994
Capacity: 49,170
Dimensions:
Left Field 332 ft
Left Center 390 ft
Center Field 400 ft
Right Center 381 ft
Right Field 325 ft
World Series: 2010
All-Star Game: 1995

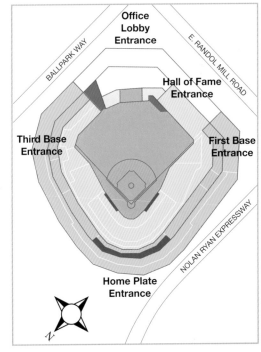

BELOW: Rangers Ballpark has a retro feel to it: brick and sunset red granite; arches and towers. (Photo cortesy Joe Mock, Baseballparks.com.)

Cincinnati is one of the very few cities that has retained their major league baseball team, although the Cincinnati Reds (originally Cincinnati Red Stockings) moved home three times until finally settling at Redland Field in 1911. The new ballpark—a rebuild of the Palace of the Fans—held 25,000 spectators at first when the Reds thrived there. The first time they got to the World Series they won it, albeit in controversial circumstances when it emerged that a number of their Chicago White Sox opponents had thrown the 1919 series.

Redland Field was a classic ballpark constructed using steel and concrete and was built for $225,000 by architect Harry Hake. Always one of the smaller major league parks, its capacity never exceeded 30,000. In 1894 legendary groundskeeper Mathias "Matty" Schwab took charge of the field and continued to oversee the grounds until he retired in 1963 aged eighty-three. Hence the affectionate nickname "Schwab's Field."

In 1933 the Great Depression hit everyone hard and the Cincinnati Reds suffered as well until it seemed the only answer was to move the franchise elsewhere. Luckily, local radio tycoon Powel Crosley Jr. thought otherwise and bought the club so it could remain in Cincinnati: the stadium was renamed in his honor the following year. The night game was becoming popular and Crosley was persuaded to follow suit: by May 1935 eight metal stanchions had been erected holding, in total, 632 individual lights. The Reds' first night game was a victory over the Philadelphia Phillies—the event was started back at the White House, where President Franklin D. Roosevelt pressed a button that lit the lights around the field so 20,422 spectators could enjoy their first night game—the first in the majors.

Between 1937 and 1938, home plate was moved twenty feet farther out to reduce the dimensions of the ground. The 1938 All-Star Game was held at Crosley and won by the National League. During the following season, roofed upper decks were added to the left and right side pavilions, supplying an additional 5,000 seats.

In the mid-1950s parking near Crosley became a big problem while crime around night games became notorious and consequently spectator numbers started to decline. The status of Cincinnati baseball got very political in 1957, especially when New York tried to poach the Reds after losing both the Giants and Dodgers to the West Coast. Crosley refused to sell out, but when he died in 1958 his estate sold the Reds within months to Bill DeWitt. At much the same time, NFL football was returning to Cincinnati but only on condition that it had a suitable venue; agreement was reached to renovate Cincinnati's dilapidated riverfront with a multipurpose facility for the new Cincinnati Bengals and the Cincinnati Reds. The 1969 season was supposed to be Crosley Field's last, but delays at Riverfront Stadium meant their final game there was a victory against the San Francisco Giants on June 24, 1970.

After much argument and an encounter in court, the Reds sold Crosley Field to the city of Cincinnati for $2.5 million: a million less than the Reds wanted and a million more than the city wanted to pay. Crosley became an auto impound yard. In early 1972 the ballpark was stripped and many pieces sold off as memorabilia, then in April demolition started. Some of the ground is now a parking lot, but much of the site has disappeared under new buildings.

Location: Intersection of Western Avenue and Findlay Street, Cincinnati, OH
Aka: Crosley Field (from 1934), the Old Boomerang, Schwab's Field, Findlay & Western
Status: Demolished in 1972
Architect: Harry Hake
Capacity: 25,000 (1912); 29,488 (1970)
Opened: April 11, 1912
Last MLB game: June 24, 1970
Dimensions:

	Original 1912	Final 1958
Left Field	360 ft	328 ft
Left Center	380 ft	380 ft
Center Field	420 ft	387 ft
Right Center	383 ft	383 ft
Right Field	360 ft	366 ft

World Series: 1919, 1940
All-Star Game: 1938

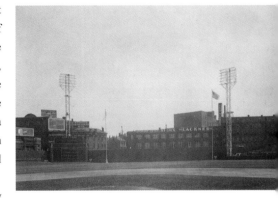

BELOW: 1939 World Series between the Reds and Yankees. Notice the terrace in front of the left-field fence. It was an incline that started twenty feet from the left-field wall and gradually increased until it reached the four-foot grade at the wall. The upper deck was extended down the left and right foul poles in 1938.

ABOVE RIGHT: Center field was dominated by a very short fence and a very large warehouse building.

CENTER and BELOW RIGHT: Compare Crosley in the 1930s (center) and a 1912 postcard. The center photograph is dated 1935 when the lights were erected. (Photos courtesy Larry Klug and Ch Foerty Meyer

Location: Edmonton, Alberta, Canada
Aka: John Ducey Park (from 1983)
Status: Demolished in 1995
Opened: 1935
Capacity: 6,500

John Ducey Park was home to the Edmonton Trappers for sixty years, before it was demolished in 1995 to make way for Telus Park, Edmonton's current baseball stadium. Edmonton has always had a huge baseball fan base, and half a million spectators regularly turned out every year to watch the games at the city's ballpark whatever the weather.

Built in 1935, the stadium was originally known as Renfrew Park, but was renamed in 1983 in honor of John Ducey, Edmonton's "Mr. Baseball." Promoter, administrator, umpire, coach, and lifelong fan, Ducey worked hard to improve the whole baseball experience in Edmonton, lobbying the council to install floodlighting, decent drainage, and sunken dugouts. In 1947 Renfrew Park became the first Canadian ballpark to have permanent lighting and the improvements pulled in more fans. A fire destroyed the wooden grandstand in 1950, and two years later a new concrete-and-steel grandstand was opened to accommodate the 100,000-plus fans that attended games in the late 1940s and early 1950s.

The first professional team to use the stadium was the Edmonton Eskimos, who became part of the newly expanded Northwest League in 1953. By 1955 they had joined the Independent Western Canadian League and remained in it until its demise in 1964.

From 1981 the Triple-A Edmonton Trappers of the Pacific Coast League played their home games at John Ducey Park and in 1984 won their first league championship, the first Canadian team to do so. Affiliated to the Chicago White Sox (1981–82), the California Angels (1983–92), and the Florida Marlins (1993–94), the Trappers provided a useful opening for many payers who went on to major league fame, such as Ron Kittle, Wally Joyner, and Juan Agosto.

In 1994 the Pacific Coast League issued new ballpark regulations and it became clear that the venerable John Ducey Park did not meet the requirements for a Triple-A facility. The city of Edmonton decided to demolish the old stadium, replacing it with the groundbreaking Telus Field on the same site.

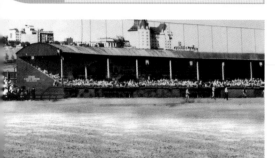

ABOVE and BELOW: A concrete-and-steel grandstand replaced the wooden one after the 1950 fire.

Location: 1137 Second Avenue West, Birmingham, AL
Status: Oldest surviving pro baseball park in the United States
Opened: August 18, 1910
Capacity: 10,800
Dimensions:

	Original 1910	Final 1987
Left Field	400 ft	325 ft
Center Field	470 ft	395 ft
Right Field	334 ft	335 ft

The oldest surviving professional ballpark still in use today dates from 1910, when it cost $75,000 to build. It is still in perfect condition as every possible effort has been made to preserve the authentic atmosphere and early stadium but with all the best in modern facilities and comforts. Rickwood Field is listed on the National Register of Historic Places and is now owned by the City of Birmingham. The stadium was built for the Birmingham Barons in 1910 by successful local businessman and passionate baseball fan Rick Woodward.

When Rickwood opened in 1910 it could entertain a capacity crowd of a little over 10,000 spectators. Over the years Rickwood has been home to many teams, from the minor league Birmingham Barons to the Black Barons of the Negro National League and then the Negro National League.

In those early days the white Birmingham Barons would play one Sunday and the Black Barons alternated on the next the following week; however, while black fans were allowed to watch the white Barons game, they were not allowed to mingle with the white fans but

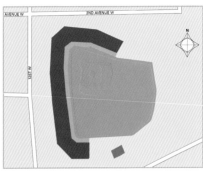

ABOVE: Footprint of Rickwood Field.

ABOVE LEFT: The five old seventy-five-foot light towers were put in place in 1936, when Rickwood became one of the first minor league parks to host night baseball.

BELOW: Rickwood Field has been preserved and is undergoing restoration—since 1992 it has been under the care of the Friends of Rickwood and will be used as a working museum.

had to sit in separate stands behind the outer right field wall. Conversely, when the Black Barons played their fans filled the ballpark—extra bleachers were often procured for the huge crowds—and any white fans had to sit in the segregated bleachers.

In 1988 the Barons moved on to Hoover Metropolitan Stadium, but—thanks to the Friends of Rickwood—pro baseball is still played at Rickwood, most notably the annual Rickwood Classic, when the Barons return to play a game at their old home.

Every effort has been made to create the nostalgic atmosphere of the early twentieth century ball game, including authentic replicas of early advertisements on the outfield fences. A nice touch is the replica press box on top of the roof of one of the stands.

Touted as the closest thing baseball has to a time machine, Rickwood is the oldest ballpark still in use in the world today. Every measure has been taken to preserve the stadium and create an authentic atmosphere of the early twentieth century.

Ridgewood Park, also known as Grauer's Ridgewood Park (Ridgewood Park I) or Wallace's Ridgewood Park (Ridgewood Park II), was a baseball ground located in Ridgewood in the New York City borough of Queens. The grounds were used, on occasion, by the Brooklyn Bridegrooms baseball club of the American Association as their home park from 1886 to 1889, and by the Brooklyn Gladiators, of the same association, for the 1890 season.

Residents of Brooklyn regularly headed across the county line to enjoy a picnic or see a ball game in Ridgewood Park in the 1880s. In 1885 George Grauer purchased a ten-acre lot next to the picnic grounds and laid out a new diamond with the intention of staging regular games to large crowds. Charlie Byrne's Brooklyn squad traveled to the grounds of the Long Island Athletic Club, Grauer's "new and unfinished field," and thrashed the home team, the Ridgewood Park Base Ball Club. Byrne then scheduled a number of American Association Sunday matches for his Brooklyn squad on the field. The Long Island Athletics continued to play their brand of semipro ball throughout 1886.

Location: Myrtle Avenue, Queens, New York, NY
Aka: Grauer's Ridgewood Park, Ridgewood Park I, Wallace's Ridgewood Park, Ridgewood Park II
Status: Disappeared under development
Last pro game: September 13, 1886
Opened: c. 1883

Ridgewood Park

Location: 201 East Joe Nuxhall Way, Cincinnati, OH

Aka: Cinergy Field (from 1996)

Status: Demolished in 2002

Architect: Heery & Heery and Finch, Alexander, Barnes, Rothschild and Pashal

Capacity: 52,952 (1970); 40,008 (2000)

Opened: June 30, 1970

Last MLB game: September 22, 2002

Dimensions:

	Original 1970	Final 2000
Left Field	330 ft	325 ft
Left Center	375 ft	370 ft
Center Field	404 ft	393 ft
Right Center	375 ft	373 ft
Right Field	330 ft	325 ft

World Series: 1970, 1972, 1975, 1976, 1990

All-Star Game: 1970, 1988

THIS PAGE: Riverfront Stadium met with a huge round of applause when it opened on June 30, 1970. Players were thrilled to have a modern clubhouse, announcers had real booths to broadcast from, and the press had air-conditioned accommodation. Time passed and then the Baltimore Orioles built Oriole Park at Camden Yards and everyone wanted a retro classic. And so the Great American Ball Park was planned where center field was currently sitting. To begin creation of the Reds' new dream park, it was necessary to tear down the entire center field grandstand and turn Cinergy Field into a configuration that more resembled Shea Stadium. Seating capacity went from 52,000 to 39,000 in 2001, as the three-tiered center field grandstand came crashing down.

The need for a new ballpark in Cincinnati started in the late 1940s but the agreement to build a multipurpose stadium on the downtown Ohio River front wasn't reached until 1968. Work began on a $50 million "cookie cutter" stadium in 1968 and took two years to complete. When finished it was remarkably similar to Three Rivers Stadium in Pittsburgh and they were often mistaken for each other by sportscasters.

When Riverfront Stadium opened in 1970 it could accommodate 53,000 spectators to enjoy the new NFL franchise, the Cincinnati Bengals, as well as the Cincinnati Reds. The home plate from Crosley Field had been taken by mayor Gene Ruehlmann via helicopter to Riverfront, where it was installed in the artificial turf. The first game was against the Atlanta Braves on June 30, 1970. That same year the Reds contested the World Series but lost out 4–1 to the Baltimore Orioles.

The artificial turf was controversial: some loved it, most hated it. It paid dividends to players who relied on speed and strength, but players who used subtlety floundered. Some areas were still dirt, namely cutouts around first, second, and third base—so-called sliding pits—the pitcher's mound, and home plate areas.

In September 1996 Riverfront was renamed Cinergy Field following sponsorship by energy company Cinergy Corporation. The aging stadium lacked modern amenities and was

getting badly dated, so new premises were required for both MLB and NFL games. In 2000 the Bengals moved to Paul Brown Stadium and in 2001 the seating capacity was reduced to 39,000 to make room for the construction of Great American Ball Park. At the same time the artificial turf was removed and the stadium remodeled for baseball only. Much of the left and center field stands were removed and the fences brought in by five feet: for a time the two venues were twenty-six inches apart at their closest point.

On December 29, 2002, Riverfront Stadium was destroyed by implosion, watched by thousands of people.

RIGHT: Cinergy Field is imploded; to the right is Great American Ball Park.

Location: 901 W. Arcadia Avenue, Dawson Springs, KY
Status: Overwhelmed by floodwater, c. 1935
Opened: 1914
Dimensions
Left Field 335 ft
Center Left 365 ft
Center Field 405 ft
Center Right 365 ft
Right Field 335 ft

LEFT and BELOW: Riverside Park is a complete re-creation of the former spring training home of the Pittsburgh Pirates.

Riverside Park was built in 1914 and it served as a spring training home for the Pittsburgh Pirates from 1915 to 1917. It is the only ballpark in Kentucky to have hosted a major league team. Records also show that the Boston Red Sox and the Cincinnati Reds played exhibition games here in the early 1920s. But even after the major league teams left in 1917, Riverside Park remained the center of baseball for western Kentucky, hosting games of the Kitty League.

The first incarnation of this park survives only in pictures that show a beautiful wooden ballpark.

The waters of Dawson Springs were believed to have medicinal qualities, and in the early years of the twentieth century a sizable tourist trade grew up as thousands of "the sick, the lame, the well came for the curative waters and to enjoy the social activities" (as a surviving sign in the town relates). Both the crowds and the springs lured the Pittsburgh Pirates to Dawson Springs. But at some point in the 1930s (the date remains unclear) the Tradewater River that runs alongside the park was swollen by an almighty storm and washed away the entire ballpark. It was not rebuilt, presumably because these were the financially troubled years of the Depression.

In 1999 the mayor of Dawson Springs, Stacia Peyton, succeeded in re-creating the old ballpark, building an exact copy from the 1914 blueprints, entirely in wood. She faced opposition from some of the public who thought that city funds could be spent in other ways, but the new ballpark is a thing of beauty and now home to a new baseball team, the Tradewater Pirates.

Riverside Stadium

Location: 1 Championship Way, City Island, Harrisburg, PA

Aka: Metro Bank Park (since 2005)

Status: Current home of the Harrisburg Senators

Architect: 360 Architecture

Opened: 1987; renovation 2001

Capacity: 6,302 (1987); 6,187 (2010)

Dimensions:

	Original 1987	Final 2010
Left Field	335 ft	325 ft
Center Field	400 ft	400 ft
Right Field	425 ft	325 ft

RIGHT: Riverside Stadium was but a stone's throw from the Susquehanna River.

BOTTOM: The original Island Park.

BELOW and OPPOSITE, TOP: The $45 million renovation produced a unique and exciting ballpark that has tremendous atmosphere, comfort, and distinct features. It dwarfs the Double-A home of the Nationals and former Expos: Metro Bank Park looks more like a Triple-A park.

Once located on City Island in the middle of the Susquehanna River, Riverside Stadium was home to the Harrisburg Senators. Harrisburg has one of the most unique settings for professional baseball yet the former Riverside Stadium was perhaps the ugliest ballpark in baseball, one with absolutely no soul. The only thing that it did have was the history and distinction of being located in the same historical spot where the game had been played since 1901. Island Park was a Tri-State League, original NY-Penn League before today's Single-A system, an Interstate League, and even a Triple-A International League ballpark.

The original wooden stadium, Island Park, was washed away in floodwaters during the 1950s and baseball wasn't played there again until Riverside Stadium was rebuilt in 1987 and was basically a pile of aluminum with very little soul.

The new Riverside Stadium was to be built on the site of the old stadium in 2005 and the $448 million funding was supposed to have been available in 2005, but persistent delays pushed the ballpark's building schedule back four years. Construction finally began in 2008 and the first level of the rebuild was complete by 2009. Finally in 2010, the ballpark was finished and renamed Metro Bank Park. The decision to go with aluminum was a controversial one as it certainly contributed to Metro Bank Park being one of the ugliest stadiums ever built. However, the franchise had the right architects to handle the job. The firm, 360 Architecture, knew they could do something unique with the metal to make Metro Bank Park look different from any other ballpark in the country. With a large seating capacity, it looks more than a Double-A stadium and, if the call came, this ballpark could be easily raised to Triple-A standards.

Location: 15th and Yale, Tulsa, OK
Aka: Tulsa County Stadium (1982–1989), Drillers Stadium (since 1989)
Opened: 1981
Capacity: 8,000 (1981); 10,997 (2010)
Dimensions:
Left Field 335 ft
Center Field 390 ft
Right Field 340 ft

Robert B. Sutton Stadium

LEFT: Today, Drillers Stadium has lost its team to a new park closer to Tulsa.

The Tulsa Oilers' old Driller Park collapsed in April 1977 and it was four years before the team had a permanent new home, one originally named Robert B. Sutton Stadium after its benefactor, but it looked a lot different than it did during its final incarnation as Drillers Stadium. The original ballpark was renamed Tulsa County Stadium in 1980 but when it opened in 1981 the Robert B. Sutton Stadium was far from cohesive, as the four sections were completely separate. Despite this, it was light-years ahead of Driller Park, where the front base lines had been made of folding chairs and simple wooden bleachers made up the total of the grandstand. Attendance jumped at the new ballpark.

When it was announced that the entire stadium would be getting a Triple-A makeover in 1987, attendance jumped even more, despite the miserable play. When the renovations were done, the ballpark had been transformed into a potential Triple-A venue with over 10,000 seats—the most in the Double-A Texas League. The renovation was so extensive that the original stadium and the newly named Drillers Stadium should really be listed as two different ballparks. Tulsa may not have gotten its Triple-A team, but the Drillers continued to compete, although attendance began to fall. The team threatened to abandon the city, but their bid for a new ballpark was approved—2009 was their final season at Drillers Stadium and they moved to ONEOK Field for the next season.

ABOVE: Sutton Stadium contained berms, not grandstands, down the first base line. Down the third base line, there was a series of nondescript, unroofed bleachers and when it first came into play the aluminum-based stadium was only single-decked. It could seat 4,800.

Robison Field

Location: Natural Bridge Avenue and Vandeventer Avenue, St. Louis, MO

Aka: New Sportsman's Park, League Park, Cardinal Field

Status: Defunct

Opened: April 27, 1893

Closed: 1877

Capacity: 14,500 (1893); 15,200 (1899); 21,000 (1909)

Dimensions:

	Original 1893	Final 1909
Left Field	470 ft	380 ft
Left Center	520 ft	400 ft
Center Field	500 ft	435 ft
Right Center	330 ft	320 ft
Right Field	290 ft	

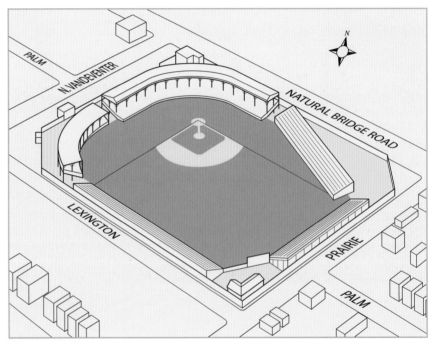

ABOVE: Artist's impression of Robison Field.

The newly named St. Louis Cardinals moved into Robison Field (New Sportsman's Park) in 1893. Opposite the Fair Grounds amusement park, the new ballpark occupied two city blocks and was taken by Cardinals owner Chris von der Ahe on a fifteen-year lease. He built a new grandstand and pavilion at a cost of around $45,000 to be ready for the new season. In 1893 the ballpark opened with great fanfare and festivities and proclaimed itself as "one of the most beautiful base ball and athletic parks in America."

The main entrance sat at the corner of Vandeventer and Natural Bridge. The wooden grandstand was supported by steel arches and beams and separated by tall fences from the grandstands on either side. Under the shelter of the grandstand was a large (in play) beer garden serving refreshments, and a ladies' restroom was located at the rear. On the grandstand roof sat three private boxes reserved for VIPs, officials, and the press. The scoreboard stood centrally in front of the clubhouse. Behind the grandstands lay open bleachers along Lexington, Natural Bridge, and Prairie.

In 1895, much to the fans' disgust, van der Ahe installed a horse racetrack around the playing field, in the course of which some bleachers and the grandstand had to be altered. He also allowed the ballpark to be used for a wide range of other popular entertainments, such as Wild West shows and dog racing.

During a game between the Browns and the Chicago Cubs on April 16, 1898, a fire started in the stands; by the time it was extinguished the left field bleachers and the grandstand were destroyed, one person was dead, and over a hundred carried serious burns. Van der Ahe was forced into bankruptcy and the Browns put up for auction: the buyers already owned the Cleveland Spiders and swapped team players between the cities with St. Louis the beneficiary. Robison Field was improved with new and closer bleachers, a refurbished grandstand, and increased capacity to around 15,500.

Another fire during a game in May 1901 destroyed the office, grandstand, and pavilion, but this time no one was hurt. The insurance money paid for a new grandstand and pavilion. In 1908 the ballpark was refurbished and capacity extended to over 20,000.

By 1918 the ground was known as Cardinal Field and in a bad state of repair; rather than invest in expensive improvements, the Cardinals were moved back to their old home at Sportsman's Park. In 1922 Cardinal Field was taken for Beaumont High School.

BELOW: A fire is ripping through League Park, formerly Robison Park, on May 4, 1901.

BOTTOM: Over 100,000 fans walk through the gates of Roger Dean Stadium each season, making this the best attended ballpark in the Florida State League.

Roger Dean Stadium

Location: 4751 Main Street, Jupiter, FL

Status: Home to the Jupiter Hammerheads, Palm Beach Cardinals, St. Louis Cardinals for spring training, Florida Marlins for spring training, the Gulf Coast Cardinals, and the Gulf Coast Marlins

Architect: HOK Sport

Opened: February 28, 1998

Capacity: 6,870

Dimensions:

Left Field 335 ft

Left Center 380 ft

Center Field 400 ft

Right Center 375 ft

Right Field 325 ft

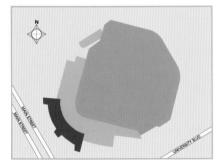

TOP: No other ballpark anywhere sees more professional games in a single season than Roger Dean Stadium. In fact, from February until September, it hardly ever has even a day off.

ABOVE: Footprint of Roger Dean Stadium.

No other ballpark anywhere sees more professional games in a single season than Roger Dean Stadium. It is home to not one but two major league teams in March, the St. Louis Cardinals and the Florida Marlins. Two Single-A teams take over for the summer, the Jupiter Hammerheads (affiliated to the Marlins) and the Palm Beach Cardinals (affiliated to the Cardinals). In addition, two teams in the Gulf Coast League use the stadium as their base, the Gulf Coast Marlins and the Gulf Coast Cardinals.

Until 2002, the Montreal Expos shared the stadium with the Cardinals. They swapped with the Marlins when Marlins owner Jeffrey Loria orchestrated a convenient multimillion dollar trade. With the arrival of the Marlins and their Triple-A Hammerhead colleagues, Roger Dean became home to some future stars. In 2002, Miguel Cabrera, who wasn't quite the home run hitter he later became, managed to get a league-leading forty-three doubles! Josh Willingham was the big home run leader on the team, hitting 17 while batting .274.

Jupiter is located nineteen miles north of West Palm Beach on the east coast. Roger Dean Stadium was built in 1998 to replace West Palm Beach Municipal Stadium, which was demolished in 2002. Costing $28 million and designed by HOK, it is still considered to be one of the top ballparks in the state, despite being over ten years old. It features a cloverleaf field of four training ballparks, and has a capacity just short of 7,000, with seating for 6,600 and space for another 200 or so on the grass berms. Roger Dean is by far the best-attended ballpark in the Florida State League, with both the Cardinals and the Hammerheads regularly drawing over 100,000 spectators during the course of the season.

The $28 million ballpark was named for the automobile magnate in 1994 in exchange for a $1 million donation from Dean's daughters, Patty and Janie.

LEFT: Roger Dean Stadium cost $28 million and was designed by HOK Sports.

Location: 1 Blue Jays Way, Toronto, Ontario, Canada
Aka: SkyDome
Status: Home of the Toronto Blue Jays
Architects: Rod Robbie and Michael Allen
Opened: June 5, 1989
Capacity: 50,516
Dimensions:
Left Field 328 ft
Left Center 375 ft
Center Field 400 ft
Right Center 375 ft
Right Field 328 ft
World Series: 1992, 1997
All-Star Game: 1991

The home of the Toronto Blue Jays is the multiple-entertainment facility near Lake Ontario in downtown Toronto formerly known as the SkyDome but now called the Rogers Centre. Built in the late 1980s, it was intended to accommodate both baseball and football, as well as a wide range of other sporting disciplines. It was then—and still is—far more than just a sports venue; for example, part of the complex is a huge 348-room hotel, with seventy rooms overlooking the playing field.

Sport in Toronto is at the mercy of the weather, and the need for a covered stadium became overwhelmingly apparent after the near wash-out of the 1982 Grey Cup Canadian football championship at the open-air Exhibition Stadium. Following vocal public demands, the architectural, location, and funding possibilities for an alternative sporting venue were investigated for a few years. Finally an industrial area comprising an old Canadian National Railway yard near Union Station and west of the CN Tower was chosen and the financing was provided by a complicated public-private partnership.

The stadium was to be the first of its kind in the world with a huge, fully retractable, four-paneled domed, motorized roof that takes around twenty minutes to close. It is the highest of all the domed arenas in MLB at 310 feet. The field was originally covered with AstroTurf as the surface need to be removed for non-sporting events. It is now covered with a synthetic fiber, rubber, and sand-based AstroTurf (only Tropicana Field in Florida in MLB also uses artificial turf). The pitcher's mound is raised and lowered hydraulically as required.

Seating is in five levels from right center field to home plate and to left center field. The original

ABOVE: The SkyDome is famous for having one of the biggest digital scoreboards in the history of baseball. Beneath the scoreboard is a restaurant, and above is something unique: the Hotel Renaissance, which has rooms overlooking the playing field. These are the glass windows that you see surrounding the scoreboard. You can book a room and watch a major league game right from your hotel window!

BELOW LEFT: Footprint of the stadium showing entrances.

BELOW: The tall pole is the CN Tower—the tallest free-standing structure in the world. You can travel up into it and look down through the glass at the field below and get views such as the image at the top of page 312.

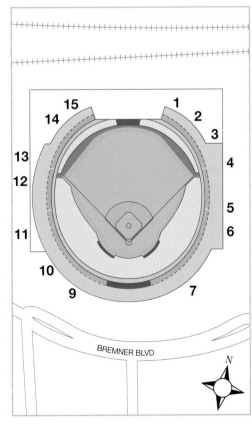

scoreboard was the huge video display JumboTron at 33 feet high and 110 feet side to side, but this was replaced by the equally huge LED scoreboard called "JaysVision."

In February 2005 the owners of the Blue Jays, Rogers Communications Inc., bought the complex and changed its name to the Rogers Centre, and set about improving the already well-equipped venue.

ABOVE: The SkyDome is testimony to the greatest technology in stadium building, but after it and U.S. Cellular Field opened, ballpark architecture went into "retro mode."

RIGHT: During nice weather, the ballfield is exposed to the elements. The SkyDome is the first ballpark ever built with a working retractable roof.

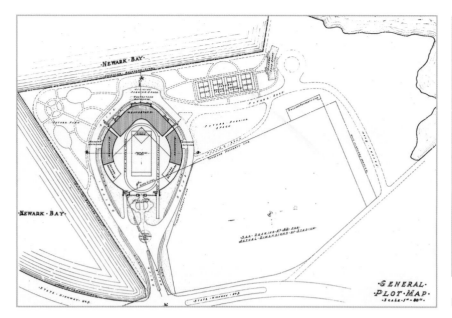

Location: Danforth Avenue and New Jersey Route 1, Jersey City, NJ
Aka: Jersey City Roosevelt Stadium
Status: Demolished in 1985
Architect: Christian H. Ziegler
Opened: April 23, 1937
Capacity: 23,000
Dimensions:
Left Field 330 ft
Left Center 377 ft
Center Field 411 ft
Right Center 377 ft
Right Field 330 ft

LEFT: Footprint of the stadium.

BELOW: 1940 view of the main entrance.

BOTTOM: Aerial view of the stadium in 1955. Jackie Robinson made his professional debut for the Brooklyn Dodgers' Triple-A Montreal Royals at Jersey City's Roosevelt Stadium in 1946.

Roosevelt Stadium was built in 1936, and began its professional life in 1937 as a home for the Jersey City Giants of the International League. This was often the last stop for any rookie ballplayer before becoming a member of the New York Giants. The Giants would use the ballpark for fifteen years until 1951, when the organization moved their International League team to Lansdowne Stadium in Ottawa, Canada. During that time, almost every famous ballplayer in New York had played at least one exhibition game here at the 23,000-seat Roosevelt Stadium.

In 1946 Jackie Robinson made his professional debut for the Brooklyn Dodgers' Triple-A Montreal Royals at Jersey City's Roosevelt Stadium. Schools were closed and the stadium sold 50,000 tickets. The controversial signing of the first black ballplayer had created quite a stir. Jackie Robinson got four hits that day, including a three-run homer, and added a pair of stolen bases. He brought an electricity to the ballpark that left a lasting impression on everyone—even his detractors.

The Brooklyn Dodgers made this their alternate home for two seasons. In 1956 and 1957 the Brooklyn Dodgers moved 10 percent of their home games from Ebbets Field to Jersey City in an attempt to draw fans. This was a difficult period for professional baseball, which was adversely affected by the impact of television. The Dodgers moved the franchise to the West Coast in 1958, bringing an end to professional baseball at Roosevelt Stadium for three years.

It returned in interesting circumstances, prompted by Fidel Castro's revolution in Cuba. On July 26, 1960, during a game in Havana between the Rochester Red Wings and the Havana Sugar Kings, shots rang out at Gran Stadium, hitting Rochester third base coach Frank Verdi and Sugar Kings shortstop Leo Cardenas. While neither was seriously injured, the Sugar Kings immediately escaped to Jersey City and finished their season at Roosevelt Stadium.

From 1961 until 1978, Roosevelt hosted football games and pop concerts, until in 1978 the Eastern League began to use the stadium. Roosevelt was finally demolished in 1985 after several years lying empty.

Location: 1250 First Avenue S and S. Atlantic Street., Seattle, WA

Status: Home of the Seattle Mariners

Architect: NBBJ

Opened: July 15, 1999

Capacity: 47,116 (1999); 38,177 (2010)

Dimensions:

Left Field 331 ft

Left Center 390 ft

Center Field 405 ft

Right Center 387 ft

Right Field 327 ft

All-Star Game: 2001

THIS PAGE and OPPOSITE:
The final design for Safeco Field included an unusual feature. The roof would be a completely independent nonfolding structure of three panels that would simply roll over the ballpark like a big hat when the weather was inclement, and roll out across the railroad tracks below to allow the sun to shine in when Seattle's summer sun made an appearance.

In July 1999 the Seattle Mariners left the unloved Kingdome for Safeco Field, a modern 47,772-seat retro ballpark. The stadium has a brick facade and an asymmetric playing field, and features a retractable roof that is left open to the skies whenever the forecast is good.

For the players the stadium boasts cedar-lined dugouts and elevated bullpens while the fans enjoy the wide concourses and numerous franchises. It is claimed that it took a massive $517 million to move from one of the very worst venues to one of the very best, but the fans are very happy with Safeco and its numerous facilities. There are nice retro touches such as the old-fashioned, hand-operated scoreboard alongside the eleven state-of-the-art video display boards. As for the field, the grass is a mixture of bluegrass and perennial rye laid over around thirty miles of undersoil heating coils.

The stadium consists of five levels; the field level, main concourse, club level, suite level and upper concourse are full of numerous food and drink opportunities (and plenty of restrooms). Scattered around the venue are numerous artworks, including a chandelier made up from 1,000 resin baseball bats, and a nine-foot-high bronze baseball glove.

But the single most expensive item is the retractable roof that covers the stands and the field but allows fresh air to blow in through the sides. When it is open, spectators on the right-side upper deck can enjoy views over Puget Sound and downtown, although other seating does not overlook the city. There are strict rules covering the deployment of the roof: if the weather suddenly turns bad, the roof can be closed in the middle of an inning. However, once the roof is closed during a game it cannot be reopened, but if the game starts with the roof closed it can be opened between innings, although the visitors can challenge the decision if they wish.

BELOW LEFT: The bullpens are alongside the left-field foul post and the left-field bleachers are a great place to watch a game.

BELOW: Footprint of the stadium showing entrances.

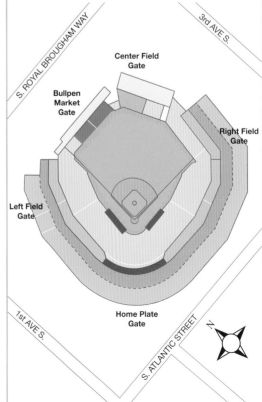

Location: Staten Island, NY

Opened: 1880s

Aka: St. George Grounds

Status: Demolished

Capacity: 4,400 or more

There was more to watch from the grandstands of this old ballpark than the game due to some outstanding views—at one stage during its heyday a fan could look out and see the Statue of Liberty being assembled. Two teams called it home—the American Association's New York Metropolitans in 1886–1887 and the New York Giants of the National League in 1889. In 1886, a ticket got you into the game and a ferry ride from Manhattan, as one Erastus Wiman owned the ballpark, the ferry, and the team.

During the Giants' year there the ballpark was rocky and bare from second base to center field because a production of *Nero, the Fall of Rome* was being staged and the same rains that caused the Johnstown flood forced the team to put wooden planks down in the outfield because the grass was too soggy to run on. The St. George Cricket Grounds had "illuminated geysers," just like those at Kauffman Stadium in Kansas City today.

RIGHT: St. George's two-tier grandstand could seat at least 4,400.

Location: St. Petersburg, FL

Aka: Waterfront Park

Status: Demolished 1947

Today the site of Progress Energy Park, perched on the edge of Tampa Bay, the St. Petersburg Athletic Park opened in 1921. It was a wooden structure also known as Waterfront Park and became the winter home of the Boston Braves from 1921 until 1937 (a marker stands just north of Progress Energy Park identifying this). They were joined by the New York Yankees in 1923, and legends of the game, such as Babe Ruth and Lou Gehrig, played here. The Braves were succeeded by the St. Louis Cardinals in 1938, whose long association with the field was to last fifty years.

Waterfront Park was a simple stadium with uncovered bleachers and a roof that was held up by poles, and in 1947 the Cardinals rebuilt it, constructing a concrete ballpark.

Location: 7555 North Pima Road, Scottsdale, AZ

Status: Spring training facility for the Arizona Diamondbacks and the Colorado Rockies

Architect: HKS

Opened: 2011

Capacity: 11,000

Dimensions

Left Field 345 ft

Center Field 410 ft

Right Field 345 ft

Winner of Digitalballparks.com Ballpark of the Year Award in 2011

This 140-acre, $100 million stadium complex is located in the Salt River Pima-Maricopa Indian community and is the newest MLB spring training facility, being home to the Arizona Diamondbacks and the Colorado Rockies since its opening. It is also the first major league park to be built on Native American land.

Construction began on November 17, 2009, with an aggressively fast-tracked schedule to get the stadium done by the 2011 spring training season. Each team has an 85,000-square-foot clubhouse, six full-size practice fields, two infield-only practice diamonds, and batting cages. The Diamondbacks occupy the facilities along the left field and the Rockies are in the right field.

The architects were HKS of Dallas, Texas. Founded in 1939 by Harwood K. Smith, it is one of the largest architectural firms in the county, and well-versed in ballpark design. Among their accomplishments are the Dell Diamond in Round Rock, Texas; Banner Island Ballpark in Stockton, California; Dr Pepper Ballpark in Frisco, Texas; Miller Park, home of the Milwaukee Brewers; the Ballpark at Arlington, home of the Texas Rangers; and the $118 million renovation of U.S. Cellular Field. They were also resposible for the Los Angeles Dodgers' spring training home, Camelback Ranch—Digitalballpark's top spring training ballpark until Talking Stick was built.

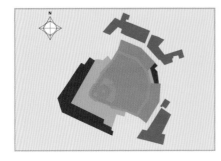

THIS PAGE and OPPOSITE, BELOW: The entrance, footprint, and internal views of Salt River Fields at Talking Stick, which is billed as "Two Tribes … Two Teams … One Home" and is the spring home of the Arizona Diamondbacks and of the Colorado Rockies.

Location: 9449 Friars Road, San Diego, CA

Aka: Jack Murphy Stadium (1980–1997), "the Murph," Qualcomm Stadium (since 1997), "the Q"

Status: No longer used for baseball

Architect: Gary Allen (Frank L. Hope & Associates)

Capacity: 50,000 (1967); 67,544 (1997)

Opened: August 20, 1967

First MLB game: April 8, 1969

Last MLB game: September 28, 2003

Dimensions:

	Original 1969	Final 1982
Left Field	330 ft	327 ft
Left Center	375 ft	370 ft
Center Field	420 ft	405 ft
Right Center	375 ft	370 ft
Right Field	330 ft	327 ft

World Series: 1984, 1998

All-Star Game: 1978, 1992

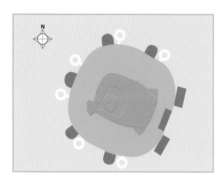

In the middle of the 1960s, Jack Murphy, sports editor of the *San Diego Union,* started a campaign to find a suitably impressive home for the San Diego Chargers of the NFL and a home for a much-hoped-for expansion MLB team. The public responded enthusiastically to his rally cry, and when it was put to a public referendum whether to fund the $28 million, the response was a resounding 72 percent "yes." The selected site was 166 acres in Mission Valley and construction work started immediately on the $27.75 milllion project.

The first occupants of San Diego Stadium were the Chargers, who arrived in August 1967. At that time the venue was a horseshoe-shaped three-tier grandstand capable of holding about 50,000 spectators. Half the lower-level seating was built of concrete on the south side and the rest of movable steel and aluminum frames that, for the baseball configuration, would be moved into the western quadrant along the third-base, left-field side.

In 1968 the Triple-A San Diego Padres played their last season at San Diego Stadium before being folded by their owner, C. Arnholt Smith, who wanted to transfer their name to the new MLB franchise he and San Diego had just been awarded. The following year, the new San Diego Padres joined the National League West Division and played their first game on April 8, 1969; they stayed for three decades.

ABOVE: The Padres spent more than thirty years at San Diego Stadium before moving to PETCO Park.

BELOW: The main problem with cookie-cutters is the distance you are from the field—as this picture shows.

In 1980 the venue was renamed Jack Murphy Stadium in honor of the man who had done so much to inspire the building of the sports arena and who had died in September that year. When the stadium was renamed seventeen years later in 1997 as Qualcomm Stadium after the local telecommunications company donated $18 million so the facility could be fully enclosed, the stadium site was named Jack Murphy Field so his memory would live on.

The Padres' original lease expired at the close of the 1999 season, but they managed to get an extension to September 28, 2003, when they played their last game there. During the last few years the city had been constructing a downtown ballpark near the waterfront, but the lack of sufficient funds delayed the project by two years. The Padres finally moved into state-of-the-art PETCO Park 2004.

ABOVE and BELOW: Aerial views of the stadium in 1971 (below) and 2007 show its enclosure. Initially, there was no seating from right field to center field. The right-field bleachers were added for 1983 and then double-decked in 1997.

Location: 7408 E. Osborn Road, Scottsdale, AZ

Status: Demolished in 1991

Opened: 1956

TOP: Scottsdale Stadium from behind home plate.

ABOVE: Scottsdale Stadium looking over to Camelback Mountain.

RIGHT: The main entrance. The original stadium served as the former Cactus League home of the Baltimore Orioles, Boston Red Sox, Chicago Cubs, and Oakland A's.

The first Scottsdale Stadium was built at the intersection of Osborn Road and Drinkwater Boulevard in the middle of Old Town Scottsdale, Arizona. Completed in one year in 1956, it enjoyed the stunning backdrop of Camelback Mountain. The venue cost $72,000 and the first major league team to play here was the Baltimore Orioles. In 1982 the San Francisco Giants came to Scottsdale for the first time for their spring training. After the last game ended on April 3, 1991, the old venue was torn down and a new one was built within a year.

Location: 7408 E. Osborn Road, Scottsdale, AZ

Status: Home to the Scottsdale Scorpions and the Arizona League Giants; spring training facility for the San Francisco Giants

Architect: HOK Sports

Opened: March 12, 1992; renovated 2006

Capacity: 12,000 (11,500 seats)

Dimensions:

Left Field 360 ft

Center Field 430 ft

Right Field 340 ft

Built in 1992, the second version of Scottsdale Stadium was designed by HOK Sports with a capacity of around 12,000. It was the first modern ballpark in Arizona and set the standard for the Cactus League. The stadium was built using red brick and dark green wrought iron, on eleven acres of landscaping filled with over 200 trees.

The main scoreboard is in left center while two smaller boards are attached on opposite sides of the grandstand. The upper grandstand has aluminum benches with seat backs while the lower stand has green plastic chairs. Bleacher seats are fixed down both the left and right field lines, while a concourse completely encircles the entire ballpark with the main section behind the grandstand.

Between 1992 and 1997, Scottsdale was the home of the Phoenix Firebirds of the Pacific Coast League until they moved to Fresno; the Arizona Diamondbacks moved in for the 1998 season. However, the stadium is probably most famous for hosting the San Francisco Giants in spring training and for games in the Cactus League.

In 2006, after a renovation costing around $23.1 million, Scottsdale became a greatly improved facility. For the upgrade, the Giants extended their playing agreement to stay for an additional twenty years, until 2035. At Scottsdale they attract some of the top attendance numbers for the Cactus League. Traditionally, the mayor of Scottsdale throws out the first pitch on the opening day of each season.

The new facilities include the construction on the eastern side of the stadium of a full and half-size practice field, the expansion of the stadium clubhouse, new right-field deck and seating, and new walkways connecting the left- and right-field berms.

The Scottsdale Scorpions play here in the Arizona Fall League, and the Arizona League Giants play in the Arizona League in the summer.

LEFT: The 1992 Scottsdale Stadium sets the stadium standard for the Cactus League.

BELOW: The second Scottsdale Stadium looking over to Camelback Mountain. The ballpark is well-liked by fans who small admire the atmospher of a spring training venue smack in the middle of downtown Scottsdale. The fact that it's the home of the 2010 World Champions helps swell the crowds and being able to watch batting and pitching practice—particularly if it's on the main field—is a real bonus. Because of these factors, attendances can be high: the record in 2008 was 11,999 fans against the Chicago Cubs

Location: Intersection of 16th and Bryant Streets, San Francisco, CA

Status: Demolished in 1959

Opened: April 7, 1931

First MLB game: April 15, 1958

Last MLB game: September 20, 1959

Capacity: 16,000 (1931); 18,500 (1946); 22,900 (1958)

Dimensions

	Original 1931	Final 1959
Left Field	340 ft	365 ft
Left Center	375 ft	375 ft
Center Field	400 ft	410 ft
Right Center	397 ft	360 ft
Right Field	385 ft	355 ft

ABOVE and BELOW: Seals Stadium did not have a roof because of the high temperatures and sparse rainfall.

Between 1931 and 1959, Seals Stadium in San Francisco was the home of the Pacific Coast League San Francisco Seals and their rivals, the Mission Reds. Accordingly, the stadium had three locker rooms, one each for the Seals and Reds, as well as another for the visiting team.

The stadium opened on April 7, 1931, in downtown San Francisco during the Depression, when workmen slaved for $3 a day; the ballpark cost $600,000 to construct. The resulting ballpark was accused of possessing little character with its open-air, single-tier grandstand made of steel and concrete that extended down both foul lines. Most of the spectators sat in the grandstand, but there was also a small bleacher section in right field. For a few years, a seal was kept in a water tank underneath the grandstand.

The scoreboard was positioned in center field, but the outfield grass ran right

up to the fence as the playing field lacked a warning track. Night games were lit by six tower banks of lights and were generally considered the best in the minor leagues. In 1938 the Missions moved on and out of Seals Stadium to become the Hollywood Stars.

The New York Giants arrived on the West Coast in 1958 to play in the National League's West Division and chose to play at Seals Stadium. On moving they became the San Francisco Giants (their namesake minor league team had to move out of Seals). A second open-air outfield bleacher was added in left field on their arrival to accommodate the extra demand for tickets. Starting on April 15, 1958, they stayed for two seasons until Candlestick Park was ready for them: the Giants left after their last game on September 20, 1959.

In November 1959 Seals Stadium was demolished, but many of the light stanchions and fold-down seats reappeared at Cheney Stadium in Tacoma, Washington. A discount department store was built on the site, and then in the early 1990s it became the location of the Potrero Center shopping mall.

TOP: A separate uncovered bleacher section was added in left field when the New York Giants moved to San Francisco in 1958.

ABOVE RIGHT: A still from a film: *"Opening Day at Seals Stadium: First Major League Game Ever in San Francisco."*

RIGHT: Hamm's brewery was next door to the stadium, and the Hamm's beer glass at Seals Stadium was a popular landmark.

LEFT: The Giants played at Seals Stadium for two years, attracting over two million fans before moving to their new home. The scoreboard was in center field, above the batter's eye. Note the absence of the bleachers that were added for the Giants' arrival.

Location: 1 Line Drive, Des Moines, IA

Aka: Principal Park (since 2004)

Status: Home of the Iowa Cubs

Architect: Populous

Opened: April 16, 1992; renovated 2005–2006

Capacity: 11,500

Dimensions:

Left Field 335 ft

Center Field 400 ft

Right Field 335 ft

All Star Game: 1997

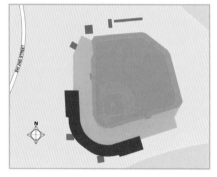

TOP: The impressive right-field grandstand was renovated in 2005.

ABOVE: The footprint of Principal Park shows its size. Triple-A players have to get used to playing in larger ballparks before larger crowds, in order to deal with the intensity of the "Show." They certainly do that here: 15,188 fans watched an Iowa Cubs game against the New Orleans Zephyrs and the franchise attendance record is 576,310 in 2007.

RIGHT: This photograph shows clearly the twelve skyboxes added in left center field in 1995. This building also serves as the clubhouse for the Cubs. There's a weight room, manager's offices, locker room, family center, and an indoor batting cage. It also shows, over the batter's eye, less than a mile away, the stunning Iowa State Capitol building, which is illuminated at night.

In 1947 the original Sec Taylor Stadium was built at the confluence of the Des Moines River and the Raccoon River. At that time it was called Pioneer Park. In 1991 it was completely rebuilt at a cost of $12 million. This was not a renovation. The old ballpark was completely demolished and Sec Taylor Stadium II rose out of the ashes. Pioneer Park had been similar to many of the ballparks built in its era, such as Sam T. Wolfson Park and Bill Meyers Stadium. It was certainly a beautiful stadium. It had a great rustic quality to it, and a real old-time ballpark vibe. The Iowa Cubs, however, are a Triple-A team—all Triple-A parks had to be brought up to high standards in the early 1990s or face being decomissioned. It was easier just to begin anew.

It was money well spent. Since its inception, Sec Taylor Stadium has done well at the box office. The Cubs have drawn crowds as high as 13,660, and in the 2002 season 509,000 fans passed through its gates.

In 2004 the naming rights were bought by Principal Financial Group in a $2.5 million deal, which helped fund a $6.8 million renovation project that included the addition of over a thousand new seats in the right-field grandstand, replacement of the other seats, new right-field bleachers, scoreboard and video board, stadium field lighting system, and other structural changes. This expenditure ensured that the agreement with the Chicago Cubs ran through 2012, and that the I-Cubs remained the Triple-A affiliate of the Cubs.

Location: 123-01 Roosevelt Avenue, Flushing, NY

Status: Demolished 2008–2009

Architect: Praeger-Kavanagh-Waterbury

Capacity: 55,300

Opened: April 17, 1964

Dimensions:

	Original	
	1964	2008
Left Field	341 ft	338 ft
Left Center	371 ft	371 ft
Center Field	410 ft	410 ft
Right Center	371 ft	371 ft
Right Field	341 ft	338 ft

World Series: 1969, 1973, 1986, 2000

All-Star Game: 1964

The New York Mets arrived in Shea Stadium (official name: William A. Shea Municipal Stadium) in the borough of Queens, New York City, in 1964 after a long history at the three variations of the Polo Grounds. Built in Flushing Meadows for $31 million and within ear-splitting distance of La Guardia Airport and next to the site of the 1964–65 World's Fair, this was a stadium with distinct character.

Sitting in a forty-five-acre plot—the very same one that Walter O'Malley, owner of the Brooklyn Dodgers, had rejected before taking his squad to Los Angeles—the stadium started construction in fall 1961 but was not completed until April 1964, delayed by over a year

ABOVE: Shea Stadium on August 30, 2007. The Mets' new home—Citi Field—is under construction alongside.

BELOW: View from the top tier, showing off the skill of the ground crew.

due to appalling winter weather in 1962 and 1963 and numerous labor disputes. While the venue was under construction it was called Flushing Meadow Stadium, but a popular campaign was started to name it instead to honor local attorney William A. Shea, whose tireless work to bring the Mets to Queens needed acknowledgment.

For its time, Shea was a showpiece. Circular in shape, it had five tiers of seating all pointing toward center field; additionally, there were two rotating stands of 5,000 seats for conversion between baseball and football. Both sections were moved by motor-operated equipment that rolled on subterranean railroad tracks; to convert for football the left-field stands moved clockwise to center field and the right-field stands moved counterclockwise to center field so both sections were parallel to the sidelines.

The original plans included a dome, but that was dropped after feasibility studies declared it problematic and expensive. The grounds included a scoreboard weighing over sixty tons that was 175 feet wide and 86 feet high and showed scoring information, out-of-town scores, color slides, and messages. A real convenience for most fans were the twenty-one escalators, and numerous public restrooms. Another innovation was the installation of a light ring instead of the usual light towers. In this way, banks of lights were built around the top of the stadium to illuminate the playing area.

The end came for the Mets at Shea at the finish of the 2008 season. In line with New York City law, the old stadium was dismantled rather than imploded: the venue was stripped of memorabilia that was sold off to fans and collectors. A plaque in the Citi Field parking lot marks the location of Shea's home plate.

ABOVE: View from the parking lot, including the back of the huge scoreboard.

BELOW: Shea Stadium could hold over 55,000 spectators. In addition to sports, the venue was a concert location for almost every major modern musical act from Janis Joplin to the Beatles, Rolling Stones, Jethro Tull, Bruce Springsteen, and many others.

Location: In a plot bounded by West Somerset Street, North 21st Street, West Lehigh Avenue, and North 20th Street

Aka: Connie Mack Stadium (1953–1976)

Status: Demolished in 1976

Architect: William Steele and Sons

Opened: April 12, 1909

Last MLB game: October 1, 1970

Capacity: 23,000 (1909); 33,608 (1970)

Dimensions:

	Original 1909	Final 1960
Left Field	378 ft	334 ft
Left Center	358 ft	405 ft
Center Field	502 ft	447 ft
Right Center	355 ft	400 ft
Right Field	340 ft	329 ft

World Series: 1910, 1911, 1913, 1914, 1929, 1930, 1931, 1950

All-Star Games: 1943, 1952

Shibe Park was named after Benjamin Shibe, one of the original owners of the Philadelphia Athletics. They had moved to Shibe after leaving Columbia Park in October 1908 because it had become too small: they replanted a sod of dirt from Columbia Park at Shibe.

Built and styled to impress, Shibe Park was designed by manager (and co-owner) Connie Mack with a distinctive brick-and-stone French Renaissance facade with a Beaux Arts–style cupola above the main entrance. But, in fact, Shibe was the first of the modern concrete-and-steel ballparks in the majors and cost an impressive $300,000. When it first opened, the field dimensions were huge (500 feet in center), but over time the foul posts were brought in. However, the biggest change came in 1925 when all the grandstands were double-decked and a left-field grandstand was constructed.

In the 1920s the Athletics drew such big crowds that nearby flat owners on Twentieth Street built their own bleachers and charged fans an entry fee. A furious Connie Mack took them to court but lost, so during winter 1933 he oversaw the building of the fence to thirty-three feet high, blocking the unauthorized view: it became known as the "spite fence." Ironically, the form of the A's dropped away, as did the crowds.

In midseason 1938, the National League's Philadelphia Phillies moved into Shibe to share expenses with the American League's A's; they stayed as co-tenants until 1954, when

ABOVE: As with most of the jewel-box parks, Shibe was built in a city block and had stands around three sides. This photograph shows off the two-tier grandstand and single-tier pavilions roofed in 1913.

LEFT: The impressive French Renaissance tower topped off by a cupola and columns along the outside of the grandstand made Shibe a distinctive structure. It was the first modern ballpark and revolutionized the way ballparks looked—more so when one considers today's interest in retro fields.

ABOVE: 1910 panorama of the World Series game between the Philadelphia A's and the Chicago Cubs. The home team won 9–3 and went on to win the title.

BELOW: A packed house for the A's playing the St. Louis Cardinals, October 5, 1931.

the A's moved away to Kansas City. After guiding the A's to five World Series victories, Connie Mack finally retired in 1950 at the age of eighty-eight.

The Phillies bought the stadium outright in 1954 and renamed it Connie Mack Stadium. But by the 1960s the Phillies started agitating for a new multipurpose stadium.

On August 20, 1971, the statue of Connie Mack was ceremonially rededicated at Veterans Stadium; however, back at Shibe a serious fire broke out and destroyed the left-field stands, collapsing one of the walls.

That year the Phillies left Connie Mack Stadium for their new home at Veterans Stadium. During the last game on October 1, 1970, fans disrupted the game as they scavenged for souvenirs. Now owned by the city of Philadelphia, in October 1975 the stadium was ordered to be razed; it has since been built over by the Deliverance Evangelistic Church.

Location: 2700 Rainier Avenue South, Seattle, WA
Aka: Sick's Seattle Stadium
Status: Demolished in 1979
Opened: June 15, 1938
Closed: 1976
Capacity: 11,000 (1938); 25,420 (1969)
Dimensions:

	Original 1938	Final 1969
Left Field	325 ft	305 ft
Center Field	400 ft	405 ft
Right Field	325 ft	320 ft

Sick's Stadium was built in 1938 at a cost of $350,000 to replace the old wooden Dugdale Field, which had burned to the ground in 1932 after a Fourth of July celebration.

Seattle's professional baseball team was purchased by Emil Sick, who quickly built a new stadium for the team over the footprint of the old Dugdale Field. Upon completion of the sale, the Seattle Indians changed their name to the Seattle Rainiers, not because of Sick's Stadium's proximity to Mount Rainier, but because Sick was owner of the Seattle Rainier Beer Brewery.

The minor league Rainiers proved to be more than comfortable in their new digs, winning 100 games and making the playoffs, although they lost in the first round. By 1940 the Rainiers got their act together and won a monstrous 112 games during the regular season. They plowed through the playoffs and then defeated the Los Angeles Angels to win their first Pacific Coast League championship, a feat they repeated in 1941 and 1942.

In 1946 Sick's Stadium was granted another professional baseball franchise that would play home games whenever the Rainiers were on the road. The new team, the Seattle Steelheads, was part of the Negro West Coast Baseball Association. Despite the talent, the Steelheads didn't draw well at the box office, and they would call it quits before the end of the season.

The Rainiers continued until 1968, winning the PCL in 1951 and 1955. When the Sick family sold the team, they became known as the Angels from 1965 to 1968.

Major league baseball arrived at Sick's Stadium in 1969, but although the fans were delighted, the stadium as far from ready for its new role. Preparations and renovations were incomplete by the time of the Seattle Pilots' opening game, and facilities remained inadequate. It was the death knell for Sick's Stadium and for major league baseball in Seattle until the construction of the Seattle Mariners' Kingdome. In 1979 Sick's was demolished, leaving just a memory of its glory years in the 1940s and 1950s.

TOP and ABOVE:
Contrasting views from 1969 (above) and 1941 (top) showing the extra seating in left field.

BELOW: Panorama looking toward the grandstand and a less than full house. Trouble was that by the end of the first MLB season, the team had finished in dead last and drawn only 690,000 fans because the stadium just wasn't up to scratch. (Photo courtesy Paul Hamaker.)

South End Grounds I
Location: Boston, MA
Aka: Walpole Street Grounds, the Union Baseball Grounds, the Boston Baseball Grounds, the Boston National League Base Ball Park
Status: Demolished in 1887
Opened: 1871

South End Grounds II
Aka: Grand Pavilion
Status: Destroyed by fire in 1894
Opened: 1888
Capacity: 6,800

South End Grounds III
Status: Closed in 1914
Opened: May 16, 1894
Capacity: 6,800
Dimensions
Left Field 250 ft
Center Field 440 ft
Right Field 255 ft

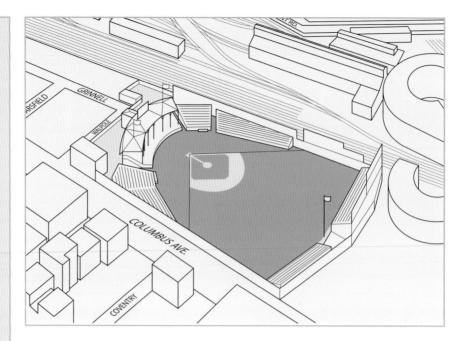

ABOVE: Artist's impression of South End Grounds III.

ABOVE: South End Grounds II—the Majestic Pavilion. There is a digital re-creation of this at the Hall of Fame in Cooperstown.

South End Grounds refers to any one of three baseball parks that the Boston Braves—who played in the National Association and the National League from 1871 to 1914—called home. The stadiums had many different names. The first South End Grounds was opened in 1871 and the Boston Red Stockings played there from 1877. Attendance varied from 55,000 in the first year, slumping to 34,000 in 1880, and rising to 260,000 in the final year. The second stadium opened the following year. Sometimes called the Grand Pavilion—as can be seen from the photograph below, it was indeed a grand affair, but it was destroyed in the Great Roxbury Fire of May 1894 which was started by children beneath some bleachers and quickly spread. After a season under the Red Stockings name, the team became the Beaneaters.

The third ballpark was built in a mere ten weeks on the site of the old stand. The Beaneaters were hit badly when their players were poached by the American League startup in Boston. Attendance fell from a high of 335,000 in 1897. The change of name in 1912 saw the Braves appear, and in 1914, the last season at South End Grounds, they staged a miraculous comeback, moving from last place to first. They played the last few games and the World Series, which they won, at Fenway Park until Braves Field was completed in the 1915 season. Attendance in 1914 was a record 380,000.

RIGHT: The Boston Beaneaters playing at South End Grounds II; May 24, 1888.

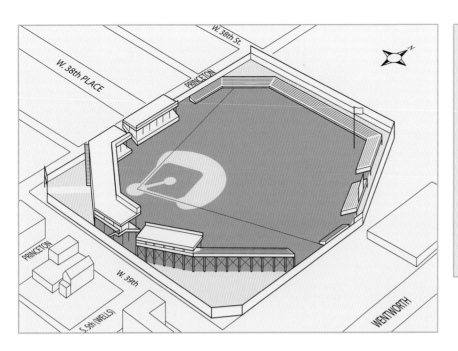

South Side Park III
Location: W 39th Street (now called Pershing Road) between South Wentworth Avenue and South Princeton Avenue, Chicago, IL
Aka: Brotherhood Park, Schorling's Park (from 1911)
Status: Destroyed by fire in 1940
Opened: 1890
Capacity: 15,000
World Series: 1906; 1924 and 1926 (Negro Leagues)

South Side Park was the name used for three different ballparks that were located just a few blocks from each other. The first was the home of a short-lived team in a location around 39th Street and South Wabash Avenue.

The second was located at 35th Street and South Wentworth Avenue. The Chicago Pirates played there in 1890 and the Chicago Colts, forerunners of the Chicago Cubs, in 1891–1893. Charles Comiskey played and managed the Chicago Pirates.

The third South Side Park, the best known and longest lived, was at 39th Street (now called Pershing Road) between South Wentworth Avenue and South Princeton Avenue, where it served as the playing field for the Chicago Wanderers cricket team during the 1893 World's Fair.

Comiskey moved the St. Paul Saints to South Side as the White Stockings. He built a 7,000-seat wooden grandstand on the site in 1900, and gained immediate success, winning the American League 1901 and 1906 pennants, and the 1906 World Series over the Cubs. The White Sox clinched the only all-Chicago World Series on October 14, 1906, at South Side Park in front of an overflow crowd of 19,266. When the White Sox moved to Comiskey Park in 1910, South Side Park became the home of the newly formed Chicago American Giants of the Negro League, in 1911. It was renamed Schorling's Park after their owner Rube Foster's business partner, John C. Schorling. The Giants played there until the 1940 season, when the third version of South Side Park was destroyed by fire on Christmas Day.

ABOVE: Artist's impression of South Side Park, home to the White Sox 1901–1910.

BELOW: White Sox vs. Cubs, City Championship series, October 9, 1909, at South Side Park.

Location: 2 South Mickey Mantle Drive, Oklahoma City, OK
Aka: The Brick, SBC Bricktown Ballpark, AT&T Bricktown Ballpark (from 2001), RedHawks Field at Bricktown
Status: Home to the Oklahoma City RedHawks
Architect: Architectural Design Group
Opened: April 16, 1998
Capacity: 13,066
Dimensions
Left Field 325 ft
Center Field 400 ft
Right Field 325 ft

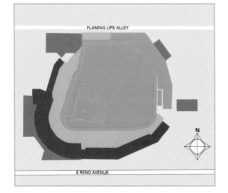

TOP: RedHawks Field also hosts the season-ending Bricktown Showdown Triple-A championship game, fought out between the International League and Pacific Coast League winners. It is also the venue for the Big 12 Conference tournament.

ABOVE: Footprint of the stadium.

BELOW: Looking over to first base from third shows off well the size of this ballpark.

Built in 1998 for $34 million, the AT&T Bricktown Ballpark is one of the latest and greatest modern ballparks built for Triple-A baseball. The ballpark is a major league facility in many ways, just scaled down for the smaller numbers of the minor league market. For many years the Oklahoma RedHawks were Triple-A members of the Texas Rangers organization and the Pacific Coast League, but have recently come under the wing of the Houston Astros. The ballpark's name has changed several times, though, from Southwestern Bell Bricktown Ballpark to SBC Bricktown Ballpark, AT&T Bricktown Ballpark, and now RedHawks Field at Bricktown.

The RedHawks themselves came from rather humble beginnings. Before 1998, they were known as the Oklahoma City 89ers, and played at All Sports Park at the Oklahoma fairgrounds. The stadium was built in 1962 and was a large one, built into a bowl with a 12,000-seat capacity—certainly large enough for Triple-A baseball. Though a bit utilitarian, it was actually a rather nice ballpark. However, it was light-years away from Bricktown Ballpark's major league feel.

Bricktown Ballpark is a completely enclosed stadium that seems to take you into its own world. The 13,000-seat stadium is almost like a little city within itself, catering to all of your ballpark-related needs, including food and beer. Though less than half the size of Pittsburgh's PNC Park, the stadium has all the facilities normally associated with the major leagues, including statues of Hall of Fame players associated with Oklahoma, such as Johnny Bench, Mickey Mantle, and Warren Spahn. It's a popular venue and the ballpark regularly draws over 500,000 fans annually, putting its attendance figures in the top fifteen of minor league teams.

Location: 5800 Stadium Parkway, Melbourne, FL
Status: Home of the Brevard County Manatees; spring training facility for the Washington Nationals
Opened: 1994
Capacity: 8,100
Dimensions:
Left Field 340 ft
Center Field 404 ft
Right Field 340 ft
All Star Game: 2008 (Florida State League)

LEFT: The stadium was created for the Florida Marlins, which accounts for the colors. A makeover has since changed the stadium into the Nationals' colors.

Built in 1994, Space Coast Stadium is relatively close to the Kennedy Space Center, and the architects of the ballpark tried to incorporate the intergalactic theme into the design. The stadium was built as the spring training facility for the Florida Marlins, the team that was created in 1993 as part of the expansion of Major League Baseball. It is currently the spring training home for the Washington Nationals and the regular training ground for the Brevard Country Manatees, the Triple-A affiliate of the Milwaukee Brewers.

With a capacity of 8,000, it cost around $8 million to build, and the Marlins called it home every spring for eight seasons. There are five training fields, two half-fields, and an award-winning stadium. Until 2008, the stadium colors remained those of the Marlins, and the teal and gray seating gave the stadium a very Floridian feel. A makeover in 2008 changed the decor to the Washington Nationals' colors of blue and red, as well as improving the scoreboard system and installing a new roof.

In 2003, the Marlins and the Montreal Expos swapped stadiums. Together with their Triple-A franchise, the Expos trained at Roger Dean Stadium at Jupiter, while the Marlins and their minor league team, the Manatees, used Space Coast. In a complicated maneuver, Jeffrey Loria, onetime owner of the Expos, bought the Marlins in 2002 and therefore owned Space Coast Stadium, a facility he simply disliked. So he leased it back to the Expos and installed his Marlins at Roger Dean Stadium, a facility he believed in. In a further twist, the Expos moved to Washington in 2004, becoming the Washington Nationals, who took up residence at Space Coast in 2005.

The Brevard County Manatees play at Space Coast during the regular season as part of the Florida State League.

ABOVE RIGHT: The foul poles are memorials to the two space shuttle disasters, *Columbia* and (as here) *Challenger*.

RIGHT: Space Coast Stadium has a mini space shuttle monument to emphasize its proximity to the Kennedy Space Center.

Speranza Park

Location: In a block bounded by Cherry Street, Frederick Street, and Franklin Avenue, Toledo, OH
Status: Closed October 2, 1890
Opened: May 1, 1890

Speranza Park was the short-lived home of the Toledo Maumees, a team that played in the American Association during the 1889 season, and was located at a site bounded by Cherry Street, Frederick Street, and Franklin Avenue. The term *speranza* means "hope" in Italian and the ballpark was supposedly named after the owner's personal yacht. The Maumees' first home game took place on May 1, 1890, but their season's performance was distinctly poor. The team finished a few games above .500, and twenty games back of first place, ending whatever hopes the club had of major league status. They ran out for their final game at Speranza Park on October 2, 1890.

Sportsman's Park (1882)

Location: Grand and Dodier, St. Louis, MO
Opened: 1882
Capacity: 6,000 (1882); 12,000 (1886)
Status: Burned down in 1891
Closed: 1892
Dimensions:
Left Field 351 ft
Center Field 460 ft
Right Field 285 ft

The first important ballpark in St. Louis was called the Grand Avenue Ball Grounds and sat at the corner of Grand Avenue and Dodier Street. Set out in 1867 on a single square block, it became the home of the St. Louis Brown Stockings of the National Association in 1875—they stayed for two years.

In 1880 the St. Louis Brown Stockings—now members of the American Association—were bought by Alfred Spink, and he ordered the existing structures removed and instead built a new wooden, covered grandstand. The new ballpark was named Sportsman's Park and stood on the southeast corner of the block nearest Grand Avenue. In 1891 the all-wood grandstand burned to the ground. The Browns needed a better ballpark and found what they needed a few blocks north. They called it New Sportsman's Park (it would become Robison Field). That same year, 1892, the National Association folded and the Browns transferred to play in the National League and at the same time changed their name to become the St. Louis Cardinals.

RIGHT: The St. Louis Browns from the American Association are posed in a photo collage inside Sportsman's Park. This photograph is dated 1884 and the wooden grandstands can be seen in the background.

Sportsman's Park (1902)

Location: Grand and Dodier, St. Louis, MO
Capacity: 18,000 (1907)
Opened: April 23, 1902
Status: Rebuilt as Sportsman's Park III
Dimensions:
Left Field 368 ft
Center Field 430 ft
Right Field 335 ft

The second incarnation of Sportsman's Park was the shortest-lived. The American League Browns moved to St. Louis from Milwaukee in 1902 and built new grandstands at Sportsman's Park. The diamond and main stands were in a different position to the one adopted in Sportsman's III. The period is perhaps best remembered for football rather than baseball. It was here that St. Louis University's football team played and perfected the aerial pass in 1906.

In 1909 the Browns made changes. The diamond was repositioned at the southwest corner, and a new steel-and-concrete grandstand was built—only the third such in the major leagues. The previous curved grandstand continued to be used until 1912 as the left-field bleachers, but was soon replaced with permanent bleachers.

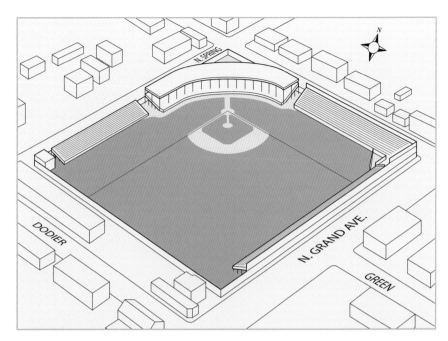

LEFT: Artist's impression of the second Sportsman's Park, the last wooden version.

BELOW: Aerial view of Sportman's Park III before 1940, when the lights went in.

BOTTOM: The lights were roof-mounted on the grandstand with four towers, two each in left and right field (see also photo at top of page 336).

Location: Grand and Dodier, St. Louis, MO

Aka: Busch Stadium (1953–1966)

Status: Demolished in 1966

Architect: Osborn Engineering

Opened: April 14, 1909; renovated 1925

Last MLB game: May 8, 1966

Capacity: 17,600 (1909); 30,500 (1954)

Dimensions

Left Field 351 ft

Left Center 379 ft

Center Field 422 ft

Right Center 354 ft

Right Field 310 ft

World Series: 1926, 1928, 1930, 1931, 1934, 1942, 1943, 1944, 1964

All-Star Games: 1940, 1948, 1957

Sportsman's Park (1909)

The Browns played in Sportsman's Park from 1909. They were joined by the Cardinals, who moved back to the grounds, playing their first game there on July 1, 1920. Improvements were soon made to the grounds in 1925: seating capacity was increased to 30,500 and the grandstands were covered and double-decked to the foul poles on both left and right. Bleachers encircled the outfield, with the right-field bleachers covered. A press box was installed on the stadium roof and a huge scoreboard was placed above the left-field seats. In May 1940 Sportsman's Park held its first night game under lights.

In 1953 the Browns moved to Baltimore, leaving the Cardinals alone at Sportsman's Park. Owner Bill Veeck sold out to Anheuser-Busch, owner of the Cardinals, and in April 1953 Sportsman's Park became Busch Stadium. Busch

initiated some $500,000 worth of renovations, including an improved clubhouse and new box seats, but most dramatically, he had a huge Budweiser eagle installed on top of the scoreboard that would dramatically flap its wings after each home run.

After the move to Sportsman's Park, the Cardinals became one of baseball's glory teams. Between the mid-1920s and mid-1940s they captured nine NL pennants and six World Series titles.

On May 8, 1966, the Cardinals played their last game at Busch, a loss to the Giants, and at the end of play the home plate was helicoptered over to the new Busch Memorial Stadium in downtown St. Louis. Sportsman's Park III was being demolished even as the fans exited the ground. The ballpark was replaced by the Herbert Hoover Boys and Girls Club.

Stotz Field

Location: Memorial Avenue and Demorest Street, Williamsport, PA
Aka: Carl E. Stotz Field
Status: Birthplace of Little League Baseball
Opened: 1939
World Series: 1947–1958

TOP: The World Series opener on October 7, 1946.

ABOVE : Every single measurement and every Little League rule was devised by Carl E. Stotz at this endearing little ground.

BELOW: Sun City Stadium lacked a roof, and enjoyed a brief heyday as a spring training ground in the 1970s.

Carl E. Stotz Field in Williamsport, Pennsylvania, is the birthplace of Little League Baseball and home to the first twelve Little League World Series.

Carl E. Stotz came to this ballfield in 1939 and began to draw the very same lines that are still here today. This is the true birthplace of Little League Baseball—every rule, every distance, every single measurement was designed by Stotz right here. These are his base paths, his mound, his home plate.

Just a handful of teams started here, and then like wildfire, news of the league spread throughout the U.S. Maybe it was the times . . . World War II was just beginning. Stotz knew the idea was brilliant when he came up with it while playing baseball with his nephews: dress children up in real uniforms like big leaguers, and have them play on real baseball fields with real baseballs.

Stotz saw that popularity would bring unwelcome commercialization, and he did not like it. While he was happy to have enthused over a million children, he was unhappy with the changes that brought. After many fierce battles over sponsorship with his Little League board, the Little League threw Stotz out of his own organization in a court battle in 1955. Stotz never attended another World Series, and the Little League removed his recognition as the founder of the league.

Upon building Volunteer Stadium in 2001, the Little League erected a stone in honor in Stotz. This was their first attempt to make amends. Unfortunately, Stotz had already passed away by then. This little ballpark is how Stotz saw the innocence of his game. It's doubtful, however, that this small grandstand would have held the 71,000 fans that attended the 2004 Little League World Series.

Could he have ever imagined that the Little League World Series, which he established in 1947 (at this park), would eventually be covered by the major networks and ESPN, and be attended by over 70,000 fans throughout the tournament?

Location: 10801 Oakmont Drive, Sun City, AZ
Status: Demolished in 1995
Opened: 1971
Capacity: 5,000

ABOVE: After the Brewers left for Chandler and a more modern facility, Sun City Stadium tried to attract other tenants. The construction of nearby Peoria Sports Complex, a modern, two-team pro baseball training facility, made the job much more difficult. (Photo courtesy Stephen Carroll.)

Sun City Stadium was built at a cost of $1.1 million in 1971 to replace Sun City Ballpark, which was home to the Sun City Saints, a women's professional softball team that was tremendously popular and drew huge crowds.

Del Webb, co-owner of the New York Yankees from 1945 to 1964 until they sold out to CBS, was a real estate developer who had built the ballpark. He had hoped that a major league–sized stadium would not only increase the Saints' popularity, but perhaps draw a major league team to its confines. When Sun City Stadium was completed, it quickly attracted attention. With the spotlight shining brightly on his new ballpark, Webb convinced the San Francisco Giants to move some of their spring training home games from Phoenix Muni to Sun City for the 1972 season.

The presence of Juan Marichal, Willie Mays, and Willie McCovey brought fans to see Webb's new ballpark. The presence of the press and the huge crowds drawn by the Giants gave Sun City the perfect publicity, and by the end of the spring training season, the Milwaukee Brewers applied to make Sun City Stadium their new spring training home from March 1973. A deal was struck, and the Brewers pulled their spring operations out of Diablo Stadium in Tempe, Arizona, and moved to Sun City.

When the Brewers went back to Milwaukee for the regular season, the Sun City Saints professional women's team played throughout the summer. The Saints continued to draw crowds that reached into the thousands. According to "Uncle John Poja," who sold souvenirs at the stadium, "Everyone was just crazy about the Saints. There was nothing else like it. People in the stands brought cowbells and honked horns at the games."

In 1982, the stadium was sold to the Bade Boyes Partnership. The Sun City Saints, who had been leasing out the stadium to the tune of $1 per season, were faced with a rent rise to $6,000 and moved to Phoenix the same year. When Chandler Stadium was built in Atlanta, Georgia, in 1984, the Brewers were lured away by the prospect of new facilities.

Sun City tried and failed to bring semipro baseball back to their stadium, and the stadium was demolished in 1995.

BELOW: Other events, such as games of the Sun City Saints and a senior men's league, filled seats occasionally. There were National Adult Baseball Association tournaments, and even several musical concerts. (Photo courtesy Stephen Carroll.)

Location: 2269 Dan Marino Boulevard, Miami, FL

Aka: Pro Player Stadium (1997–2004); Dolphins Stadium (2005); Dolphin Stadium (2006–2008); Land Shark Stadium (2009–2010); Sun Life Stadium (since 2010)

Status: Home of the Florida Marlins

Architect: HOK Sport

Capacity: 47,662 (1993); 38,560 (2011) but expandable

Opened: August 16, 1987; renovated 2006, 2007

First MLB game: April 5, 1993

Dimensions:

	Original 1993	Current
Left Field	335 ft	330 ft
Left Center		360 ft
Center Field	410 ft	420–404 ft
Right Center		363–385 ft
Right Field	345 ft	345 ft

World Series: 1997, 2003

RIGHT: Joe Robbie Stadium has had many name changes in its thirty-year history. As a multipurpose stadium that shares with the NFL, it has a checkered reputation with baseball fans.

BELOW: Footprint of Sun Life Stadium.

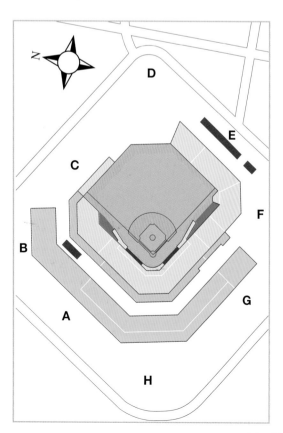

In 1991 Miami won a close battle for a major league expansion franchise and the Florida Marlins debuted on April 5, 1993, by defeating the Dodgers in front a sellout crowd at Joe Robbie Stadium. Many of the team's problems concern stadium issues, even though the Marlins have played all their home games in a relatively new facility now called Sun Life Stadium. Built in 1987 for the city's NFL team, and first named for then-Dolphins owner Joe Robbie, the football-oriented stadium was also built to accommodate baseball. After Robbie's death in 1990, Wayne Huizenga bought the Dolphins and a half share in the stadium, and started $10 million in renovations to make it better suit baseball.

Sun Life Stadium is large, arguably too big for baseball, and located far from downtown. Sadly, Miami fans have never embraced the team, and most blame the isolated, open-air stadium, which exposes fans to the heat during the day and often thunderstorms at night. However, the venue is colorful, comfortable, and a good place to watch a game. It has a hydraulically operated pitcher's mound, baseball locker rooms, a new press box for baseball media reporters, and a 200-foot manual scoreboard between left and center fields rises to a height of 33 feet, it is painted blue-green and nicknamed "the Teal Monster." To give the venue a more intimate feel for ball games, the upper deck is closed off with blue tarps to limit the capacity.

In 1997 the Marlins reached the playoffs as a wild card team and went on to take the World Series from the Indians. But then owner Huizenga embarrassed MLB by dismantling

the team and slashing the payroll; the 1998 Marlins won only fifty-four games—but his strategy paid off when John Henry bought the franchise in January 1999.

However, the Marlins' lease was set to expire in 2010 and Huizenga wanted MLB gone from his football stadium; with no sign of a new stadium for the Marlins and a rapidly deteriorating financial situation, MLB stepped in to help resolve what was quickly becoming a major headache. In 2002 the league brokered an agreement for Henry to sell the Marlins to Jeffrey Loria and purchase a majority stake in the Boston Red Sox. Loria was sure he could both field a good team and get a new stadium. He succeeded on one of those goals when the Marlins astonishingly won their second World Series in 2003, defeating the Yankees 4–2.

The Marlins then went on to have three good seasons: in 2005, 2008, and 2009, finishing third (83–79), third (84–77), and second (87–75) respectively. In 2008 Jimmy Buffett purchased naming rights and the stadium became Land Shark Stadium.

Then in January 2010 a five-year deal was signed with Sun Life Financial and the stadium name changed again to become Sun Life Stadium. A name change is also in sight for the Florida Marlins, who will become the Miami Marlins and in 2012 will move into a new home with a retractable roof on the site of the legendary Miami Orange Bowl.

ABOVE and BELOW: Images of Sun Life Stadium. In 2007 there were $250 million in renovations, which included an improved club level, new concessions, and upgraded video equipment.

Surprise Stadium

Location: 15946 North Bullard Avenue, Surprise, AZ

Status: Home of the Surprise Rafters; spring training facility of the Texas Rangers and Kansas City Royals

Architect: HOK Sport

Opened: 2002

Capacity: 10,500

Dimensions:

Left Field 350 ft

Center Field 400 ft

Right Field 350 ft

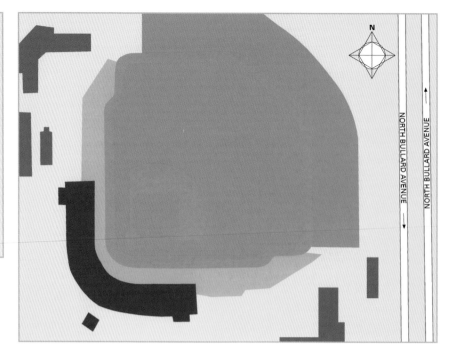

Surprise Stadium has been the spring training home of the Kansas City Royals and the Texas Rangers since 2003, and was the home of the Arizona Fall League's Surprise Rafters since 2007. It has hosted not only spring training games, but plenty of Little League, high school, and college sports tournaments, too. It is located on a 124-acre site that includes six full practice fields and a half-field, as well as separate clubhouse and office facilities.

LEFT and BELOW: As befits the spring training grounds of a team (the Texas Rangers) that contested the World Series in 2010, Surprise Stadium is well-appointed and receives rave reviews from fans.

Swayne Field—named for Noah H. Swayne Jr., son of U.S. Supreme Court justice Noah Haynes Swayne, who donated the land—was the first double-decked stadium in the American Association and was constructed at a cost of $300,000. The former home of the Toledo Mud Hens, it replaced Armory Park, which the team had used since 1897.

Made of iron and concrete, following Forbes Field, which had opened a few weeks earlier, the main grandstand seated 5,800, of which 1,000 were on the upper deck. The bleachers were asymmetric, with those in left field seating 2,500 and 3,500 in right. The wooden bleachers were replaced in 1928 with concrete-and-steel structures, and a new center-field bleacher section was added.

The Mud Hens had little success over the years and attendance diminished. In mid-1952 the team transferred to Charleston, West Virginia. Another AA club—the Milwaukee Braves—transferred to Toledo for 1953. As the Toledo Sox, they revived Swayne Field, drew over 343,000 fans, and won the AA pennant under coach George "Twinkletoes" Selkirk. It was too good to last. After three years they left to go to Wichita, and Toledo was left without professional baseball for a decade. Swayne Field was demolished soon after. It is now the Swayne Field Shopping Center.

Location: In a block between Monroe Street, Detroit Avenue, and Council Street, Toledo, OH
Status: Demolished in 1955
Opened: July 3, 1909
Capacity: 11,800 (1909); 14,800 (1928)
Dimensions:
Left Field 382 ft
Center Field 505 ft
Right Field 326 ft

BELOW LEFT: Two views of the first game at Swayne Field in 1909. (Photo courtesy Bruce Orser.)

BELOW: Fans of the TV series *MASH* will remember Corporal Klinger's allegiance to the Mud Hens. This is the view after the 1928 renovation.

After years of bargaining—since the mid-1990s—for a new stadium, the Twins and Hennepin County agreed on a new $390 million stadium on a smallish site in the old Mills District near the Mississippi River. Surrounded by Minnesota fir trees, Target Field was finished in time for the 2010 opener against Boston on March 27. Made of local limestone, this stadium has no roof—which would have cost an extra $110 million or so—and is open to all that the Minnesota weather can throw at it. However, the Twins can enjoy playing on home grass for the first time in twenty-eight years.

The stadium seats 39,504 spectators in the open air, although it has a full roof canopy that projects out over the seating and offers some protection to fans. Additionally, there are "warming shelters" for when things get really cold and there is undersoil heating. It has the fourth-largest scoreboard in MLB and the flagpole is the same one relocated from Metropolitan Stadium.

The new ballpark has been well received by fans, with attendance passing the three million mark in 2010.

Location: 1 Twins Way, Minneapolis, MN
Status: Home of the Minnesota Twins
Architect: Populous
Opened: March 27, 2010
First MLB game: April 12, 2010
Capacity: 39,504
Dimensions:
Left Field 339 ft
Left Center 377 ft
Center Field 404 ft
Right Center 367 ft
Right Field 328 ft

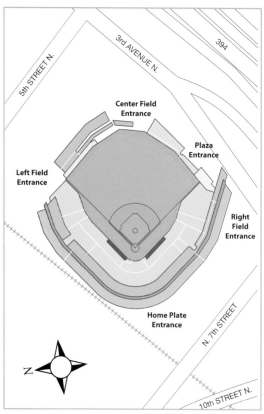

LEFT: Footprint of Target Field. Note the railroad line that has a stop outside the stadium (visible in picture opposite, below).

ABOVE: Nighttime view of Target Field and the Minneapolis skyline.

TOP and BELOW: The Minneapolis skyline as construction nears an end in 2009. Note at left the Budweiser roof deck, which boasts the only bonfire in the majors.

ABOVE: Right-field entrance on March 23, 2010. The first game at the field took place a few days later on the 27th.

BELOW: The stadium's limestone cladding, swooping roof, and downtown skyline stand out in this July 2, 2010, shot.

Tecumseh Park

Location: London, Ontario, Canada
Aka: Labatt Memorial Park, the John Labatt Memorial Athletic Park
Status: Home of the London Majors and the oldest continually operating baseball grounds in the world
Architect: Tillman Ruth Mocellin (2001 renovation)
Opened: May 3, 1877; renovated 1937 and 2001
Capacity: 5,200
Dimensions:
Left Field 300 ft
Center Field 402 ft
Right Field 330 ft

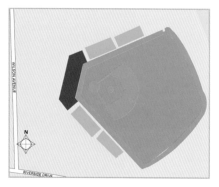

ABOVE: Footprint of Tecumseh Park.

Tecumseh Park, which is today known as Labatt Memorial Park, was built on common playing fields near where the Thames River forks in central London, Ontario. The almost nine-acre plot has, since December 1936, been owned by the City of London, Ontario. It is generally considered to be the oldest continually operating baseball grounds in the world, with a history dating back to 1877, although this claim is challenged by Fuller Field in Clinton, Massachusetts.

In 1937 the Thames River flooded spectacularly and all but wiped out the ballpark. The local Labatt Brewing Company contributed to the fund for a new grandstand and clubhouse, and also donated the ground to the City of London, so that it remains a public athletic park forever; in return, the park was renamed the John Labatt Memorial Athletic Park.

The London city council formally designated the ballpark as an historic site in May 1994, and a ceremonial plaque was unveiled at the front gates on July 1 (Canada Day), prior to a doubleheader between the London Majors and Toronto Maple Leafs of the Intercounty Baseball League. The park's historical designation occurred after a six-month lobbying effort spearheaded by the Friends of Labatt Park, a not-for-profit body, which has done much to bring the ballpark to a wider audience.

Telus Field

Location: 10233 96th Avenue NW, Edmonton, Alberta, Canada
Aka: The Phone Booth
Status: Home of the Edmonton Cracker Cats
Opened: May 2, 1995
Capacity: 10,000
Dimensions:
Left Field 340 ft
Center Field 420 ft
Right Field 320 ft

RIGHT: Telus Field sports an artificial infield and a natural grass outfield. The only other ballpark to share this odd quirk is Lawrence Dumont Stadium in Wichita, Kansas.

During the 1980s up to half a million baseball fans regularly turned out each year to cheer on the local Edmonton Trappers, but to continue to play in the Pacific Coast League in the early 1990s, the local ballpark had to be upgraded. Telus Field was built in 1995 as a state-of-the-art Triple-A facility to replace the popular, but faded, sixty-year-old John Ducey Park (Renfrew Park).

It is the most northerly professional ballfield in North America and has an unusual combination of artificial turf on the infield and real grass on the outfield to cope with the harsh climate and long winters. An interesting quirk of Telus Field is the luxury boxes. The "high-brow" sections are tucked underneath the main section of the grandstand, at field level. Each windowed box has a set of outdoor seating in front, allowing the fans to choose whether to stay in the luxury of the leather couches, with catered food and in-house broadcasts, or be a part of the game right next to the action.

Telus Field, which was built on the site of the old ballpark, opened to rave reviews and very healthy attendance in 1995. The Trappers went on to win three PCL titles over the next decade, in 1996, 1997, and 2002, and winning became the new tradition in Edmonton. The Trappers were affiliated to the Oakland Athletics from 1995 until 1998, followed briefly by the Anaheim Angels (1999–2000), the Minnesota Twins (2001–2002), and finally the Montreal Expos (2003–2004). Although they qualified for the playoffs in 2003, they were defeated. In 2004 the team was sold and, to the horror of fans, moved to Texas.

Suddenly, Edmonton's ballpark was empty and abandoned by minor league baseball. Edmonton's fate was reflected throughout Canada, and by 2007 only two minor league teams remained.

The Edmonton Cracker Cats, who began play in the Northern League in 2005 and are based at Telus Field, have done much to restore Edmonton's faith in baseball, not least by stirring up an intense rivalry with neighboring Calgary.

BELOW: In 1995, Telus Field had opened to rave reviews. Almost half a million fans would come to see the Trappers play at their new ballpark.

The Los Angeles Angels have been loyal tenants at Tempe Diablo Stadium in Arizona for nearly twenty years, returning every spring to train in the Arizona climate. The stadium was built in 1968 for the team that was then the major league's newest franchise, the Seattle Pilots. Sadly, the Pilots were a very short-lived team and changed their affiliation toward the end of the 1970 season, when they moved to Milwaukee and were renamed the Brewers. They also moved out of Tempe Diablo pretty quickly, leaving in 1973 for Sun City Stadium.

Tempe Diablo did not have another major league franchise in residence until 1977, when the Seattle Mariners arrived. They stayed for eighteen years, gradually building up their strength and playing in the Cactus League every spring. In 1994 the Mariners moved to a new stadium in Peoria and the Angels took their place at Tempe Diablo.

The Angels played well at the stadium. Tempe loved the Angels and it seemed that the Angels were quite happy here as well. In March 2006, when it seemed as though Tempe Diablo's aging charms were beginning to fade, the Angels shocked the baseball world by signing a new contract and agreeing to an $8 million renovation project for the stadium.

New green tarp covered the concourses, all new seating, was installed, and new concessions and a striking entrance made Tempe Diablo look like new again. The old ballpark was now able to compete with many of the newer stadiums. Many of the biggest renovations, however, are unseen by the fans. Most important to the team and the players are new clubhouses and batting tunnels. While the fans are just concerned about the ballpark, players and coaches want the best in training facilities.

Location: 2200 West Alameda Drive, Tempe, AZ
Status: Home of the Tempe Angels; spring training facility of the Los Angeles Angels of Anaheim
Opened: 1968; renovated 2002
Capacity: 9,785
Dimensions:
Left Field 340 ft
Center Field 420 ft
Right Field 360 ft

Tempe Diablo Stadium

BELOW and BELOW LEFT: Entrance and footprint of Tempe Diablo Stadium.

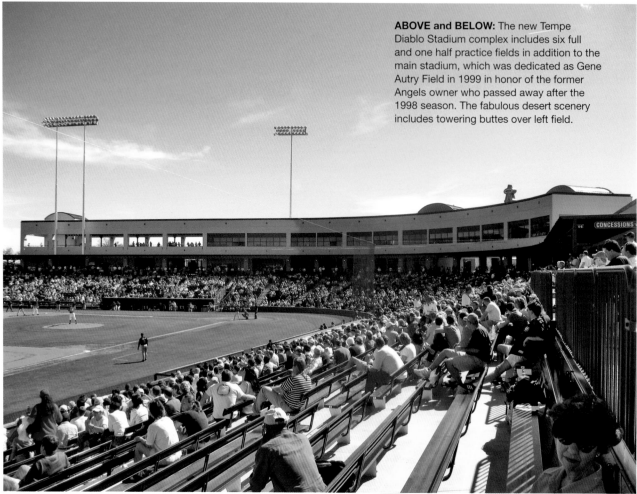

ABOVE and BELOW: The new Tempe Diablo Stadium complex includes six full and one half practice fields in addition to the main stadium, which was dedicated as Gene Autry Field in 1999 in honor of the former Angels owner who passed away after the 1998 season. The fabulous desert scenery includes towering buttes over left field.

Location: 3410 Palm Beach Boulevard, Fort Myers, FL
Aka: Park T. Pigott Memorial Stadium (from 1995)
Status: Extensively used for college baseball
Opened: 1925; rebuilt in 1943 after fire and in 2004 after hurricane
Capacity: 600 (1925); 3,000 (1955); 900 (2004)
Last MLB game: 1989
Dimensions
Center Field 415 ft

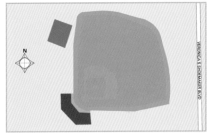

ABOVE: Footprint of Terry Park.

TOP: Destroyed by a hurricane, little of the old grandstand remained. The city decided not to rebuild, even though it had an official historic marker given in 1995. Instead a small 700-seat structure went up.

BELOW: What Terry Park looked like before the hurricane. (Photo courtesy Bob Busser.)

There was a ball field at Terry Park from the 1920s, when the Terry family donated pastureland to Lee County and a small wooden grandstand was erected among the grazing cattle. This structure burned down in 1943, and it was eventually replaced in 1955 by a concrete-and-steel ballpark. In 2004 Hurricane Charlie devastated the Gulf Coast, inflicting serious damage on the 5,000-seat grandstand, and the Fort Myers authorities decided to demolish the grounds as the grandstand was condemned as unsafe. However, the council had a change of heart and the grounds were reprieved but at the cost of the destruction of the old grandstand and the construction of a smaller, metal-covered grandstand. The renovations cost $701,697 and of the former grandstand only the original girders were retained.

The Pittsburgh Pirates had spent many years flitting from one spring training ground to another, but with the construction of Terry Park, they finally found a place to call home. They remained until 1968, moving out to Bradenton, another historic ball field. The new Kansas City Royals took over Fort Myers and played the first exhibition games of their franchise history here. They would spend nineteen years training at Terry Park II.

In 1978 the Royals brought a new team to Terry Park, the Fort Myers Royals. The new full-season Single-A Florida State League franchise finally made Terry Park more than just a "one month a year" stadium. Terry Park was now a full-season home to the Royals' Single-A affiliation, and they remained for ten years, from 1978 until 1988.

The Royals performed strongly, finishing in first place twice, and winning the FSL championship in 1985. Many future impact major leaguers would call this dugout their first professional home, including Bret Saberhagen, Kevin Seitzer, Brian McRae, and Tom "Flash" Gordon.

When the Royals left for Baseball City in 1987, it seemed that major and minor league baseball had ended at Terry Park. There was one last fling, however, when the Fort Myers Sun Sox came to town in 1989.

The Sun Sox were part of the Senior Professional Baseball Association, which featured former major league stars who played during the winter months when there was no professional baseball in the area.

Location: 4400 E. 15th Street, Sandusky and Urbana Avenues, Tulsa, OK

Aka: Tulsa County Stadium, Oiler Park, Driller Park (1977)

Status: Demolished in 1980

Opened: July 11, 1934

Capacity: 5,194 (1935); 7,200 (1948); 3,780 (1979)

Dimensions:

Left Field 330 ft

Center Field 390 ft

Right Field 330 ft

Texas League Park, which was sometimes known as Tulsa County Stadium, Oiler Park, or Driller Park, was located in the Tulsa County Fairgrounds. The ballpark replaced the old fairgrounds stadium where Tulsa's minor league teams had been playing since 1930, and opened to rave reviews in 1934. The new ballpark was a huge concrete structure built to last for decades probably because the older Athletic Park in Tulsa had collapsed in the late 1910s, injuring many fans.

The Tulsa Oilers occupied the ballpark from its opening until the team was moved to New Orleans and replaced by the Tulsa Drillers after the 1976 season. However, the stadium became more and more dilapidated and suffered a partial collapse, injuring seventeen people during a full-capacity major league exhibition game in April 1977. The rest of the grandstand was demolished as quickly as possible, and bleachers were put in its place. The new temporary grandstand was named Driller Park and would be used for three years until a new stadium was built in the fairgrounds. Oiler Park's days were over.

TOP and ABOVE: Following the April 3, 1977, partial collapse of the grandstand, the remainder was demolished as quickly as possible. Under a new name—Driller Park—the facility would be used for three more years. (All photos courtesy Wayne McCombs.)

RIGHT: 1960s photograph of the home plate entrance after the the Cardinals had come to town in 1959. They signed the Tulsa Oilers to a long agreement that finished in 1977.

Location: Old Orchard Beach, ME
Status: Home of the Raging Tides
Opened: 1984; rebuilt 2010
Last game: 1988
Capacity: 6,000 following renovations

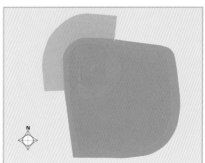

The Ballpark at Old Orchard Beach was once home to the Philadelphia Phillies' Triple-A Maine Guides, from 1984 until 1988. The Ballpark is owned and operated by the town of Old Orchard Beach and has a capacity of 6,000.

Opened in 1984, the Ballpark was intended to cater to the large number of tourists who frequented Maine every summer, and attendance hovered at a respectable 107,000–150,000 spectators per season. However, the Ballpark suffered from several problems that limited its success:

Every summer the area was infested with irritating Maine blackflies that made life uncomfortable for the fans. And that was after they had dealt with chaotic traffic on their way to the stadium—there was only one road leading to and from the Ballpark, so traffic inevitably backed up. Finally, the Ballpark was completed just before the Triple-A park standards were raised. Players expected higher standards from the facilities and backers wanted a larger capacity to increase their revenue. At 6,000, the Ballpark was about 4,000 fans short.

In 1988 the Guides (renamed the Phillies for this last season) left for Pennsylvania and the Ballpark ceased to live up to its name. It was leased to a performing arts company, which hired it out for concerts. From 1997 the Ballpark sat idle and neglected—as can be seen from the accompanying photographs—until the town of Old Orchard Beach began a volunteer program to revive it. Before this could begin, a lightning strike caused a fire that destroyed a section of the skyboxes in June 2007.

The residents of Old Orchard Beach rallied to fix this fine stadium, and did so by dint of hard work and enthusiasm. Their efforts were rewarded in 2011 when the New England Collegiate Baseball League announced it would be moving their Lowell All-Americans franchise, the Raging Tides, to Old Orchard Beach for the 2011 season.

ABOVE: This is what it should have looked like (enhanced photograph).

BELOW: Today it's hard to believe that these photos show what was once home of the Philadelphia Phillies' Triple-A affiliate, the Maine Guides. It hasn't been used by a professional team since 1988.

Location: 3400 East Palm Valley Boulevard, Round Rock, TX

Status: Home of the Round Rock Express

Architect: HKS, Inc.

Opened: August 16, 2000

Capacity: 8,722

Dimensions:

Left Field 330 ft

Center Field 407 ft

Right Field 325 ft

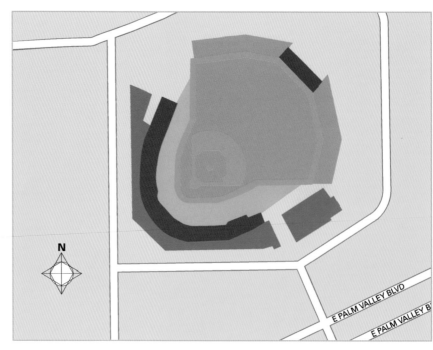

RIGHT: Footprint of the Dell Diamond.

BELOW and BOTTOM: The Dell Diamond was voted the best Double-A ballpark in the country by *Baseball America* magazine in 2003.

The Dell Diamond is located in Round Rock, Texas (about nineteen miles north of Austin), home of Nolan Ryan's Round Rock Express.

Hall of Famer Ryan began building the Dell Diamond in a suburb just north of Austin in 1999. He assured everyone that this would be one of his greatest triumphs yet. With a price tag of over $20 million, Ryan built his field of dreams. He made sure that his ballpark exceeded the code of Double-A baseball, building in a capacity of 10,000, installing exceptional facilities for families, such as a climbing wall and fifty-foot pool, not to mention state-of-the-art facilities for the players.

By 2000, the Dell Diamond was ready to open its doors. With Nolan Ryan's son Reid Ryan at the helm as president, and son Reese Ryan in the front office, they officially moved their team, the Jackson Generals, to Round Rock. On opening day in 2000, over 10,000 fans showed up at the Dell Diamond, and by season's end, the Round Rock Express had blown away every record for a Double-A franchise in the history of baseball. Over 660,000 fans attended the Round Rock Express games.

Affiliated to the Houston Astros, the Express continued to draw record-breaking crowds, and in 2004 the team was renamed the Corpus Christi Hooks, allowing the Ryans to purchase the Pacific Coast League's Edmonton Trappers in 2005 and move them south.

With the Hooks and the Express, the Ryan family now owns the top two franchises in the Houston Astros' minor league system. The Ryans continue to have tremendous successes every season at the Dell Diamond. In 2004, they drew more than 13,000 on one particular night, and just under 700,000 for the season.

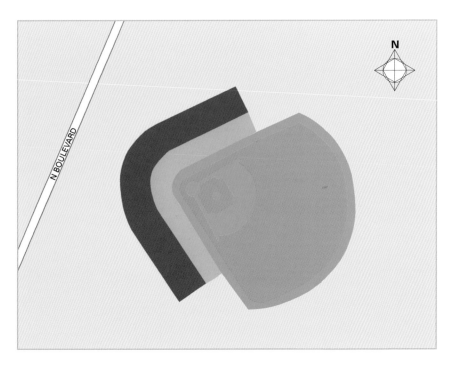

Loaction: 3001 N Boulevard, Richmond, VA
Status: Home of the Richmond Flying Squirrels
Opened: 1934
Capacity: 9,560
Dimensions:
Left Field 330 ft
Center Field 402 ft
Right Field 330 ft
All-Star Game: 1992

LEFT: Footprint of the Diamond.

BELOW: The Flying Squirrels have already started renovating the Diamond, tearing out benching and putting in individual seats—there are now 6,200. There are two new party decks now in the upper level.

BOTTOM: You have to love concrete to find this beautiful!

The Diamond is one of the largest stadiums in minor league baseball, with seating for over 12,000 in a very steep rotunda. All 12,000 seats are located around the home plate, stretching out only just past first and third base, and the grandstand is probably higher than any other minor league ballpark in history.

The Diamond was built on the site of the old Parker Field that had served Richmond's baseball community from 1954 until 1984. When it opened in 1985, the Diamond ushered in a new era of Atlanta Braves baseball. Atlanta was still a fledgling team but on the cusp of becoming a dynasty that would last for well over a decade, and many of its future stars began their careers with the Triple-A side, the Richmond Braves, at the Diamond.

In most seasons before it was demolished, Parker Field steadily broke the quarter-million mark in attendance, peaking in 1983 when 293,000 fans came to the ballpark to see the Richmond Braves contend for the International League championship but lose in the finals. The new ballpark broke records when it opened, with 379,000 watching the Braves win their first championship in the new stadium in 1986.

During the 1990s the talent that stalked the Diamond was incredible and unstoppable. Tom Glavine, Jeff Blauser, David Justice, and John Smoltz began their careers in the late 1980s.

In 2001, attendance at the Diamond began its slow slide and in 2008 the Atlanta Braves abandoned the team they had been affiliated to for forty-two years. The Richmond Braves played their final game in September 2008, and a new Eastern League Double-A team moved to the Diamond. The Richmond Flying Squirrels have begun a $1.5 million restoration program to the Diamond, which means that it will be preserved for the foreseeable future.

Location: 525 Northwest Peacock Boulevard, Port St. Lucie, FL
Aka: Tradition Field (2004–2010), Digital Domain Park (since 2010)
Status: Home of the St. Lucie Mets; spring training home of the New York Mets
Opened: 1988; renovated 2004
Capacity: 7,160
Dimensions:
Left Field 338 ft
Center Field 410 ft
Right Field 338 ft

ABOVE and BELOW: Interior and exterior of the stadium.

Built in 1988, Thomas J. White Stadium became Tradition Field as part of an $11 million renovation in 2004, and Digital Domain Park in 2010. The New York Mets have used it for spring training since 1988, and the Port St. Lucie Mets, their Triple-A affiliates, call it home for the rest of the year. The original stadium needed renovations in 2004 to repair hurricane damage. They also added much-needed character to the whole facility. The press boxes that are in place today right above the rim of the grandstand were once just holes. The lovely tiered picnic area down the left-field line with several rows of permanent seating parallel to the ball field replaced sixteen rows of metal-slat bleachers; the berm in right field was introduced. The most striking feature is the cantilevered roof, which provides some protection for the elements.

Much of the Mets' future talent has played in Port St. Lucie, including Edgardo Alfonzo, Jeromy Burnitz, and Rey Ordonez in the 1990s. The Port St. Lucie Mets would win the Florida State League championship in 1996 and 1998.

The presence of these great players and the continued success of the Port St. Lucie Mets means that attendance at Digital Domain Park is rising and fans continue to flock to this popular ballpark—over 90,000 in 2011, a bit short of the recent record of 99,988 in 2008.

Location: 600 Stadium Circle, Pittsburgh, PA
Status: Demolished in 2001
Architect: Osborn Engineering, Deeter Ritchy Sipple, Michael Baker
Opened: July 16, 1970
Last MLB game: October 1, 2000
Capacity: 50,500 (1970); 47,687 (1993)
Dimensions:

	Original 1970	Final 1975
Left Field	340 ft	335 ft
Left Center	385 ft	375 ft
Center Field	410 ft	400 ft
Right Center	385 ft	375 ft
Right Field	340 ft	335 ft

World Series: 1971, 1979
All-Star Games: 1974, 1994

In June 1970 Forbes Field, then the oldest venue in the National League, was closed and the Pittsburgh Pirates moved to Three Rivers Stadium to share the venue with the NFL's Pittsburgh Steelers. Built in Old Allegheny at the point where the Allegheny and Monongahela Rivers joined to form the Ohio River, it was built on much the same site as Exposition Park, where the Pirates played around the turn of the twentieth century.

Three Rivers was the quintessential "cookie cutter" ballpark—the fifth to be built—and opened in summer 1970 following a two-year build. Nationally hailed as the future of sports venues, once the novelty wore off it became apparent that the stadium lacked character and fan appeal. On opening, the stadium had five levels of red and yellow seating, making the venue instantly recognizable and very colorful. In the 1990s blue seats were installed in the lower deck. Movable seats along the first and third base lines were used to convert the stadium with two ground-level sections holding 4,000 seats. Despite this, the stadium favored football.

The scoreboard was originally above the outfield fence but was later changed to sit along the rim of the upper deck. The original bullpens were behind the right-field fence. They were moved around the stadium but ended up back in the same position. Various artificial surfaces, including AstroTurf, were used and eventually an underground drainage system was installed after the original vacuum system proved ineffective. The most significant change came in 1975 when, in an attempt to facilitate more home runs by shrinking the outfield dimensions, the fences were moved ten feet closer to home plate.

In 1993, to give the stadium a more intimate feel, tarps were put over much of the upper deck, in the process reducing the capacity to 47,687. As the years passed the Pirates began to lobby for a new stadium, and in October 2000 the Pirates played their last game at Three Rivers, a 10–9 loss to the Chicago Cubs.

On February 11, 2001, Three Rivers Stadium was imploded with thousands of people watching. It took under a minute and cost $5.1 million.

ABOVE and BELOW: Interior and exterior of the ultimate cookie-cutter.

Blues Stadium opened in 1963 as an American Legion field on the Mid-South Fairgrounds (next to the Liberty Bowl) with a capacity of around 8,800. In 1968 minor league baseball in the shape of the Memphis Blues arrived, and a covered grandstand and press boxes were added to the ground to improve the facilities.

The Blues came from Russwood Park and were a farm club for the New York Mets, but they left after eight years in 1976. With seating close to the field, Blues was a small and intimate ballpark that was popular with the fans for its roomy environs enlivened by different food outlets, souvenir stands, and other diversions. It briefly became Chicks Stadium when the Memphis Chicks arrived, but was soon renamed Tim McCarver Stadium in 1978, after local celebrity and major league catcher (and later commentator) Tim McCarver. The Chicks remained there until 1997. The crowds were raucous and—on one occasion in 1986 when the Cardinals played an exhibition game against the Royals—reached 14,000.

After a few years AstroTurf was installed across the infield—the outfield remained grass—so that the Kansas City Royals could practice before moving to their new AstroTurfed home at Kauffman Stadium.

Finally, in 1998, Memphis joined the Pacific Coast League with the Memphis Redbirds, an affiliate of the St. Louis Cardinals, but they only stayed for a year before moving to their new home at Autozone Park in downtown Memphis. The stadium was left to the occasional semipro game and has been used as a car lot. It was demolished, generally unlamented, in early 2005.

Location: Mid-South Fairgrounds, next to the Liberty Bowl, Memphis, TN
Aka: Fairgrounds #3, Blues Stadium (1968–1976), Chicks Stadium (1978)
Status: Demolished in 2005
Capacity: 8,800 (1999)
Opened: 1963
Last game: 1999
Dimensions:
Left Field 323 ft
Center Field 398 ft
Right Field 325 ft

Tim McCarver Stadium

Location: 1610 West Church Street, Orlando, FL

Status: Used for amateur games

Opened: 1914

Capacity: 1,500 (1914); 5,100 (2009)

Dimensions:

Left Field 340 ft

Center Field 425 ft

Right Field 320 ft

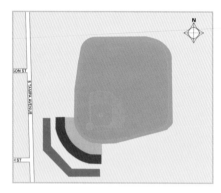

TOP: When Griffith Stadium in Washington, D.C., was demolished, nearly 1,000 of the stadium's seats were moved to Tinker Field, where they remain today.

ABOVE: Footprint of Tinker Field.

BELOW: Tinker Field sits in the shadow of the Florida Citrus Bowl.

Tinker Field is one of Florida's most venerable stadiums, having opened in 1914. It is now overshadowed by the neighboring Citrus Bowl football stadium, but it served Orlando for over eighty-five years, finally being decommissioned in 2000.

Tinker Field began serving the major leagues as a spring training home in 1923, when the Cincinnati Reds began an eight-year stay, before moving to Tampa in 1931. In 1934, the Los Angeles Dodgers began sharing Tinker Field with the Washington Senators. The Dodgers would remain for only two years, before moving to Green Field in Clearwater, Florida. The Senators, however, would call Tinker Field their spring home for almost their entire existence. The Senators (or Nationals, as they were called then) remained until 1942.

The Senators returned in February 1946, and wouldn't leave their much-loved spring home again. In 1960, the Senators moved from Washington, D.C., to Minneapolis, Minnesota, and become the Minnesota Twins. While the Senators were reincarnated in 1961 (eventually to become the Texas Rangers), the Twins would not give up Tinker Field. The Twins would continue to utilize Tinker Field as their spring home for another twenty years. After the Twins' departure in 1991, Tinker Field lacked a major league team until 1998, when the Atlanta Braves used Tinker Field for two years.

Tinker Field's minor league history is just as compelling from the Florida State League's Orlando Caps in 1919 to the Sun Rays in the 1990s.

Minor league teams continued to use the stadium until 1999, when the Tampa Bay Devil Rays were the last occupants. Since the Rays left, various youth teams have played at Tinker Field, and its future is under some debate.

Tinker Field is named for Hall of Famer Joe Tinker—of "Tinker to Evers to Chance" fame—who retired to Orlando and is buried nearby.

Sunlight Park, an all-wood stadium and the first ballpark in the city, was built for $7,000 as a home for the International League's Torontos, who were eventually to be renamed the Toronto Maple Leafs.

Originally called Toronto Baseballl Grounds, Sunlight Park was located to the south of Queen Street East and to the west of Broadview Avenue, near the Don River. The ground became Sunlight Park after the Lever brothers' Sunlight Soap Works was built beyond the outfield. The stadium hosted the city's first professional baseball championship in 1887. The team and league folded in 1890 and the stadium lasted until 1896, when the team's new owners abandoned the park for their new Hanlan's Point Stadium.

The site is now a city park but a nearby street, Sunlight Park Road, hints at the location of the old ballpark.

Location: Queen Street East and West Broadview Avenue, Ontario, Toronto, Canada
Aka: Sunlight Park
Status: Closed in 1896
Opened: 1887
Last MLB game: 1886
Capacity: 2,200

Travelers Field was built in 1931 to replace the aging Kavanaugh Field, former home of the Southern Association's Little Rock Travelers. The new ballpark, named after the home team, promised to be one of grandest ballparks in the land. When it debuted, however, it far exceeded everyone's expectations.

A gleaming steel-and-concrete creation, Travelers Field was home to the Arkansas Travelers for seventy-five years (with the exception of a two-year hiatus in the 1960s), as well as hosting countless games of the Negro League. Little Rock has always proved tremendously loyal to the Travelers, who even became part of a fan-owned enterprise in 1960.

The Travelers have enjoyed mixed fortunes during their long history, which has been reflected in the attendance figures at Travelers Field. Their career at the new facility began during the Depression, so perhaps they can be forgiven for drawing only 44,000 in 1934, but the team's performance didn't really help. The appointment of manager Doc Prothero began to turn the team's fortunes around from 1936. The Boston Red Sox moved their Class A team to Little Rock and in 1937 Travelers Field hosted an exhibition game between the World Series champion New York Yankees and the Cleveland Indians. The Travelers themselves performed so well, with ninety-seven wins in the 1937 season, that attendance rocketed to 160,000.

In 1944 Ray Winder and former Cleveland Indians pitcher Willis Hudlin began their legendary partnership. Travelers Field was improved with the addition of more seating behind the plate and down the lines. The bullpen was pushed into the grandstands, allowing fans to intermingle with the players as they wished. The field was renamed in 1966 after the man who had done so much for the team.

Location: 400 West Broadway Street North, Little Rock, AR
Status: Closed in 2011, scheduled for demolition
Aka: Ray Winder Field (from 1966)
Opened: 1931
Capacity: 6,083 (1999)
Dimensions:
Left Field 330 ft
Center Field 390 ft
Right Field 345 ft

BELOW LEFT: Ray Winder Field's bullpens were located in the grandstand, so fans and players could mingle easily.

BELOW: The wooden seats—dating back to 1932—were sold off to the highest bidder.

The 1950s were a miserable period for the Travelers, culminating in the removal of the team to Shreveport in 1959, leaving Little Rock without a team. The city and fans clubbed together, buying shares in "Arkansas Travelers Inc." and the team returned to improved fortunes, winning the Southern Association playoffs and finishing third overall. There was also an agreement with the St. Louis Cardinals. Everything went well and Ray Winder Field remained home to the Arkansas Travelers until the construction of a new ballpark in 2005. After the Travelers left, the ballpark stood empty for five years. There was some interest in an attempt to preserve the ballpark but that fell through and the city confirmed it could be demolished.

BELOW: It was announced in January 2011 that UAMS—who bought the stadium from the City of Little Rock—planned to tear down the stadium.

Triborough Stadium

Location: Manhattan, New York, NY

Aka: Randall's Island Stadium, Downing Stadium (after 1955)

Status: Demolished in 2002

Architect: Works Progress Administration

Opened: July 1936

Capacity: 22,000

RIGHT: The stadium is at center right in this photograph.

BELOW: The Newark Eagles play the New York Black Yankees at Randall's Island Stadium.

Triborough Stadium was only infrequently used for baseball. It was first known as Randall's Island Stadium and then renamed Downing Stadium to honor John J. Downing, a director at the New York City Department of Parks and Recreation, in 1955.

Built on Randall's Island in the East River as a Works Progress Administration project, some 15,000 witnessed Jesse Owens compete in the Olympic Trials on July 11, 1936, the opening night event at the stadium, but it became increasingly associated with soccer. The stadium was also used for some Negro League baseball games in the 1930s. After Downing Stadium stopped hosting major sporting events, it was occasionally used as a venue for rock concerts. It was finally demolished in 2002, to be replaced by a newer complex, Icahn Stadium, which opened in 2004.

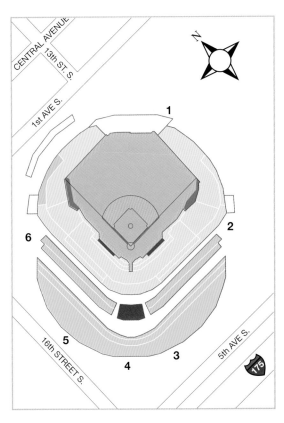

Originally called the Florida Suncoast Dome, Tropicana Field was built at a cost of $85 million in St. Petersburg, with the intention of attracting a Major League Baseball team to the Tampa Bay area. Ready in 1990, it had no tenants but a seating capacity of over 45,000. From seasons 1993 to 1995, it was occupied by the Tampa Bay Lightning hockey team and called the Thunderdome.

In 1995 MLB expanded and finally awarded the Tampa Bay area its own franchise. The following year the naming rights for the stadium were sold to Tropicana Products. For the new franchise, the stadium was renovated at a cost of $70 million, which included the laying of AstroTurf. The Devil Rays arrived in 1998, with their first game in March against the Detroit Tigers, a loss of 11–6.

Tropicana Field has a cable-supported Teflon-coated fiberglass fabric dome with a diameter of 688 feet, all supported by twenty-four concrete columns. Crucially, it is nonretractable and angled at a slant (towards the outfield) to deflect hurricanes and to reduce the interior volume so cooling costs are lower. Four interior catwalks hang from the ceiling and complicated game rules apply when a ball hits one of the catwalks. When the Rays win a home game the dome is lit up with orange lights to celebrate the victory. For 2000 the field was relaid with more forgiving FieldTurf plus a dirt infield, but it was changed back to AstroTurf in 2011.

Prior to the 2006 season Tropicana had a $25 million facelift, plus a further $10 million worth of improvements. A new attraction was a 35-foot, 10,000-gallon tank containing live cow nose rays (collected from Tampa Bay waters) situated behind the center field wall.

Location: 1 Stadium Drive, St. Petersburg, FL
Aka: Suncoast Dome (1990–1992); Thunderdome (1993–1995); Tropicana Stadium (from 1996)
Status: Home of the Tampa Bay Rays
Architect: HOK Sport
Capacity: 45,200
Opened: 1990; renovated 1998
First MLB game: March 31, 1998
Dimensions:
Left Field 315 ft
Left Center 370 ft
Center Field 404 ft
Right Center 370 ft
Right Field 322 ft
World Series: 2008

LEFT: Tropicana was bought by Pepsi in 1998, but there have been no name changes.

Before the start of the 2007 season even more improvements were made, including new video display boards and family-oriented entertainments.

The first year saw 2.5 million fans pass through the turnstiles, but thereafter the novelty soon wore off and in 2003 the Devil Rays were watched by just over a million. That proved to be the nadir, and improved results saw attendance pick up. Between 2008 and 2010 over 1.8 million watched the Rays—the "Devil" was dropped in 2008.

THIS PAGE: Interior views of Tropicana Field. Note the catwalks at the top of the top picture: when they are struck in play, complicated rules apply. The field itself started off with an AstroTurf surface, which was was replaced by the softer FieldTurf in 2000. A improved version of FieldTurf—FieldTurf Duo—went in for the 2007 season. The big difference between Tropicana and other stadiums that use artificial turf is that Tropicana has full dirt basepaths and pitching mound.

Built in 1998, Tucson Electric Park was one of the great stadiums that were built for spring training baseball. Boasting one of the most beautiful mountain views of any ballpark, Tucson Electric Park is the model upon which many other ballparks were created. Even by today's standards, this ballpark is huge. It is one of the two biggest spring training facilities, and every one of those seats is needed during the Cactus League season. The stadium was named for the local utility company until 2010, when the name was changed to Kino Veterans Memorial Stadium.

This huge complex, with a dozen baseball fields and associated facilities, was spring training home of the National League's Arizona Diamondbacks (1998–2010) and of the American League's Chicago White Sox (1998–2008). It also hosted the Pacific Coast League's Tucson Sidewinders during the regular season (1998–2008). With a capacity of 11,000, it was usually sold out, especially since the Diamondbacks make Arizona their full-time home, so the majority of spectators in Arizona are die-hard Diamondbacks fans.

From 1998 until 2008, Tucson Electric Park was the home of the Pacific Coast League's Tucson Sidewinders, the Triple-A affiliate of the Arizona Diamondbacks.

In 2008 the White Sox wanted to end their contract early and negotiated a deal that introduced a Major League Baseball academy to Tucson. In 2011 the San Diego Padres announced that their Triple-A affiliate, the Tucson Padres, would move in.

With the construction of the new Salt River Fields at Talking Sticks, Arizona, in 2011, the Diamondbacks have also announced their departure to a new spring training home, which they will share with the Colorado Rockies.

Location: 2500 East Ajo Way, Tucson, AZ
Aka: TEP (1998–2010), Kino Veterans Memorial Stadium (from 2010)
Status: Home of the Tucson Padres
Opened: 1998
Capacity: 11,000
Dimensions:
Right Field 340 ft
Center Field 405 ft
Left Field 340 ft

Tucson Electric Park

RIGHT: Down the foul lines there is bleacher seating on the upper concourse.

BELOW: The majestic backdrop of the Santa Catalina Mountains makes Kino Veterans Memorial Stadium the perfect setting for baseball.

Location: 755 Hank Aaron Drive, Atlanta, GA

Aka: Atlanta 1996 Summer Olympic Stadium, Centennial Olympic Stadium

Status: Home of the Atlanta Braves

Architect: Atlanta Stadium Design Team

Opened: July 19, 1996

First MLB game: March 30, 1997

Capacity: 49,304

Dimensions:

Left Field 335 ft

Left Center 380 ft

Center Field 401 ft

Right Center 390 ft

Right Field 330 ft

BELOW: Aerial photo with the Grand Entry Plaza on the north end at the top of the picture. Adjacent to the plaza on the north side is the Ivan Allen Jr. Braves Hall of Fame Museum.

OPPOSITE, ABOVE: Panorama from third base side.

OPPOSITE, BELOW: The HD video display board stands above the batter's eye in center field. The scoreboard is 71 feet tall by 79 feet wide. Built by Mitsubishi, it cost $10 million and made its debut in 2005.

Originally built as the centerpiece of the 1996 Olympics, Turner Field has a huge 85,000 capacity. The Olympics arrived in Atlanta just as the Braves needed a new home, so a deal was struck between the city and Ted Turner, owner of the Braves. Atlanta contributed $207 million for the brick-and-limestone Olympic stadium that was built in the parking lot of Atlanta-Fulton County Stadium. Following the Olympics, the Braves spent a further $35 million converting the stadium for baseball only: among other changes, 35,000 seats were removed and the grandstands pulled down, dugouts appeared, and the basement TV studio became the home locker room.

In summary, the Braves received a ballpark that many believed to be an instant classic, with a state-of-the-art, symmetrical designer field that boasted seats angled toward home plate and fantastic viewing positions. Near the ticket windows lies Monument Grove, where statues of Hank Aaron, Phil Niekro, and Ty Cobb were relocated from Atlanta-Fulton and placed alongside other baseball-themed attractions.

More controversially, the stadium was named after Ted Turner rather than local hero and one of the greatest players of all time, Hank Aaron. Instead, the seats are decorated with a silhouette of Aaron in tribute to his remarkable career. The sports complex includes a museum as well as numerous food and games concessions.

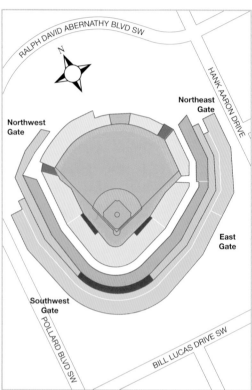

Union Base-Ball Grounds was also sometimes called White Stocking Park as it was the home of the National Association's Chicago White Stockings in 1871, a professional independent team that had spent the previous season playing at Dexter Park race course and Ogden Park. The ballpark was bounded by Michigan Avenue to the west, by Randolph Street to the north, and by railroad tracks and the lakeshore on the east. The October 1871 Great Chicago Fire totally destroyed Union Base-Ball Grounds and, after completing the season on the road, the club did not field a team for the next two seasons. The ballpark was not rebuilt.

The White Stockings returned to the original site in 1878 to take up residence in a new ballpark that was usually called Lake Shore Park, Lake Front Park, or simply Lake Park until being renamed Grant Park in 1901. The team played there to the end of the 1884 season. Led by Hall of Famer Cap Anson, the team won the National League pennant in 1880, 1881, and 1882.

The city reclaimed the land after the 1884 season and the White Stockings became a road team for the first couple of months of 1885 while awaiting completion of West Side Park.

Location: Michigan Avenue and Randolph Street, Chicago, IL
Aka: White Stocking Park, Lake Front Park, Lake Shore Park, Lake Park, Grant Park
Status: Destroyed by fire in 1871
Status: Closed in 1884
Opened: 1871

Union Base-Ball Grounds

Union Grounds, Brooklyn

Location: Built in a block enclosed by Harrison Avenue, Rutledge Street, Lynch Street, and Marcy Avenue, Brooklyn, NY
Status: Demolished in 1883
Opened: 1862
Last MLB game: July 1878

Union Grounds was the first park completely ringed by a fence, and a pagoda stood in center field. During its early years it was home to several clubs, including the Brooklyn Eckfords in 1872 and the Brooklyn Atlantics from 1873 to 1875, while the New York Mutuals arrived during 1868 from Elysian Fields in Hoboken, New Jersey.

After the formation of the National Association of Professional Base Ball Players, the New York Mutuals called Union Grounds home from 1871 to 1876. It also hosted the "Hartford of Brooklyn" team during the 1877 National League season.

The final major league game was played in July 1878 but the ballpark continued to stage barnstorming major league, amateur, and independent games through the 1882 season. Union Grounds was demolished in July 1883 and today, sadly, there is no evidence left of its significance to baseball.

Union Grounds, St. Louis

Location: In a block enclosed by Cass, Jefferson, Howard, and the present 25th Street, St. Louis, MO
Aka: Union Base Ball Park; Lucas Park
Status: Demolished c.1888
Opened: 1884
Last MLB game: September 23, 1886
Capacity: c.10,000

Investors in the St. Louis Maroons included a local brewer, Adolphus Busch, but another local, Henry Lucas, held the majority of the shares in the club. He brokered a five-year lease for a plot in northern St. Louis, at a site bordered by Cass to the south, Jefferson to the west, Howard on the north, and what is now 25th Street to the east. Although some referred to the stadium as the Palace Park of America, almost all news reports during its life as a major league ballpark refer to it simply as the Union Grounds or the Union Base Ball Park, although it was called Lucas Park on occasion. Henry Lucas spent more than $15,000 on the stadium, making it an all-round sports venue. Bluegrass and clover covered the outfield, which was ringed by a cinder track for running and bicycling.

Features to specifically cater for baseball fans included wire netting behind the home plate and a large scoreboard at the southeast corner that showed not only the Maroons' game tally but also telegraphed progress reports from other Union Association games. A white-painted wooden grandstand was built at the northwest corner of the ballpark with its wings running to the east and south. The main entrance was at the northwest corner, where there was a double ticket office and stairs leading to the grandstands. There was another entrance farther south on Jefferson and a third on Cass that led to the park's carriage yard. Lucas also purchased two billiard tables for the clubhouse's reception room and shower rooms for all the athletes who used the stadium.

Union Park

Location: Corner of North, Grant, and Pennsylvania Avenues, Allegheny City, Pittsburgh, PA
Aka: Recreation Park, Pittsburgh Coliseum
Status: Demolished
Capacity: 17,000

Union Park, also known as Recreation Park, was located in Allegheny City during the late nineteenth and early twentieth centuries before it was subsumed by Pittsburgh in 1907. It was the first official home of the Pittsburgh Pirates, the city's major league franchise, as well as the University of Pittsburgh's football team, then known as the Western University of Pennsylvania. In November 1892 the ballpark hosted the first ever professional American football game, between two local teams. After such sporting events had moved elsewhere, Recreation Park was renamed the Pittsburgh Coliseum and was used for motorized bicycle riding. The stadium, which stood at the corner of North, Grant, and Pennsylvania Avenues on Pittsburgh's north side, originally had a capacity of just 2,500 but was subsequently expanded to hold many times more.

Prior to 1876, three amateur baseball teams—the Enterprise Club, the Xanthas, and the Olympics—regularly competed at the ballpark. After that year an Allegheny club, an antecedent of the present Pittsburgh Pirates, played its first game against Xanthas at Union Park. The first major league team to play at the stadium was the Union Association's Pittsburgh Stogies, but they did not stay long.

Due to the flooding of Exposition Park II, the American Association's Pittsburgh Alleghenys arrived in the late 1880s and their owner, William A. Nimick, switched them from the American Association to the National League in 1887, paving the way for them to evolve into the Pittsburgh Pirates. After the collapse of the Players' League's Pittsburgh Burghers in 1891, the Alleghenys moved into Exposition Park III, which had originally been built to house the Burghers.

Location: 333 West 35th Street, Chicago, IL

Aka: New Comiskey Park

Status: Home of the Chicago White Sox

Architect: HOK Sports (now Populous)

Opened: April 18, 1991

Capacity: 40,615

Dimensions:

Left Field 330 ft

Left Center 377 ft

Center Field 400 ft

Right Center 372 ft

Right Field 335 ft

World Series: 2005

All-Star Game: 2003

U.S. Cellular Field opened for the 1991 season when the Chicago White Sox left Comiskey Park after eighty-one years. Originally called New Comiskey Park, it changed to U.S. Cellular Field in 2003 when U.S. Cellular bought the naming rights for twenty years for a cool $167 million. It is situated directly opposite the old Comiskey Park, which is now the parking lot for the new stadium, and was the last of the big ballparks to be built before the fashion for retro-classic ballparks started in the 1990s.

Its most notable feature is the "exploding scoreboard," a nod to the original 1960s version in the old ballpark. The park has one of the highest upper decks in the game because the stadium was built with the upper deck set back over the lower deck: some people have complained of vertigo after sitting at the top. In fact, the seats in the first row of the upper deck are as far away from the field as the highest upper deck seats at Comiskey. Fans also didn't like the modern look of the park or the way the original roof only partially covered the upper deck. After listening to the fans, the owners have put the stadium through seven

ABOVE: The new roof, put up before the 2004 season, is visible around the top of the stands.

BELOW: A 2000 aerial view of Comiskey Park before it was renamed and revamped. In this guise, some people complained about the vertiginous upper-deck seating.

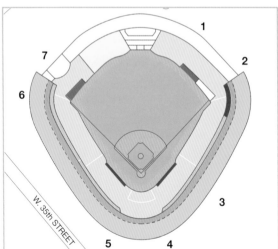

revamps. Most notably, 6,600 seats have been removed from the top of the upper deck and the fences have been altered to become less symmetrical. The venue has been themed in forest green and black colors and, similarly to the old stadium, murals have been painted along the interior concourses. Among numerous improvements and to generate more revenue, there are 103 luxury suites to accommodate high-spending fans.

TOP: The outfield concourse gives fans 360-degree access to the field (as long as they stay on the concourse level and they have a ticket with some sort of field level seating). The outfield has a party deck located in dead center field, covered at the bottom in ivy to help the batter's vision.

ABOVE: The footprint of U.S. Cellular Field showing entrances.

RIGHT: Field level view gives a feel for the height of the stadium.

Varsity Park, which was later renamed Pete Beiden Field, stands in the campus of the California State University, Fresno, and is the home of the Fresno State Bulldogs. Former baseball coach Pete Beiden led the team to 600 wins in twenty-one seasons from 1948 to 1969. Prior to the opening of Grizzlies Stadium in 2002, the park also was home to the Triple-A Pacific Coast League's Fresno Grizzlies minor league team. It has hosted eight NCAA Regionals since 1979. The park was redesigned at a cost of $2.2 million in 1993, which was raised by the DugOut Club and a community-wide fund drive, and accommodated 5,422 people after the refit. Since the renovation, Fresno State has been among the nation's attendance leaders every year.

The park was upgraded again in 1998. The project included the installation of a $300,000 state-of-the-art scoreboard, a new public address system, and the addition of 2,000 bleachers down both left- and right-field lines. The left-field bleachers were removed in the 2004 season to make room for indoor batting cages and a team clubhouse. Further improvements included a turf "halo" surrounding the infield and a new sound system after the 2010 season. The stadium is also equipped with a modern press box, with facilities for more than forty members of the media.

Location: North Cedar Avenue, Fresno, CA
Aka: Beiden Field, Pete Beiden Field
Status: Home of the California State University, Fresno, baseball team
Opened: 1966; renovated 1993 and 1998
Capacity: 5,422 (1993); 6,500 (2010)
Dimensions
Left Field 330 ft
Left Center 370 ft
Center Field 400 ft
Right Center 370 ft
Right Field 330 ft

LEFT: In 2001 Bob Bennett guided Fresno State to its twenty-fifth consecutive winning season. He became the first coach in Fresno State history to have his number—26—retired. It will live forever on the left-field wall of the facility he helped build.

Vaughn Street Park was opened in 1901, financed by E. I. Fuller and C. F. Swigert, owners of nearby trolley lines who hoped to profit from professional baseball, both at the box office and via fares from lines. The stadium's main tenants were the Portland Beavers, formerly the Portland Webfoots, of the Pacific Coast League. During a time when the club was nicknamed the "Lucky Beavers," the ballpark was also known as Lucky Beavers Stadium. The stadium also briefly became home to the Portland Rosebuds, a team from the short-lived West Coast Baseball Association that disbanded after just two months.

Initially, the stadium had a single 3,000-seat grandstand but seating grew to 6,000 in 1905. With the construction of additional seats in 1912, capacity rose to 12,000. Multnomah Stadium opened two miles south in 1926 and it was thought that the Beavers would move, but they elected to stay at Vaughn Street. The left-field bleachers burned in 1947 and the new owners announced that they would tear it down in 1955. The Beavers moved to Multnomah Stadium the next year, and nothing of Vaughn Street remains today except a plaque.

Location: NW 24th & Vaughn, Portland, OR
Aka: Lucky Beavers Stadium
Status: Demolished in 1956
Opened: 1901
Capacity: 6,000 (1905); 12,000 (1912)
Dimensions:
Left Field 331 ft
Center Field 368 ft
Right Field 331 ft

LEFT: Vaughn Street Park.

Veterans Stadium

Location: Packer Street and Pattison Avenue, Philadelphia, PA

Aka: The Vet

Status: Demolished in 2004

Architects: Hugh Stubbins; George Ewing; Stonorov & Haws

Capacity: 56,371 (1971); 66,744 (1980s)

Opened: April 4, 1971

Last MLB game: September 28, 2003

Dimensions:

Left Field 330 ft

Left Center 371 ft

Center Field 408 ft

Right Center 371 ft

Right Field 330 ft

World Series: 1980, 1983, 1993

All-Star Games: 1976, 1996

Veterans Stadium in Philadelphia has the dubious distinction of being one of the worst venues in baseball history. The Phillies and the NFL's Philadelphia Eagles both wanted a new multipurpose stadium to showcase their games. It took almost a decade to build it, cost $50 milllion—one of the most expensive ballparks at the time—to construct, and the players and public alike all hated it. The AstroTurf was notorious for its bumpy and uneven surface and tendency to create bad bounces. Nevertheless, the Vet had the largest seating capacity in the entire National League for most of its existence.

As the 1990s progressed the old stadium really began to deteriorate and lobbying started for a new venue. In April 2004 the Phillies moved on to Citizens Bank Park, much to general approval all around.

Starting in 1976 the Phillies won the East Division three straight years, and later added four more division titles—in 1980, 1981, 1983, and 1993. Over that stretch the team played in the 1980, 1983, and 1993 World Series, winning only the first, defeating the Royals in six games. On March 21, 2004, the Vet was imploded. The stadium had stood for thirty-three years and disappeared in sixty-two seconds. The site is now a parking lot and dedicated fans can search out granite spaces marking the locations of home plate, the pitcher's mound, and three bases.

TOP and ABOVE LEFT: On October 21, 1980, in game six of the World Series, the Phillies clinched their first world championship, beating the Kansas City Royals in front of 65,838 fans. That year 2,651,650 fans came to watch—but the late 1990s saw a dropoff, as these pictures show. In contrast, in 2010 at the new ballpark the year's attendance was 3,777,322.

LEFT: Veterans Stadium was part of a complex that also included the Spectrum, home of both the Flyers (NHL) and 76ers (NBA), and JFK Stadium, site of the annual Army-Navy college football game.

366

This little-known early venue for professional baseball in St. Louis lay just north of the Missouri Pacific Railroad tracks. Conveniently located in the central city on the west side of Compton Avenue at Gratiot, this six acres of level ground saw baseball as far back as 1867, when the inaugural game of that year's St. Louis City Championship series between two amateur clubs, the Unions and the Empires, was held at what was then the Veto Grounds. Then a local amateur club, the St. Louis Red Stockings, built a grandstand behind home plate and enclosed the field with a wooden stockade fence in 1874. The diamond lay near the southeast corner of the lot, with the home plate facing northwest. The following season, the club turned pro and joined the National Association of Base Ball Players.

Although the team's stay in that first professional association was brief, the park continued to support various amateur and semipro clubs until at least 1898. As time passed, the ballpark became better known as Compton Avenue Park. The land where the stadium stood eventually passed to the Bi-State Development Agency, a public transit company, and today its repair facilities cover the area where the Unions and Empires contested the city's first fully professional baseball game. A bridge now passes over that spot and most locals are unaware of the little bit of baseball history that was played out beneath their feet.

Location: Compton Avenue, St. Louis, MO
Status: Demolished in 1898
Opened: 1875
Capacity: 1,000

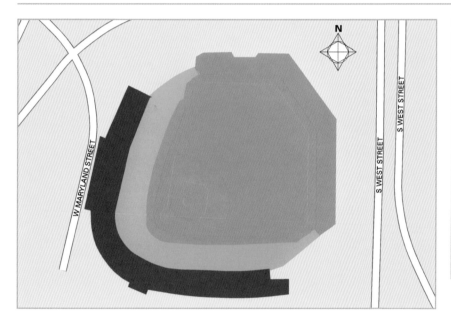

Location: 501 West Maryland Street, Indianapolis, IN
Status: Home of the Indianapolis Indians
Architect: HOK Sport (now Populous)
Opened: 1996
Capacity: 15,596
Dimensions:
Left Field 320 ft
Center Field 402 ft
Right Field 320 ft
All-Star Game: 2001

Victory Field is the name of the current minor league park that is the home of the Indianapolis Indians of the International League and the Triple-A affiliate of the Pittsburgh Pirates. It replaced Bush Stadium, which had also been called Victory Field for some twenty-five years of its existence.

The $20 million ballpark is also home to the annual city, county, and high school baseball state championships and in July 2001 it hosted the Triple-A All-Star Game.

The new Victory Field is considered one of the finest facilities in the minor leagues and has been dubbed the "Best Minor League Ballpark in America" by *Baseball America* and *Sports Illustrated*.

THIS PAGE: Victory Field has some 12,500 seats, space for 2,000 on the outfield lawns, and room for some 1,000 standing.

Location: Wahconah Street, Pittsfield, MA

Aka: Nokona Stadium at Wahconah Park (2008)

Status: Home of the Pittsfield Colonials

Opened: 1892

Capacity: 3,500

Dimensions:

Left Field 334 ft

Center Field 374 ft

Right Field 333 ft

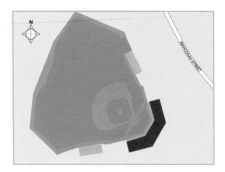

RIGHT: Footprint of Wahconah Park.

Wahconah Park is a city-owned venue located in a working-class neighborhood of Pittsfield and is one of the very few remaining stadiums in the United States with a wooden grandstand. The stadium hosted the Pittsfield Dukes—later the American Defenders—from 2005 until 2009 and it is now the home of the Canadian American Association of Professional Baseball's Pittsfield Colonials. Through the park's history, which has seen more than a dozen franchises take up residency at one time or another, more than 201 Pittsfield players have made it into the major leagues.

Pittsfield city officials had reached an agreement with Dan Duquette for the Pittsfield Dukes, a New England Collegiate Baseball League summer team, to play at the park from 2005 and it paid off. During the 2007 season, the Dukes attracted a total attendance of 28,955 for twenty-one home games, an average of 1,378 spectators per game. Duqette teamed up with the Nokona glove company and the U.S. Army team in late 2008 to create the Pittsfield American Defenders and, as part of the deal, Wahconah Park was renamed Nokona Stadium at Wahconah Park. With the newly received injection of money, Nokona Stadium received a makeover, including a brand-new infield, bathrooms, offices, and press box.

Location: 213–269 Dodge Street, Buffalo, NY

Aka: Roesch Memorial Stadium (1937), Grover Cleveland Stadium (1937–1938), Civic Stadium (1938–1960), the Rockpile

Status: Demolished in 1988

Opened: 1937

Capacity: 35,000 (1939); 46,500 (1960)

RIGHT: The mid-1960s upper-deck addition increased seating capacity substantially. (Photo courtesy Bob Gaver.)

BELOW: As always, baseball was not a great game for the football stadium footprint.

Built as part of Roosevelt's New Deal via the Works Progress Administration project, groundbreaking took place in 1935. It was named Roesch Memorial Stadium (after mayor Charles Edward Roesch, who died in 1936) to begin with and opened in 1937. It boasted a classic football bowl that did not sit easily with baseball, but it had a cozy feel that allowed fans close proximity to the players. In 1938 it was renamed Civic Stadium but didn't see much sport. Buffalo didn't have a pro football franchise and it was used mainly for civic gatherings. Things improved with the advent of the Buffalo Bills in 1947 but the team didn't gain an NFL slot, and during the 1950s the stadium was best known for stock car racing.

Everything changed in 1960. Renamed War Memorial Stadium, it became home for the Buffalo Bisons of the International League when Offermann Stadium closed, as well as the newly created NFL Buffalo Bills franchise. To increase the capacity, an upper deck was built along the north stands, but the changes had come too late for the stadium. It was starting to show its age, and during the 1960s the fans stopped coming in numbers. The Bisons struggled financially and in 1971 relocated to Winnipeg only to disband at the end of the year. Meanwhile, the Bills opened Rich Stadium and moved away. By 1973, War Memorial Stadium stood unused.

Six years later, in 1979, the revived Buffalo Bisons (a new Triple-A team relocated from Wichita) took up tenure. They played at War Memorial Stadium until 1988, when they moved to a new stadium at Pilot Field. All the while the stadium was getting much shabbier, which ironically made it the ideal location for the classic baseball movie *The Natural,* starring Robert Redford. After the Bisons left, "the Rockpile" was soon demolished.

RIGHT: End-on view shows clearly how the stand was added in the 1960s.

Over the winter of 1899–1900 a ballpark was built in Indianapolis on railroad-owned land south of Washington Street. On two city blocks at the intersection of Gray and East Washington Streets, the ballpark was laid out with a wooden grandstand in the southwest corner. From the marshaling yard to the south of the grounds, railroad workers, dubbed "railbirds," used to catch a free view of the players as they went about their business.

The Indianapolis Indians were founded in 1902, making them the second-oldest minor league franchise in professional baseball, and initially played at Washington Park in the American Association in 1902 and 1904. After being demolished, the site became the Wonderland Amusement Park until it burned down in 1911. It was never rebuilt and the lot became used for commercial and residential purposes.

In 1905 the Indianapolis Indians moved home across town to Washington Park II, where they remained until 1912. After a lapse of three years they returned for the 1915 season and stayed there until mid-season 1931, when they moved to Perry Stadium on 16th Street. The site is currently an industrial and commercial area.

Location: I: 3001 East Washington Street, Indianapolis, IN; II: 1235 West Washington Street
Aka: I: East Washington Street Park; II: West Washington Street Park
Status: I: Demolished c. 1905; II: Demolished in 1931
Opened: 1900
Capacity: 20,000
Dimensions: (for I)
Left Field 375 ft
Center Field 400 ft
Right Field 310 ft

Located at Washington and Hill Streets, Washington Park was near an amusement park called Chutes Park at Washington and Main. The Angels initially played in the California League on a field at the north end of Chutes Park between 1903 and 1911, before moving two blocks west to Washington Park, where an area had been designed for baseball. The grounds contained a covered, single-deck grandstand.

Washington Park was the home of the Los Angeles Angels of the Pacific Coast League from 1912 until they moved during the 1925 season to Wrigley Field in Los Angeles. The owner of the Angels as of 1921 was chewing gum magnate William Wrigley Jr. The story goes that, as part of his ambitions for the park, he wanted to create an underground parking lot but was not given permission by the authorities, who clearly were not interested in developing the ballpark. So instead he built a new ballpark of his own,which he called Wrigley Field, and moved his men there. Washington Park was demolished in the mid-1950s.

Location: Hill Street between Washington and 21st Streets, Los Angeles, CA
Status: Demolished c. 1955
Opened: 1911
Capacity: 12,200

BELOW: Washington Park, Los Angeles, around 1911. The amusement park's water slide and building are visible behind right field.

Location: Third and Fifth Streets and Fourth and Fifth Avenues, New York, NY

Status: Burned down in 1889

Opened: 1883

Capacity: 2,000

Washington Park opened in 1883 on land where George Washington's Continental Army fought the battle of Long Island and where his temporary headquarters of Gowanus House still stands. That same year the Brooklyn Bridegrooms became the first baseball team to call New York home; in time they became better known as the Brooklyn Dodgers. Within a year Washington Park had become the recognized home of New York baseball.

Located at Third Street and Fourth Avenue, the site was the home of three Washington Park baseball grounds: the ballparks were positioned diagonally across the intersection with Washington Park I directly opposite Washington Park II, and then later Washington Park III built on the same site as Washington Park II.

Washington Park I was built into a slight hollow in a lot bounded by Third and Fifth Streets and Fourth and Fifth Avenues that also contained Gowanus House (which they used as the clubhouse). The two-decked wooden grandstand could seat around 2,000 fans. The minor league Brooklyn Bridegrooms first played baseball here in 1883, the following year they joined the American Association and then changed again in 1890 to join the National League. For the 1892 season the Bridegrooms intermittently played at the more modern Eastern Park in Brooklyn and then moved there permanently. But the move proved too far away for the majority of their fans and attendances fell. Also, the rent was high, so after six years the Dodgers (though still officially the Bridegrooms) returned to their old stomping grounds but this time across the other side of the intersection. By then they had acquired the nickname "Trolley Dodgers" in reference to the nearby trolley tracks at Eastern Park. The old ballpark was consumed by fire in May 1889.

Location: First and Third Streets and Third and Fourth Avenues, Brooklyn, NY

Status: Demolished in 1926

Opened: April 30, 1898

Capacity: 3,000 (1898); 18,800 (1914)

Dimensions

	Original 1898	Final 1908
Left Field	335 ft	300 ft
Center Field	500 ft	443 ft
Right Field	215 ft	275 ft

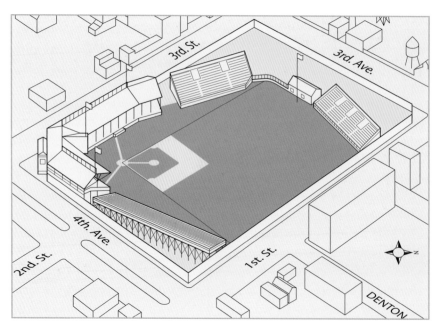

RIGHT: Artist's impression of Washington Park II in 1908 after the seating capacity was increased.

In 1898 and still playing in the American Association, the Brooklyn Bridegrooms (who would become the Dodgers) returned to Washington Park but in a slightly different location; the entrance was now on Third Street and Fourth Avenue. This time there was a covered grandstand and open seating down the right field line. The park officially seated 3,000 fans, but with many more standing: the clubhouse was once again the old Gowanus House.

The Dodgers played their first game back in Brooklyn on April 30, 1898, in front of 15,000 spectators and stayed for fifteen seasons, but all the while their owner, Charlie Ebbets, was buying up plots of land around Flatbush, slowly acquiring an entire block. By 1913 Ebbets had what he wanted and the Dodgers moved to their new home at Ebbets Field.

The Brooklyn Tip-Tops of the Federal League moved into Washington Park and played there for two years until the Federal League folded. The grandstand and surrounds were demolished in 1926, but parts of the twenty-foot-high left field wall still remain on Third Avenue.

Location: First and Third Streets and Third and Fourth Avenues, New York, NY
Status: Demolished c. 1915
Opened: 1914
Capacity: 18,800
Dimensions
Left Field 300 ft
Left Center 443 ft
Center Field 400 ft
Right Center 300 ft
Right Field 275 ft

In 1913 the abandoned ballpark site was bought for the Brook-Feds of the Federal League. The old structure was pulled down and replaced in 1914 with a new wood-and-concrete grandstand and the ballpark was embellished with Native American symbols on the outfield fence. Despite the changes, the ballpark was still called Washington Park. A 220-foot flagpole made from the yacht *Reliance*—which successfully defended the America's Cup in 1903 and was broken up in Brooklyn in 1913—stood centrally behind the scoreboard. The scoreboard itself stood on supporting legs in center field and was the occasional cause of inside-the-park home runs when fielders had to scramble underneath the board to retrieve a fair ball. But after two years the Federal League dissolved in 1915; the park lost its tenants and was demolished.

LEFT: The famous scoreboard and flagpole of Washington Park's third incarnation. This photograph of the flag raising on April 10, 1915, shows the legs on which the scoreboard stood.

Built in 1948 on the site of Exhibition Park, a wooden ballpark that had burned down twice (in 1939 and 1944), Watt Powell Park was home to several minor league franchises until 2005, when it was replaced by Appalachian Power Park and allowed to decline.

With a capacity of 4,500, Watt Powell's dimensions favored pitchers—there was a remarkable lack of power hitting at games there. The height of the outfield walls may have influenced this, as at twelve feet high, they were higher than most. Another interesting feature is the ballpark's location next to the CSX railroad, which enabled impecunious fans to watch the game from there, rather than paying for a seat. Apparently the view was great.

Charleston had hosted professional baseball since 1910, but it was not really until the 1970s that teams of the International League made a real commitment to the city. In 1987 the Charleston Alley Cats brought minor league baseball back to Charleston after a three-year absence and they played at Watt Powell until 2004. In 2005 their name was changed to reflect their sponsors, West Virginia Power, and they moved out to Appalachian Power Park.

In 2005 the stadium was sold to the University of Charleston and demolished gradually piece by piece.

Location: MacCorkle Avenue and 34th Street SE, Charleston, WV
Status: Demolished in 2005
Opened: 1949
Capacity: 5,500
Dimensions
Left Field 340 ft
Center Field 406 ft
Right Field 330 ft

Werner Park

Location: 12356 Ballpark Way, Papillion, NE

Status: Home of the Omaha Storm Chasers

Architect: DLR Group

Opened: 2011

Capacity: 9,023 (6,434 seated)

Dimensions

Left Field 310 ft

Center Field 402 ft

Right Field 315 ft

BELOW and RIGHT: The first game at Werner Park was between two local high schools, six days before the Storm Chasers took to the field for the first time on April 16, 2011.

Werner Park is the current home of the Omaha Storm Chasers of the Pacific Coast League. The club, formerly known as the Omaha Royals, moved from Johnny Rosenblatt Stadium into Werner Park on April 16, 2011. The ballpark was budgeted to cost $26 million to construct and groundbreaking for the new stadium took place on August 12, 2009. The Storm Chasers announced that they had reached an agreement with the Omaha-based company and long-time Royals sponsor Werner Enterprises for the ballpark's naming rights in November 2010.

The omens didn't seem good when the Storm Chasers had to delay their inaugural game by a day because of bad weather. When it did happen, on April 16, C. L. Werner, founder and chairman of Werner Enterprises, threw out the ceremonial first pitch. The game was played in front of a sellout crowd and the Storm Chasers defeated the Nashville Sounds 2–1. The news from Papillon has gotten better and better, as a May 2011 press release said:

"In 42-plus years of Triple-A baseball in Omaha, fans have never consistently supported a team like this. The Omaha Storm Chasers, just 19 home dates into the inaugural 2011 season at Werner Park, have hosted a record 13 games in a row with at least 4,000 fans in attendance. That shatters the previous all-time high at Rosenblatt Stadium and is a full eight games longer than any single streak from 2001–2007."

West End Park

Location: 1400 South Park Street, Little Rock, AR

Aka: Highland Park Baseball Field, Kavanaugh Field (from 1915)

Status: Demolished in the 1930s

Opened: 1895; rebuilt 1915

Closed: 1931

Capacity: 2,000 (1895); 4,450 (1915)

The groundbreaking work on this now long-gone stadium began in 1894 and the Little Rock Travelers of the Southern Association were the first baseball team to move in the next year. They would call West End Park their home for that season as well as two other somewhat longer periods, first from 1901 to 1909, and for a third and final time from 1915 to 1931.

The person responsible for the return of professional basebal to Little Rock was Judge William M. Kavanaugh, who had been president of the Southern League since 1903. Unfortunately, he died suddenly on February 21, 1915, and did not see the return. The stadium was renovated before the Travelers returned to the renamed Kavanaugh Field. The diamond was set back to make the field larger, and the original grandstand was demolished to make way for a new 3,500-seat wooden one—the extra seating more than doubling its total capacity.

The venue was also used for major league spring training on a number of occasions, in 1895, 1898, and from 1907 to 1910. However, when the Travelers moved out, the stadium, which had been the scene of the first ever night baseball game played in Arkansas in 1894, was closed down and demolished.

RIGHT: The end of an era—this photograph shows the final home opener at Kavanaugh Field on April 15, 1931.

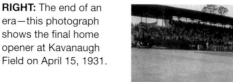

Location: 715 Hank Aaron Drive, West Palm Beach, FL

Status: Demolished in 2002

Opened: March 9, 1963

Capacity: 4,200 (1963); 5,000 (1986)

Dimensions

Left Field 350 ft

Center Field 410 ft

Right Field 350 ft

LEFT: 1995 view of the stadium with Expos and Braves spring training dates identified.

BELOW: Many future major league players would call this ballpark their Single-A home. (Both photos courtesy Bob Busser.)

The first tenants in West Palm Beach Municipal Stadium were the Atlanta Braves, who moved their spring training operations to West Palm Beach from Bradenton's McKechnie Field. The Braves would make West Palm Beach their spring training home for thirty-five years, from 1963 to 1997.

In 1963 the Braves moved their Single-A operations to West Palm Beach. The Montreal Expos shared the Braves' facilities for the first four years of their existence,

from 1969 until 1973, when they moved on to Daytona Beach's Jackie Robinson Ballpark. The Expos' minor league club, the West Palm Beach Expos, remained at the site even when the parent club moved on, staying for a remarkable twenty-nine years from 1969 until 1997. Many of the Expos' future stars played their first professional games for the Single-A Expos.

A new winter league, the Senior Professional Baseball Association, came to town in 1989 and 1990, and was a senior circuit of ex–major league stars. There were eight teams in total and the West Palm Beach Tropics called the stadium home.

BELOW: This 1995 photograph shows the view from right field.

With Jupiter's new Roger Dean Stadium in full operation hosting two major league spring training teams and two Florida State League teams, West Palm Beach Municipal Stadium was taken out of commission in 1998, and this excellent ballpark was demolished in 2002.

West Side Park (1885)

Location: In a block enclosed by Congress, Loomis, Harrison, and Throop Streets, Chicago, IL
Status: Demolished in 1920
Opened: June 6, 1885
Capacity: 10,000
Dimensions:
Center Field 560 ft
Right Field 216 ft

The first West Side Park was a replacement for the Chicago White Stockings' (later Chicago Cubs) Lakefront Park from 1885 to 1891. Although the park's useful life turned out to be just seven years, it was a memorable time, as the team won the National League pennant in their first two seasons. The park was located on a small, elongated block that gave a decidedly odd shape to the park. In addition to the diamond, the park held a bicycle track around the playing field.

The Cubs had to secure a new property after 1884, and it took longer than anticipated. The club spent the first five-plus weeks of the 1885 season on the road before playing at West Side Park, but captured the National League pennant that season and also went on to lose the league crown in 1886 to the St. Louis Browns.

In 1891 the team split their playing schedule between West Side Park and South Side Park I. West Side Park was abandoned after the 1891 season, with the team playing exclusively at South Side the next year.

In May 1893 the Chicago Cubs opened their second West Side Park, which was sometimes called West Side Grounds, a few blocks west-southwest of the first stadium and then made it their permanent home the following year. The stadium was the home of the Cubs' most successful teams of the twentieth century, as they won four National League pennants and two World Series championships between 1906 and 1910. However, by the early 1910s the wooden ballpark was visibly showing its age, a result in large part of its neglect by Charles Murphy, the unpopular owner of the Cubs, and the ballpark found itself competing unsuccessfully with newer steel-and-concrete venues.

When the Federal League folded after the 1915 season, Charles Weeghman, owner of the now-defunct Chicago Whales, was allowed to buy a substantial interest in the Cubs. One of his first acts was to abandon West Side Park II and move to Weeghman Park for the next season. Weeghman Park survives today as Wrigley Field. West Side Park II continued to host semipro and amateur baseball events for a few years but was eventually torn down. The site is now occupied by the University of Illinois Medical Center.

Location: In a block enclosed by Taylor, Wood, Polk, and Lincoln Streets, Chicago, IL
Status: Demolished in 1920
Opened: 1893
Capacity: 16,000
Dimensions
Left Field 340 ft
Center Field 560 ft
Right Field 340 ft

LEFT and BELOW LEFT: Two views of West Side Park both with the White Sox playing the Cubs in the first City Championship series, on October 10, 1909.
The lower image is from the fifth game of the 1906 World Series, October 13, 1906.

Westgate Park was located in the Mission Valley region of San Diego and was home to the Pacific Coast League's San Diego Padres from 1958 to 1967. Westgate was built to replace the deteriorating Lane Field, and the $1 million build was paid for by the Padres' owner, C. Arnholt Smith. It was a neat modern stadium and there were unrealized plans to increase its capacity to major league levels. The Padres played their first game at Westgate in April 1958, a day-night doubleheader against the Phoenix Giants.

A particular problem at Westgate Park was the drainage of the field, especially in right field. This was because the nearby San Diego River had its high-water mark only a little below the playing field. In wet weather the water was unable to drain away and the playing field remained sodden.

However, the American Football League's San Diego Chargers wanted a new home to replace the 1915-vintage Balboa Stadium. With Major League Baseball soon to arrive, the city decided to build a single multipurpose stadium to host both baseball and football. The new facility was initially called San Diego Stadium but would eventually become known as Qualcomm Stadium. The announcement spelled the end of Westgate. The minor league Padres played the 1968 season in the cavernous new stadium knowing they were about to disappear when the major league San Diego Padres appeared the next year.

Location: Friars Road, San Diego, CA
Status: Demolished in 1968
Opened: April 28, 1958
Last MLB game: 1967
Capacity: 8,268
Dimensions:
Left Field 320 ft
Center Field 410 ft
Right Field 320 ft

Wiedenmeyer's Park

Location: 258 Wilson Avenue, Newark, NJ

Aka: David's Stadium (1926–1931), Bear Stadium (1932–1933), Ruppert Stadium (1934–1953), Newark Memorial Stadium (after 1953)

Architect: Charles A. Davids

Status: Demolished 1967

Opened: 1900

Last MLB game: 1949

Capacity: 19,000 (1925)

Dimensions:

Left Field 305 ft

Center Field 410 ft

Right Field 305 ft

World Series: 1946 (Negro League)

OPPOSITE, TOP: A simple two-tiered design makes up Wrigley's architecture. The broadcast booth seems to hang precariously behind home plate. That second tier was added twelve years after the ballpark opened.

OPPOSITE, CENTER: Footprint of the ground showing entrances.

OPPOSITE, BELOW: A full crowd at Wrigley Field. The Cubs had a good season in 1929, reaching the World Series. Attendance averaged over 19,000 a game with a record 1,485,166 on the year—a figure that would not be bettered until 1969, the year the Cubs blew the pennant by losing 17 out of 25 games from mid-September. The record year now is 2008, when 3,300,200 turned out.

BELOW: Season-opening game between Rochester and Newark, 1910.

This minor league park housed several stadiums and hosted a succession of teams over its sixty-plus years of use, reflecting the great minor league tradition that thrived in Newark.

Wiedenmeyer's Park was built at the beginning of the twentieth century for half a million dollars by George Wiedenmeyer, a successful Newark brewer. Wiedenmeyer's Park began hosting the International League in 1902 (then known as the Eastern League, but still in existence today) and was home to several Triple-A minor league teams. The Newark Sailors played home games there from 1902 to 1907, and they were succeeded by the Newark Indians (1908–1916) and the Newark Bears (1917–1918).

Occasionally used as an alternate Sunday base by the major leagues, on July 17, 1904, Wiedenmeyer Park hosted its only major league fixture when the Highlanders (later known as the New York Yankees) played the Detroit Tigers. Future Hall of Famer Clark Griffith took the mound for the Highlanders and pitched a three-hit complete-game shutout.

The wooden stadium burned down in 1925 (at the same time that Prohibition caused Wiedenmeyer's brewing empire to collapse), but it was quickly replaced by a new steel-and-concrete structure. Owned by the Yankees organization, the new stadium was originally named after its designer, Charles A. Davids. The name altered again eight years later, changing to that of the owner, another brewer, Jacob Ruppert.

From 1926 until 1949 Ruppert Stadium was home to the International League's Newark Bears, a farm club of the New York Yankees. They won the league title four times, in 1937, 1938, 1940, and 1945, and several major league players began their careers in Newark, including Charlie Keller, Spud Chandler, and George McQuinn.

New owner Colonel Jacob (Jake) Ruppert was a politician and wealthy brewer but was perhaps best known as the owner of the New York Yankees for twenty-four years, during which time he turned them into a great team. By 1937 the Bears had become one of the greatest minor league teams of all time.

The Newark Eagles, who were formed in 1936, also used Ruppert as their home stadium. In 1946, supported by stars such as Larry Dobbs, Monte Irvin, and Leon Day, the Eagles won the Negro League World Series at their home grounds.

The stadium was next to a garbage dump and games could be delayed by smoke and noxious smells from burning garbage. The crowd found it difficult to get in, as the stadium was a good distance from Newark, so most spectators had to take a long public trolley from downtown Newark, but in the 1930s and 1940s both teams played exciting baseball and pulled in the crowds. But when they both moved on, the stadium was left to decay. By 1950 it was empty and in December 1952 was sold to the Newark Board of Education for around $250,000. By mid-1953 the stadium was renamed Newark Memorial Stadium, but nothing came of the plans for it and it was soon deteriorating. In 1967 the stadium was demolished.

Wilmington Park

Location: Governor Printz Boulevard and E 30th Street, Wilmington, DE

Status: Demolished in 1963

Opened: May 1, 1940

Capacity: 7,000

Dimensions:

Center Field 370 ft

Wilmington Park cost $185,000 to build and was located at the corner of 30th Street and Governor Printz Boulevard, and was owned by the local Carpenter family, which also controlled the Philadelphia Phillies. It was home to the International League's Wilmington Blue Rocks, a Phillies farm team also owned by the Carpenters, between 1940 and 1952. Many Negro League games were played at the ballpark in the 1940s. The Philadelphia Stars of the Negro National League, who had replaced the Hilldale Club as the Philadelphia-area Negro League representative, played many of their home games at Wilmington Park after losing their Philadelphia lease in 1947.

The stadium was also home to the University of Delaware football team from 1940 to 1952, and the Wilmington Blue Rocks of the Class B Interstate League from 1940 to 1952.

Location: 1060 West Addison Street, Chicago, IL

Aka: Weeghman Park (1914–1920), Cubs Park (1920–1926), the Friendly Confines

Status: Home of the Chicago Cubs

Architect: Zachary Taylor Davis

Opened: April 23, 1914

First MLB game: April 20, 1916

Capacity: 14,000 (1914); 42,000 (2011)

Dimensions:

	Original 1914	Current
Left Field	345 ft	355 ft
Left Center	364 ft	368 ft
Center Field	440 ft	400 ft
Right Center	364 ft	368 ft
Right Field	356 ft	353 ft

World Series: 1918, 1929, 1932, 1935, 1938, 1945

All-Star Games: 1947, 1962, 1990

Weeghman Park was built in 1914 by Charlie Weeghman for $250,000, specifically for his ball team the Chicago Federals, who played in the Federal League. That league failed to challenge the majors and folded within two years, leaving Weeghman with an empty stadium. His solution was to go in with ten other principals and buy the Chicago Cubs and move them into his ballpark.

The Cubs had been formed in 1876 and went through several name changes and ballparks before finally settling as the Chicago Cubs at Weeghman Park in 1916. The Cubs had appeared in four World Series in five years, twice winning the championship against the Detroit Tigers in 1907 and 1908. They reached the World Series again in 1918, but came up short against the Red Sox, losing 4–2.

One of the owners of the Cubs was William Wrigley Jr., a member of the Wrigley chewing gum family. In 1919 he bought the Cubs from Weeghman and the other owners and renamed the stadium Cubs Park; in 1926 the stadium was renamed for him. It has remained so ever since.

Wrigley Field is regarded as one of the last places to really enjoy old-fashioned baseball as it used to be with all its excitement and personality. The second-oldest active MLB ballpark (after Fenway, by two years), it still retains its classic vine-covered brick outfield and old-fashioned, hand-operated, 1937-vintage scoreboard, which is situated above the center field bleachers. Such features are especially enjoyed on long summer afternoon games that have become a popular feature of Chicago sporting life.

However, as an inner city venue, Wrigley has to be particularly sensitive to neighborhood disturbance and local residents for years blocked attempts to stage night games until August 1988, when Wrigley became the last ballpark in the major leagues to install floodlights, although the number of night games is strictly limited.

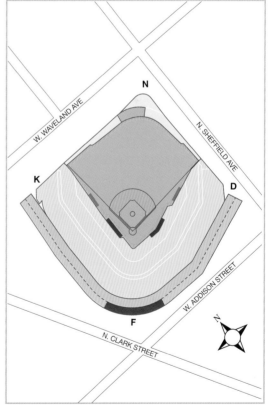

377

ABOVE: Fans gather outside Wrigley Field in the 1920s.

RIGHT and BELOW: Wrigley Field today—the steel structure obstructs sightlines but adds to the atmosphere. The bleachers and the scoreboard didn't make their debut till 1937. The famous ivy walls also debuted that year, thanks to Bill Veeck. The ivy can be voracious—and the ball is sometimes lost, leading to a ground-rule double.

Location: Intersection of 42nd
Place and Avalon Boulevard, Los
Angeles, CA
Status: Demolished in 1966
Architect: Zachary Taylor Davis
Opened: September 29, 1925
First MLB game: April 27, 1961
Last MLB game: October 1, 1961
Capacity: 22,000 (1925); 20,712
(1961)
Dimensions:
Left Field 340 ft
Left Center 345 ft
Center Field 412 ft
Right Center 345 ft
Right Field 338 ft

Named after the chewing gum magnate William Wrigley Jr., the venue was built in south Los Angeles and housed minor league ball teams for almost thirty years during the early to mid-twentieth century. The stadium was built in Spanish-style architecture as a smaller version of the Chicago Cubs' ballpark, Cubs Park, that in turn became Wrigley Field a year after the Los Angeles Wrigley Field was named.

Between 1925 and 1957 the Los Angeles Angels of the Pacific Coast League (owned by William Wrigley Jr., who also owned the Chicago Cubs) played at Wrigley Field. From 1926 to 1938 Wrigley Field was also home to the Angels' rivals, the Hollywood Stars, until they moved to their own ballpark at Gilmore Field. Minor league baseball ended at Wrigley when the Brooklyn Dodgers transferred to Los Angeles in 1958: they considered the stadium but turned it down. Then in 1961 the expansion Los Angeles Angels briefly used the stadium for the season after a $275,000 facelift until they moved into their new home at Dodger Stadium.

Inevitably being so handy for the Hollywood studios, a number of movies used Wrigley Field as a location. It was also used as a boxing venue for six world boxing title bouts. After 1961 no other teams took up residence; even the movie work had moved on to Dodger Stadium, and in the mid-1960s the park was demolished. The lot has since been built over.

ABOVE: The Los Angeles Wrigley was a clone of the famous Chicago ballpark, save for the 150-foot office tower whose clock was visible from the field. The ballpark was used in a number of Hollywood movies, including *It Happens Every Spring* with Ray Milland (1949), *Fear Strikes Out* (1957), and *Damn Yankees* (1958).

BELOW: Wrigley Field was a home run hitter's paradise. In 1961, Crosley Field's record 219 home runs in a ballpark in one season was smashed with 248—a record that lasted until 1996, when 271 home runs were hit in the mile-high atmosphere of Coors Field.

RIGHT: Wrigley Field in Los Angeles also hosted boxing matches as shown here.

Wrigley Field of Avalon

Location: Santa Catalina Island, CA
Status: Demolished in 1966
Architect: Zachary Taylor Davis
Opened: 1921
Dimensions
Left Field 340 ft
Left Center 345 ft
Center Field 412 ft
Right Center 345 ft
Right Field 338 ft

In 1919 the chewing gum magnate and millionaire William Wrigley Jr. bought a controlling interest in the Santa Catalina Island Company. In 1921 he combined his two passions, his Chicago Cubs and his love of Santa Catalina, twenty-two miles southwest of Los Angeles off the California coast, when he took his Cubs there for spring training. A small grandstand was completed in time for the beginning of the 1922 training season. The stadium was built in Spanish-style architecture with the same dimensions as Cubs Park, which became Wrigley Field a year after the Los Angeles Wrigley Field was named. It became the spring training facility for the Cubs until 1951.

The ball field was a paradise for many players, as Catalina Island was, and still is, considered to be a resort town. There was general admission bleacher seating along the third base line. The only "permanent seating" was in the small wooden grandstand on the first base line. The little grandstand is no longer located on the island, but much of the original field remains, including the clubhouse that housed the team's lockers and now features a restaurant, bar, and a wealth of Chicago Cubs memorabilia.

Known as the "Field of Dreams," it hosted a variety of local sports, but bad weather began to batter the island during the late 1940s and early 1950s. Storms forced the Cubs to move spring training to the Los Angeles Wrigley Field for the 1948 and 1949 seasons.

After training proved to be difficult again in 1951, the Cubs moved to the Arizona desert, where there was less possibility of bad weather. The move to Rendezvous Park in Mesa ended a tremendous history of professional baseball on Santa Catalina Island. In all, nineteen future Hall of Famers would train here and step up to the plate. While Mesa would eventually become endearing to the ballplayers, many still remembered this ballpark with tremendously fond memories.

ABOVE, LEFT, and RIGHT: Wrigley Field of Avalon had the same dimensions as the Cubs' Chicago home but a vastly different setting. The link between the Cubs and the island paradise of Santa Catalina ended thanks to bad weather and the promotion of Mesa, Arizona, by Dwight Patterson and the HoHoKams.

Location: East 161st Street and River Avenue, Bronx, NY

Aka: The House That Ruth Built

Status: Demolished in 2009

Architect: Osborn Engineering (1923); Praeger-Kavanaugh-Waterbury (1976)

Opened: April 18, 1923; rebuilt 1974–1975

Closed: September 21, 2008

Capacity: 67,000 (1923); 82,000 (1927); 56,937 (final)

Dimensions:

	Original 1928	Final 1988
Left Field	301 ft	318 ft
Left Center	460ft	399 ft
Center Field	490 ft	408 ft
Right Center	429 ft	385 ft
Right Field	295 ft	314 ft

World Series: 1923, 1926–28, 1932, 1936–39, 1941–43, 1947, 1949–53, 1955–58, 1960–64, 1976–78, 1981, 1996, 1998–2001, 2003

All-Star Game: 1939, 1960, 1977, 2008

Few structures house more memories than the old Yankee Stadium that was demolished at the end of the 2008 season. Ruth, Gehrig, DiMaggio, and Mantle are among the legends who made history on these ten acres in the Bronx. Opened during the Harding presidency and still filling seats thirteen presidents later, the majestic, triple-decked structure hosted heavyweight championships, fabled football games, international soccer matches, world leaders, two popes, and music concerts. Yankee Stadium became synonymous with the most successful sports franchise in America, hosting thirty-seven World Series.

America was dotted with ballparks in 1923 when the Yankees opened the first baseball field to be dubbed a "stadium." Like the team that called it home, there was nothing modest or understated about its confines. Three decks of grandstands, originally intended to encircle the park to deprive non-paying bystanders a free look, rose above home plate, with a distinctive copper frieze decorating the roof of the top deck. Babe Ruth himself, a left-handed hitter who enjoyed the advantage of a short right-field porch, hit the park's first home run to the roaring approval of the New York faithful, who quickly called it the "House That Ruth Built."

ABOVE: 1920s photograph showing stadium being built.

BELOW: 1939 aerial view. By 1937 the wooden bleachers had been replaced by permanent bleachers and the grandstands had been completed, with all three decks extended around the right-field corner.

ABOVE and ABOVE RIGHT: The lights came on in Yankee Stadium in 1946. Note the grandstand frieze that was removed in the 1975 renovation but which has been reproduced in the new stadium.

BELOW: 1966 view of the exterior of Yankee Stadium. Mickey Mantle said: "To play eighteen years in Yankee Stadium is the best thing that could ever happen to a ballplayer." He was honored with a plaque in the stadium's Monument Park, one of twenty-eight that included two popes, the victims of 9/11, and some of the most famous names in baseball, from Babe Ruth to Reggie Jackson.

In 1921 the New York Yankees purchased a ten-acre plot of land from William Waldorf Astor. It cost $675,000 and the new stadium opened in 1923 to a crowd of 74,000 fans who came to see the Yankees play (and defeat) the Red Sox. In baseball's glory years, from the 1930s until the 1960s, this was where many baseball players wanted to play, and the great names did, drawing crowds in the tens of thousands.

The horseshoe-shaped grandstand was the first three-tiered stadium in the United States, and it was designed partly to accommodate the left-handed slugging of Babe Ruth. Raised in only 284 days, it was built mainly of steel and concrete. It was expanded within five years of its construction, with capacity increasing from the initial 58,000 and reaching nearly 80,000 in 1937. Floodlighting was installed in 1946, which enabled night games, and a new scoreboard was added in 1959.

By 1973 the stadium was in serious need of improvement, and it was closed for renovations in the 1974 and 1975 seasons, during which the Yankees played at Shea Stadium. The appearance of the stadium was altered considerably, and die-hard fans consider the Yankee Stadium of post-1974 an entirely new building. The playing field was lowered by about seven feet, allowing several additional rows of box seats to be squeezed in, and the outfield dimensions were reduced, thus altering the asymmetrical layout. Some complained that a baseball relic had been turned into another cookie-cutter design. Nonetheless, the upgrade added at least three decades to the stadium's life, which ended with the 2008 season.

It was here, just across the Harlem River from the Polo Grounds (which the Giants and even the Yankees once called home), that Joe McCarthy and Casey Stengel managed the Yankees to a combined eighteen pennants, where Ruth hit his sixtieth home run, and where Roger Maris hit his sixty-first. Cemetery-sized monuments to manager Miller Huggins and,

later, Gehrig and Ruth were placed in deep center field, ten feet from the wall. Patrons could pay homage to their heroes as they exited through the center field gate, and watch as balls hit sharply to center field occasionally rattled around the monuments. Plaques to DiMaggio and Mantle were added in 1969, and as others were installed in later years, what became known as Monument Park gradually became an open-air museum to the Yankees' finest.

ABOVE: The 1975 renovation added three decades to the life of Yankee Stadium.

BELOW: The old and the new—this 2008 aerial shows just how similar the original and new Yankee Stadiums are.

Yankee Stadium (2009)

Location: East 161st Street and River Avenue, Bronx, New York, NY

Status: Home of the New York Yankees

Architect: Populous

Opened: April 16, 2009

Capacity: 52,325

Dimensions:

Left Field 318 ft

Left Center 399 ft

Center Field 408 ft

Right Center 385 ft

Left Center 314 ft

World Series: 2009

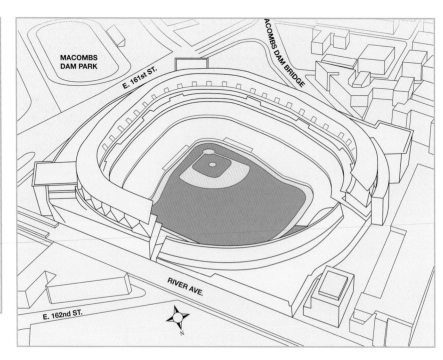

RIGHT: Footprint of Yankee Stadium with Macombs Dam Park in the background. In April 2010, on the rooftop of the two-story Ruppert Plaza Garage, an upgraded, $35 million Macombs Dam Park was opened, giving residents back the green space they had lost when Yankee Stadium was constructed.

BELOW: This aerial view of Yankee Stadium emphasizes the size of the scoreboard and the similarity between old and new—compare the limestone-and-granite outer skin with that shown in the photograph on page 382.

The new Yankee Stadium had to be in the Bronx and it is, right next door to the old stadium. Siting it there was controversial as it is built over what was Macombs Dam Park, a popular twenty-four-acre public facility. For fans familiar with the old Yankee Stadium, the Yankees' new home reflects much of the original ballpark's mystique and character, although it was built at a staggering cost of $1.6 billion.

Ceremonial shovels wielded by prominent New Yorkers broke the first ground on August 16, 2006, coinciding with the fifty-eighth anniversary of the great Babe Ruth's death. The limestone-and-granite outer wall mimics the style of its predecessor's 1923 exterior. Also, to most fans' delight, the distinctive copper frieze that lined the old stadium until 1973 has been replicated around the entire upper deck. Monument Park—honoring more than two dozen former Yankee players, managers, and executives with plaques and monuments—

is located in center field. The dimensions of the playing field are the same as those used in the final season at the previous Yankee Stadium in 2008, and the bullpen locations are in the same positions.

The grandstand seating stretches beyond the foul poles and there are bleacher seats beyond the outfield fences just like at old Yankee Stadium, with cutouts to show the passing subway trains. The biggest change is that the majority of the seating (about two-thirds) is in the lower bowl, as opposed to being in the upper at old Yankee Stadium. To allow for bigger seats and more leg room, the new stadium has "lost" 4,000 seats. The number of luxury suites has been increased from the old stadium's nineteen to sixty-eight and there are currently 4,300 club seats. The playing field is covered with Kentucky bluegrass over an elaborate drainage system that can be ready for play within an hour of two inches of rain falling.

The huge high-definition scoreboard is one of the biggest anywhere, at 59 feet by 101 feet, but there are also manually operated auxiliary scoreboards built into the right- and left-field fences as at the old pre-renovation Yankee Stadium.

Inside the very modern interior there are many more retail outlets, restaurants, and far better amenities—to lessen the blow of the rather higher prices. The interior is decorated with hundreds of photographs charting the historic progress of the Yankees through the decades.

The fans' reaction to the stadium has been mixed but mostly positive, although the high ticket prices exclude many would-be visitors. The high number of home runs the stadium produces is a subject of great debate about whether it cheapens the game or not, and how much the wind currents and temperatures are causal to the way the balls fly through the air.

ABOVE: The new stadium proudly displays a frieze modeled on the old—compare with the picture on page 382.

BELOW and BELOW LEFT: The impressive facade is made from Indiana limestone. Inside, on a non-game day, the interior Great Hall runs events such as trade shows, dinners, and concerts. It is lined with larger-than-life banners of Yankees legends.

385

Location: 6000 Airline Drive,
Metairie, LA

Aka: The Shrine on Airline

Status: Home of the New Orleans
Zephyrs

Architect: Populous

Opened: April 11, 1997

Capacity: 10,000

Dimensions:

Left Field 330 ft

Center Field 400 ft

Right Field 330 ft

All-Star Game: 1999

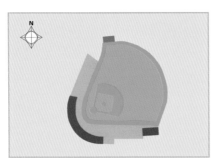

When it was built in 1997 for $25 million, 10,000-seat Zephyr Field provided New Orleans with its first permanent baseball home in forty years. Since the demolition of Heinemann Park (Pelican Stadium) in 1957, the city's baseball teams had shared football stadiums, which were just not suited to the needs of baseball fans.

Zephyr Field became home to the New Orleans Zephyrs, the Triple-A team affiliated to the Houston Astros. The inaugural year at Zephyr Field was a memorable one, as the Zephyrs won the Pacific Coast League championship. New Orleans, meanwhile, proved just how much it loved finally having baseball as a permanent sport in the "Big Easy," and

the Zephyrs drew over half a million fans during its first season. The Zephyrs' overall attendance came back down to earth, but still averaged between 380,000 and 420,000 throughout the Astros' reign in New Orleans.

Since the Astros' departure, the Zephyrs have been affiliated to a succession of teams: the Washington Nationals (2005–2006), the New York Mets (2007–2008), and currently the Florida Marlins. The support of these teams has ensured a flow of talented players destined for major league teams.

In the wake of the devastation caused by Hurricane Katrina in 2004, Zephyr Field has provided an oasis of calm, providing a sense of normality for a few hours at the ball game. After Katrina had passed, Zephyr Field was one of the few buildings still standing in the area. The ballpark did sustain millions of dollars in damages, but that was light compared to rest of the city. When the team announced that it would continue to play despite the fact that New Orleans was now in ruins, it brought a sense of relief to the city.

Zephyr Field also hosts collegiate games, mostly those of the Tulane University Green Wave, as well as the annual grudge matches between local rivals Tulane, the University of New Orleans, and Louisiana State University.

THIS PAGE: Zephyr Field footprint and interior views. Attendance for college games is substantial: 12,069 were in attendance on April 19, 2005, to see Tulane defeat LSU, 11–8.

Adelaide Avenue Grounds Providence, RI

Built in 1875, the Adelaide Avenue Grounds was an alternate site used by the New Haven Elm Citys and Boston for one game each in 1875.

Agricultural County Fair Grounds Worcester, MA

Home of the Worcester Ruby Legs from 1880 to 1882. Worcester pitcher Lee Richmond threw the first perfect game in major-league history on June 12, 1880. A granite post commemorates this on the Becker College campus. Renamed Driving Park Grounds, it hosted one more major league game in 1887. It also hosted one game for the Boston Red Stockings on October 30, 1874.

Agricultural Society Fair Grounds Rockford, IL

Home of the Rockford Forest Citys for the 1871 season.

Association Park Kansas City, MO

Located on Prospect Avenue, between Olive Street and 18th Street. Home to the Kansas City Cowboys for the 1886 season; later became the location of Blues Park.

Athletic Park Kansas City, MO

Located near Southwest Boulevard and Summit Street and home of the Kansas City Cowboys/Unions after they transferred from Altoona, PA, for the last games of the 1884 season.

Athletic Park Minneapolis, MN

Located behind the West Hotel at 6th Street and 1st Avenue North, near present-day Target Center and Target Field, and home of the Minneapolis Millers from 1889 to 1896. The small playing area allowed many home runs at a time when they were rare. Sold during the 1896 baseball season, the Millers had to move to Nicollet Park.

Athletic Park Washington, D.C.

Located at S Street NW, T Street NW, and 9th Street NW, and home to the Washington Nationals, aka "Statesmen" in 1884: the Nationals folded before that season ended.

Avenue Grounds Cincinnati, OH

Aka Brighton Park and Cincinnati Baseball Park, 1875–1900. Used for amateur baseball until c. 1900; the grandstand could seat up to 3,000 fans. Home to the Cincinnati Reds from 1876 to 1879, when poor form saw the team drop out of the league. The Reds revived for 1880, relocated to the Bank Street Grounds.

Bacharach Park Atlantic City, NJ

This former greyhound racetrack was converted into a baseball stadium and was the home of the Atlantic City Bacharach Giants 1896–1926.

Bank Street Grounds Cincinnati, OH

Located at the intersection of Bank Street and McLaren Avenue, this was home to three MLB teams: the Cincinnati Reds in 1880, the Cincinnati Outlaw Reds for 1884, and the current Cincinnati Reds 1882–1883. The former won the inaugural season of the AA, and

competed against the Chicago White Stockings for the first exhibition World Series. There were two games, both held at Bank Street Grounds, with each team winning once.

Bay View Park Toledo, OH

Located on Manhattan Boulevard at Summit Street, this was the home of the Toledo Swamp Angels/Mud Hens from 1896 to 1900 for Saturday and Sunday games only.

Belair Lot Baltimore, MD

Located within a block bounded by Forrest Street, Low Street, Orleans Street, and Gay Street, Belair Lot was home to the UA Baltimore Monumentals for the 1884 season.

Brookside Stadium Cleveland, OH

Used c. 1915 and located a little south of Denison Avenue, between Fulton Road and West 46th Street, this was home for the amateur Omaha Luxus sponsored by Krug Brewery, the White Autos, and the Cleveland Blues (who became the Cleveland Naps in 1903).

Brotherhood Park Cleveland, OH

Home to the Cleveland Infants for the 1890 season.

Bruce Grounds Indianapolis, IN

Aka Bruce Park. Located outside the city limits in an area known as Broad Ripple, at Bruce Street (now 23rd) and College Avenue. This was home to the Indianapolis Hoosiers in 1884. The Indianapolis Hoosiers also used Bruce Grounds for Sunday games in 1887 thanks to the blue laws. However, it was too far out of town and the Hoosiers moved to Indianapolis Park for 1888–1889.

Bugle Field Baltimore, MD

Located at the corner of Federal Street and Edison Highway, this mostly wooden ballpark was the home of the Baltimore Elite Giants from the 1920s until the park was demolished during the 1949 Negro National League Championship Series. It was also home to the Baltimore Black Sox between 1932 and 1934, when the team folded.

Bulldog Park Indianapolis, IN

Located on the campus of Butler University, Bulldog Park has its own press box and can seat up to 500 fans. Built as a multi-purpose baseball and football practice field, it became baseball-only in the 1990s when bleachers, dugouts, and a permanent fence were added.

Capaha Field Cape Girardeau, MO

Located at 1400 Broadway, inside Capaha Park, and home to the Southeast Missouri State University Redhawks and the Capahas, who claim to be the oldest amateur baseball team in the country. Local American Legion teams also play here.

Capitol Grounds Washington, D.C.

Aka Capitol Park, it was located in a block bounded by C Street NE, Delaware Avenue NE, B Street NE (now Constitution Avenue), and First Street NE, and northeast of the Capitol building. It was the home of the Washington Nationals during the league's only season in 1884. The grounds had a seating capacity of 6,000.

Catholic Protectory Oval New York, NY
Located in the Bronx in the grounds of a famous orphanage, Sunday semi-pro and amateur games had been played here for twenty years or so before it became the home of the Negro League's New York Lincoln Giants in 1923. The bleachers from their demolished home at Olympic Field in Harlem were moved here in 1920 to accommodate the considerably larger crowds they attracted. The field closed in 1939.

Cedar Avenue Driving Park Cleveland, OH
In the 1880s this was the home field of the Cleveland Spiders. It was a large racetrack and fans would line their carriages around the outfield perimeter. The vehicles were in play, so fielders would have to crawl under the carriages to retrieve the ball.

Centennial Field Tallahassee, FL
Built in 1924 to celebrate Tallahassee's hundredth anniversary, it was used for minor league baseball and football 1924–1935.

Chessline Park Philadelphia, PA
Briefly home for the start of the 1928 season of the Philadelphia Tigers before the circuit was disbanded in June. The Tigers tried to continue but folded that July.

Clark Field Austin, TX
Home field of the University of Texas Longhorns from 1928 until 1974, when it was replaced by UFCU Disch-Falk Field. The irregular outfield featured a 30-foot limestone cliff that ran from center field to left center. The Longhorns used its irregular bounce to their advantage: fielders could either play in front of the cliff or on top of it!

Compton Avenue Baseball Park St. Louis, MO
Aka Compton Park, Red Stocking Baseball Park, located in a block bounded by Compton Avenue, Gratiot Street, Theresa Avenue, and Scott Street and home to the St. Louis Red Stockings for the 1875 season, the ground was used irregularly until it was demolished in the late 1890s. A marker was placed in September 2008 to commemorate the site location at 3750 South Compton.

Dartmouth Grounds Boston, MA
Aka Union Park, it was located near present-day Copley Square and home of the Boston Reds for the 1884 season. The iron grandstand held 1,523 spectators and underneath contained locker rooms, a restaurant, bathrooms and a Western Union office. The ground had a total capacity of 4,570.

De Quindre Park Detroit, MI
Aka Linton Field, Cubs Park, it was located in a block enclosed by Dequindre Avenue, Modern Street, Orleans Street, and Riopelle Street. It was the first home—for the 1937 season—of the Negro National League's Detroit Stars.

Dexter Park Queens, NY
Located north of Eldert Lane and Jamaica Avenue almost on the county line with Brooklyn, the original venue was a racetrack. This was replaced by a recreation park in the nineteenth century, and then became a ballpark and home of the Negro League's Brooklyn Royal Giants in the 1920s and 1930s. In 1923 a steel-and-concrete grandstand was built, and by 1924 the ground held some 8,000 fans. Lights were installed in 1930. When the Negro League declined, attendance dropped and the park was demolished in 1955.

Diamond Park Toronto, Canada
Probable location was southeast of Dufferin Street and King Street West. It was the home of the Toronto Maple Leafs c. 1902–1909.

Ducks Park Dayton, OH
Located on the south side of W. Third Street, Ducks Park was home for the Dayton Old Soldiers for a decade from 1932. The name changed to Hudson Field in 1942, from 1946 to 1951 the ground was used by the Dayton Indians minor-league farm team for the Cleveland Indians and St. Louis Browns.

Dugdale Park Seattle, WA
Located at the corner of Rainier Avenue S and S McClellan Street, Dugdale Park was built in 1913 and was home for the Seattle Indians from 1919. The stadium had a double-deck wooden grandstand, electric lights, and seating for 10,000, but on July 5, 1932, fire broke out and destroyed the ground. Originally considered an accident, it transpired three years later that it was the work of a notorious arsonist. Sick's Stadium was later built on the same site.

Eastern Park Brooklyn, NY
Located between Eastern Parkway, Vesta Avenue, Sutter Avenue, Powell Street, and the Long Island Railroad, it was the home of the Brooklyn Ward's Wonders in 1890. The following year it became the part-time home of the Brooklyn Dodgers and their permanent home 1892–1897 (excepting two stints at Washington Park). After the Dodgers left, various other sports were played there. It was demolished in about 1898.

Estadio Cerveza Tropicale Havana, Cuba
Aka La Tropical, Estadio Pedro Marrero following the Cuban revolution, the stadium was built in 1929 and is home of CF Ciudad de La Habana. This multipurpose stadium holds 28,000 and has held many Cuban League baseball games as well as hosting the 1937 Bacardi Bowl. It is still used, mostly for soccer matches.

Estadio de Beisbol Monterrey, Mexico
Located at Avenida Manuel L. Barragan, this is the home of the Mexican League's Sultanes Monterrey team. It is the largest baseball stadium in Mexico and holds 27,000 spectators.

Euclid Beach Park Collinwood, OH
Only used twice by the Cleveland Spiders in 1898 when blue laws prohibited Sunday baseball, three years earlier the ballpark was

built as part of an amusement park. On June 19, 1898, during the second game with the score at 4–3 to the Spiders, the police arrived and arrested all the Cleveland players. No more baseball was played here.

Fairview Park Dayton, OH
Located at the northwest corner of Fairview Avenue and North Main Street, this multi-attraction amusement park opened in 1897. The velodrome in time became Fairview Park Baseball Field and home to the Dayton Old Soldiers from 1899 to 1911. The amusement park closed in 1915.

Fairview Park Fair Grounds Dover, DE
Aka Dover Grounds, a game was played here on June 24, 1875, by the Philadelphia Athletics.

Federal League Park Buffalo, NY
Aka International Fair Association Grounds, it was located in a block bordered by Northland Avenue, Lonsdale Road, Hamlin Road, Oriole Road, and Wohlers Avenue. The ballpark was built on part of the old fairgrounds and was home to the FL Buffalo Buffeds and the Buffalo Blues between May 11, 1914 and September 29, 1915.

Federal League Park Indianapolis, IN
Located at the southwest corner of Kentucky Avenue and South Street, the ballpark was constructed in 1913 and was home to the Indianapolis Hoosiers in 1914. The park was demolished in 1916 after the failure of the Federal League.

Federal League Park St. Louis, MO
Aka Handlan's Park, Steininger Field, Laclede Park, Market and Grand Park, and Grand and Market Park, located in a block formed by Grand Avenue, Laclede Avenue, Theresa Avenue, and Clark Avenue, it had a capacity of 15,000. Used from 1914 to 1915 when it was the home of the St. Louis Terriers. Later, the National Negro League's St. Louis Giants played occasional games here in 1920 and 1921.

Ferris Field Spokane, WA
Built in 1936 in the northwest corner of Spokane Fairgrounds on money granted by the Works Progress Administration, this was the home field for the Spokane Indians from 1937 to 1956.

Forepaugh Park Philadelphia, PA
Located at Broad and Dauphin Streets, this was the home of the Philadelphia Athletics for 1890 and 1891, and the Philadelphia Quakers in 1890.

Freeman's Park Oakland, CA
Located at the northwest corner of 59th and San Pablo, it was built in 1899, held seating for 7,000 fans, and was home to the Oakland Oaks and PCL teams until 1904. They moved away for three years but returned in 1907 and stayed until 1913.

Geauga Lake Base Ball Grounds Geauga Lake, OH
Built in 1887, in 1888 three MLB games were played here on Sundays by the Cleveland Blues.

Giants Park St. Louis, MO
Aka Kuebler's Park and Metropolitan Park, it was located at North Broadway, Clarence Street, East Taylor Street, and Hall Street and was the home of the Negro National League's St. Louis Giants from 1920 to 1921 for most of their home games. The St. Louis Giants got new owners in 1922 who changed their name to the St. Louis Stars, they played their first nine games here before moving to their new ballpark, Stars Park. The Stars disbanded following the 1931 season but six years later a new team with the same name became part of the Negro American League and played here in 1937. Giants Park disappeared under new development around 1950.

Gill Stadium Manchester, NH
Built in 1913, with grandstand seating capacity of 2,220 and total capacity of over 3,000, Gill Stadium was originally called Textile Field. It has hosted professional baseball: the Manchester Blue Sox (1926–1930), Manchester Giants (1946–1947), and various Eastern League teams—the Yankees, Nashua Angels, and most recently the Fisher Cats—but today is used by amateur teams.

Gloucester Point Grounds Gloucester City, NJ
Located in an area bounded by 5th Street, Jersey Avenue, 7th Street, Charles Street, and Pine Street, this was the home of the Philadelphia Athletics from 1888 to 1890.

Gordon and Koppel Field Kansas City, MO
Located in an area bounded by the Paseo, 47th Street, Tracy Avenue, and Brush Creek and home to the FL Kansas City Packers in 1914 and 1915, it was prone to flooding from the adjacent creek. The field was abandoned after the collapse of the Federal League.

Grand Avenue Park St. Louis, MO
Aka Grand Avenue Ball Grounds. The home field for the St. Louis Brown Stockings from 1875 to 1877. The venture was not successful and the park was abandoned after October 1877. The site went on to become Sportsman's Park (1881–1952) and then Busch Stadium (1953–1966), making this the longest-used baseball site in the world.

Grays Field Pittsburgh, PA
Home of the Negro League's Homestead Grays in the 1930s and 1940s: the Grays were one of the most popular and best-known Negro League teams.

Hamilton Field Fort Wayne, IN
Aka the Grand Duchess, its probable location was at the corner of West Main Street and Camp Allen Drive. It was the home of the Fort Wayne Kekiongas for the 1871 season.

Hamilton Park New Haven, CT
Aka Brewster Park and Howard Avenue Grounds, Hamilton Park was

located at the intersection of Whalley Avenue and West Park Avenue. From 1870 until the mid-1880s the park was used by Yale University for sports competitions. It was the home of the New Haven Elm City baseball team in 1875.

Hardware Field Cleveland, OH

Located at E 79th and Kinsman and used occasionally by the National Negro League's Cleveland Cubs (formerly the Elite Giants) in 1931. Following the collapse of the league in 1931, the team moved to the Negro Southern League and Nashville and became the Elite Giants again.

Hartford Trotting Park Hartford, CT

The old ballpark was located near Granby Turnpike (now Blue Hills Avenue) on the southern side of Albany Avenue. It was the home field of the Middletown Mansfields for three games in 1872. The Hartford Dark Blues used the field as home in the 1870s.

Hartwell Field Mobile, AL

Located at Ann and Tennessee Streets, Hartwell Field (aka Hartford Trotting Park) was home to the minor league Mobile Bears. In July 1931 they moved to Knoxville, Tennessee, but returned to Hartwell Field in July 1944 when the seating was extended to accommodate 9,000 fans. During the 1940s and 1950s the club was a farm system affiliate of the Brooklyn Dodgers, and then the Cleveland Indians. The Bears left Hartwell Field in 1961.

Highland Park Stadium Kokomo, IN

Aka Highland Park CFD Investments Stadium, Highland Park was built in 1955 and served as the home of minor-league teams for many years—first the independent Kokomo Giants, then the Kokomo Dodgers, an affiliate of the Brooklyn Dodgers, and later of the Los Angeles Dodgers. The original ballpark was rebuilt in 1985 and has a capacity of 3,000.

Holcomb Park Des Moines, IA

Located at Sixth Avenue and Holcomb, the field was built in 1914 and was the location of the first ever night game on May 2, 1930, when 12,000 spectators watched the Des Moines Demons beat the Wichita Aviators. The May 3, 1930, *Des Moines Register* wrote, *"One hundred forty six projectors diffusing 53,000,000 candle-power of mellow light and the amazing batting of Des Moines' nocturnal-eyed players made the opening night of the local baseball season a complete success Friday night. Baseball was played successfully after dark on an illuminated field and the Demons won 13–6 in a contest that was normal in every respect so far as the playing was concerned."*

Honolulu Stadium Honolulu, HI

Located at the corner of King and Isenberg Streets in the Moʻiliʻili district of Honolulu, this multipurpose stadium was built in 1926 and demolished in 1976.

Hooper Field Cleveland, OH

Located at Sykora and Beyerle Roads, it originally opened in 1921 as Tate Field, home field of the Tate Stars. In 1923 the team folded and the new home team was the Cleveland Browns of the Negro National League and the venue's name was changed to Hooper Field. The Browns lost the franchise in 1925; the following year the Cleveland Elites played here and in 1927 the Cleveland Hornets. After this Hooper Field was abandoned and then demolished in 1932.

Hyde Park Stadium Niagara Falls, NY

Aka Sal Maglie Stadium since 1983, it is located in a block formed by Hyde Park Boulevard, Gill Creek, Robbins Drive, and Linwood Avenue. When it opened in 1939 it mainly hosted football; the stadium was set up for baseball in the 1950s and properly converted in the late 1990s. For the 1967–1968 season it was the home field of the Buffalo Bisons of the International League.

Indianapolis Park Indianapolis, IN

Long since disappeared, the location of Indianapolis Park was within a block enclosed by New York Street, Arsenal Avenue, East Ohio Street, and Hanna Street. It was the home field for the National League's Indianapolis Hoosiers from 1887 to 1889 for Sunday games only.

Iron Pier Syracuse, NY

Located within the Iron Pier amusement park, it was the alternative field for the Syracuse team of the American Association. Scheduled for use for a Sunday game in 1890, both teams were warned not to play by the local police chief. Syracuse turned up, opponents Louisville didn't, so they forfeited the game.

Island Grounds Wheeling, VA

The venue for one game only, in front of 15,000 people on September 22, 1890, when the Pittsburgh Alleghenies (now Pirates) played the New York Giants.

Jennings Stadium Augusta, GA

Also called Municipal Stadium, Jennings Stadium was built in 1928 and was home to the Augusta Tygers (named after former teammate Ty Cobb), and later, the Augusta Tigers, Augusta Wolves, Augusta Rams, and Augusta Yankees. After the 1965 season the Yankees moved to Golden Park in Columbus, Georgia, and Jennings Stadium lost professional baseball. The stadium was demolished in 1964 soon after the Yankees left, and Augusta went without baseball until Heaton Stadium was built in 1988.

John Affleck Park Ogden, UT

Home of the Triple-A Ogden A's, affiliate of the Oakland Athletics, for the 1979 and 1980 seasons. The park was demolished in 1985.

Keystone Park Philadelphia, PA

Located in an area defined by Broad Street, Wharton Street, Moore Street, and 11th Street on the grounds of Forepaugh Circus, it was the home ground for the 1884 season of the Philadelphia Keystones.

Lakeside Park Decatur, AL
Between 1957 and 1961 this was the home of the longest running franchise in Negro League history—the Kansas City Monarchs.

Lawrence Stadium Norfolk, VA
Home of the Portsmouth-Norfolk Tides (1961–1962), who became the Tidewater Tides (1963–1992), and since then today's Norfolk Tides. They played at Lawrence Stadium from 1961 until 1968 before moving to Met Park.

League Park Toledo, OH
Located within a block formed by Monroe Street, 15th Street, Jefferson Avenue, and 13th Street and home of the Toledo Blue Stockings between May and September 1884.

Long Island Grounds Maspeth, NY
Located at the intersection of Grand Avenue and 57th Street, this was the home for the amateur Skelly Base Ball Club in 1886. Despite attracting huge enthusiastic crowds, the team moved away in 1886.

Louisville Baseball Park Louisville, KY
For the 1876–1877 seasons home of the Louisville Grays, a charter member of the National League. The ground has long since been built over for housing.

Ludlow Baseball Park Ludlow, NY
Based in a natural amphitheater, this was the home of the National Association's Philadelphia Whites in 1875.

Luna Bowl Cleveland, OH
Based in an amusement park, this was the home field of the Negro League's Cleveland Stars (1932), Cleveland Giants (1933), and Cleveland Red Sox (1934). It was largely destroyed by fire in 1938.

Mahaffey Park Canton, OH
In 1890 this was the home for one game only for the Pittsburgh Pirates, and then for three games in 1902–1903 for the Cleveland Indians.

Maier Park Vernon, CA
Aka Vernon Park, located at the intersection of Santa Fe and East 38th Street, the ground had a capacity of 7,000 and was home of the Vernon Tigers from 1909 to 1912 and then again from 1915 to 1925.

Martin Park Memphis, TN
Located at 494 E.H. Crump Boulevard, this was the home of the Negro National League's Memphis Red Sox between 1924 and 1930. They were one of the few NNL teams to own their own ground. The ballpark was demolished in 1949.

Maryland Baseball Park Baltimore, MD
Home of the Baltimore Black Sox from 1923 to 1928, then the Negro American League's Baltimore Black Sox for the 1929 season, the park also hosted the Negro League World Series in 1924 and 1926.

Milwaukee Base-Ball Grounds Milwaukee, WI
Located at West Clybourn, North 10th, and North 11th, this was the home field for the Milwaukee Brewers in 1878. The ground is now lost under a freeway.

Mission Stadium San Antonio, TX
Located in a block enclosed by Mission Road, Mitchell Street, and Steves Avenue and home to the San Antonio Missions from 1959 to 1963. The multipurpose stadium opened in 1947 with a capacity of 10,000. It was closed in 1964, abandoned, and demolished ten years later.

Monitor Park Weehawken, NJ
Hosted one game in 1887 for when the Monitors beat the Poughkeepsies 14–7.

Monumental Park Baltimore, MD
The Baltimore Monumentals played one game here in the 1884 season but the ground was too uneven, so they returned to their usual home at Belair Lot.

Mounds Ballfield Mounds, IL
Home of the New Orleans–St. Louis Stars just for August and September 1939. The struggling team moved to New Orleans the following year to try to revive their fortune.

Nationals Grounds Washington, D.C.
Located at 16th Street and R Street, this was home to the Washington Nationals during April and May 1872.

Newington Park Baltimore, MD
Located in West Baltimore on Pennsylvania Avenue, it was the home of the Lord Baltimores from 1872 to 1874; the Marylands in 1873; and the Baltimore Orioles for the 1882 season.

Northwestern Avenue Grounds Indianapolis IN
Home of the Indianapolis ABCs from 1920 to 1926. They had their best year in 1922 when they finished second in the Negro National League with a record of 46–33.

Oakdale Park Jersey City, NJ
Located beside a coal yard and wagon works along Oakland Avenue, this was where the New York Giants played the first two games of the 1889 season after they lost the Polo Grounds.

Paradeway Park Kansas City, MO
Training home of the Kansas City Monarchs from 1923 to 1930. The Monarchs were the longest running of the Negro League teams and won the World Series in 1924 and 1942.

Passon Park Philadelphia, PA
Home of the Philadelphia Bacharach Giants for the 1934 season. The venue was named for their white promoter, Harry Passon, who ran the team between 1931 and his death in 1942.

Pelican Stadium New Orleans, LA

Constructed on the site of the White City amusement park at the corner of Tulane and Carrollton Avenue, it was home of the Double-A New Orleans Pelicans and the Negro National League's Black Pelicans. Built in 1915 and demolished in 1957, it was originally known as Heinemann Park after A.J. Heinemann, the Pelicans' owner who shot himself at the park during the stock market crash. The name changed to Pelican Park in 1938.

Perry Park Keokuk, IA

Home to the Keokuk Westerns in 1875—their sole season of professional baseball.

Piqua Park Piqua, IL

Home of the Chicago American Giants—for over twenty years the best and most successful Negro League team—for the 1920 season.

Riverside Grounds Buffalo, NY

Located within a block made by Fargo Avenue, Rhode Island Street, West Avenue, and Vermont Street, this was the home of the Buffalo Bisons from 1878 to 1883. However, the landowner wanted to develop the plot for housing, and so demolished the stadium in 1883.

Riverside Park Albany, NY

Home of the Troy Trojans from 1880 to 1882, after which they moved to New York City to become (eventually) the New York Giants. Long balls hit over the fence could land in the Hudson River—not an automatic home run in the 1880s.

Rocky Point Park Warwick, RI

The Rocky Point Amusement Park held many attractions, including a baseball diamond. This became the venue for Sunday games between 1891 and 1917 when the Sunday laws prohibited professional baseball.

Satchel Paige Memorial Stadium Kansas City, MO

Located at 51st Street and Swope Parkway, the stadium was renovated in 1982 and named for the legendary Cleveland Indians pitcher. He died shortly afterward.

South End Park St. Louis, MO

Part-time home of the New Orleans–St. Louis Stars in 1941.

South Street Park Indianapolis, IN

Located at Delaware Avenue, South Street, and Alabama Street. It was home for the Chicago White Stockings for a few games in 1878, and home ground for the full season for the Indianapolis Blues. That year South Street Park was also a neutral ground for some Chicago White Stockings games.

Speedway Park Indianapolis IN

Between 1920 and 1926, this was the home field for the Indianapolis ABCs.

Sprague Field Bloomfield, NJ

Home of the Newark Browns for the 1932 season.

Sprague Field Montclair, NJ

Located on the campus of Montclair State University, this multipurpose venue is the home field for the university sports teams. The venue holds 5,700 spectators.

Spurgeon Stadium Colorado Springs, CO

Located in Memorial Park at 1315 E. Pikes Peak Avenue, it was the home field of the Colorado Springs Sky Sox from 1950 to 1958.

Star Baseball Park Covington, KY

Located at the end of the streetcar line at 17th Street and Madison Avenue. Star Baseball Park was used for one season only—1875—for neutral games by the Philadelphia White Stockings.

Star Park Syracuse, NY

A number of Star Park ballparks existed in Syracuse. The first was the home of the National League's Syracuse Stars for the 1879 season. The second was home of the American Association's Syracuse Stars (same name, different team) for 1890: they folded before the following season. They had played at Star Park in the minor leagues between 1885 and 1889, and then again from 1902 to 1904.

Stars Field New Orleans, LA

Home for the 1960–1961 season for the Detroit-New Orleans Stars.

Stars Park St. Louis, MO

Home field for the St. Louis Stars from 1922 to 1931. In 1922 the venue could accommodate 10,000 fans.

Swampoodle Grounds Washington, D.C.

Located near the Capitol Building in a block enclosed by North Capitol Street NE, F Street NE, Delaware Avenue NE, and G Street NE, it was also known as Capitol Park. It could hold 6,000 fans and was home of the Washington Nationals between 1886 and 1889. The site has long since been built over.

Swinney Park Fort Wayne, IN

Located northeast of the junction of Jefferson and Washington Streets and named after a prominent local landowner who gave his land to the city for use as a park in 1874. It was used for one game between Chicago and Providence, in front of a crowd of 600, on October 24, 1882.

Tate Park Cleveland, OH

The home of various Negro League teams—Cleveland Tate Stars (1922); Cleveland Tigers (1923); Cleveland Browns (1924); and the Cleveland Elites (1926).

Tingley Field Albuquerque, NM

Aka Rio Grande Park, it was located at the intersection of 10th Street and Atlantic Avenue. The stadium was built for $84,000, funded by the Works Progress Administration, and opened in 1937. It was home for the Class D St. Louis Cardinals. The facility could seat 3,000 fans with another 2,000 standing. It survived until 1968 when Albuquerque Sports Stadium was built. Tingley was redeveloped.

Tom Wilson Park Nashville, TN
Opened in 1929 for the Nashville Elite Giants, this was one of only two African American-owned ballparks. It was also the spring training home of the Nashville Vols. The ballpark closed in 1946.

Tri-State Fair Grounds Toledo, OH
Located at Dorr Street and Upton Avenue, this was probably the venue for Saturday and Sunday games for the Toledo Blue Stockings in 1884.

Union Street Park Wilmington, DE
Home of the Wilmington Quicksteps for the 1884 season.

University of Pennsylvania Athletic Field Philadelphia, PA
Located at 37th and Spruce Streets, the University of Pennsylvania opened Franklin Field in 1894. The university baseball team was immediately successful in an era when professional ball players could play—controversially—on the same team as college students; professionals were banned in 1894. The facility is still in use.

Valley Field Grand Rapids, MI
Home field for the Kansas City Monarchs between 1956 and 1961.

Virginia Base-Ball Park Richmond, VA
Founded in June 1883, the Richmond Virginians played at a ballpark on farmland owned by Otway Allen. They played in the Eastern League in 1884 but disbanded by 1885. Since 1890 a statue of General Robert E. Lee has stood on the same site.

Virginia State Agricultural Society Fairgrounds Richmond, VA
Aka Richmond Fairgrounds and sometime home field for the Washington Nationals.

VJ Keefe Stadium San Antonio, TX
Located on the campus at St. Mary's College, it was built in 1960 for the university but was used by Texas League teams. The first professional game was in 1968; since then Double-A teams played here until 1994, when Nelson Wolfe Stadium was built. In 1994 the independent Texas Louisiana League had a team at Keefe, but it became home only to collegiate baseball in 1995, as it remains today.

Waverly Fairgrounds Waverly, IA
Located in a block defined by Lower Road, Haynes Avenue, and Frelinghuysen Street, this was the home for eight games of the Elizabeth Resolutes for 1873.

West End Grounds Harrisburg, PA
Home of the Harrisburg Giants for most of the 1920s.

West NY Field Club Grounds West New York, NJ
Now long built over, this was the home of the Brooklyn (now Los Angeles) Dodgers and of the New York (now San Francisco) Giants.

Windsor Beach Irondequoit, NY
Home for Sunday games between May and July 1890 for the Rochesters of the American Association.

Winnipeg Stadium Winnipeg, Manitoba
Aka Canad Inns Stadium, it was home of the Winnipeg Goldeneyes (1953–1964, 1994–1998) and the Winnipeg Whips (1970–1971).

Wright Street Grounds Milwaukee, WI
Located within a block formed by West Wright, West Clarke, North 11th, and North 12th Streets, it was the home ground of the Brewers in 1884, as well as their minor league associates from 1884 to 1888.

Acknowledgments

Eric and Wendy Pastore would like to thank those who have contributed to this book and throughout the years to Digitalballparks.com. We recommend that you visit those who have websites too, as they will give you a different perspective of the baseball stadium and its evolution and provide hours of great photos and reading…

First, however, I have to thank Wendy Pastore, who has been with me through the past twelve years of Digitalballparks, driving from city to city and living through not only some great baseball, but the crazy experiences that can only happen when you do a 7,000-mile road trip. A barnstorming baseball player herself, roaming the land from Massachusetts to Kansas City, she has the same appreciation for the game and its architecture as I do, and that makes every trip all the more fantastic.

We would also love to thank Simon Forty who has worked so diligently with us to make this book something special. We hope it will live up to his vision of creating the ultimate baseball stadium publication and look forward to future endeavors with this very charming Englishman.

Thanks to Dan Mansfield of Thunder Bay for his meticulous examination of the pages.

We would also like to thank Gord Brown of Kitchener, Ontario, who spent years researching the names of every single professional ballpark in North America so we can go find and photograph them.

We would also like to thank for contributions and their friendship: Joe Mock (Baseballparks.com); Gary Jarvis (Minorleague Ballparks.com); Paul Crumlish (Littleballparks.com); Graham Knight of BaseballPilgrimages.com; Brian Merzbach (Ballparkreviews.com); Amanda Lippert Merzbach (Baseballstadiumreviews.com); Charlie "Zeb" O'Reilly (http://mysite. verizon.net/charliesballparks /stadiums. htm); All-star pitcher Jerry Reuss (JerryReuss.com); Mike Castro at Field of Dreams (http://www.mcmas.net/fod/); Jeff LaCrone (Small-Parks.com); Tim Perry's Frontier League history guide (http://flhistory. gofreeserve. com/); and Bob Busser who visits not only ballparks but arenas as well (http://www.ballparks. phanfare.com/).

Thanks to Judith Millidge and Ian Westwell who contributed to the text and captions.

Special thanks to the Pastore brothers, Gary and Sonny; Ralph and Brooklyn Dodger-loving Karen Pastore, my parents who adored the game as I do; Bonnie Smith and Patrick Farrell for nurturing Wendy's love for the game and making sure she made it to every baseball practice; Fred Murphy for continuing that tradition and making sure my love for the New York Mets is a living hell.

Thanks to the following for their contributions to Digitalball parks.com's galleries and this publication with photographs of ballparks now long gone: Fred Sagebaum, Robert K. Shoop, Bill Mountjoy, Chris Hunter at the Schenectady Museum and Science Center and the "watcher of the skies," Steven L.J. Russo; Jerry Reuss, Stephen Carroll, Larry Klug, C.H. Foertmeyer, Jim Castle, Ed Baker, Mike Daddario, Chris Epting, Bob Busser, Jim Reynolds, Ed Johnson, Darrell T. Adkerson, Michael Collins, Sam Leon, Daniel Papillon, Paul Hamaker, Peter G. Pierce, Barbara Cassell, Bob Lipp, Adam Raine, Bruce Orser, Mark London, Joshua Maxwell, Stephen Doll, Jason Lane, Matthew Couillard, Mike Goodwin, Jordan Anderson, and Steven Bowles.

And for all those of you who wish to contribute to Digital ballparks.com to make it the greatest baseball stadium museum in the world: don't worry about the current standing ballparks. We will gladly take care of every single one of them (that is the goal of course) in high resolution panoramic photography. However, if you have photographs of a now-demolished-long forgotten minor league ballpark from yesteryear, please let us know at www.Digitalballparks.com (admin@digitalballparks.com) and we will make you your own special permanent gallery for all to see.

Last but not least, thanks to the over one million fans who have visited our website and continue to every single year. Your wonderful emails and thoughtful comments have made this worth every minute that we've spent on the road. Our sincerest appreciations.

Eric and Wendy Pastore